SMILE WHEN YOU CALL ME A HILLBILLY

JEFFREY J. LANGE

SMILE

WHEN YOU CALL ME A HILLBILLY

COUNTRY MUSIC'S STRUGGLE FOR RESPECTABILITY, 1939-1954

THE UNIVERSITY
OF GEORGIA PRESS
ATHENS AND LONDON

© 2004 by the University of Georgia Press
Athens, Georgia 30602
All rights reserved
Designed by Mindy Basinger Hill
Set in Bulmer MT by Bookcomp, Inc.
Printed and bound by Maple-Vail
The paper in this book meets the guidelines for permanence
and durability of the Committee on Production Guidelines
for Book Longevity of the Council on Library Resources.
Printed in the United States of America
08 07 06 05 04 C 5 4 3 2 1
08 07 06 05 04 P 5 4 3 2 1

Library of Congress Cataloging-in-Publication Data
Lange, Jeffrey J.
Smile when you call me a hillbilly : country music's struggle
for respectability, 1939–1954 / Jeffrey J. Lange.
p. cm.
Includes bibliographical references and index.
ISBN 0-8203-2622-4 (hardcover : alk. paper) —
ISBN 0-8203-2623-2 (pbk. : alk. paper)
1. Country music—To 1951—History and criticism.
2. Country music—1951–1960—History and criticism.
3. Country music—Social aspects.   I. Title.
ML3524.L325 2004
781.642'0973'09044—dc22   2004001707

British Library Cataloging-in-Publication Data available

TO TERESA, ALEXANDRA, AND HAGAN

CONTENTS

PREFACE

This book is about the people who recorded and listened to country music in the 1940s and early 1950s and is intended for a reading audience of historians, sociologists, and appreciators of the musical genre. Ten years ago, I considered myself a casual fan of country music. Somewhere in between wayward drives on desolate backroads listening to Hank Williams and the beginning of the research on this project, I developed a deeper appreciation of country music and its universal message that prompted me to pursue a formal study of the subject. When I began the research for this project in 1996 in the basement of the old Country Music Hall of Fame on 16th Street in Nashville, there were still hundreds of country music performers that I had never heard of, let alone heard on record. After listening to thousands of records, examining over fifteen years of trade magazines, and unearthing countless primary and secondary source materials, I realized that the 1940s represented not only a key component to understanding the history of American music, but also a vital source of understanding the thoughts, feelings, and motivations of the people who listened to it as well. Like a window into the souls of its listeners, country music of the World War II era captured the mindset of a group of people confronted with monumental changes in their lives at the hands of the exigencies of war and the modernizing forces of urbanization and industrialization. Their lives would never be the same, but through country music, in part, their vital culture remained intact. In the end, I came to understand that country music represented more than just a historical document of the times; it represented a vehicle for survival, on both an individual and collective scale.

I would not have been able to reach this discovery, let alone write about this subject matter, without the support of numerous individuals along the way. Bruce Wheeler, Stephen Ash, and Charles Aiken at the University of Tennessee provided invaluable direction, whether through advice on research or through comments and suggestions on the dissertation as it progressed. Agatino La Rosa, an amicable neighbor and graduate school compatriot, offered key assistance in generating the "birthplace" maps; I sincerely appreciate the sacrifice of his time. Jim Cobb demonstrated remarkable patience throughout and was there to offer encouragement and support whenever I needed it. I am also grateful to Jim for suggesting I pursue publication of the book with the University of Georgia Press. I would like to extend my gratitude to Derek Krissoff and Sarah McKee at the

Press for their help throughout the publishing process. Additionally, Courtney Denney was immensely helpful in the final stage of copyediting.

The staff at the old Country Music Foundation in Nashville provided invaluable assistance throughout the research process. Thanks especially to Ronnie Pugh, John Rumble, Alan Stoker, and Bob Pinson. Every time I walked down the stairs at the Country Music Hall of Fame to the CMF archives, I was greeted with a smile and bolstered by the encouragement of these individuals. The old building no longer stands, but I will always remember the countless days I spent there listening to the old 78s and working with people who shared my belief in the importance of country music. My thanks also to Denny Adcock, photo curator at the new museum, for his assistance with securing photos for the project.

I am deeply grateful to my parents and family for their infinite support and understanding through the years. They are responsible for instilling within me not only the work ethic needed to complete a project of this magnitude, but also the understanding and humility that allowed me to realize that this book was about much more than country music, that it was about people turning to their families, their friends, and their faith as a means to persevering in the face of adversity.

Finally, I would like to thank my wife, Teresa, for giving me the strength and the time to finish this project. She was with me in spirit on all the drives back and forth from Knoxville to Nashville and in the thousands of hours spent researching and writing. Unwavering throughout, she never stopped believing. This book is dedicated to her; my daughter, Alexandra; and my son, Hagan. As the source of my faith, they give my life purpose and meaning.

SMILE WHEN YOU CALL ME A HILLBILLY

INTRODUCTION

The urban presses and most of the American populace called it hillbilly music, but the people who enjoyed listening to it cared much less about what others thought than they did about the music itself. To thousands of white working-class southerners in the 1940s and early 1950s, the musical genre now known as country was simply the music they grew up with, the music they heard in church, around the house, in the fields where they worked, or during social gatherings. Country music legend Hank Thompson recalls, "I don't remember any other kind of music [except country]. To me, that's the only music that anybody listened to."[1]

Today, country music enjoys a national audience that transcends economic and social boundaries; sixty years ago, however, hillbilly music attracted an audience composed primarily of white, rural southerners. This music gave a collective voice to these people, who were marginalized from American society by their economic and social status, and provided them with a means for defining themselves in a period when their lives remained in an almost constant state of flux. In the 1940s and early 1950s, southern society experienced a tumultuous upheaval initiated by the advent of World War II. The war brought sweeping changes to the southern economy that led to increased urbanization and a veritable revolution in lower- and middle-class employment opportunities. Such a striking alteration in the lifestyles of country music's most ardent listeners naturally affected the genre. Exhibiting remarkable flexibility in a period of dynamic change, country music managed to retain the loyalty of its initial listeners while broadening its appeal to an expanding audience of nonsoutherners. From humble beginnings, country music emerged in the early 1950s as a highly profitable art form with an audience that was neither as rural nor as unsophisticated as the one in the late 1930s.

The changes occurring within country music in the period between 1939 and 1954 parallel the changes in the lives of its listeners. A product and a reflection of developing southern culture, country music responded to the social upheavals precipitated by World War II, adapting itself to the altered lyrical and musical preferences of its audience. The different styles of country music produced in the period demonstrate the genre's various responses to the sociocultural tumults experienced by its listeners. The development of these styles, in the wake of social and musical changes precipitated by World War II, led to the modernization of country music, its evolution from a regional folk art form aimed at a white southern rural audience to a nationwide phenomenon seeking to expand its core of listeners beyond a regional folk base.

Changes in the manner in which artists presented their songs to their audience (performance styles) demonstrate the process of acculturation into the American mainstream experienced by country music and its audience in the 1940s and early 1950s. The major performance styles (subgenres) were progressive, western swing, postwar traditional, honky-tonk, country pop, and country blues. Progressive country refers to performers of the late 1930s who attempted to expand the country music audience through a variety of musical, vocal, and lyrical approaches that de-emphasized the genre's rough-hewn qualities in favor of evocative singing, domestic lyrical themes, and musical innovation. Western swing began in Texas and attracted listeners in the urbanizing Southwest and southern migrants in California. Its performers differed from their progressive counterparts principally in their use of electric instrumentation and in the primacy of musical presentation over lyrical meaning. Postwar traditionalists appealed primarily to rural southerners grappling with the spiritual exigencies of the post–World War II era. Some of these performers emphasized old-time (prewar) instrumentation; others built on that tradition by developing and perfecting the country music style now commonly referred to as bluegrass. Honky-tonk singers and musicians gained the favor of rural southerners transplanted in urban environments in the mid- to late 1940s. Lyrically, these performers indirectly voiced the alienation and dislocation their listeners experienced. Musically, they utilized southwestern instrumentation with more emphasis on vocal presentation. From strident beginnings, honky-tonk evolved in the early 1950s into a music with more emphasis on lighthearted lyrical material and refined vocal techniques. Country pop and country blues refer to performers' efforts to fuse country music with American popular music and African American rhythm and blues respectively. Country pop was popular among an expanding urban middle class, in the South and throughout the nation. With their understated, unobtrusive singing styles and sense of decorum, country pop performers gained the attention of the national media as well as a national audience. Country blues singers emerged in California after the war on the heels of the western swing phenomenon, securing an audience of dance hall regulars on the West Coast. In the early to mid-1950s, the focus of country blues shifted eastward, culminating with the advent of rock and roll, which appealed to youths in southern cities initially, then in urban areas nationwide.

These six subgenres do not represent completely homogeneous musical styles; vocalists and musicians used a variety of approaches to each. Carl Smith and Hank Williams performed in very distinct styles, yet both belong beneath the honky-tonk umbrella. Red Foley and Eddy Arnold blended elements of American popular music with country music in different ways, but both shared a vision of country pop that would appeal to a wide spectrum of listeners. The basic terminology for these six subgenres is essentially modern. Bob Wills played western swing in the late 1930s, but no one called it that until the mid-forties. Similarly, honky-tonk did not receive its common label until well after the style developed. Most of the performers discussed in this book considered themselves hillbilly, country, or old-time performers. Some refused categorization as country performers; others preferred any label except hillbilly. In hindsight, historians can clearly see the development of distinct subgenres in the period, although the appropriate placement of performers within them can elicit debate, as can nomenclature. However, breaking country music down into individual subgenres provides a viable model for discussing how the dynamic genre responded to cultural changes as well as explaining its expanding appeal.

The modernization of country music essentially began with the implementation of stylistic changes designed to broaden the genre's audience beyond its initial rural, southern, working-class base. This phenomenon was more an intensification of early efforts at country music promotion than it was a novel development. In 1939, country music was essentially a folk art form, but even then, as a business, it never existed in a cultural vacuum. Soon after its inception in the early 1920s, the process of commercialization began to dilute the music's southern folk qualities. A conglomeration of centuries of ethnocultural, interregional, and rural-urban interaction, the music genre was never a pure folk cultural product. Additionally, with male performers dominating the early period, emphasizing what D. K. Wilgus termed the "public tradition," country music neglected much of the music heard in southern homes and churches at the time. In the mid- to late 1930s, country music directed itself more toward this domestic tradition, but it also embraced musical experimentation, moving away from folk simplicity. This latter development reflected early efforts to promote the acceptance of the genre beyond the rural South, as evidenced in the recordings of progressive performers, such as Roy Acuff, Jimmie Davis, and Bill Monroe, who strove to reach a wider audience and gain respectability for their music.

Before gaining a nationwide audience in World War II, country music performers directed their product at a predominantly rural and regional audience of working-class southerners. Only in Texas, a southern state that underwent early urbanization, did country performers consciously reach out to urban listeners via the western swing subgenre. During the war, many members of the country music audience moved to urban areas; simultaneously, many urban listeners from around the country discovered country music. Displaying remarkable elasticity, the genre in the war years responded to these developments by adopting elements of urban country music from the Southwest as well as pop stylings.

When country music recordings started selling in large quantities to a national audience during World War II, efforts to enhance the genre's reputation stepped up dramatically. This movement took many forms, from changing the way performers dressed to altering the music itself, making it more palatable for new listeners. In the postwar period, many acts reasserted country's southern roots, through the postwar traditional subgenre (southern and rural based) and the honky-tonk subgenre (southern and urban based), while enjoying a peaceful coexistence with acts that downplayed the genre's regional and rural characteristics, resulting in country pop and country blues. With country music's profits increasing every year and record companies growing more interested in the music, however, efforts to de-emphasize country music's southernness intensified. When the musical genre known as rockabilly emerged as a formidable threat to country music, the latter's regional and rustic characteristics fell by the wayside. Ironically, country music in the late forties and early fifties achieved the respectability it sought so earnestly since the 1930s by turning its back on the listeners (rural and working-class southerners) who ensured its early survival. In doing so, however, country music in the postwar years attracted a variety of new listeners, including urban southerners, members of the middle class (both rural and urban) nationwide, and America's youth.

Four major developments occurred in country music from 1939 to 1954: the popularity of country music subgenres over the period fluctuated, reflecting modifications in audience tastes and changes in southern society brought about by World War II; country music became more sophisticated and musical styles altered with emerging country music industry trends and the expansion of the audience to urban and nonsouthern areas; country music styles combined with one another and with American popular music, and subsequently, alternative subgenres emphasizing country music's southernness emerged; and Nashville was established as the hub of country music with the concurrent decrease in the relative importance and influence of other centers. The sum of these developments was the modernization of country music: a reflection of sociocultural changes in southern society and of the genre's transformation from regional peculiarity to national acceptance.

The scope of this book begins in 1939, the year that the *Grand Ole Opry,* soon to become country music's most prominent radio show, received network status, and closes in 1954, with the beginning of the rock and roll era. Six out of the seven chapters trace the transformation of the country music subgenres prominent in the period. The remaining chapter deals with World War II and the effects of that era on country music. Within each chapter dealing specifically with the six country music subgenres is an analysis of the recording output of the most significant performers in each field as well as biographical sketches of these artists and a discussion of their roles in each subgenre's development over the period. In some cases, performers played an important role in the modernization of country music; in others, they contributed to the maturation of a specific subgenre, the popularity of which either peaked or plummeted during the era. The discussion of each subgenre's musical and lyrical profile placed in historical context explains the reasons for the fluctuations in a subgenre's success.

The primary determinant for selecting the most significant performers in each subgenre was the artist's contribution to a subgenre's development; retail sales were considered as well, but to a lesser extent. As such, for instance, Lefty Frizzell deserves recognition as a prominent honky-tonk performer, George Morgan as a country pop journeyman, and so forth. Two performers do not fit as neatly into the subgenres as others do. Hank Snow could easily be placed in the honky-tonk or even in the postwar traditional category, but in terms of vocal style and musical accompaniment he conforms to the country pop model. Similarly, many view Merle Travis as a honky-tonk or a western swing performer, but upon examination of his entire repertoire, he fits into country blues. Ten performers are discussed in each of the chapters on the progressive, western swing, postwar traditional, and honky-tonk subgenres to reveal various approaches to each type of country music. Only six recording artists each were chosen for the chapters on country pop and country blues because of these performers' dominance in their respective fields and the relative ease of breaking down the nuances of these two subgenres. The fact that two groups, Bill Monroe's Blue Grass Boys and the Delmore Brothers, played important roles in the evolution of two different subgenres brings the total number of performers analyzed to fifty (table 1).

Gauging the popularity of each subgenre during the 1940s and early 1950s was determined primarily by the *Billboard* charts that measured the retail sales and radio and jukebox plays of country music selections. As the nation's premier musical trade publication, *Billboard* was the first major periodical to rate the success of country music recordings with its inception of a jukebox popularity chart in 1944. Unfortunately, little consistency existed in the number of selections, ranging between two and fifteen per week over the period. Unlike today's computer-calculated charts, the early *Billboard* tabulations were rudimentary at best. The small number of selections on the charts excluded several recordings that enjoyed considerable sales success. In 1946, for example, the author of *Billboard*'s country music column reported that Ernest Tubb's "There's a Little Bit of Everything in Texas" had sold over two hundred thousand copies, an impressive seller by contemporary standards, yet it never made the magazine's jukebox popularity list. Additionally, several artists sold thousands of records on a subregional scale that never appeared on the national charts. Nevertheless, I ascertained fluctuations in each subgenre's popularity using the *Billboard* listings by awarding points to the top twenty-five singles of each year on a high-low basis (for example, number one was given twenty-five points, number twenty-five was given one point). For the period 1939 to 1943, when no *Billboard* charts existed, the approximated charts determined by Charles Faber were used to assign points. Faber estimated these charts based on the reissuance of recordings and the frequency with which the songs appear in country music anthologies and standard publications. Categorizing each of the top twenty-five songs of each year into a specific musical subgenre provided the means for measuring a subgenre's annual success (table 2). A discussion of the reasons for the fluctuations in subgenres' popularity follows in the appropriate chapters.[2]

Although an analysis of musical styles for the sake of categorization of performers and determination of subgenres' popularity must disregard lyrics, the importance of the words to country music songs merits recognition. Speaking of lessons learned throughout a long life as procurer and producer of country music dating back to the early 1920s, Art Satherley notes that "it is not the guy that can sing the best that can get you the best results; it's the guy that's got words and the lyrics that the people will accept." In country music, the tune nearly always plays second fiddle to the words, resulting in the primacy of the story over the song, the message over the musicianship.[3]

There are many ways to define country music, but most of the genre's performers usually do so in the context of its lyrical qualities. The country music lyric bases itself primarily in realism, in the mundane, and in the hopes and fears of its listeners. In essence, Ray Price points out, "country music is music expressing deep feelings of folks in areas pertaining to their work . . . their religious experience . . . their ups and downs, joys and disappointments. . . . It concerns everyday happenings about everyday people about things that touch directly on them." To Roy Acuff, "it's the music of our people and our places." Johnny Cash summed up the subject matter of most country songs: "I love songs about horses, railroads, land, judgment day, family, hard times, whiskey, courtship, marriage, adultery, separation, murder, war, prison, rambling, damnation, home, salvation, death, pride, humor, piety, rebellion, patriotism, larceny, determination, tragedy, rowdiness, heartbreak and love." Finally, Maybelle Carter had this to say about the genre's primary lyrical concerns: "Country music reflects to us a way of life. . . . When we sang, we sang of people and places that were familiar to us . . . when we sang, we sang of problems—hard work, poverty and sorrow—problems that were part of everyday life . . . when we sang, we sang of hopes and prayers. . . . And when we sang, we sang to others who knew the same people, places, and problems, and who had the same hopes and prayers."[4]

In the analysis of the most prominent artists' recorded output in the period, the songs are informally categorized by their subject matter. The purpose of this general approach is simply to provide insight into a specific performer's lyrical inclinations and to shed light on the lyrical preferences among performers as a whole in a specific subgenre. An examination of the subject matter of all songs that made the Faber and *Billboard* charts between 1939 and 1954 indicates fluctuations in the popularity of lyrical themes (table 3). Several observations are worth noting. Generally considered the most popular of country music lyrical themes, melancholy selections about lost love dominated the charts in only four of the sixteen years covered in this study, with the war years representing their apex. Straightforward love songs steadily became more popular after the war, especially in the early 1950s. Songs about breakup without regret reached their high tide in 1945, a year that witnessed a staggering rise in divorce rates. Ultimately, the most popular lyrical theme of the period, and of the postwar years in particular, was the upbeat and humorous novelty song, representing 28 percent of all selections that made the Faber and *Billboard* charts.

Coupled with a description of evolving musical styles placed in the context of industry trends, lyrical theme analysis helps to explain why the modernization of country music took place between 1939 and 1954. To a lesser extent, the chapters in this book place this phenomenon within the context of regional developments in an effort to demonstrate how country music's modernization reflected the modernization of southern society. Richard Peterson and Melton McLaurin argue that three factors preclude the use of country music lyrics as a means to accurately encapsulating the southern mindset: the absence of taboo subjects (such as race), record companies' influence on an artist's repertoire, and the artist's reluctance to stray from an existing image. Augmentation of lyrical theme examination with subgenre musical analysis and a study of chart popularity patterns placed in the context of southern history, however, opens the door to viewing developments within country music as a barometer of broad changes in southern society. Merle Travis termed the evolution of country music lyrical themes as "part of the revolution." As a significant component of white southern culture, country music served as a vessel of indirect commentary on social developments. Exploring the reasons why it changed over the course of the period provides the basis for an understanding of how its audience and the South changed as well.[5]

Country music offers this unique perspective on changes in southern culture in the postwar period mainly because the majority of the genre's performers in this period hailed from the South. Approximately 74 percent of country music performers who placed at least one record on the Faber and *Billboard* charts between 1939 and 1954 were born in the South (map 1). Of performers with three or more charted singles in the period, the South produced about 79 percent (map 2). Of the southern states, Texas and Tennessee bore the largest percentage of chartmakers, particularly in the three or more category. The majority of success-ful country music performers—in terms of record sales and radio and jukebox popularity—were of southern origin.[6]

What, then, of the land that produced these country music stylists? The South comprises the states Alabama, Arkansas, Florida, Georgia, Kentucky, Louisiana, Mississippi, North Carolina, Oklahoma, South Carolina, Tennessee, Texas, Vir-ginia, and West Virginia and is considered as a cultural entity defined in greater part by its distinctiveness in manner and thought than by geographical boundaries. Several scholars over the years have dissected southern distinctiveness using this paradigm. Wilbur Zelinsky points out that "the South is ostensibly a cultural rather than physical entity, being simply an area occupied by a population that thinks and behaves distinctively." Writing in 1941, W. J. Cash noted, "There exists among us by ordinary [people]—both North and South—a profound conviction that the South is another land, sharply differentiated from the rest of the American nation, and exhibiting within itself a remarkable homogeneity." Cash refers to a shared mindset among southerners shaped by historical experience and the evo-lution of regional folkways. George Tindall maintains that several factors such as climate, an African American presence, a powerful religious heritage, persistent rurality, and a distinct history produced the "southern" phenomenon. Other scholars, such as Charles Roland and John Shelton Reed, add such factors as common speech patterns, diet, and the persistence of rural and folk values to the equation. Lyrical themes in country music songs of the 1940s and early 1950s demonstrate these cultural traits and reveal consistencies in southern culture as well as alterations in it brought about by socioeconomic change.[7]

In its relative isolation from American society, the rural South of the prewar years remained immersed in folk tradition. The South's persistent rurality facili-tated an agrarian mindset that shaped a folk culture increasingly distinguishable within an urbanizing nation. David Potter notes, "The culture of the folk sur-

Map 1. Birthplaces of Performers with One or More Charted Singles, 1939–1954

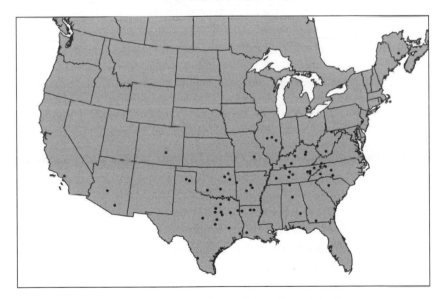

Map 2. Birthplaces of Performers with Three or More Charted Singles, 1939–1954

vived in the South long after it succumbed to the onslaught of urban-industrial culture elsewhere." Defined by E. B. Reuter as "the simpler, uneducated and less sophisticated members of a population," the "folk" and their culture persevered in the South largely due to their isolation from the American mainstream and their substantiality in number.[8]

If folksiness can be equated with lack of sophistication, the South of the 1940s can certainly be described by and large as a folk society. Less than half of all dwellings occupied by white southerners in 1940 were equipped with working indoor plumbing. Less than one-quarter of white southerners' homes in rural areas had working toilets and sinks; only 41 percent had electricity. The fact that nearly two-thirds of white southerners lived in rural areas in 1940 compounds the importance of these statistics. More of an indicator of folk culture than a defining factor, a lack of sophistication helps to statistically pinpoint folk societies more than it does to describe them. Many folk societies, including the prewar rural South, are rich in tradition and estimable in cultural values; labeling the rural South unsophisticated merely states the condition in which the culture developed. In any event, as the majority of country music performers and listeners in 1940 hailed from rural, southern areas, it stands to reason that the genre was primarily a product of folk culture intended for a folk audience. Country music's popularity certainly transcended regional borders and even crept into several cities, but hillbilly music in 1940 was essentially a folk phenomenon.[9]

As a derivative of southern folk culture, country music bore the impression of many characteristics of white southern society. Howard Odum observed that "the way of the South . . . is the way of the folk, symbolic of what the people feel, think, and do as they are conditioned by their cultural heritage and the land which Nature has given them." Odum described folk culture as revolving around a sense of place, the importance of family, and social interdependence; to its southern version, he added ruralism, religiosity, and a reverence for the past. Another contemporary sociologist, Fred Voget, stressed the binary relationship of folk and urban societies, stating that "urban secularism and heterogeneity contrast sharply with folk sacredness and homogeneity." Several other historians and sociologists, including C. Vann Woodward and John Shelton Reed, stress the importance of a distinct historical experience and cognizance of regional differences when defining the culture of the modernizing South. Country music in 1939 reflected white southern folk values as well as regional and even subregional identifications. Bound together by a folk culture and a common historical experience, rural white southerners in 1939 found something familiar in country music that they could identify with on both an individual and collective scale.[10]

Chapter 1 discusses at length the characteristics of the folk culture prevalent in the rural South before World War II as a starting point on the southern culture continuum. Lawrence Levine maintains that "culture is not a fixed condition, but a process: the product of interaction between the past and present." Sociologist Howard Odum termed culture "the sum total of all the processes and products of a given people and their society at any given time and region in which they grow up." Southern culture exhibited a remarkable degree of fluidity in this period of veritable revolution in lifestyles while also displaying remarkable survival skills. Enduring the onslaughts of nationalization and urbanization that threatened its very existence, southern culture survived as a bastion against such threats. Southerners turned to their core value system as a means of sustaining a way of life that defined their existence. Clifford Geertz views culture as a vehicle for people to "communicate, perpetuate, and develop their knowledge about and attitudes toward life." Country music was a major exponent of southern culture, and southerners turned to the medium as a catharsis to their lives' tumults. As the product of incessant change, southern culture would not survive the period unaltered; southern music, however, helped to ensure that it would not emerge unduly adulterated. [11]

While country music of the period affirmed and reflected southern culture, its principal purpose remained twofold: as an entertainment vehicle for its listeners and as a grounding force amid sweeping changes in audience lifestyles. The near-ubiquitous presence of comedy acts in country music road shows of the 1940s illustrates the entertainment function of the genre. In between songs about mother, infidelity, and love won and lost, country musicians from honky-tonkers to postwar traditionalists inserted comedy acts into their performances. As comedienne Minnie Pearl pointed out, "what we were trying to do, right from the start was to entertain people and bring a measure of release and love and a little surcease from daily cares." [12]

In musical repertoire and lyrical inclination, some country music subgenres, particularly western swing, functioned primarily as escapist vehicles for their working-class audience. Others, such as the postwar traditional and honky-tonk subgenres, intentionally displayed more seriousness in their approach and presentation. Regardless, the function of the music as an instrument for coping with social, economic, and cultural upheavals, both on an individual and collective scale, remained constant. Bluegrass historian Robert Cantwell categorizes early southern rural musical performances as "social and participatory, in which the lines between musician and audience were diffuse." Recollections of artists and listeners suggest similar interaction in country music performances on the eve of World War II. From 1939 to 1954, however, the gatherings in which southern whites congregated to hear country music became steadily less participatory as audiences became more introspective, particularly after the war. In essence, the country music audience turned inward at the expense of communality.[13]

The notion of authenticity provides one answer to the question of why country music audiences preferred certain subgenres over others. Defined forthrightly by Richard Peterson as the product of believability and originality, authenticity centers on the connection listeners feel toward performers. The ability of country musicians to forge this bond helped distinguish the genre from popular music in the 1940s and played a major role in country music's remarkable success story over the course of the period. Country music performers exhibited their authenticity primarily through their interaction with the audience and the composition or selection of song lyrics immediately relatable to their listeners. Country music lyrics reveal the mosaic of the southern social landscape in their description of southerners' relationships with one another, their land, and their God. The concept of authenticity helps explain why progressive and postwar traditional performers attracted a greater portion of rural listeners, why honky-tonk emerged as the predominant postwar subgenre, and why an expanding audience turned to country pop and country blues acts.[14]

Although the South is a distinct cultural entity, it is by no means a monolithic one. Within its mythical boundaries lies a complex myriad of hamlets and urban centers, of churches and barrooms, of ramshackle shacks and palatial homes. The southern mindset is an amalgam of hedonism and generosity, of violence and graciousness, of sullenness and celebrative excess. Country music not only captures the dichotomies of the South and its inhabitants, it thrives on it. A country musician's ability to reach his or her audience and to speak to their daily concerns and perpetual beliefs often determined the degree of his or her success. The dynamic nature of country music in the 1940s and early 1950s allowed it to adapt to cultural developments while retaining its authenticity. The inherent subjectivity of authenticity, however, splintered the genre's audience into those who embraced changes in musical and lyrical styles and those who resisted prevailing trends.

Beyond presentation and song selection, country musicians substantiated their authenticity by displaying a colloquial manner of speech and acceptable visual appearance. Roy Acuff once said, "If you aren't a country boy, you can't write or sing country music." Beyond the gender bias, there lies a considerable amount of truth in that statement in terms of authenticity. Hank Williams stated the case more bluntly: "You got to know a lot about hard work. You got to have smelt a lot of mule manure before you can sing like a hillbilly. The people who have been raised something like the way the hillbilly has knows what he is singing about and appreciates it." Historian Bill Malone elaborates on the performer and audience bond: "The music reflected the kind of life we shared, and it was performed by people like ourselves who could have, and often did, come out of our own communities." Most performers did hail from small communities and the vast majority began their professional careers within familiar parameters, mostly via informal gatherings or local radio shows, where they often performed without pay.[15]

Those fortunate enough to make it as professionals discovered that the proper image often secured their success. Some male performers opted to don a western style of dress, others the guise of the country gentleman or country bumpkin. Some leaned toward a retro look, fostering an image of rugged individualism representative of the American cowboy. Others dressed in more casual attire, some in sport coats, some in suspenders and flannel shirts. In choosing an appropriate image, performers hoped to avoid alienation of a prospective audience on the one hand while sustaining the loyalty of core fans on the other. In 1940, the prospective audience might be listeners in another county or another southern state or, in a few cases, a national audience, but the base consisted of loyal rural, working-class radio listeners and personal appearance regulars. By 1954, the prospective audience became increasingly national in scope while the base demographic became more urban, more sophisticated, and more middle-class. As the period wore on, the cowboy image increased in popularity among country music's most successful performers, many eager to separate themselves from the hayseed image of southerners prevalent among Americans in the prewar years.

Female country music performers projected an image that adhered more to prevailing stereotypes than estimable representations. Country music songs performed by male and female performers in the 1920s and 1930s accentuated the preconception of women as virtuous homebodies providing a refuge from the corrupting influences of secular society. The infamous tribute to mother reflected this projection of women more than anything else, as did songs that placed females' roles squarely within the boundaries of southern womanhood. Gradually, however, as women gained more independence both in country music and in southern society, particularly due to the Depression and World War II, these stereotypes began to wane somewhat. A proliferation of songs about mother by male artists and songs by female artists extolling southern female virtues continued after the war, but the war dealt a blow to the image of the docile and faithful female. A rising divorce rate and new freedoms experienced by women opened the door to profiles of feminine strength and assertiveness that challenged earlier stereotypes. For the most part, women remained marginalized by the country music industry well into the 1950s, but a notable few served as vanguards to a feminist movement in country music that only recently has come to full fruition.

In addition to influencing the images chosen by performers, changes in southern society affected the lyrical content of country music songs. With audience expansion and demographic reshuffling came changes in listeners' tastes and lyrical theme preferences. Together with the use of appropriate musical presentation, the choice of appealing lyrical subject matter determined the success of both an individual performer and a particular subgenre. An examination of these two ingredients furnishes the key to understanding why a particular subgenre's success peaked at one point in the study period instead of another. For instance, why did the progressive country category enjoy more popularity before and during the war than after; conversely, what brought about the mercurial success of honky-tonk after the war? These questions are answered by placing the popularity of each subgenre within the context of country music trends and the background of southern history and through an analysis of prevalent lyrical themes of the period.

The country music audience in 1940 was overwhelmingly white, rural, and working-class. Country music performers in the late 1930s geared their lyrics and musical approach to this core audience. Southern urbanites displayed indifference to hillbilly music, at best tolerating its presence; occasionally, they became openly hostile to its performers. Over the next fifteen years, this antagonism began to wane and country music grew in popularity among nontraditional listeners both outside the South and within southern cities. Simultaneously, many members of the traditional audience entered the middle class and settled in urban areas. The modernization of country music took place within the context of these evolving audience demographics; in essence, country music had to change in order to survive. The metamorphosis that occurred led to the emergence of more cosmopolitan country music styles and the transformation of more bucolic ones. Every country music subgenre experienced some type of transformation during the period as a means to sustaining its appeal among an existing (but modified) audience or to gaining popularity among an expanding one.

Although the country music audience was not exclusively southern, a look at how southern society evolved in the 1940s provides several clues as to why the modernization of country music took place within this period. The South of 1940 was predominantly rural; in fact, 65 percent of white southerners lived in areas of 2,500 inhabitants or less. Only about 16 percent of urban southerners lived in cities with a population of 50,000 or more (table 4). By 1950, the percentage of white southerners residing in rural areas dropped from nearly two-thirds to just over one-half (53 percent); simultaneously, the white population of large southern urban areas (50,000 or more) grew by 5 percent (from 16 to 21 percent; table 5). The 1940s witnessed a period of massive white exodus from the southern countryside. Many came to cities looking for war-industry jobs; others experienced displacement from farms due to changes in southern agriculture. Some found a better life and entered the middle class; others encountered novel problems and struggled to achieve financial independence. Country music spoke to the urban integration sought by some and the alienation felt by others. Bill Malone notes that "its performers and audience were torn by opposing desires, clinging to a self-image of rustic simplicity while at the same time striving to be accepted in an urban, middle-class milieu." Some country music subgenres appealed to listeners seeking to break free from rustic roots, while others drew an audience grappling with the rural/urban dichotomy. Many listeners who remained in the countryside still liked the old stuff; some preferred to hear it in a new way. As musical styles began to merge near the end of the period, the country music audience splintered into stratified groups drawn to the musical and lyrical nuances of the subgenres.[16]

Country music was able to achieve its successful transformation from regional folk art form to national phenomenon through its ability to reach its listeners with musical styles and lyrical themes that appealed to changing tastes and lifestyles while holding steadfast to its original homespun approach. To an increasing number of Americans in the 1950s attracted to its honesty and unpretentiousness, country music offered an alternative to popular music's insipidity. Through its realistic depictions of everyday life, country music seemed to capture the essence of Americans' contemporary concerns. To many white southerners, it simply continued to be the music they grew up with, the music of their communities produced by men and women of similar cultural background. But the South had changed, and so had the music the region produced. Between 1939 and 1954, country music and the South underwent a modernizing process. Along the way, country music performers, purveyors, and promoters struggled to achieve respectability and acceptance on both a regional and national scale in the face of prejudice and indifference. In the end, they succeeded in their efforts by producing a music that simultaneously spoke to the concerns of a regional, base audience in socioeconomic flux and appealed to a nation searching for simplicity amid the intricacies of postwar life.

PART

ONE

THE NATIONALIZATION OF COUNTRY MUSIC

1 | RADIO BARN DANCES, SCHOOLHOUSE SHOWS, AND "HILLBILLY" DOMESTICATION
PROGRESSIVE COUNTRY MUSIC IN THE PREWAR ERA

The initial stages of country music's modernization took place in a region on the verge of a social revolution. In 1939, the American South found itself amid social changes precipitated by the New Deal. Principally, the mechanization of southern agriculture accelerated the migration of southern sharecroppers to cities, both North and South, as farming became increasingly less labor intensive. But the heyday of migration and mechanization was still on the horizon, and the South of the late 1930s closely resembled the South of the 1920s; many places within the region, in fact, looked as they did in 1900. Historian David Goldfield points out that on the eve of World War II "the South was still a rural, agrarian region in the midst of an urban, industrial nation. Its cities were modest and the characteristic urban settlement was the small town." The vision of a "New South" proclaimed by Henry Grady in the late 1800s proved unfounded in 1939, not only in an economic sense, but in a sociocultural one as well. Although some elements of progressivism crept into southern cities, the hinterland remained predominantly unaffected by the early-twentieth-century phenomenon. When the South began its major economic transformation in the 1930s, it hesitantly strolled into modernity unsure of the social costs. For the time being, the region remained sectionalized and undaunted by the cultural homogenization occurring on a national scale.[1]

In its isolation from American society, the rural South clung to the values and customs that shaped its identity. For many rural white southerners, country music manifested their worldview in addition to offering an avenue for entertainment. White southerners listened to country music because its lyrics captured the particulars of their lives while the music provided a reason to congregate with friends and family. In their daily lives, country music listeners worked at a variety of manual labor jobs, from farming to mining, and lived in an assortment of dwellings, from comfortable homes to shanties. Merle Travis's recollection of life growing up in a coal-mining town in Kentucky captures the domestic surroundings of many country music listeners in the area: "Dad never owned a car, a horse or a mule from the time I was born and Mom never had any rugs for the floor, an ice box or anything more modern than a coal stove and five-gallon crock churn. We never had electricity or water-works and money was out of the question. . . . We never had a bit of paint on the house. . . . There was no locks on the door. And there was no inside plumbing. We got our water from a spring down the hill." In northern Alabama, the Louvin Brothers' parents eked out a living as semisubsistent farmers. The family hauled the cotton they plowed with mules to Chattanooga and occasionally sold food crops locally for cash. Up the road in Elkmont, Alabama, the Delmore Brothers' parents worked the rocky red clay as tenant farmers. As a sharecropper's son, Johnny Cash had to put in a full day's work picking cotton upon reaching the age of twelve. Some families turned to moonshining to augment their meager earnings.[2]

White working-class southerners in the 1930s worked hard and maintained unsophisticated lifestyles. Social gatherings usually centered on family functions. Starved for entertainment, they were naturally excited at the announcement of a local dance or the performance of a musician coming to their town. White southerners looked on music as an important social and religious part of their lives. Music could be heard everywhere: mothers sang old popular ballads around the house, men sang in the fields, children sang in schools, and everyone sang in church. Music often provided the impetus for domestic social gatherings, many taking place in parlors emptied of furniture and rugs to make room for dancing. Barbecues, house raisings, fish fries, candy breakings, and corn shuckings also allowed for social interaction, with omnipresent musicians furnishing the necessary milieu. Roy Acuff recalls the religious and social gatherings that he attended as "the only contact I had with the outside world" before his family acquired a radio.[3]

The radio itself provided another reason for assembly, especially among those who could not afford the device. Southerners without radios often gathered at a local store on weekends to hear their favorite musical shows. Johnnie Wright recalls: "I remember that me and my brothers liked to go down to the store [and listen to the *WSM Barn Dance*]. We'd lie there on one-hundred pound feedsacks and listen until the music stopped." In the absence of radios, many people simply gathered around a local business in the evening to hear an impromptu performance by amateur local musicians. Music was everywhere, and southerners sang, played, and listened to it every chance they could get.[4]

Southerners' fascination with regional music stems from its historical roots, which date back to the first settlements of the South. As Bill Malone points out, "hillbilly music . . . evolved primarily out of the reservoir of folksongs, ballads, dances, and instrumental pieces brought to North America by Anglo-

Celtic immigrants." Trans-Atlantic migrants brought this musical baggage to both the northern and southern colonies, but as the eighteenth century progressed, the Anglo folk musical tradition tended to remain more prevalent in southern social circles. The influx of non-British immigrants to the North in the mid-1800s certainly had a great deal to do with the erosion of Anglo folk music's presence in the region, as did northern urbanization. D. K. Wilgus explains, "By the end of the eighteenth century, the North was receiving newer material and newer styles than the South and was under pressure to conform to emerging urban 'popular' styles and to accept the products of the growing urban commercial entertainment industry." The South, meanwhile, though neither ethnically homogenous nor without urbanization, maintained a preference for older, rural English musical styles. The folk culture that developed in the region as a result of its agrarian economy and sectional isolation fostered a music that tended to reaffirm conservative rural values. The presence of a variety of ethnic groups in the South, including Germans, Mexicans, Poles, French, and especially African Americans, led to the dilution of the British musical matrix, but a substantial English legacy survived the eighteenth century.[5]

The Civil War precipitated a course of events that fundamentally altered the nature of southern music and set the groundwork for its commercialization. Immigration to and emigration from the South increased cultural interaction while railroads advanced interregional communication. The South's economy remained primarily rural based, but manufacturing and extracting industries began devoting more attention to opportunities within Dixie's borders. These developments laid the foundation for both the commercialization of southern music and the rise of professional musicians. Norm Cohen notes that "the surge in urbanization and industrialization provided both the means and the market for a mass-produced entertainment medium." Simultaneously, the products of northern songwriters penetrated the southern market, primarily through traveling medicine and minstrel shows.[6]

Often touring with nomadic circuses, the semiprofessional minstrels introduced southerners to northern music while popularizing the African-derived banjo. Sometimes they performed alone at rural courthouses; other times they played in tandem with other musicians, initiating the string-band sound with their conglomeration of fiddle, banjo, tambourines, and a variety of percussive instruments. Medicine shows also provided work for musicians, many of whom went on to become country music performers, such as Jimmie Rodgers, Uncle Dave Macon, Roy Acuff, and Hank Williams. The medicine show, Roy Acuff explains, "was the vaudeville of America's South, at least the small towns and hamlets of the South." This type of show often employed balladeers to sing many of the sentimental pieces popularized in the North near the end of the 1800s. Centered on New York's Twenty-eighth Street, near Union Square, the song-publishing houses of Tin Pan Alley were the source for many of these ballads, which remained popular in the South well after the dance craze of the early 1900s diminished their popularity in the North. War weariness in the postbellum period and economic dislocation into farm tenancy drew many southerners to sentimental pieces of the Victorian era, which appealed to their traditional value structure and penchant for nostalgia.[7]

Through exposure to professional entertainers and sheet music, southerners brought back home a considerable amount of commercial music in the late nineteenth and early twentieth centuries. In their parlors, they played pianos and sang many Tin Pan Alley compositions. At frolics, country fiddlers began to augment their repertoire of Old World dance music with ragtime tunes, waltzes, and other products of popular entertainment. Meanwhile, the guitar and mandolin, increasingly available through mail-order catalogs, began to encroach on the popularity of the banjo and fiddle. The fiddle remained supreme at public gatherings, but fiddlers increasingly sought the accompaniment of guitarists and banjoists for rhythmic purposes. In many southern homes, women continued to sing older folk songs and hymns a cappella, but more and more pianos and dulcimers entered homes along with newer song material.[8]

By 1920, southern music represented the product of three centuries of ethnic intermingling and approximately fifty years of exposure to commercial influences. The evolution of southern music began the first time American colonists added provincial ingredients of American society to a British folk song. First through racial and ethnic interaction, and later through the creation of Protestant hymnals, the transformation of southern music occurred in a series of stages, constantly evolving and adapting itself to contemporary conditions. In the postbellum period, southern music absorbed the influence of popular ballads and the repertoires of traveling professional and semiprofessional entertainers.

For all the encroachment of American popular culture, rural white southern music in the early twenties remained peculiarly and distinctly southern. In the mid-twenties, the relatively new recording industry recognized the economic potential of southern music and set about marketing it to an isolated audience. In the process of commercializing the music of rural white southerners, these companies ushered in the next stage of southern music's transformation, one characterized by the exportation of local styles to regional markets.[9]

The inauspicious birth of commercially recorded rural white southern music (hereafter referred to as country music) took place on July 1, 1922, in New York City. Fresh on the heels of playing for a Civil War veterans' reunion in Virginia, Arkansas-born A. C. "Eck" Robertson and Oklahoma-born Henry Gilliland appeared at the offices of Victor Records. Uninvited and unannounced, the two must have received a cool reception, but the company's directors permitted the recording of a few tunes, and Victor subsequently released Robertson's solo fiddle version of "Sallie Gooden." Although Robertson's disc enjoyed some success, country music found its first commercially viable performer in Fiddlin' John Carson. A champion fiddler born in the hill country of northern Georgia, Carson gained his musical reputation from performances in political campaigns, various social gatherings, and especially at the Old Time Fiddlers' Association Convention in Atlanta, where he won the championship at least seven times between 1913 and 1922. In the mid-1920s, Ralph Peer, a representative of the General Phonograph Corporation, traveled to Georgia to record Carson. Okeh Records tentatively shipped five hundred copies of two selections from the Carson session to the Atlanta area. When the initial pressings sold out within a month or so, Okeh signed Carson to an exclusive recording contact, and so began the commercialization of rural white southern music.[10]

Recording companies' interest in the music of rural whites actually began in 1919, two years after the publication of Cecil Sharp's *Folksongs from the Southern Appalachians*. Previously confined to the music of Native Americans and rural blacks, Americans' vision of folk music soon expanded to the realms of white folk music via cowboy songs and Appalachian ballads. Record companies initially marketed the recordings of these folk idioms primarily to urban audiences, often using performers of urban origin. The music that covered the southern countryside struck the American public as much less romantic and the record companies as much less profitable. The Scopes Monkey Trial of 1925 heightened Americans' disdain for all things southern and helped to confine the promotion of early country music to a rural, white southern audience. Although the companies attempted to soften the inelegant roots of country music with such labels as "Olde Time Fiddlin' Tune" and "Familiar Tunes on Fiddle, Banjo, Harmonica, and Accordion," they could not veil the music's unadorned rusticity. In 1925, Ralph Peer labeled a band he was recording Hill Billies, and by late 1926 the term *hillbilly music* appeared in *Variety* as a label for what most Americans viewed as more "southern" than "folk" music.[11]

Initially viewed as status symbols at the turn of the century, records gradually became more affordable in the 1920s, largely due to plummeting sales brought about by the emerging popularity of radio. The increased availability of records brought about two important developments in country music: the expansion of its audience within its original demographic market and the initial intermingling of subregional styles. Although the extent of the former development is difficult to gauge, the fact that the country music industry survived both the initial misgivings of the record companies and the crippling effects of the Great Depression suggests there was an expansion of the audience. Merle Travis's parents did not have a great deal of disposable income, yet he recalls his father ordering a record from the Sears Roebuck catalog if enough money was left over after the purchase of necessities. The establishment of Decca Records in 1934 had a great deal to do with this phenomenon. Founder Jack Kapp's introduction of a lower-priced record line nudged other companies to do the same, with most reductions coming in their folk catalogs. With record prices falling, as Chet Atkins recalls, "suddenly there was more music for everybody."[12]

While broadening the country music audience, the availability of records also allowed for the commixture of various performing styles. The complex roots of the genre ensured that from the beginning it would bear the imprints of American popular music and the ethnic and racial conglomeration of the southern states. Together with the vigorous presence of radio, records provided the opportunity for performers to absorb the intricacies of other musicians and vocalists. Ever so slowly, country moved closer to an identifiable hybrid of folk, pop, and peculiarly southern music. To many northern listeners, it may very well have all sounded the same from the start, but the process of sculpting country music into its modern form took nearly thirty years. By no means complete by 1939, the molding process was certainly under way, with records playing an ever-increasing role in the process.

No single artist played a more prominent role in stylistic diffusion than Jimmie Rodgers. Appropriately termed the "Father of Country Music," Rodgers had a profound influence on performers of the 1930s and 1940s and spawned a flock of imitators and disciples. In every aspect, from his manner of dress to his singing and performing style, Jimmie Rodgers made an impression on his audience that directly influenced country music's development for nearly twenty years. Writing in 1953, Ralph Peer reflected on Rodgers's importance: "The impetus which he gave to so-called hillbilly music . . . set in motion the factors which resulted in making this sector of the amusement business into a matter of world-wide importance and a source for a high percentage of our popular hits." Initially recorded by Peer in 1927, Rodgers became the most popular country music entertainer of the Depression. At the time of his death in 1933, he was selling two to three times more records than any other contemporary country music performer. Nolan Porterfield, Jimmie Rodgers's biographer, notes that even at the height of the Depression people often spent a day's pay for a Jimmie Rodgers record. With a combination of personal magnetism and sexual appeal, Jimmie Rodgers attracted both urban and rural listeners, but, according to Hank Snow and Ernest Tubb, it was his sincere manner of singing that drew the attention of southern youths: "Jimmie set a pattern in singing folk songs to sing the way the song feels. . . . This free way of singing made an impression on all of us that followed."[13]

Jimmie Rodgers's legacy lay not only in his vocal style but also in his musical repertoire. Rodgers's penchant for singing and playing a variety of musical styles, from blues to pop to jazz, opened the eyes and ears of many of his listeners to country music's potential. His most enduring selections of lyrical material, however, remained firmly rooted in the southern soil. From blues songs to hobo laments to rambler struts, Rodgers's repertoire served as the lyrical foundation for a genre drifting away from its instrumentally inclined base. His popularity ensured that a country music performer's commercial success would forever be linked to his or her ability to reach listeners with lyrics that touched their lives.

Jimmie Rodgers's pushing of the musical boundaries of country music coupled with his lyrical legacy set the stage for the 1930s as a transitional period for the genre. Younger performers influenced by Rodgers began to supplant older performers on radio and records. Unlike their predecessors, these progressive performers did not find contentment as part-time musicians, for Rodgers's success proved that they could make a living, perhaps even a lucrative one, as country music performers. Although they grew up in an atmosphere of conservative folk music, they recognized the commercial viability of incorporating less austere musical idioms as blues and ragtime into the country music repertoire. Many grew up listening to radio and records. As historian Robert Coltman points out, "they were already at one remove from the source. . . . They had an idea that they might be able to learn new licks and tricks from pop crooners, blues singers, orchestras, Latin dancers, ragtimers, jazzers." They borrowed ideas from one another as well as from other musical genres, and more important, they wrote many of their own songs. Their lyrics reflected their rural, southern upbringings, but their instrumental backup became more experimental, augmentations of the traditional string-band sound with mandolin, stand-up bass, and acoustic steel guitar. Their vocals became smoother and softer, often employing harmony to create an atmosphere in marked contrast to the musical rusticity of earlier performers. These younger performers embraced the benefits associated with commercialization and clearly subscribed to the notion that country music needed to advance beyond its folk roots in order to expand its audience base. [14]

The term *commercialization* implies a pollution of something pure, but it is doubtful that the younger performers of the thirties viewed their actions as contaminative to country music's authenticity. Country music in the 1930s could not remain static with radio and records encouraging the cross-fertilization of American musical styles. In enhancing the commercial viability of country music, younger performers served as vanguards for the modernization of country music that took place in the 1940s. Judging from these performers' success, the country music audience did not view them as inauthentic country artists. Some performers stuck close to country music's folk roots, while others disregarded all parameters in their experimentations. Listeners picked and chose their favorites as country music sauntered away from its folk isolation. Bill Ivey points out that the process began as early as the mid-twenties: "From the moment it appeared on radio and on commercial recordings . . . country music began to gain sophistication and to lose some of the rough-hewn purity that characterized the white southern folk tradition." By 1940, country music continued to reflect its southern origins while its audience remained primarily rural and southern in composition. Along with records, radio laid the groundwork for country music's breakthrough in the World War II era. [15]

Radio served as a vitally important cultural medium in the 1930s, and therefore as a great agent for country music expansion and change. The relatively young radio industry underwent considerable growth in the thirties, mainly due to its ability to provide inexpensive entertainment in the midst of the Depression. In 1930, 40 percent of American homes reported having one or more radios; by 1940, the figure doubled to 81 percent. Even in the poverty-stricken South, 60 percent of whites owned a radio in 1940. In the days before television, radio was an important source of entertainment for southerners whose economic status precluded more expensive avenues of leisure. Chet Atkins explains, "Most of the small towns in the South depended on the radio as their contact with the outside world." In the early mornings and then again at noon, southerners could tune in to hear performers on regional stations. In the days before radio stations proliferated the airwaves, a listener in North Carolina could hear a small 1,000-watt station one or two states away in addition to local programming. High-wattage stations, such as WSM and WLS, enjoyed clear-channel status, enabling listeners from around the country to tune into them. At night, the infamous outlaw X-stations blaring from Mexico with tremendous wattage transmitted country music between near-ubiquitous commercials. And on the weekends, a selection of radio barn dances blanketed the South.[16]

The first American radio station, KDKA, went on the air in Pittsburgh in 1920, and within a couple of years radio stations began to appear in the South. In the absence of network programming (NBC and CBS were not formed until 1926 and 1927, respectively), stations turned to local talent for music and talk shows. Fiddlin' John Carson's appearance on Atlanta's 500-watt WSB in the fall of 1922 signaled the beginning of country music programming in the South. Inspired by the communal rural gatherings of previous centuries, the radio barn dance offered listeners a variety program of comedy and down-home music. WBAP in Fort Worth initiated the barn dance format on the night of January 4, 1923, with its broadcast of an hour and a half of square dance music, but the era of the weekly barn dance began on April 19, 1924, when the *WLS Barn Dance* in Chicago went on the air.[17]

Initially skeptical of the profitability of a program centered on nostalgic country dances, heart songs, and novelty numbers, WLS's owners, Sears Roebuck, soon discovered its potential when telegrams and letters began pouring into the station after the *Barn Dance*'s first broadcasts. Gradually, as the station's wattage increased (from 500 to 5,000 watts in 1925), so too did its roster of *Barn Dance* performers. The station's hiring of Bradley Kincaid in 1926 symbolized its effort to target a national rural audience, composed of southerners and nonsoutherners alike. Like many other radio stations that broadcast north of the Ohio River, WLS promoted a style of "country" music that exhibited less affiliation to the southern hybrid and more attention to a conglomeration of the English folk tradition and the northern and midwestern ethnic music mix. Kincaid brought to WLS the English and mountain folk songs and hymns his mother sang to him as a child growing up in Kentucky. When the *Prairie Farmer* purchased the station in 1928, the new owners continued the policy of emphasizing folk talent that would not alienate northern listeners. D. K. Wilgus points out, "Early WLS artists performed in styles lacking some of the sharp, regional characteristics of the South." Glenn Snydor, WLS manager after 1932, termed rural southern music "hungry hillbilly" and kept smoother-sounding groups, such as the Prairie Ramblers, on the program to offset the presence of a band of southern singers and musicians called the Cumberland Ridge Runners. George Biggar, one of *Barn Dance*'s early program directors, commented on his dislike of the term *hillbilly*: "We use the terms 'folk music' for traditional music, and 'modern folk music' for more recently written songs." In 1954, WLS performers Homer and Jethro used the phrase "uptown hillbilly" to describe the music heard on the *National Barn Dance* since its inception. Another country music show out of the Midwest, the WHO *Iowa Barn Dance Frolic*, similarly emphasized a variety of singing styles more rural than southern in approach. Despite their initial trepidations, the midwestern barn dances introduced northern listeners to "country" music and paved the way for the genre's audience expansion of the 1940s. [18]

By 1935, some five thousand radio programs across the nation featured some type of country music. With network programming in its infancy, most stations still relied on local shows to fill airtime. This was especially true in the South and Southwest because only 45 of the regions' 137 radio stations maintained an affiliation with the networks. Most stations broadcast under 20,000 watts because the absence of airwave competition increased their coverage area. Some, like 5,000-watt WWVA, in Wheeling, West Virginia, reached audiences in the Northeast as well. In April 1933, the station began broadcasting the *World's Original WWVA Jamboree,* and some of the show's stars, such as Doc Williams, soon gained a following in the northern states. Two personalities on two Knoxville stations, Cas Walker (WROL) and Lowell Blanchard (WNOX), dominated eastern Tennessee radio in the 1930s and 1940s. Walker emphasized local talent and early morning live shows. The WNOX station manager hired Blanchard in 1936 with specific instructions to acquire hillbilly performers. The *WNOX Mid-Day Merry-Go-Round* (officially named in 1936) supplemented country music with Dixieland, swing, and a heavy dose of comedy to create a true variety program. Blanchard also introduced a Saturday night program, eventually named the *Tennessee Barn Dance,* in 1942 that introduced its Appalachian listeners to several polished vocalists and musicians as well as traditional mountain music. Other early barn dances included the *Old-Fashioned Barn Dance* (KMOX, Saint Louis, begun around 1930), the *Crazy Barn Dance* (WBT, Charlotte, 1934), the *Boone County Jamboree* (WLW, Cincinnati, 1936), the *Old Dominion Barn Dance* (WRVA, Richmond, 1938), the *KWKH Round-Up* (Shreveport, 1939), and the *WSB Barn Dance* (Atlanta, 1940). Many of these stations increased to 50,000 watts in the late 1930s and early 1940s; the overall effect was an enlargement of the country music audience and a breakdown in the isolation of regional musical tastes. Primarily through the barn dance programs, radio became the chief exponent of southern music to the nation in the 1930s. Roy Acuff explains, "There's no question, it helped to popularize country music. It carried 'hillbilly' music far beyond the hills and into the living rooms of people everywhere, and turned it into 'country' music." Reciprocally, radio exposed white southern musicians to other regional and nationally popular styles that profoundly influenced country music's creative development. One country music show, however, the *Grand Ole Opry*, demonstrated considerable more interest in exporting southeastern musical stylings than it did in incorporating other regional singularities into its program.[19]

The *Grand Ole Opry* made its debut as the *WSM Barn Dance* on November 28, 1925, and within a month became a regularly scheduled Saturday evening program. The *Opry* was essentially the creation of "Judge" George Hay, a radio announcer whose career began in Memphis and continued in Chicago, where he became a popular announcer, before his arrival in Nashville in late 1925. Armed with an influx of telegrams supporting the first *Barn Dance* broadcasts, Hay convinced the station's owners, Nashville's National Life and Accident Insurance Company, of the potential of a variety program that appealed to rural listeners. Like the Midwest barn dances, the first WSM country shows revolved around an eclectic mixture of nostalgic, popular, and rural music, but by 1928 the program (by then called the *Grand Ole Opry*) focused on instrumental string bands. Hay discouraged the development of "stars," but two solo performers, an African American harmonica player named De Ford Bailey and an irrepressible older banjoist known as "Uncle Dave" Macon, emerged as popular featured acts by the time the station's wattage increased to 50,000 in 1932.[20]

In 1925, Hay seemed content to promote the *Opry* as a show featuring folk music with amateur performers. Gradually, however, Hay became more interested in popularizing the show as a barn dance featuring authentic southern rural musicians. Despite the fact that some of the *Opry*'s early performers came from urban and even professional backgrounds, Hay insisted on their cultivating a rustic, bucolic image. Hence, the group Dr. Bate and His Augmented Orchestra became the Possum Hunters and began dressing in hillbilly attire. The *Opry*'s evolution into a stage show with a live audience had a great deal to do with this development. David Cobb, who came to WSM as an announcer in the early 1930s, commented that "mostly lower-middle class people [of] mostly rural background" comprised the bulk of the show's live audience. Musicians and singers popular in other parts of the country often experienced a cool reception from the *Opry* crowd. *National Barn Dance* superstar Bradley Kincaid found his career in Nashville short-lived: "I never did feel at home on the *Grand Ole Opry* like I did at WLS. I'd say that I was just fairly popular on the *Grand Ole Opry*—not like I was on WLS." Grandpa Jones, who toured with Kincaid on a successful tour of the Northeast, offers this explanation as to why: "The audience in Nashville was different from audiences in New England. Bradley was doing songs . . . that you've really got to listen to because they are slow and tell a story. The *Opry* audiences were into a lot of noise and hand-slapping and more of the band sound was taking over."[21]

Hay's famous line of advice to *Opry* performers, "Keep it down to earth, boys," symbolized his awareness of audience tastes as well as his own musical preferences. More than anything else, Hay fought the intrusion of electric instruments into *Opry* broadcasts. Sam McGee, one of the *Opry*'s more recognized guitarists, discovered that the policy applied to everyone, regardless of popularity: "I got by with [playing an electric guitar on the *Opry*] about two Saturday nights; about the third one, [Judge Hay] come in and patted me on the shoulder: 'Now you wouldn't play that on the *Grand Ole Opry*. You know we're going to hold it down to earth.' And I said, 'Well, thank you, Judge, I won't bring it back any more.' " As WSM increased in wattage and the *Grand Ole Opry* gained in stature, however, Hay found his control of the show circumvented by Harry Stone, who replaced Hay as station manager of the *Opry* in 1930. Historian Charles Wolfe describes Stone's demeanor and the vision he brought to WSM: "[He] was cool, efficient, businesslike, and thoroughly professional. He saw that the show would have to attract full time, professional acts, and he set about trying to make it possible for WSM to support full-time musicians." To this end, Stone formed the WSM Artists' Service Bureau in 1934 to systematically promote the personal appearances of *Opry* acts. Additionally, he hired nontraditional (and nonsouthern) acts such as the Vagabonds to soften Hay's hard-edged approach. Stone could point to the fact that only 15 percent of the 60,000 weekly letters to the station came from Tennessee listeners, with at least 20 percent originating from nonsouthern states such as Ohio, Michigan, and Pennsylvania. At least in part due to Stone's actions, the *Grand Ole Opry*'s popularity increased dramatically as the 1930s progressed. The show's institutional status was confirmed on October 14, 1939, when NBC broadcast a thirty-minute segment of the show sponsored by R. J. Reynolds's Prince Albert Tobacco on its national Red network. By July 1940, thirty-five NBC stations were carrying the thirty-minute portion of the six-hour local broadcast coast to coast. Within a span of fifteen years, the *Grand Ole Opry* had made the transition from an informal local program centered on amateur musicians to a nationally broadcast show featuring professional performers playing in a variety of musical styles.[22]

While George Hay fought the onslaughts of the star system and sophistication, John Lair was concocting his own vision of a program revolving around folk talent. As a youth growing up in Kentucky's Renfro Valley, Lair developed a deep appreciation of American folk music and Appalachian culture, an affection that he brought in spirit and body (in the form of the Cumberland Ridge Runners) to WLS in the early 1930s. The polish of the *National Barn Dance* format, however, proved incongruous with Lair's idea of an authentic rural program, and he eventually moved to Cincinnati's WLW, bringing many of the Ridge Runners with him. Not content to simply simulate a barn dance, Lair came up with the idea of broadcasting an actual one from a rural site. Not surprisingly, he chose Renfro Valley as the locale, and with three members of the Ridge Runners, he purchased a tract of land in the area. The first *Renfro Valley Barn Dance* was broadcast from Cincinnati in October 1937, but on November 4, 1939, the show debuted on Louisville's WHAS from a rural site near Mount Vernon, Kentucky. The show went on to enjoy considerable success both as a radio program and as a tourist attraction. By 1941, plans were under way to construct a hotel on the site to accommodate the average Saturday night crowd of five thousand people who could not be housed in the settlement's lodge and tourist cabins. The barn could only house one thousand people at a time, so Lair scheduled several shows on Saturday afternoons and evenings. Eventually picked up by network radio, the show became an unqualified success. Like Hay, Lair enforced a strict yet unconventional dress code for the show's performers. Homer Haynes and Jethro Burns recall that Lair kept a close eye on everything from a performer's haircut to his costuming. Lair also came up with several characters for the show, including Old Joe Clark and the Coon Creek Girls.[23]

As pioneers of the barn dance format, John Lair, George Hay, George Biggar, and others demonstrated the potential of rural-based programming in the Depression. Unlike country music recordings, which were distributed primarily in the South, the radio barn dance freely disseminated the music of the rural, white South to a national audience. The acquisition of a nonsouthern audience inevitably led to efforts to broaden country music's scope beyond its rough-hewn beginnings. The WLS *National Barn Dance* was particularly influential in this development through its promotion of vocalists and female artists. As the paramount communications medium of the 1930s, radio effectively challenged the southern rubric that confined the public performance of country music to instrumental, male-dominated groups.

The radio barn dances offered women the opportunity to reassert their role as carriers of distinct southern musical traditions and furnished them with a source of supplemental income or even possibly a career. Prior to the commercialization of rural white southern music, women preserved English ballads through their informal (and often a cappella) singing in domestic settings. Although men provided the music for secular public gatherings, women exercised their influence on songs heard around the house and in church. With the popularity of parlor pianos and sheet music in the late nineteenth and early twentieth centuries, women also exposed their children to sentimental Victorian ballads and the offerings of Tin Pan Alley songwriters. In addition to transmitting songs and singing styles to future generations, women played a variety of instruments in homes, from banjo to guitar, and in some cases, even the fiddle. In dominating the musical environment of the domestic sphere, southern women played a major role in shaping the development of the region's distinct musical characteristics.[24]

As an outgrowth of public performances, early commercial southern music largely reflected the male-dominated southern string-band and frolic traditions. Musically, this meant an emphasis on a rather abrasive combination of banjo, guitar, and short-bow fiddling. Reflecting the early commercial period's public performance roots, vocalists often sang in a full-throated, resonant style. Lyrically, their song repertoire ranged from folk songs and popular tunes to original and traditional blues numbers. The domestic tradition of sentimental ballads, nostalgic pieces, and hymns was never completely eclipsed in the 1920s and early 1930s, but record companies' penchant for fiddle-based music and bluesy vocals, coupled with southern social norms, ensured the male domination of early country music. Robert Coltman estimates that only 3 percent of individual artists and groups in country music recorded between 1922 and 1931 were women soloists or all-women groups. In general, few string bands admitted women as musicians, leading some, such as Samantha Bumgarner and Eva Davis in 1924, to form their own bands. More often, they played backup roles as vocalists or accompanists in family bands or in religious-based groups. It was not until Ralph Peer recorded the Carter Family in August 1927 that record companies began to recognize women's role in the country music equation.[25]

Several factors contributed to the Carter Family's success, with their undeniable musical talents and lyrical repertoire topping the list. The harmonic blending of Maybelle Carter's alto and Sara Carter's soprano created one of country music's finest vocal pairings, and Maybelle's distinct rhythm guitar style inspired thousands of young southern guitarists. Lyrically, their songs explored religious and domestic themes, emphasizing sentimental and fundamentalist imagery in a marriage of church and parlor traditions. Bill Malone points out, "The Carter Family sang of an America that was gradually disappearing, an America whose values had seemed inextricably interrelated with rural or small-town life." Although their records sold more steadily than spectacularly, the Carter Family's achievements demonstrated the commercial viability of the domestic country tradition. More important, their success invalidated the precept that associated female performers with immorality. Shielded by the male presence of A. P. Carter (as chaperon and occasional vocalist), Sara and Maybelle Carter exuded virtuousness in their presentations of songs about home and God. Until their retirement from records in 1941 and radio in 1943, they remained one of early country music's most durable and successful acts, setting an important precedent for other performers of the Depression era.[26]

While a few female performers, such as Patsy Montana and Louise Massey, enjoyed commercial success via record sales, the vast majority of women who built careers in country music did so through radio. Mary Bufwack points out, however, that even on radio they remained an unmistakable minority, representing only about 10 to 15 percent of barn dance acts during the Depression. The WLS *National Barn Dance* featured female performers more prominently than its southern counterparts, and several of those women gained national popularity. Myrtle Eleanor Cooper, who was also known as Lulu Belle, arrived at WLS in 1932 as a comedienne and singer; by the mid-thirties she had emerged as one of country music's most popular female performers as well as one of the nation's top radio personalities. Dolly and Millie Good, the Girls of the Golden West, joined the *National Barn Dance* in 1933; by 1935, their appealing western repertoire garnered them a spot as regulars on Rudy Vallee's national radio show broadcast from New York City. Eventually, they landed in Cincinnati on WLW's *Midwestern Hayride,* where they remained a popular staple into the 1950s. In their employment of western imagery, the Girls of the Golden West broke free from the shackles of the domestic lyrical tradition. WLS promoted other female performers as farm girls, with the DeZurick Sisters representing one of the most successful acts in this vein.[27]

In the South, women found more radio opportunities as comediennes. Minnie Pearl (née Sarah Ophelia Colley) developed a country girl persona that the *Grand Ole Opry* audience fell in love with soon after her arrival at WSM in 1940. The daughter of an affluent Tennessee sawmill owner, Colley started her career as an actress, but soon found the opportunity that "Minnie Pearl" presented more lucrative. Cousin Emmy (Cynthia May Carver), another comedienne, learned to play a variety of instruments growing up in Kentucky. After becoming the first woman to win the National Old-Time Fiddlers' Contest at Louisville in 1935, she joined WWVA in Wheeling and over the course of the next fifteen years became a very successful regional performer. In commenting on Cousin Emmy's attributes and legacy, Mary Bufwack notes that "she relied on her native wit and intelligence to survive as country music's first independent, unmarried, self-supporting female touring attraction." Through their caricatures of Minnie Pearl and Cousin Emmy, Colley and Carver broke into the southern barn dance fraternity to emerge as independent stars in their own right.[28]

Another barrier for female country music performers fell with the formation of the first all-female string band, the Coon Creek Girls, in 1937. Lily May Ledford, the group's founding member, journeyed from her native Kentucky to the WLS *National Barn Dance* in 1936. A year later, she took part in the exodus of WLS talent to Cincinnati led by John Lair. True to form, Lair encouraged Ledford and the Coon Creek Girls to maintain a hill folk appearance. As a staple on the *Renfro Valley Barn Dance,* the Coon Creek Girls excelled as a first-rate string band capable of holding their own among their male counterparts.[29]

By the end of the 1930s, women had established their presence in the country music field mainly through the inroads they made into the radio barn dances. The Carter Family and Lulu Belle certainly set precedents in the country music recording industry, but female performers in general remained second-class citizens in the eyes of the record companies. The radio barn dances, on the other hand, recognized the audience appeal of female singers and comediennes and reserved a place for women on their programs, often as frontliners. More opportunities existed for female performers in the North than in the South, primarily due to the persistence of derogatory images of female performers in the southern states. Despite the limitations imposed by their gender, southern women in the 1930s proclaimed their right to be acknowledged as country music performers and re-established their influence on southern music.

Male performers paid meager attention to these developments. Their primary concern lay in establishing a name for themselves in the still-uncertain country music business. For the vast majority, this meant obtaining a spot on a local radio station that enabled them to advertise their personal appearances. Some country music performers sold quite a few records, but most relied on the income derived from their show dates. Charlie Louvin maintains, "You didn't need a record contract in those days. If you worked on the radio, you could play all the show dates that you wanted." Personal appearance dates may not have been as readily available as Louvin implies, but his observation is well founded. According to Merle Travis, phonograph sales were relatively unimportant to artist promotion in the days before World War II: "What did a record mean? It was something you'd stick inside an old phonograph that you couldn't half hear anyhow. Nobody cared about records." Radio, on the other hand, reached countless southerners.[30]

Most radio programming was local, especially during the day throughout the week, and stations naturally turned to native performers to fill airtime. In the South, station owners saw in hillbilly artists an inexpensive source of entertainment that appealed to rural listeners. Generally placed on the air in the early morning hours and around noon—corresponding to rural families' breakfast and dinner times—country music shows, usually fifteen to thirty minutes in length, featured a collage of music, comedy, and advertisement. Almost all performers publicized their personal appearances; others fortunate enough to have sponsors promoted products as well. Some performers offset their nominal compensation for their services by selling songbooks to faithful listeners. Although radio performing did not provide a particularly lucrative living, many artists preferred it to farmwork. Upon discovering their musical talent, many, such as Eddy Arnold, opted for the alternative lifestyle: "[Once] I got to playing at parties . . . I guess I was sixteen, seventeen years old. I decided well now, by george, there's got to be something better than looking up a mule's rear end."[31]

Typical country music radio performers in the late 1930s were white, Protestant males who learned to play music from family members or neighbors living in or near the rural southern communities of their births. They often inherited musical instruments from siblings and other family members and gained exposure to a variety of songs and singing styles through their mothers' warbles, informal social gatherings, radio, and records. Some sought out musical training from African Americans in adjacent communities; others taught themselves to play fiddles, guitars, banjos, and other stringed instruments. Many pursued careers in music rather tentatively, beginning as part-time musicians while fulfilling their obligations on family farms or at a local mill. In Texas, Tom Yarbro arranged his radio programs around his schedule at an oil company. More notable acts like Johnnie and Jack and the Louvin Brothers began their careers in the late 1930s and early 1940s in much the same way, with the Louvins heading to their cotton mill jobs in Chattanooga after their morning show and Johnnie and Jack maintaining day jobs at cabinet and hosiery companies in Nashville. Marty Licklider of the Missouri Fox Hunters describes the experience shared by many others who progressively became full-time musicians: "We were on one program a week and were working in a factory for our living. Gradually, one act after another dropped off the station until ours was the only one left. Then, in May, 1940, we started on the air every day, quit our jobs in the factory, and went into it right." In Chicago, Kentucky migrants Karl Davis and Harty Taylor worked at "factories and things" until Bradley Kincaid was able to secure them a spot on WLS. Countless other performers remained in limbo, biding their time in bands without the benefit of broadcast. In 1941, Virginian Edwin J. Malechek wrote in to the *Mountain Broadcast and Prairie Recorder* describing his situation: "We are still not on the air, but we play dance engagements three nights a week and are doing fairly good. . . . My brothers have good jobs and are making good money and they hate to quit to play on the air again. They are working in a paper factory here. I am also working but I am not happy at the work I am doing. All my life I wanted to play music, and when I work that's all I have been thinking about, music."[32]

Country music performers of the late 1930s and early 1940s usually developed their affection for performing at an early age, often encouraged by their neighbors. As youths, the Louvin Brothers honed their craft with performances at community cakewalks and ice cream suppers. Pat and Russell Jackson of the Dixie Playboys cut their musical teeth at local square dances in a farm community south of Nashville. As Pat Jackson recalls, "Most times they'd have a wood-cuttin' or somethin' and everybody'd gather in and help the man get his wood, then they'd have a big dance at night. Clear out one of the rooms and dance all around. You could feel the old houses shakin' up and down."[33]

From community performances, country musicians secured radio spots on the basis of their local reputations or via impromptu auditions before an owner of a station. Many remained sectional performers throughout their careers. Acts fortunate enough to secure radio spots faced a rather feverish existence if they chose to become full-time musicians. Many drifted from town to town until an area was "played out." Charles Wolfe points out, "It took its toll on the lives of countless entertainers who had to live rootless, nomadic lives bouncing from station to station while they tried to keep their families fed, marriages together, and fresh songs coming." An extended stay on a particular station by no means signified stability. As Russell Jackson recalls, groups had to rectify daily road show commitments in every direction with their daily obligation to their home base: "It was a rough life. . . . You'd get up and play fifteen minutes in the morning and hit the road and ride all day, and then play a couple of hours and then head back." Country music performers weathered the inconveniences of this arrangement as a necessary evil of their occupation.[34]

In many cases, radio acts willingly accepted nominal fees for the opportunity to advertise their personal appearances. These "sustaining programs" offered a great deal of exposure in the days before promoters and record company advertisements in trade magazines. Making a fairly decent living from personal appearances, the Monroe Brothers threw away the first letter they received from a company seeking to record them. When the Monroes finally agreed to a session, they stipulated a limit to its length: "We finally went up to their studio in Charlotte, but we told 'em we didn't have much time, that we had to get back in time to play a school that night." Merle Travis similarly accentuates the expediency of putting radio shows before records: "In those days, records wasn't the thing. Being on the radio was the big thing. . . . If you were on the radio, people [would] write to you, send you chocolate cakes, and all that stuff. Then when you'd go to town, everybody'd come out to see what you looked like and . . . you'd pick their favorites." Most performers viewed records as just another form of advertisement or a means to enhance their reputations. Personal appearances provided the major part of their income.[35]

Local schoolhouses were the most common setting for country music performers' personal appearances in the late 1930s and early 1940s. Roy Acuff explains, "We played schoolhouses mostly, but there were courthouse appearances and church basements, and any sort of place where there was a stage." Shows offered music and comedy for around two hours at a cost of about twenty-five cents for admission. For the use of the facility, school principals and local PTAs generally accepted 40 to 50 percent of a show's proceeds. As Pat Jackson points out, "they were lookin' for a way to make a little bit of money for the schoolhouse, so they was glad to have 'em. Most all of them would welcome you." On the other hand, Bill Bolick of the Blue Sky Boys remembers some schools refused to let country acts play at their institutions: "A lot of the teachers, and especially the principals and the higher ups in the schools, felt that this music wasn't conducive to a good way of life and they were pretty much opposed to it." In any event, once an act secured a venue, the time came for promotion of the show. Performers fortunate enough to have radio shows broadcast their upcoming dates, while others depended more on the distribution of printed circulars. A receptive schoolhouse might actually participate in the advertising process, as Pat Jackson explains: "You'd leave [the circulars] with the school and then the kids would carry them home with 'em and put 'em up and that was a pretty good way of getting it out." Chet Atkins recalls hooking up a public address system to a car battery to promote personal appearances to people who did not have radios. Through whatever means necessary, performers found ways to disseminate information about their upcoming shows.[36]

Personal appearances satisfied rural southerners' hunger for entertainment while providing radio entertainers with much-needed revenue. Russell Jackson recollects, "Most times we had a pretty good crowd. Well, there wasn't else much to do, see, actually. Either sit at home or come and watch us." Quite often, an act remained unsure of a crowd turnout until the time of the show, as Grandpa Jones explains: "I remember one time we had to drive up a dry creek bed—that was the only road—to a little old schoolhouse. We figured there wouldn't be nobody there, but when eight o'clock came, here come lanterns down the mountains. And they filled it up. They knew about us some way." Arriving at a desolate spot in rural Mississippi with Roy Acuff, *Grand Ole Opry* announcer David Cobb remembers expressing his doubts to Acuff about the prospective turnout. With showtime arriving, Cobb's uncertainties proved unfounded: "Boy, did they come. Flatbed wagons drawn by tractors with twenty people of all ages sittin' on 'em and cars and wagons of all descriptions."[37]

The environment at personal appearances undoubtedly made an impact on performing styles. Zeke Morris of the Morris Brothers and Hank Snow both recall the need to both play and sing loud in the absence of amplifiers and microphones. Some schoolhouses provided electricity, but as Chet Atkins recalls, "most of the rooms were so small that you didn't really need amplification." At more rudimentary locales with no stage or electricity, performers simply improvised. Jim and Jesse McReynolds, for example, recall attending a Carter Family personal appearance where the featured act played by the light of kerosene lamps in a corner of an old schoolhouse. The "kerosene circuit," as many performers referred to it, provided family entertainment in a communal setting for thousands of rural southerners, many of whom did not possess automobiles or radios. Although country music acts might occasionally dress in costumes for their performances, little if anything else distinguished them from their listeners. The participants of the communal gatherings in the rural schoolhouses of the South shared common beliefs and similar backgrounds. At no other time in country music's history would its audience have such an infusive impact on the genre's development. Despite the trend toward commercialization via radio and records, country music on the eve of World War II remained a grassroots, folk phenomenon primarily due to the reciprocal relationship established between the performer and the audience at the personal appearance shows.[38]

Some of the most convincing evidence of the genre's prewar folksiness can be found in the prevalence of rural and regional imagery in country music lyrics during the period. The English ballads and Tin Pan Alley songs played through-out the South prior to country music's commercialization tended to focus on the tragic, the nostalgic, and the sentimental. Certainly, a number of humor-ous pieces popularized by minstrels remained popular, as did some nonsensical ditties, but for the most part southerners gravitated toward songs with more somber or nostalgic themes. With commercialization and the subsequent need for fresh material, country music writers continued to emphasize these traditional themes. Gradually, more and more songs appeared dealing with male-female relationships, many containing the same humorous or tragic elements present in earlier folk songs. Fascination with liberal African American blues themes ignited a white blues phenomenon in the late 1920s and early 1930s, leading to the appearance of several rather risqué country music songs that utilized double entendre, a lyrical technique popularized by African American blues performers.

The domestication of country music that occurred in the mid-1930s as a result of radio expansion and personal appearance tours inevitably encouraged writers to explore more conservative themes as the decade progressed. In the midst of the Depression, religious and calamitous songs began to soar in popularity, along with others that predicated traditional norms. Bill Malone points out, "Rural southerners responded affectionately to songs which reaffirmed the values of home, family, mother, and God, and they took to their hearts songs about dying orphans, neglected mothers, blind children, maidens who died of broken hearts, and eastbound trains that carried penniless children to see their poor blind convict fathers." In their penchant for graphic imagery, southern songwriters set the precedent for realism in country music lyrics. Art Satherley elucidates on this development: "In [country] music . . . we concentrate on the emotions. The country people, these so-called hillbillics, are tremendously sensitive people, with deep emotions. Whereas the sophisticated city person likes these humbug, boy-girl love songs, with everything pretty-pretty, the mountaineer is a realist. His songs deal with loneliness, misery, death, murder."[39]

In the 1930s, southerners found the strength to overcome their adversities and rise above their economic plight via the tenets of their religion and their communal ethos. They congregated in rural churches and schoolhouses to tap into these fortifying resources. Rural white southerners gravitated to country music and its performers because the lyrics spoke to their hopes, pains, and aspirations, while the music itself provided them with the opportunity to gather as a collective whole in much the same way as they did on Sunday mornings.

Country music also fostered a collective consciousness by providing a source of pride for many southerners. Through country music, white southerners acquired a means to define themselves and their culture. Northern politicians disparaged the South's sluggish economic development, but country music performers sang the praises of the region. The grassroots localism of country music begat several tributes to areas within the South, but many writers also lauded the region in general. Romantic and nostalgic images of childhood homes and the southern landscape appear frequently in country music songs of the thirties, ranging from the subtle to the sublime. Southern songwriters' fascination with trains rose to new heights in this period as well. Alton Delmore describes his attraction to the iron horses: "A train had the most awesome force about it I had ever experienced. It would come chugging down the tracks like a gigantic dragon, belching out smoke and steam and keeping a steady rhythmic roar that was fascinating to a small boy like me." Through country music songs, southerners found sources of pride in their trains, their homes, their religion, and their region.

In expounding on the virtues of southern culture in the prewar years, country music songwriters furnished a generation of southerners with the ammunition to defend their lifestyles and their beliefs from the onslaughts of urban and national prejudice.[40]

In many ways, one country music performer, more than any other, personified the pre–World War II regional culture that rural white southerners clung to in the face of social and economic obstacles. Roy Acuff's voice blended the emotionalism of an evangelist with the vociferousness of a medicine show performer. Applied to sentimental, religious, and nostalgic lyrics, it became the ultimate conduit for expressing the trials and tribulations of a generation of Americans besieged by economic depression and war. Colin Escott points out, "His voice rang clear and true through the ethers, it was a perfect radio voice, full-throated and wracked with emotion." Acuff's distinctly southern voice stood in marked contrast to that of his northern radio counterparts. He explains: "Most of the people back then were crooners. They sang soft, and they sang harmony, where I would just open my mouth and fill my lungs with air, and let it go with force." Musically, the Acuff band sound reflected its Appalachian roots: "We . . . stuck to the style of the old mountain string band, with a fiddle, rhythm guitar, string bass, five-string banjo [played with the old-time frailing technique] and Dobro guitar. Once in a while we used a harmonica or mandolin or even a piano, but the instrument I always favored was the Dobro." Bluegrass historian Robert Cantwell succinctly points out that "Acuff sounded old."[41]

Prior to Roy Acuff's rise to popularity in the late 1930s, string bands remained dominated by instrumentalists, with fiddlers usually taking center stage. An outgrowth of the banjo-fiddle duets that performed at square dances and other social gatherings, a string band generally revolved around a fiddler's lead part, with the banjoist initially providing the necessary rhythm for dancing. As the guitar grew in popularity after the turn of the century, string bands became three-piece ensembles. The domination of the fiddle continued unabated well into the 1930s, on radio as on records. George Hay termed the fiddle-based groups that dominated the *Opry*'s first decade "hoedown bands," even as fiddle playing drifted away from the shuffling dance styles. Two fiddlers, in particular, accelerated this trend. Arthur Smith's more melodic-based approach to the instrument smoothed out many of the frontier characteristics of string-band fiddling, while Clayton McMichen infused pop and jazz elements into traditional-based styles. Commenting on the bands he played with growing up in Georgia, McMichen attributes their popularity to his ability to play the fiddle louder than anyone else did. By the mid-1930s, however, the "louder the better" axiom no longer held sway. People still danced to country music, but with the popularity of radio and barn dances, they increasingly became interested in listening to it as well. The popularity of Jimmie Rodgers, based on his bluesy guitar runs and gift for storytelling, sealed the fate of the hoedown fiddler. Rodgers proved once and for all that you did not need to play danceable rhythms to be a successful country music performer. Rodgers's success also contributed greatly to the ascendance of the guitar in the mid- to late 1930s, as it became the primary rhythm instrument for country music acts. Meanwhile, the mandolin and slide guitar began displacing the fiddle as lead instruments in the southeastern acoustic-based bands that dominated the country music scene in the late 1930s.[42]

On the heels of the demise of old-time fiddling and banjo picking came the rise of the vocalists. This too represented a deviation from traditional precepts. Bill Malone describes singing in country music's early period as "incidental to instrumentation." He goes on to point out that "much of the vocals of early country music . . . was merely tangential to the string-band emphasis." Vocal "stars" on country music records like Fiddlin' John Carson, Charlie Poole, Riley Puckett, and Jimmie Rodgers represented a distinct minority in an era dominated by musicianship. The radio barn dance format, particularly WLS's *National Barn Dance*, offered far more opportunities for singers. In general, however, country music lagged behind the popular music trend that placed vocalists in front of bands. On country radio in general, and the *Grand Ole Opry* in particular, vocalists remained in the background, as *Opry* stage manger Vito Pellettieri explains: "The string bands were the main thing. What little singing there was, begun with Uncle Dave [Macon], and [the] Delmores and Sam and Kirk [McGee]. But there wasn't a lot of it. We hadn't got to the star business yet, not until the coming of a curly-headed fiddler." The curly-headed fiddler was Roy Acuff, who arrived at the *Opry* in February 1938 and soon thereafter became a regular on the show. Acuff set the precedent as the first featured vocalist backed by a band. In the years that followed, he became a major figure in the popularization of country music and the *Grand Ole Opry*.[43]

Born in 1903, Roy Acuff developed an interest in fiddle and gospel music at an early age growing up in east Tennessee. His parents taught him many religious songs at home, and he learned several more at the local Missionary Baptist Church. Acuff's father was a civil servant and minister, but he also played fiddle on occasion. While recovering from a sunstroke that ended a potential career as a professional baseball player in 1929, Acuff took the time to learn to play the fiddle by listening to his father's record collection of old-time fiddle tunes. After recovering from the illness, he set off on a career as a professional entertainer, joining a medicine show in 1932. By his own account, Acuff acquired his full-throated singing style playing to the large medicine show crowds. After several local performances, Acuff acquired a spot on a local Knoxville radio station, and by 1935 he and his band, the Tennessee Crackerjacks, became a regular feature on Lowell Blanchard's noontime show. In March 1936, the band left for rival Knoxville station WROL, where they acquired a new name, the Crazy Tennesseeans, and continued making personal appearances in the area. A CBS talent scout's discovery of the band led to a recording session in October 1936. In the meantime, Acuff hatched a plan to get his band on the *Grand Ole Opry,* making several unsuccessful trips to Nashville in the mid-thirties. Acuff knew that the Knoxville area would soon be "played out" and saw a move to clear-channel, 50,000-watt WSM as an alternative to the traditional station-to-station approach: "The *Opry* was reaching way on out yonder, and if you could build your name up on the *Opry,* you didn't have to change every year." At the behest of J. L. Frank, one of country music's first full-time promoters, WSM finally invited Acuff and his band to the *Opry* as a possible replacement group. Acuff's heartfelt performance of "The Great Speckled Bird" in February 1938 elicited a huge response from the radio audience, which deluged the station with letters voicing their approval of the singer. As David Stone explains, the management at WSM initially harbored misgivings about Acuff's talent: "Come Monday, the powers-that-be of the station wanted to know who was that guy on the radio Saturday night singing about a bird." According to Stone, once the sacks of listener mail started pouring in expressing their approval of Acuff, "they changed their opinions very suddenly." Two weeks later, Acuff became a full-time member of the *Opry* cast. [44]

Acuff's arrival at the *Grand Ole Opry* made a considerable impact on the show as well as on the direction country music would take in the next few years. Acuff views the professionalism that he brought to the *Opry* as one of his most enduring legacies: "[When I first came to WSM] all the bands that were on the *Grand Ole Opry* had other jobs, or they worked on a farm. . . . They made their living that way. But when I came here . . . I *had* to make a living out of country music. After I got to doin' good, other people saw that money could be made out of country music." Acuff explored several avenues for increasing his income through his radio appearances. One way was through the sales of songbooks: "I started selling songbooks about forty or forty-one, because everybody was wanting my songs. I put 'em in a little folder like these picture-postcard folders and sold 'em for a quarter. . . . I advertised the first one on Saturday night, and by Wednesday there was 10,000 quarters laying in WSM." In mid-1943, *Billboard* estimated Acuff's income of the previous year at around $200,000. Also in 1942, the *Opry*'s biggest star teamed with veteran song publisher and writer Fred Rose to establish Acuff-Rose Publications, the first American publishing house dedicated solely to country music. Acuff's presence and popularity eroded much of country music's provincial outlook. Suddenly, a lucrative career as a country music performer no longer seemed inconceivable. As Hank Williams once explained: "He's the biggest singer this music ever knew. You booked him and you didn't worry about crowds. For drawing power in the South, it was Roy Acuff, then God." While tremendously popular in the Southeast, Acuff also maintained a substantial following in California, evidenced in the large crowds that turned out at his shows. One show in particular, at Los Angeles's Venice Pier, stood out in Merle Travis's memory: "So many people tried to get on the pier, the fire department had to stop them, lest a few thousand factory workers and Roy Acuff fall into the Pacific Ocean."[45]

Through his popularity on the Grand Ole Opry and his extensive personal appearances throughout the country, Roy Acuff became the first country music performer to slip into the national consciousness and break through the regional barriers that segregated white southern music. Acuff was uncompromising and starkly rural in his style and music presentation, and his ascendancy in country music represents the pinnacle of old-time music's popularity on a national scale and the Appalachian sound on a regional basis. Nearly single-handedly, Acuff revived the string-band sound in a period when country music was veering in other directions. Concurrently, he introduced several innovations to the genre, namely the emphasis on vocals and the use of the relatively new Dobro sound.

Essentially an aluminum resonator–equipped Hawaiian guitar, the Dobro rose in popularity among country musicians in the 1930s fascinated by the acoustic volume it provided and the weeping sound that could be obtained by moving a metal bar back and forth between its frets. James Clell Summey played the instrument on Acuff's earliest recordings, but he, along with two other members of the band, left in 1939 over Acuff's refusal to perform more pop-oriented material. Beecher "Pete" Kirby, also known as Bashful Brother Oswald, took Summey's place and remained with Acuff for the next fifty years. Kirby was born in Sevierville, Tennessee, in 1911 to a family of musicians, but left for Flint, Michigan, at the age of eighteen for a job with the Buick Motor Company. With the advent of the Depression, the job never panned out, and Kirby began performing at local dances and parties for money. He soon became enamored with a Hawaiian guitar sound he heard at one of these gatherings, and he began reproducing that sound, using a knife for a slide. Eventually, he returned to Tennessee, where he occasionally filled in for Summey. Once hired by Acuff full-time, he traded in his Hawaiian guitar for a Dobro, and his playing style soon became the cornerstone of the Acuff sound.[46]

Kirby wasted no time in helping to make his Dobro work an integral part of the Acuff sound. Less bluesy than his predecessor in his approach to the instrument, Kirby emphasized tremolos more in his playing, often creating a crying sound that accented Acuff's plaintive vocals perfectly. On slow numbers, such as "Drifting Too Far from Shore" and "The Precious Jewel," the early string-band sound, characterized by the banjo and fiddle, is noticeably absent, and Kirby's playing creates a lonesome, woeful atmosphere. On occasion when Acuff tackled more straightforward material, such as "Be Honest with Me" (1941), Kirby's Dobro work ensured that the overall sound never drifted too far from its Appalachian source. On such up-tempo tunes as "Fireball Mail" and "Night Train to Memphis," Kirby demonstrates the rollicking potential of the Dobro sound, again in the absence of the banjo or fiddle. Occasionally, Acuff would insert a hoedown tune into the repertoire, and Kirby or Rachel Veach would pluck the old-style banjo to Acuff's exuberant fiddle playing. For the most part, however, Acuff opted for the Dobro-oriented approach in the late thirties and early forties. He also began to emphasize religious and lovelorn song material that seemed so perfectly suited to the Acuff-Kirby combination.

Acuff's affinity for train imagery permeates many of his songs of the prewar period. In early recordings ("Streamlined Cannonball," "Just to Ease My Worried Mind"), Acuff employs a whistle to simulate a train sound; in the forties, Kirby's Dobro or Jimmie Riddle's harmonica provides the rhythmic locomotive effect. Several of Kirby's disciples, namely Joe Talbot, used the electric steel guitar to emulate the train sound, but Acuff and his band for the most part rejected this amplified approach throughout most of the period. Kirby and other country musicians shared Acuff's appreciation for acoustic instrumentation. Some, like Old Joe Clark in Renfro Valley, displayed more outspokenness when commenting on the increased presence of electric instruments as the forties progressed: "That ain't a thing in the world but show-off to a bum bunch of musicians showing another bunch of musicians just how damn loud they can get. . . . It's not music, it's a damn noise." Minnie Pearl and other *Grand Ole Opry* members lamented what they viewed as the inevitable: "I remember the first time an amplified instrument came on [the *Grand Ole Opry*], and Roy and all of us just went all to pieces. I remember Roy saying, 'Well, that'll just ruin everything. It'll just ruin everything.' " The winds of change eventually displaced Acuff from his position as the most dominant country music performer of the early 1940s. Even with decreased record sales after the war, however, Acuff continued to draw huge crowds wherever he played. He also remained an important fixture on the *Opry* well into the 1980s as a country music icon. In the long run, Acuff survived the changes that occurred in country music because he embodied three of the genre's defining characteristics: sincerity, folksiness, and southern virtue. A maverick force with a recalcitrant approach to the string-band sound, Roy Acuff was country music's first prewar progressive. [47]

Wade Mainer is another progressive country music performer steeped deep in southeastern cultural and musical roots. Born in Weaverville, North Carolina, in 1907, Mainer joined the ranks of the workers at a local sawmill around the time he reached fifteen. He developed his unique, two-finger style of banjo picking while playing at weekend square dances, entertaining the crowd when the regular musicians took a break. In the early 1930s, he teamed with his brother, Joseph Emmett (J.E.), and the two eventually secured a radio show in Charlotte. In 1935, Mainer's Mountaineers made their first recordings for the Victor label. Although several of these songs convey an old-time string-band feel, their most successful recording, "Maple on the Hill," a sentimental ballad sung with Zeke Morris, portended the musical direction Wade would take after parting ways with his brother in 1937 to form his own band, the Sons of the Mountaineers. Mainer's new group de-emphasized the fiddle, focusing increasingly on harmony vocals and a stark guitar and banjo–centered sound. The group had a sizable hit with the up-tempo "Sparkling Blue Eyes" in 1939, but the flip side, "We Will Miss Him," describing a country family's attempts to deal with the loss of a loved one, more accurately captured the group's lyrical focus. Songs of a serious nature comprised most of the group's repertoire, and religious themes were common. Even on a rounder tune like "Ramblin' Boy" the lyrics lead back to the consequences of one's actions, in this case, the impact of a young rambler's absence on a fatherless country family. Only "Old Reuben" offers a portrait of a remorseless drifter and murderer; tellingly, it is one of the few songs of Mainer's prewar sessions that showcases his innovative two-finger banjo style. [48]

With the addition of Jack and Curley Shelton to the group in 1941, Mainer's band began to augment their sound with additional instruments and vocals. The group's implementation of Curley Shelton's mandolin work on the group's final prewar sessions, as on "Shake My Mother's Hand for Me," and addition of four-part vocal harmonies, as on "I Can Tell You the Time," serve as precursors to the approach many later bluegrass groups took to religious material. Immediately after the war, Mainer began recording again, this time adding an old-time fiddle to his prewar guitar, banjo, and mandolin musical base. In "He's Coming to Us Dead" and "Searching for a Soldier's Grave," Mainer demonstrates his gravitation toward solemn lyrical subject matter, in these cases addressing the emotional impact of the human cost of war. Through his uncompromising dedication to traditional country imagery and plaintive banjo-playing style, Wade Mainer eluded the demise of many early string-band performers by veering a steady course between those who refused to alter their cacophonous approach and those who repudiated their unsophisticated roots. Undoubtedly, this helps to explain why Alan Lomax selected him (along with Josh White and Burl Ives) to perform at the White House in 1941 as a representative of American folk music. Mainer eventually retired in the early 1950s; he worked for General Motors in Flint, Michigan, for twenty years before returning to performing.[49]

Many historians view Wade Mainer as a transitional figure between old-time and bluegrass music, largely due to his emphasis on traditional country lyrical themes and his popularization of the five-string banjo. Mainer, however, rarely displayed the velocity that characterized so much of early bluegrass. The Carlisle Brothers, on the other hand, merged old-time lyrics and newer instrumentation with speed in a way that unmistakably presaged bluegrass. Although Bill and Cliff Carlisle never became bluegrass figures, their work with mandolinist Shannon Grayson on the eve of World War II places them squarely in a very small group of performers who laid the musical foundation for bluegrass.

Bill and Cliff Carlisle's early years in central Kentucky exposed them to a variety of musical styles. From their father, who taught music at a local church, they learned hymns, and local string bands introduced them to old-time standards. Cliff developed an interest in Hawaiian music at an early age and later merged the acoustic steel guitar sound with the blues he heard African Americans play at the local courthouse. In the 1920s, Cliff and guitarist Wilbur Ball traveled with a number of vaudeville troops and tent shows, eventually ending up on Louisville radio in 1930. In the wake of Jimmie Rodgers's popularity, Carlisle became a successful solo artist in the early 1930s, billed as "The Yodelin' Hobo." Despite starting out as a Jimmie Rodgers clone, Carlisle soon stepped out of Rodgers's shadow with his pioneering use of the Dobro steel guitar. Around 1935, he began a professional collaboration with his brother Bill, working at a variety of southeastern radio stations, together and separately, before settling in at Knoxville's WNOX in 1940. Bill was also a very capable yodeler and singer, but he excelled as a flat-top guitarist, and he often created two-guitar patterns on his own.[50]

The two brothers and Shannon Grayson traveled to New York City in July 1939, and again in September 1940, for a series of recordings for the Decca label. Lyrically, the songs explored a gamut of themes, ranging from the sentimental

("There'll Come a Time," "Somewhere Someone's Waiting for You") to the risqué ("Three Women to Every Man"). In this, they scarcely differed from most other string bands of the late 1930s. Musically, however, the trio's chemistry proved explosive, particularly on numbers that showcased the interplay between Bill Carlisle's unique cross-picking guitar playing and Grayson's rapid-fire mandolin solos. "Don't Let Me Worry Your Mind" and "Gonna Raise a Ruckus Tonight," in particular, roll along at a breakneck pace and spotlight Grayson's abilities, while "Broken Heart" and "Go and Leave Me If You Wish To" illustrate Bill Carlisle's impressive playing style. The group's lower-pitched singing, Cliff Carlisle's bottleneck steel guitar, and the absence of a rolling banjo all preclude these selections from being termed bluegrass, but they certainly represent a departure from the string-band tradition and point toward the modernization of the old-time sound after the war. Surprisingly, the Carlisle Brothers took another direction upon returning to recording in 1945. "Maggie, Get the Hammer" and "Baby, You Done Flubbed Your Dub on Me" reveal Bill Carlisle's postwar proclivity to novelty tunes, while "Roll on Your Weary Way" displays Cliff Carlisle's attachment to the white country blues style popular in the mid-thirties. In "Rainbow at Midnight," the group experiments with a mainstream country approach with commercially successful results. "Dollar Bill Mama Blues" suggests what Jimmie Rodgers might have sounded like with an electric-guitar backing, while "Cast on a Sea of Sorrow" experiments with the postwar boogie beat. Cliff Carlisle drifted in and out of retirement in the late 1940s before giving up performing completely in the early 1950s. Bill organized a new group, the Carlisles, and eventually joined the *Opry* in 1953 on the heels of some very successful novelty recordings. The Carlisle Brothers' most important contribution to the modernization of country music was their willingness to experiment with traditional country music sounds, merging Jimmie Rodgers's blues with fast-paced solos in an attempt to help bring country music into a new era of showmanship. Groups like the Carlisle Brothers provided a model for a younger generation of acoustic musicians.[51]

In their emphasis on individual showmanship and innovative musical techniques, the Carlisle Brothers and Roy Acuff reconfigured the complexion of the country string band. Several other groups also experimented with newer sounds, although few enjoyed anything close to Acuff's measure of success. Some, like Roy Hall and His Blue Ridge Entertainers, developed a strong subregional following. Born in 1907 in Haywood City, North Carolina, Roy Hall and his brother Hugh grew up in an area rich in the Appalachian musical tradition. They approached a career in music rather tentatively, however, opting for full-time employment in the Carolina cotton textile mills while only occasionally performing at local social gatherings. The two brothers were still working in the mills at the time of their first recording session in 1937. Soon thereafter, they acquired a radio spot on WSPA in Spartanburg, South Carolina. Within a year or so, the two brothers went their separate ways, with Roy staying on at WSPA with his newly formed band, the Blue Ridge Entertainers. After acquiring Dr. Pepper as a sponsor, the group moved to Roanoke's WDBJ in 1939, retaining their sponsorship at the new locale. As a result of the group's broadcasts, their following in the Shenandoah Valley mushroomed quickly, and the band divided into two touring entities in order to meet all their personal appearance requests. Prior to Hall's death in 1943, the Blue Ridge Entertainers stood on the verge of national popularity.[52]

A basic two-guitar sound characterized Roy Hall's recordings with his brother, but his recordings with the Blue Ridge Entertainers fall into the category of progressive country music. Tommy Magness's old-time fiddling style dominates many of the group's recordings, showcased particularly on "The Natural Bridge Blues," "Pole Cat Blues," and a version of "The Wabash Cannonball." Hall's singing style, likewise, contrasts many of the smoother sounds appearing on country radio in the late 1930s. Nevertheless, Hall was progressive in his incorporation of the nationally popular western song type into both his radio and record repertoire and in his occasional emphasis on the Dobro, played to great effect by Bill Brown on such numbers as "Don't Let Your Sweet Love Die" and "Little Sweetheart, Come and Kiss Me." Hall's eclectic tendencies turned up more frequently on his radio shows. In one particular program from 1941, he follows a songbook pitch with a hymn, plugs his Dr. Pepper sponsor, then croons the western standard "South of the Border," before ending the program with a raucous breakdown. In style and repertoire, Hall offered an example for many other southeastern string bands to follow as a means to surviving the changes of the 1930s, namely, one characterized by the blending of western popular material with progressive instrumentation such as the Dobro.[53]

A few southeastern bands viewed even the Dobro as retrogressive. Hank Penny, for example, resisted suggestions to drop his electric steel guitar player from his radio band: "When the *Opry* told me that they would add our Radio Cowboys to their stable if Noel Boggs would drop the steel guitar and play Dobro—that infringed on our rights as free musicians to create and grow. . . . We considered Acuff too hillbilly for our tastes." Penny represented a younger group of musicians entranced by the electric and swing sounds coming out of the Southwest. Prior to World War II, however, they remained a distinct minority on the southeastern country music scene.[54]

Penny was not alone in his attempt to wrench country music out of its rural, southeastern predilections in the 1930s. Clayton McMichen is another noteworthy performer that experimented musically, only to meet similar resistance. As a boy growing up in northern Georgia, McMichen learned to play Viennese waltzes as well as traditional square dance numbers on the fiddle from his father and uncles. In his early twenties, he traveled to Atlanta, where a fellow musician taught him a longer-bowed, lower-pitched fiddling style that allowed for jazzy improvisations. He made some unsuccessful recordings in this style around 1925 and even went so far as to assist in the creation of a new Fiddlers' Association designed to counteract the limitations of old-time fiddling. Ironically, by the late twenties he helped form the Skillet Lickers, country music's most prolific traditional string band of the early commercial period. Eventually, he left the band to form his own Georgia Wildcats in 1931, gradually drifting further away from old-time country music. Norm Cohen points out that over 90 percent of the Skillet Lickers' repertoire consisted of traditional fiddle tunes and ballads, but about two-thirds of McMichen's recording output with other groups were more contemporary and popular numbers. Cohen states that "McMichen . . . did not distinguish between 'country music' and 'pop music' or 'jazz,' but rather between 'old-fashioned music' and 'modern music.'" McMichen objected to the term *hillbilly* and endeavored to shake the dust off traditional country, to bring more variety to the old-time repertoire. In 1935, he organized a Dixieland jazz band that remained a fixture on Louisville radio in the 1940s, but in general, he and others like Hank Penny were unsuccessful in their attempts to inoculate jazz and popular components into the pervasive southeastern string-band arrangement.[55]

The Southwest provided an environment much more conducive to musical experimentation. D. K. Wilgus terms the southwestern folk "urban hillbillies" because of the region's relatively early urbanization (as compared to the Southeast) and its willingness to acculturate to nonsouthern and nonrural social norms. Louisiana and Texas had over 20 percent of its white citizenry living in large cities in 1940. Socially, the Southwest of the 1930s grew increasingly less rural and more urban. Musically, by the mid-1930s, the popularity of western swing opened the door for many southwestern musicians to begin experimenting with electrified instruments and jazzy solos. Some musicians, such as Charles Mitchell, began their careers as steel guitar players in the Hawaiian string bands that enjoyed popularity in the twenties. Eventually, Mitchell teamed up with Jimmie Davis in the 1930s to create some of the most groundbreaking country music of the decade.[56]

One of eleven children born to a tenant farmer's family in Jackson Parish, Louisiana, Jimmie Davis grew up in a household filled with music. His father enjoyed playing the fiddle and his mother often sang traditional country songs and old-time hymns around the house. Davis was also drawn to the music of the nearby African American churches and to the blues he heard on records and in the nearby cotton fields. As a child, he sang at school, in churches, and at various social gatherings like so many other southern youngsters in the period. More atypically from many other children of similar demographic backgrounds, he attended college, where he sang in a gospel quartet. He also performed on street corners to earn enough money to pay his tuition. In 1927, he received a Master of Arts degree from Louisiana State University and accepted a teaching job at the Dodd College for Women in Shreveport. The following year he began appearing on Shreveport's KWKH and recorded his first sides for the station's local label. In the late 1920s and early 1930s, he recorded several Jimmie Rodgers–like blues numbers for the RCA-Victor label, but his first real success as a country music performer came in 1934, when he recorded his first hit, "Nobody's Darlin' But Mine," for the Decca label. As the 1930s progressed, he began drifting away from an acoustic guitar–dominated sound and began incorporating more fiddle and electric instrumentation into his arrangements. By 1939, Charles Mitchell's amplified steel guitar–centered band was backing him on his Decca sessions. Davis then altered the rhythm acoustic–steel guitar–fiddle sound that he established with Mitchell when he added a trumpet player and pianist to the group in early 1940. With "You Are My Sunshine," Davis began experimenting with Dixieland jazz, while "Walkin' My Blues Away" hinted at western swing.[57]

In Davis's singing, his vocal resemblance to Bing Crosby is offset by the distinct country feel he brings to the material, which is utterly believable and emotionally effective. In "There's a Chill on the Hill Tonight," Davis delivers one of country music's most evocative vocal performances. Many of Davis's songs evoke an up-tempo, southwestern feel, but he rarely swaggers with a western swing vocalist's flippancy. Similarly, in his choice of lyrical material, he remains embedded in the older country music traditions. Nearly 75 percent of his recordings from 1939 to 1945 pertain to failed relationships. Less than 10 percent offer lyrical material such as novelty or straightforward love songs. The shuffling upbeat tempo of songs like "Grievin' My Heart Out for You" and "Is It Too Late Now?" belies the utter despondency of the lyrics. After the war, Davis gradually drifted toward the gospel genre, but prior to 1945 he was one of country music's most prodigious vocalists. Jimmie Davis simultaneously introduced thousands of country music listeners to electric instruments while reinforcing their preference for mournful lyrics.

The Shelton Brothers represent another southwestern country act that successfully incorporated electric instruments into the string-band repertoire. No other progressive group trifled as patently with western swing as the Sheltons, but for all their experimenting, they remained one step closer to older country styles than to the newer sound coming out of the Southwest. In many ways, they are the musical manifestation of Wilgus's characterization of the "urban hillbilly."

The Shelton Brothers were born Bob and Joe Attlesey on a cotton farm in east Texas. As teenagers, they performed at several local functions before traveling to the oil-boom town of Longview in 1929, where they played in cafés for meals and at root beer stands for tips. They first appeared on radio in late 1929 as the Lone Star Cowboys in Tyler, Texas. In 1935, Dave Kapp of Decca Records approached them about making some records, and at their first session suggested they change their name. On the strength of their early collaborations with fiddler Curly Fox ("Just Because," "Deep Elem Blues"), the Shelton Brothers became one of Decca's most prolific acts in the late thirties, cutting over 150 sides for the label between 1935 and 1941.[58]

In the late thirties, the Shelton Brothers incorporated more up-tempo, bluesy numbers into their act, but they never completely excluded old-time and sentimental pieces from their performances on radio and record. Even as they drifted closer to western swing in their musical approach, they clung to their hillbilly image. In 1938 and 1939, they made several recordings with some of western swing's finest musicians, including Bob Dunn, Leo Raley, and Cliff Bruner. Raley undoubtedly influenced Joe Shelton's decision to play an amplified mandola on the group's 1939–41 sessions, showcased on such numbers as "Old Age Pension Blues" and "I'll Be Seeing You in Dallas, Alice." Lyrically, the 1939–41 sessions offered several humorous glimpses into the urban hillbilly's ambivalence toward sociocultural developments pushing southerners into modernity ("How Times Have Changed," "Parking Meter Blues," "You Can't Do That to Me"). The Sheltons' penchant for nostalgic pieces shows up on "There'll Always Be a Maple on the Hill" and "Tell Me with Your Blue Eyes." With approximately one-third of their songs centering on love and novelty themes, the Sheltons represent a departure from the characteristic progressive country music act. They also atypically add humorous touches more often to their sketches of failed relationships. Nevertheless, in the refusal to succumb completely to southwestern impulses and their unwavering leanings toward their rural roots, the Shelton Brothers sustained an affiliation with their southeastern counterparts.[59]

The Shelton Brothers were among several country music acts in the 1930s that flirted with popular and southwestern motifs. Many others explored the

possibilities of incorporating ethnic and racial musical traditions into their repertoire. The cultural interaction that took place between working-class African
Americans and whites in the South on farms and in churches laid the foundation
for this trend. Zeke Morris recalls the environment that exposed him to the musical
culture of African Americans in rural North Carolina: "Back in those days, we
didn't know what integration was, because we was raised up around black people.
We worked together, played together, and often ate at each other's houses. That's
the way it was back in those days. I've seen many a time when black people would
come to the white church. So I went to the black church to learn their spiritual
singing." On early country music recordings, the African American influence
emerges most prominently on the offerings of Dapper Dan Hutchison, Dock
Boggs, and the team of Tom Darby and Jimmie Tarlton. Other groups, like the
Allen Brothers, made liberal use of the "blues" term, incorporating it in name
only on many songs that bore little if any resemblance to the black musical genre.
Charles Wolfe explains, "Most were using the term blues cavalierly, tacking it on
to any jazzy song, or any song that had the suggestion of a lament or of double
entendre."[60]

Jimmie Rodgers did more to popularize both the symbolic blues and the real
folk blues than any other country music performer. Much of his exposure to
the blues came from his contact with African Americans while growing up in
Mississippi, but he also absorbed the music working with blacks on the railroad.
In affixing a yodel at the end of stanzas, however, Rodgers deviated from standard
blues. The effect of the blues yodel depended on the mood of the song. In cheery,
symbolic "blues" selections, the yodel accentuated the lightheartedness of the
performance, whereas on more somber songs it resounded like a lament. Rodgers
bequeathed his use of the blue yodel to a number of acts of the 1930s; few used
it as effectively as two brother duets, the Callahans and the Delmores.[61]

Walter and Homer Callahan hailed from Madison County, North Carolina,
where they began performing at local venues in their early teens. On the heels of
an impressive performance at the Rhododendron Festival at Asheville in 1933, they
began appearing on records and radio. "She's My Curly Headed Baby," recorded
in 1934, showcased their Jimmie Rodgers–influenced yodeling and became their
most identifiable song. Like so many other groups, they leapfrogged from station
to station before ending up in Texas in 1941, where they adopted their new names,
Bill and Joe, and remained for most of the 1940s.[62]

The Callahan Brothers began as a vocal and guitar duet team and continued
on in this vein for most of the 1930s. They culled much of their repertoire in
their early period from older tunes, but they also wrote and sang many songs in

the Jimmie Rodgers blue yodel tradition. Their early fondness for novelty and individualism-centered lyrics, however, waned as the decade progressed. Their recordings from 1939 to 1941, in particular, featured more melancholy, and in some cases, tragic lyrics. "Oh Lord, Show Me the Light," "The Best Pal I Ever Had," and "They're at Rest Together" all reflect on the deaths of young people, while "Dovie Darling," "Sad Memories," and "Lonesome Freight Train Blues" explore heartbroken lovers' emotional suffering. The traditional "John Henry" and comical "A Jealous Woman Won't Do," though, represent the song types most listeners associated with the Callahan Brothers. In the 1940s, they augmented their sound with Paul Buskirk's jazz-influenced mandolin playing, and after the war they began adopting honky-tonk instrumentation (weeping steel guitar, tinkling piano, and so forth). In the late 1940s and early 1950s, they toured as the Crazy Callahans, with Homer (Bill) becoming renowned for his comedic abilities. As the 1950s wore on, they gradually terminated their musical partnership; Joe returned to Asheville and Bill settled in Dallas. The Callahan Brothers stand out as one of the few Jimmie Rodgers–style acts to survive the war, mainly due to their musical flexibility and comic talent, and in doing so, they kept alive both the blue yodel and duet singing traditions.[63]

While the Callahans were blending old-time singing and folk lyrical material with the blue yodel, the Delmore Brothers were experimenting with ways to merge white country blues with a more sophisticated vocal and musical style. Unsurpassed in their collective abilities as singers, songwriters, and musicians, Alton and Rabon Delmore remain two of country music's most overlooked performers. The Delmore Brothers embraced new technology and new sounds while remaining explicitly fastened to their southern roots. They established the prototype for country music harmony and, along with Sam McGee and Maybelle Carter, popularized lead-guitar playing in the Southeast. Additionally, they excelled as songwriters, leaving behind scores of memorable lyrics and haunting melodies. The Delmores eclipsed every other country music act of the 1930s in all-around talent and rival Roy Acuff and Jimmie Rodgers in importance.[64]

Alton and Rabon Delmore grew up in northern Alabama, the sons of a sharecropper. At an early age, Alton learned the a cappella, shape-note method of singing from his uncle and mother. It was a harmonic singing style pioneered in southwest Virginia after the Civil War and popularized via hymnal publishers throughout the rural South in the early 1900s. As a teenager, Alton Delmore published his first songs in a shape-note songbook. In the mid-twenties, the brothers began performing locally, and on the strength of their appearance at a musical contest, and with the encouragement of the Allen Brothers, they began making records in the early 1930s. From the outset, their recordings blended gospel harmony with a bluesy sound. As a youngster, Alton taught himself to play guitar and was influenced largely by the Jimmie Rodgers and Riley Puckett records he listened to, as well as the African American blues he heard. Eventually, Alton developed a unique guitar style, which incorporated jazzy improvisation and bluesy chords with an emphasis on melody. Rabon also became a skilled guitarist, playing in a similar fashion on his four-string tenor guitar. In 1933, they became regulars on the *Grand Ole Opry*, bringing to the show professionalism, an image, and a soft harmonic singing style uncharacteristic of most *Opry* acts. With a vocal approach that plainly contrasted with rudimentary mountain harmony and with a rejection of standard hillbilly garb in favor of matching checkered shirts or jackets, the Delmore Brothers brought a quiet dignity to the *Grand Ole Opry* and to country music. Alton Delmore attributes a great deal of their success to the merging of their soft harmony and technology: "There was something divine in the [microphone] . . . that helped us immensely and changed us from two country farm boy singers to something 'up-town' and acceptable to listeners who bought records and listened to radio programs. That was the whole secret of our good luck. Our voices took well to the microphone." The Delmores brought country music to urbanites with crossover hits like "More Pretty Girls Than One" and popular music to rural listeners by playing instrumental versions of standards like "Stormy Weather" at personal appearances. With their intricate harmonies and complex guitar runs, the Delmore Brothers were progressive in that they bridged the gap between the Jimmie Rodgers sound of the 1930s and the bluegrass of the late forties and portended the success of the Everly Brothers and the Louvin Brothers in the 1950s.[65]

On their records of the late 1930s and early 1940s, the Delmore Brothers built on a variety of southern musical and lyrical traditions. Charles Wolfe describes their lyrical repertoire as "an odd fusion [of] the unabashed sentimentality of 19th-century popular music and the frank, realistic portrayal of marital difficulties, unrequited love, and rambling, so characteristic of modern country lyrics." Although the Delmores were quite capable of writing humorous tunes, such as "Brown's Ferry Blues" and "Go Easy, Mabel," they excelled at melancholy portrayals of lost and wandering souls constantly traveling the rivers and railroads of the South in search of an elusive contentment, as in "There's Trouble on My Mind" and "I'll Never Fall in Love Again." Like Hank Williams a decade later, the Delmores borrowed heavily from the natural landscape to convey a sense of woefulness in the face of life's disappointments. Bluesy guitar passages weave in and out and around intricate harmonies to create an atmosphere of constant motion, pulling listeners into the tales of desperation. The Delmore Brothers mesmerized audiences with their musical and vocal abilities and maintained a huge following among *Grand Ole Opry* listeners prior to their departure from the program in 1938. They maintained a two-guitar, duet harmony approach for most of the thirties and early forties, but, like the Callahan Brothers, they emerged from World War II with a willingness to experiment with newer sounds that brought renewed success. With a progressive approach to the country blues tradition of the 1930s, the Delmore Brothers elevated country music lyrics to a level of poetry while simultaneously introducing a more complex musical approach. The Delmores cast a long shadow on country music's development through their songwriting, singing, and musical innovations. Their performing style remains ageless.[66]

The shape-note school of harmony singing popularized by the Delmore Brothers in the mid-thirties spawned a number of other significant country music duets, none more popular in the Southeast than the Blue Sky Boys. Bill and Earl Bolick, the Blue Sky Boys, looked to the parlor and the church for inspiration, and in doing so, they tapped into a wellspring of material that appealed to thousands of rural southerners. To sentimental and sorrowful pieces, they brought velvet harmonies and stark instrumentation perfectly suited to radio technology. Dressed in suits and ties, singing soft and low, they repudiated the string-band tradition, offering listeners an alternative to early country music's raucousness. Uncompromising and unremitting in their commitment to the domestic tradition, the Blue Sky Boys filled a void in country music, and as a result they became one of the genre's most popular duets on the eve of World War II.[67]

Bill and Earl Bolick first heard many of the old songs that they later rejuvenated around their parents' house in western North Carolina. Their father, a shape-note school alumnus, taught them many hymns, but they also developed an appreciation of the traditional secular material that they heard in the performances of early folk singers like Doc Hopkins, Mac and Bob, and Bradley Kincaid. After a brief period on the radio in North Carolina, the two brothers, along with fiddler Homer Sherrill, traveled to Atlanta in 1936, where they began appearing on WGST. The Bolicks recorded their first sides, sans Sherrill, later that year for Victor's Bluebird label. From the outset, their recorded output stressed sentimental and religious material derived from both folk and contemporary sources. Technically, the Bolicks were not songwriters, but they excelled as interpreters, indelibly stamping every selection they sang with their own unique style. Although their radio performances often included fiddling, on records they maintained a guitar and mandolin format throughout the prewar period. To restrained and melodic instrumentation, the Blue Sky Boys added soft, close harmony to create an atmosphere of intimacy uncharacteristic of most country music of the time. Bill Bolick sums up the approach they took to their musical interpretations: "Both of us realized from the very beginning that in order to produce good, clear harmony, one had to sing at a moderate pace in order to be understood, and softly if your voices were to blend. . . . We always felt the singing was more important [than] the instrumentals, and for that reason didn't make the instrumental work outstanding. We tried to develop a style of playing that would enhance our voices."[68]

In their choice of song material, the Blue Sky Boys demonstrated a fondness for sorrowful and sentimental lyrics. In many of their selections, lost souls find strength in memories of the happier times of their youth ("Hymns My Mother Sang," "Have No Desire to Roam"); other times inspiration comes from a divine source ("Whispering Hope," "This Evening Light," "Kneel at the Cross"). Occasionally, displaced southern migrants working in the North look forward to the prospect of returning home to devoted sweethearts ("When Roses Bloom in Dixieland"), or, in the absence of loved ones, turn to one another for camaraderie ("Are You from Dixie"). More characteristically, however, tragic figures abound in their prewar recordings: a woman driven to suicide by lost love ("The Butcher's Boy"), a broken-hearted man driven to rambling and crime ("Short Life of Trouble"), a widower left to take care of a houseful of children ("Since the Angels Took My Mother Far Away"), and a poor, young man pleading with a conductor to allow him to remain on a train so he can see his dying mother ("East Bound Train").[69]

The Blue Sky Boys deliberately chose to record sentimental and tragic songs and older hymns because of the scarcity of country music acts exploring these areas. Constance Keith, columnist for the *Mountain Broadcast and Prairie Recorder,* attributes the Bolicks' success to this approach: "The boys . . . feature many songs that are not used by other artists, thereby keeping their programs just a little different." The Bolicks were separated by the war, but afterwards they returned to radio and recording using the same approach applied to more contemporary material, although augmenting their sound with a fiddle and a bass. Despite the success of their interpretations of the Bailes Brothers' "Dust on the Bible" and Karl and Harty's "Kentucky," however, their record company grew increasingly disenchanted with their stark musical approach and choice of material, a development that contributed to the brothers' decision to retire from the music industry in 1951. Although their records failed to sell substantially after the war, the Blue Sky Boys maintained a loyal following on radio and at personal appearances right up to the time of their retirement, demonstrating that their uncharacteristic approach and undeniable talents never went out of style.[70]

Several other duet-based groups flourished in the late thirties that displayed more affection for the string-band tradition than the Bolick brothers did, namely the Morris Brothers and the team of Karl Davis and Hartford Taylor, Karl and Harty. Both acts featured guitar and mandolin, but unlike the Blue Sky Boys they occasionally augmented their sound with a fiddle and a banjo. Karl and Harty, in fact, began their radio careers as part of a string band, the Kentucky Krazy Kats, with mandolin pioneer Doc Hopkins on Louisville's WHAS in the late 1920s. In the early thirties, they began appearing regularly on WLS as a duet, on a daily show as well as on the Saturday night *National Barn Dance*. In their quest for fresh material for their daily program, Karl and Harty introduced their listeners to several Carter Family numbers and old gospel tunes, but soon began writing their own songs. With songs like "I'm Just Here to Get My Baby Out of Jail" and "Prisoner's Dream," the duet established themselves among country music's first important songwriters. On their recordings, they were sometimes accompanied by a string band ("Old Rattler," "Ridin' That Hump-Backed Mule," "I'm S-A-V-E-D"); for the most part, as Karl Davis explains, they preferred a more basic approach: "A mandolin and a guitar have always gone together well. . . . They give you that simplicity that I think most anybody likes in music. . . . Too many instruments . . . [and] you lose the simplicity and the personality." Although the duo's attempts to modernize their sound and repertoire in the 1940s proved an awkward transition, they remained a staple on Chicago radio throughout the decade.[71]

Wiley and Zeke Morris are another duet act of the late 1930s that flirted with a string-band sound before settling down to a guitar and mandolin approach. Born and raised in western North Carolina, Wiley and Zeke first performed in public as a trio with their brother George. Zeke began his professional career with Mainer's Mountaineers in 1933, and in 1935 he recorded the popular "Maple on the Hill" with Wade Mainer. In 1937, Wiley, Zeke, and Mainer appeared on radio together in Asheville and Raleigh before Mainer's departure to form the Sons of the Mountaineers. By the next year, the two brothers were playing with a fiddler and a banjoist in Danville, Virginia, on WBTM. Zeke quit performing briefly in 1938 to work in a Gastonia cotton mill, but he moved with his brother to Asheville in 1939, where they resumed playing and settled in with a guitar and mandolin approach. Split up by the war, they reunited briefly in 1945 before retiring from performing to open an auto repair business.[72]

Although they appeared briefly on radio as part of a string band in Virginia, the Morris Brothers opted for a more streamlined approach on their recordings. Their first recordings featured Homer Sherrill on fiddle, but on their third session, in February 1939, their duet vocals were accompanied by only a guitar and a mandolin. "Let Me Be Your Salty Dog," a novelty number from 1938, became their first big seller, but more often they concentrated on sentimental, nostalgic, and religious pieces. Although they recorded relatively few tragic tales, they worked well in this theme, as on "The Story of Charlie Lawson," about a man who murders most of his family, and "Little Nellie," concerning the death of a child. "Dream of the Miner's Child" tells of a child's premonition of an impending coal mining accident and remains one of their most effective performances, with the highlight of Zeke Morris's bluesy mandolin solo. On their last prewar recordings, Homer Sherrill reappears on the mainstay "Wabash Cannonball, No. 2" and "One Little Word," the latter a story of childhood sweethearts kept apart by the woman's parents because of the man's economic status. In the Morris Brothers' brief reunion after the war, they continued to emphasize the tragic, as on "Grave Upon the Green Hillside," where a man driven to rambling by his love's presumed infidelity returns home to find that she has died of a broken heart. A new version of "Salty Dog Blues" suggests that the Morris Brothers may have become a successful bluegrass act had they not chosen more stable employment to support their families.[73]

Although not bluegrass groups per se, the Morris Brothers, Karl and Harty, and the Blue Sky Boys popularized the instrument that became the focal point of early bluegrass, the mandolin. Before the success of the harmony groups of the 1930s, many country musicians and fans failed to recognize the mandolin's potential. In the mountains where Zeke Morris grew up, local folks referred to the oddly shaped instrument as a "tater bug." Brought over from Europe in the 1700s, the mandolin did not become popular in the United States until the large Italian immigration of the late 1800s. Riding the wave of the mandolin fad, the Gibson manufacturing company remodeled the instrument, giving it a flat back, and began an aggressive campaign to market it through mail order catalogs after 1900. While it became increasingly popular among the middle class in the 1910s, it remained an oddity in the rural South until the early 1930s. No one really thought of the mandolin as a country music instrument before Doc Hopkins and Lester McFarland (of Mac and Bob) pioneered its use on radio barn dances in the 1920s and early 1930s. Mac and Bob's move from WNOX in Knoxville to 50,000-watt WLS in 1931 certainly did a great deal to popularize the instrument among a younger generation of country music fans. The harmony groups finalized its legitimacy in the mid- to late thirties, but one man did more than any other to bring it to the forefront of prewar country music. [74]

Bill Monroe was born in western Kentucky, the youngest of six children. Listening to his mother sing old-time songs, he developed a fondness for singing that he nurtured at church singing schools and at Sunday services. When he was around eight years old, his older brothers bequeathed to him the unpopular mandolin, which he soon taught himself to play in his own unique style. He recalls, "I wanted to have a mandolin style of my own, not play like anybody else. There wasn't many mandolin players in the country when I started." By the time he reached his teens, Monroe was accompanying his fiddle-playing Uncle Pen at local dances. From his uncle and a local black fiddler named Arnold Schultz, Monroe learned a number of fiddle tunes. Sometime in the mid-twenties, his older brothers Birch and Charlie traveled north in search of employment, eventually landing jobs in an Indiana oil refinery. Bill joined them in 1929, and the three soon began playing local dances. In 1934, Bill and Charlie accepted a sponsored radio spot in Iowa; Birch opted to stay behind. [75]

As the Monroe Brothers, Bill and Charlie became one of the Southeast's most formidable duets. In their emphasis on traditional and religious songs, the Monroes differed little from many other duet groups, but in their tendency to play faster and sing higher, they reached a level of musical and vocal dexterity matched only by the Delmore Brothers. Between 1936 and 1938 they recorded some sixty songs for the Bluebird label, many showcasing Bill's aggressive mandolin playing. Karl Davis was among the many country musicians impressed by Monroe's feverish style: "I've never heard anybody play as fast in my life. . . . Nobody ever heard a mandolin like that." After the duet broke up in 1938, Bill traveled to Little Rock, where he formed the Kentuckians; later that year, he moved to Atlanta, where he changed the band's name to the Blue Grass Boys, and began experimenting with a number of musicians and sounds. After months of rigorous rehearsals, the group auditioned for the *Grand Ole Opry* with impressive results. Monroe recalls, "Judge Hay and Harry Stone and David Stone . . . said I had more perfect music for the station than any music they'd ever heard." His propulsive performance of Jimmie Rodgers's "Muleskinner Blues" elicited a similar response from *Grand Ole Opry* listeners. His Blue Grass Boys soon became one of the show's greatest attractions and one of country music's biggest draws. [76]

An atmosphere of experimentation dominates Bill Monroe's prewar recordings with Clyde Moody (harmony vocal, lead guitar), Tommy Magness (fiddle), and Willie Egbert "Cousin Wilbur" Wesbrooks (bass). On two Jimmie Rodgers covers, Monroe displays two elements that he would later incorporate into the bluegrass sound: speed ("Muleskinner Blues") and what is commonly referred to as a "high lonesome" vocal ("Blue Yodel, #7"). Monroe sets the pace for "Muleskinner Blues" playing rhythm acoustic guitar, but he plays mandolin on the remainder of the selections. "Back Up and Push," "Orange Blossom Special," and "Katy Hill" were early attempts to modernize the string-band sound by augmenting it with mandolin or approaching it with greater velocity. Tommy Magness's fiddle dominates several tunes, including the conservative "No Letter Today" and "I Wonder Where You Are Tonight," but Monroe's mandolin steps to the forefront on such numbers as "Honky Tonk Swing" and "Cryin' Holy Unto My Lord." The prewar sessions hearken back to the old-time tradition, particularly in their emphasis on instrumental and elementary vocals, but they also show signs of innovation: Monroe clearly strives to break free of the conventional constraints through his emphasis on the mandolin and propensity to play tunes at a pace unsuitable for dancing.[77]

Monroe continued to drift farther from the older sound when he returned to the recording studio in 1945 with a revamped version of the Blue Grass Boys. The February 1945 session with an aggregation that included Tex Willis (guitar), Howard Watts (bass), Chubby Wise (fiddle), and Sally Ann Forrester (accordion) marks the closest Monroe ever came to successfully working within the constraints of mainstream country music. Attuned to what audiences wanted to hear from two years of touring, Monroe entered *Billboard*'s top ten with the self-penned "Kentucky Waltz" and his interpretation of the traditional "Footprints in the Snow." With "Rocky Road Blues" and "Blue Grass Special," Monroe clearly stood on the brink of bluegrass, but at that point he did not possess the appropriate band to make the final plunge. Monroe was not able to free himself from contemporary country influences and incarnate the vision that inspired his radical interpretation of Jimmie Rodgers's "Muleskinner Blues" until after the war.[78]

Bill Monroe's Blue Grass Boys and other progressive acts strove to adapt country music to technological changes and alterations in listeners' preferences in the late thirties and early forties. In professionalizing and domesticating country music, they essentially legitimized its existence, dispelling many of the negative connotations associated with the term *hillbilly music*. On the eve of World War II, country music continued to function primarily as a form of rural, southern entertainment, but it also steadily distanced itself from its obtrusive past. The family-friendly radio barn dances struck a fatal blow to risqué white country blues, while the microphone rendered the louder string bands passé at best, foolish at worst. Discarding the hillbilly garb of the twenties, Bill Monroe, Roy Acuff, and others sought alternative, less derogatory images for country music performers. Dressed in jodhpurs and a tie, Bill Monroe looked more like a country gentleman than a southern rube, and Roy Acuff's sport coat more accurately reflected the business savvy he possessed. Those who led the movement to sanitize, professionalize, and domesticate country music, however, encountered one impassible obstacle: the genre's continued association with the rural South. The plaintive lyrics of country music songs clearly placed the genre in the southern, rural tradition, and rustic humor continued to comprise a good portion of the radio barn dance programs and personal appearance shows. One look at the *Grand Ole Opry* audience was enough to convince many Americans that country music was a plebian pursuit. Prior to its nationalization, however, country music remained immune to the condescending and derisive remarks of northern writers. The musical genre, however, faced a more formidable foe in upper- and middle-class southerners openly hostile to its existence.[79]

As the home of the *Grand Ole Opry*, Nashville became a cultural battleground in the late 1920s and early 1930s with the city's bourgeoisie facing off against country music enthusiasts. Steel guitarist Joe Talbot points out: "Nashville simply did not want this trash in this town. The city of Nashville, as an entity, was very embarrassed and ashamed of this bunch of hillbillies that were wandering around here. . . . This city was principally an educational, religious institutional, and financial town and a country music show simply wasn't relevant to [any] of these things." The *Grand Ole Opry* became a bone of contention almost immediately after its premiere. In a 1938 article on the program, Jack Harris points out: "When the *Grand Ole Opry* started there was an immediate protest from the Nashville citizenry. Solemn Old Judge Hay was accused of making the city the laughing stock of the nation—the hillbilly capital." In the mid-twenties, an attempt to suspend the *Opry*'s broadcasts and fill its airtime with more popular music was thwarted by a torrent of letters protesting the notion. After the failure of this coup d'état, the city cultural elite begrudgingly endured a peaceful coexistence with the program and its followers. They surely seethed at the frenzy that accompanied the premiere of the movie *Grand Ole Opry* in late June 1940. A journalist from *Variety* described the scene: "With hundreds of visitors in [the] city, the 'hill folk' staged [a] mammoth square dance in Memorial Square, [in] the heart of the city. A parade of victorias, surreys, buggies and wagons, all with old-time trimmings, led the radio stars of [the] picture to the premier." In 1943, when the *Grand Ole Opry* extended an invitation to Governor Prentice Cooper to attend a party celebrating the program's coast to coast hookup, Cooper adamantly refused, stating he wanted no part in the "circus," adding that he believed Roy Acuff was disgracing the state and the city in general by making it the nation's "hillbilly capital."[80]

While Nashville was the flashpoint of the struggle between country music culture and middle-class values, contempt for the genre and its followers pervaded other southern urban areas as well. Part of this negative bias toward country music stemmed from a prejudice that many middle-class and urban southerners felt toward their rural neighbors. In some cases, members of Nashville's middle class harbored negative stereotypes of their rural neighbors; in other cases, those one generation removed from the farm sought to distance themselves from their unsophisticated social roots. The trickling migration of displaced tenant farmers to southern urban areas heightened these class issues. Jack Kirby points out that urbanites in Virginia mocked migrants from North Carolina during this period and offers this recollection of a Knoxvillian's first exposure to newcomers from the Appalachian hills: "I'll tell you I never before knew that such people existed. Most of them had come in off of the mountains somewhere and they had such a funny way of talking that plenty of times I wouldn't know what they were saying." A combination of unfamiliarity with folk culture and an unwillingness to be associated with what country music symbolized contributed more than anything else to the antagonism many upper-class southerners felt toward the genre. A prominent West Virginian expressed these sentiments in commenting on country music's rising popularity within his state: "If the name of West Virginia is mentioned, it is immediately associated with hillbilly music and a suggestion of a social inferiority which constitutes nothing short of libel upon the name of the state." Members of the nouveau bourgeoisie attempting to disassociate themselves from their rustic roots exhibited malevolence toward country music for somewhat different reasons. To this point, Roy Acuff made the following assessment of his cultural opponents: "I always felt that these same people who were putting on airs and putting down our music had the very same background I and other performers did."[81]

The lofty pronouncements of governors and journalists did not affect country music performers as much as prejudice on a local level. Dependent on radio shows and schoolhouse personal appearances for their livelihood, many encountered difficulties getting on the air and securing venues to play. Bill Bolick explains: "It was almost impossible to get a sponsor through the radio station itself. I suppose it was what they considered a necessary evil; they knew that it was popular with most of their listeners and yet they frowned upon it very much, and, I think, really tried to hold the country musician down as much as they possibly could." Performers fortunate enough to secure a radio spot next faced the task of convincing school leaders to allow them to use their facilities. The prospect of receiving nearly half of the proceeds from a country music show did not waver some schoolhouse leaders from their cultural and intellectual predilections. Whether driven by prejudice or aesthetics, they looked at the other side of the coin and cringed at the thought of where the other profits were going. In Alabama, Tommy Gentry could not persuade a local school official to let his group perform: "The principal said that he would never allow another Hill Billy show to come in and take as much money out of the community as the Delmore Brothers did." Commenting on a movement to ban country music from schools, Cliff Carlisle wrote the *Mountain Broadcast and Prairie Recorder* encouraging his fellow performers to remain steadfast in their efforts to peddle their musical talent: "Don't worry boys, the hillbilly music is here to stay as long as we have the good old farmer, the miner, the railroader, the mill-worker, the truck-drivers and all the common class of people, which outnumber the so-called dudes one hundred thousand to one. More power to all you hillbillies and cowboys, or whatever you are." Fortunately for Carlisle and many other country music acts of the late thirties, for every school administrator that turned them away, another would be down the road willing to lend them a place to perform in exchange for a portion of the proceeds. [82]

Carlisle's comments suggest that country music on the eve of World War II had yet to expand beyond its core working-class audience. Most urban and middle-class inhabitants of the South and throughout America still derisively referred to the music as "hillbilly." Some performers willingly accepted the label as one contrived for marketing purposes. Others, such as Clayton McMichen, trying to gain respectability for themselves as musicians, balked at the term: "That 'hillbilly,' we fought it, teeth and toenails . . . [because] we wanted to make [country music] popular." Ernest Tubb similarly viewed the label as counterproductive: "We'd ask people, 'do you like hillbilly music?'; they'd always be hesitant to admit that they did. Like the word 'hillbilly' was an inferior type word, that makes it inferior type music . . . they would hesitate about saying they were familiar with the music—even though they'd come out and see our shows!" When recording executive Ralph Peer unconsciously coined the term *hillbilly* in the mid-1920s, the major record companies steered clear of using the descriptor. Roy Acuff explains: "They did everything they could to keep people from thinking these were hillbilly records, or even country records. They were listed on the record label and on the paper jackets as 'Old Time Singing and Playing' or 'Novelty Singing and Playing' . . . we had a ways to go before our type of music was to become respectable." Record companies continued to keep country music segregated well into the forties by issuing country selections on their budget labels, such as Bluebird and Okeh. Of the major labels, only Decca placed its name on its country music offerings. [83]

The reasons why country music performers and their record companies tried to distance themselves from the hillbilly epithet become apparent in light of the social and intellectual climate of the times. Country music's association with the white, rural South invariably fostered prejudicial opinions of the genre. Bill Malone explains, "To many people hillbilly music was just one more example, along with Ku Kluxism, Prohibition, sharecropping, racial violence, and religious bigotry, of the South's retarded and degenerate culture." H. L. Mencken captured the mental image many northern intellectuals held of the South when he labeled the South "the Sahara of the Bozart," describing the bulk of the region as "a vast plain of mediocrity, stupidity, lethargy, almost of dead silence." Another northern writer in the mid-1920s turgidly lambasted the region's inhabitants more directly: "The 'hill-billy' is a North Carolina or Tennessee and adjacent mountaineer type of illiterate white whose creed and allegiance are to the Bible, the chautauqua, and the phonograph." These and other critics of the American South failed to mention the effects that poverty might have on working-class southerners' highbrow pursuits; in their myopic renderings of southern culture, Mencken and others hastily equated distinctiveness with inferiority. With its increased presence on national radio, southern music became an easy target for ridicule. Compared to the popular songs that featured the velvety voice of Bing Crosby and the sugarcoated lyrical offerings of New York's Tin Pan Alley's songwriters, country music seemed foreign and cacophonous to America's middle class. As the 1930s wore on, however, the climate of opinion became less hostile to both the South in general and country music in particular. In the late thirties, the region went from the nation's most unsightly blemish to its "number one economic problem," with the Washington Brain Trust and southern sociologists both exploring the reasons for the region's deficiencies and offering solutions. Through films and literature, Americans became more intrigued with southern culture, although they were often offered a distorted image of it, and through the photographs of Dorothea Lange and Margaret Bourke-White, Americans increased their awareness of the poor southerners' plight. With poverty becoming a less abstract phenomenon no longer exclusively associated with the South, Americans suddenly faced with hard times of their own became more receptive to the commonality of the country music message. [84]

Many Americans approached country music obliquely, through folk music, which usually exhibited few of country's defining characteristics. As early as the post–Civil War period, Americans developed an interest in white southern folk music, initially through Will Hays's melodies and later through the song-collecting efforts of Cecil Sharp, John Lomax, and others in the first two decades of the twentieth century. The old-time fiddlers who took part in industrialist Henry Ford's national fiddling contests in the 1910s undoubtedly introduced many other Americans to white southern music, as did the field-recording efforts of John and Alan Lomax and others affiliated with the Library of Congress's Archive of American Folk Song in the 1930s. Radio listeners could hear Bradley Kincaid singing old English ballads, Woody Guthrie delivering anthems to social consciousness, and Burl Ives offering folk ditties. While many of these artists were not country music performers per se, they did familiarize their audience with many aspects of the genre, namely acoustic instrumentation, realistic lyrical imagery, and old-time melodies. Folklorists and folk performers often drew a distinction between their music, which they viewed as authentic, and country music, which they viewed as commercial. Nevertheless, they acquainted innumerous Americans with the basics of country music, thereby enervating the abomination many of them previously felt toward the genre. Ironically, country music seemed to attract more new listeners in the North than in the South. Commenting on country music's early expansion in the 1930s, Alton Delmore observes, "The people in the North accepted country and western music much sooner than the people in the South."[85]

Through folk music, radio expansion, and increased identification among nonsouthern listeners, country music stood on the brink of nationalization in the pre–World War II period. Robert Shelton points out that in less than twenty years "country music evolved from an un-self-conscious folk music into a highly self-conscious entertainment form." On a local scale, in thousands of schoolhouses throughout the Southeast, rural white southerners continued to gather and listen to the performances of musicians often raised in nearby communities. Countless members of country music acts sustained other means of livelihood, and even full-time country music professionals maintained a popularity that remained local or subregional in scope. Performers who enjoyed a regional or even national following maintained a base of operations with a particular radio station. Country music in 1941 represented an entertainment form produced by and for the rural white inhabitants of the American South. Musically it remained acoustic and primarily derived from traditional source material, and lyrically it continued to reflect the nuances of rural southern life.[86]

Whether or not anyone realized it, however, country music was changing, particularly in respect to instrumentation and vocal style. Principally as a result of radio expansion, country music vocalists began to sing softer and more expressively, often creating an emotional bond with listeners. As listeners became more attentive to interpretive styles, vocalists stepped to the forefront of the previously instrumentally centered genre. Shape-note-based harmonies further distinguished the human voice as country music's most popular instrument of the late 1930s, reinvigorating the domestic tradition. Meanwhile, the mandolin and the Dobro displaced the fiddle and banjo in country music bands, redefining the string-band sound. Performers continued to derive material from traditional sources, but many others took to songwriting that incorporated unconventional musical styles and folk imagery. Radio and records enabled country music performers in the late 1930s to become less provincial in outlook and more interactive in the creative process. Agilely balancing tradition and innovation, country music in the autumn of 1941 stood on the threshold of a period of monumental expansion.

2 | THE GREAT BREAKTHROUGH
WORLD WAR II AND THE NATIONAL ACCEPTANCE
OF COUNTRY MUSIC

In the autumn of 1941, country music remained primarily a rural, southern phenomenon. The radio barn dances did a great deal to break the genre of its cultural isolation, but country music's core audience continued to reside within Dixie's borders. Musically, it continued to cling to its southeastern folk heritage, even as it began to smooth out many of its rough frontier edges. Domestication and radio exposure brought more emphasis on vocals and softer instrumentation, but it did not fundamentally alter country music's basics. In the last month of 1941, country music ostensibly was still music composed by rural white southerners for rural white southerners.

In the years between 1942 and 1945, country music's audience expanded far beyond the southeast quadrant of the United States. During the war, the genre became a national phenomenon, albeit one that puzzled as many Americans as it attracted. Several factors led to country music's nationalization during World War II: country music's plaintive lyrics appealed to Americans in wartime; music publishers and promoters aggressively marketed country music; a shortage of new popular music led many Americans to country music's novelty; country music embraced popular music instrumentation; country listeners and singers intermingled with persons with other musical preferences in the armed forces; rural southerners migrated to urban areas throughout the country; and the jukebox industry expanded.

Wartime population shifts proved to be the most discernible of these trends. Rural southerners on the move in search of better employment during the war flooded into cities, North and South. Rural southern areas lost 3.3 million people, or 20 percent of their population. Those who chose to remain in the South went to the naval shipyards of the Atlantic and Gulf Coasts or to interior cities such as Fort Worth, Tulsa, Nashville, Memphis, and Birmingham, where aircraft and other types of war plants were located. In the 1940s, the South's metropolitan areas grew at about three times the national average. Between 1940 and 1944, the South's two fastest-growing metropolitan areas, Norfolk/Hampton Roads and Mobile, increased their white population by 143,500 and 71,700 respectively.

Wartime struck a fatal blow to the South's agricultural nexus, with the number of workers employed in the region's production industries doubling between 1939 and 1943. Historian Francis Abernathy captures the lure of the southern city: "A farmer making a bare living on his eighty acres found out that somebody was paying a dollar an hour in the shipyards, and it didn't take him long to figure out that he could live better in the city—with paved streets, picture shows, and brick schools—than he ever thought about on the farm."[1]

Many southerners found the work easier to come by than the amenities, as the infrastructure of many southern cities failed to keep apace with the influx of migrants. A *Washington Post* reporter in 1944 described Mobile as "up to its ears in trouble." Another observer captured this image of the Alabama coast in wartime: "Sidewalks are crowded. . . . Garbage cans are overflowing. . . . In cluttered backyards people camp out in tents and chickenhouses and shelters tacked together out of packing cases. . . . Over it all the Gulf mist, heavy with the smoke of soft coal, hangs in streaks, and glittering the training planes [that] end-lessly circle above the airfields." Despite the southern city's lackluster, however, many southerners welcomed the opportunities that it offered. Many often dis-played a reluctance to abandon their rural cultural heritage, but many welcomed the prospect of escaping from the economic quagmire that so often characterized southern agricultural tenancy.[2]

Opportunities abounded in the North as well, and many southerners tracked to the Snowbelt in search of employment in war plants. Between 1940 and 1944, 42,000 whites from Alabama, Kentucky, Tennessee, and Mississippi made the journey to Detroit. Countless others from the Mid-South and South Atlantic states migrated to Ohio, Pennsylvania, Illinois, Indiana, and the Washington, D.C., and Baltimore area. In northern cities, migrants established a support network among themselves to preserve their cultural heritage and to combat the prejudices of the native population. Owners of cafés and taverns located near defense plants or hillbilly enclaves soon discovered it profitable to maintain a stock of country music selections on jukeboxes in their establishments. Osmotically, nonsouthern patrons acquired a familiarity and, in some cases, an affinity for country music. On Sundays, southern migrants gathered amongst themselves and with the native population at folk music parks or at large traveling tent show sites to hear country music.[3]

The folk music parks of the Northeast, Mid-Atlantic, and Midwest began appearing sometime in the early thirties as a product of the folk revival of the De-pression years and northern migration. As the thirties progressed, professional touring acts supplanted local amateur musicians as the main attraction on the large, outdoor stages within these parks. Recognizing the economic potential of providing outdoor entertainment for urbanites, several independent promoters in the late thirties and early forties began to organize traveling shows based on the folk music park motif. John Lair often took his *Renfro Valley* show on the road during the touring season. His troupe remained very popular in the border states throughout the war, averaging $5,000 a week in profits playing mainly small towns in 1944. Out west, Foreman Phillips emerged as a major figure on the California scene, booking such notable country music acts as Roy Acuff and Bob Wills at his refurbished Venice Pier Ballroom. In June 1942, he inaugurated the *Los Angeles County Barn Dance,* designed to entertain the multitude of transplanted southerners employed in the war industries in southern California. Enormously popular, Phillips's dances became the focal point of the Los Angeles country music scene in the mid- to late 1940s. Other successful independent promoters of the period include Oscar Davis, Hal Burns, Connie Gay, Larry Sunbrock, and Gus Foster. Foster introduced many southeastern performers, most notably the Callahan Brothers, to audiences in the Southwest, while Burns and Davis were instrumental in bringing country music to the nation at large. A February 1943 package show organized by Frank at Cincinnati's Music Hall featuring Roy Acuff, Ernest Tubb, the Carter Family, and Bill Boyd drew 13,000 in one day. The Burns and Davis shows attracted large crowds in the South as well, in dozens of war boom cities. Roy Acuff explains a contributing factor to the success of the independent promoters throughout the nation: "There were scores of farm boys who had moved to the city to work in industrial plants and in the textile mills and on the railroads, and any contact they could have with the country was important to them. Country music was this contact."[4]

The war itself facilitated the promotion of country music tours, many designed to entertain at training camps and military installations throughout the nation. Western swing performer Bill Boyd teamed with Hal Davis in late 1942 and early 1943 for an extensive tour of southern camps. Late in 1943, Boyd headed a war bond–buying tour of the West Coast. Touring constantly throughout the war, Boyd directly introduced country music to thousands of military personnel stationed in the United States. Another important wartime touring troupe, the *Grand Ole Opry*'s "Camel Caravan" spent nineteen months in 1941 and 1942 on the road entertaining troops (as well as promoting country music and cigarettes) throughout the United States and in Panama. The brainchild of J. L. Frank, the caravan perfectly amalgamated goodwill with marketing strategy to the benefit of all involved.[5]

As a business, country music promotion was less motivated by humanitarian impulse than by economic gain, and over the course of the war it became big business. Together with the booking agencies of such high-wattage stations as WLS and WSM, the promoters revolutionized the nature of the country music personal appearance tour. WLS's Dick Bergen established the precedent of teaming a group of a station's acts for large venues when he booked several *National Barn Dance* performers for a theater show in the fall of 1932. Four shows in one day grossed over $2,000, leading to the establishment of the WLS Artists' Bureau. By the 1940s, WLS's tour of fairs, then under the direction of George Ferguson and Earl Kurtze, were consistently drawing capacity audiences. The agents of stations with a large reservoir of country talent had little difficulty booking fairs throughout the war years. Bill McCluskey, manager of WLW Promotions, explained the lucrative situation to a reporter in 1943: "We have consistently broken all records in all the spots we have played on one-day stands in theaters. . . . We never consider the size of a town. All we are interested in is the size of the auditorium because we know we can bring the people in from the surrounding towns." Established in 1934 under the principal direction of Harry Stone, the WSM Artists' Service Bureau provided *Opry* members with a more secure income than the personal appearance tours and consequently attracted many upcoming stars. While the *Opry* itself paid its performers a minimal salary, the profits earned from the Artists' Service Bureau's tours furnished its members with financial stability, and the reputation gained by appearing on the show ensured a successful future.[6]

Many performers sought spots in promoter and artist service bureau–assembled package shows as a means to continue touring in a wartime atmosphere of gas and tire rationing. The remaining country bands not broken up by the enlistment of its members into armed services found themselves without the means to travel the long distances for their personal appearances. Alton Delmore explains, "The government announced they were going to ration automobile tires and gas and that was *it*." Some, such as the Carlisle Brothers, quit the business entirely to work in war plants. Country music acts dependent on records for supplemental income or as a means of enhancing their reputations for personal appearance tours faced the impediment of shellac rationing, which curtailed their releases. In April 1942, the War Production Board restricted the nonmilitary use of the material to prewar levels; by autumn, releases of new country music recordings slumped to a mere trickle. Less established acts fell victim to Darwinistic recording and releasing policies. Producer Art Satherley found his efforts to release the products of many of his recording sessions circumscribed by the government order: "From my enormous catalog of records . . . I was only allowed to put out a few, such as Gene Autry, Bob Wills, and Roy Acuff." Shellac rationing hamstrung many performers and producers, but it actually helped to increase the popularity of the genre beyond its core audience. With popular music releases restricted as well, many jukebox customers turned to country music as an alternative to repetitive plays of familiar tunes. Many found this music pleasing and continued to make country music selections after the lifting of the shellac restriction in 1944.[7]

Coin-operated phonographs, the earliest jukeboxes, first appeared in the late 1800s, and the first disc-equipped versions were invented in the early part of the twentieth century. Wurlitzer began marketing multiselection jukeboxes in the late 1920s, but sales remained slow until the repeal of Prohibition. Many of the 100,000 taverns that opened after the passage of the Eighteenth Amendment that could not afford live entertainment provided their customers with coin-operated phonographs instead. By 1940, the nation's 300,000 jukeboxes were bringing in over $90 million annually and accounting for approximately half of all records sold in the United States. During the war, the popularity of the devices skyrocketed, largely due to their presence in restaurants, taverns, and army PXs. Southern migrants in the North congregating in "hillbilly taverns" located near defense plants looked to jukeboxes to hear the songs that local radio stations virtually ignored. Not surprisingly, 50 percent of all Detroit locations equipped with a jukebox in 1944 reported the inclusion of country music selections on their machines; in St. Louis, the number rose to 70 percent. Even in a city as openly hostile to country music as New York, three in ten operators reported "folk" music on their jukes. The popularity of country music on the city's jukeboxes eventually led to the inauguration of a New York–based barn dance. Emceed by Layman Cameron, the show generated considerable interest among transplanted southerners and native New Yorkers alike. In addition to indicating the breadth of wartime migration, the popularity of country music in the North and on jukeboxes across the nation confirmed to many observers that popular music was not fulfilling the musical appetites of a significant portion of Americans. Ironically, the songwriters of Tin Pan Alley gave the country music industry a push when they invoked a strike in the spring of 1942.[8]

Prior to World War II, Tin Pan Alley remained the primary source for American popular music. These music publishing houses in New York City reigned over American music for the first quarter of the twentieth century. Sheet music sales determined the success of a song, and sales were driven by the popularization of tunes in vaudeville, Hollywood films, Broadway musicals, and traveling entertainment shows. Formed in 1914 to protect the copyrights of songwriters, the American Society of Composers, Authors and Publishers (ASCAP) fought a series of battles in the teens and twenties in an effort to establish itself and legitimize its purpose. Two attempts to combat ASCAP's increasing monopoly of the music industry—the first by the film industry in the early twenties, the second by radio in the early thirties—eventually failed. Radio, however, proved a formidable foe, and ASCAP's efforts to secure licensing fees from broadcasters met with increasing hostility as the 1930s progressed. Broadcasters began paying fees to ASCAP as early as 1922, but when rates began to reach exorbitant levels in the mid-thirties due to radio's increased popularity, the National Association of Broadcasters (NAB) moved to organize the radio industry. In 1939, when ASCAP proposed doubling the fees charged to broadcasters for the use of their copyrighted material on the air, the NAB responded by forming a rival publishing company, Broadcast Music, Incorporated (BMI), on October 14, 1939. After the expiration of their contract with ASCAP on December 31, 1940, the broadcasters turned to non-ASCAP sources for music to play on the air. Nearly all Tin Pan Alley songwriters were members of ASCAP, so BMI opened its doors to writers excluded from ASCAP's ranks, including those in the country music field.[9]

Because ASCAP excluded country music songwriters as members, many of those songwriters never took their profession seriously. As Floyd Tillman states, "I just did it for my own amusement. I never heard of anyone in Texas writing songs. I always thought they all came out of New York, which most of them did." Art Satherley explains ASCAP's blanket prejudice toward southerners that fostered such exclusion: "The head people at ASCAP at the time thought that they should get all their songs from someone in New York or Philadelphia or Pittsburgh or any metropolitan area. . . . They didn't think there was anything south of Newark." ASCAP seemed confident that most Americans shared their views, but the public outcry for the return of popular songs on radio that ASCAP banked on never materialized, and by the fall of 1941, ASCAP acquiesced to the broadcasters. In the interim of the dispute, however, BMI secured over 36,000 copyrights, many from country music songwriters. As one of the prime beneficiaries of the dispute, the country music industry gained recognition among radio listeners and the previously inimical publishing houses. Roy Acuff and Fred Rose furthered the country music cause considerably when they joined BMI in 1942. The ASCAP-BMI dispute and its aftermath effectively legitimized country music songwriters and opened the ears of millions of Americans to their products.[10]

On the heels of the ASCAP-BMI conflict, another major dispute in the music industry offered additional exposure for country music. Seeking to gain a share of the profits from the booming jukebox and radio industries, the American Federation of Musicians (AFM) and its 140,000 members went on strike in August 1943 at the behest of their spokesman, James Petrillo. Withstanding threats from the War Labor Board and the pleas of President Roosevelt, AFM eventually succeeded in securing greater compensation for the airplay and public performance of songs produced by its members, after Decca capitulated in September 1943 and the last major label followed suit the next year. During the strike, Americans gradually turned to alternative music in the absence of new releases. Radio stations that regularly played popular music recordings soon found themselves seeking out country music discs. Louis R. Cook, an employee of a Fort Worth radio station during the ban, explains how the dearth of new pop material led to the airplay of country songs:

> I was asked by the station's general manager to go with him to a station just out-
> side Fort Worth that was going out of business . . . to buy the station's record
> library. Being a rural station, it had a much larger collection of "old familiar"
> recordings than we did at KFJZ. We were very glad to get these records as they
> [relieved] the monotony of our having to play what few popular recordings we
> had on hand. . . . The letters we received about these old songs prompted us to
> continue a program of old-time folk music after the recording ban was lifted.

While country music performers participated in the strike, many of the independent labels they recorded for reconciled with Petrillo sooner than the majors. Whether through the discovery of prewar recordings or the newer selections released by the independents, Americans gained further familiarity with country music during the Petrillo ban. [11]

While the music industry wrangled over the distribution of profits, changes in popular music itself facilitated country music's growth in the war years. Big bands dominated the prewar years, but vocalists stepped into the limelight in the early 1940s. Martin Laforse and James Drake point out, "To young couples separated by the war, vocal music seemed more personal than the music of a large orchestra or dance band." The modern ballad style, crooning, popularized by Bing Crosby in the 1930s, flourished during the war, evidenced most noticeably in the rise of Frank Sinatra. The interest in sentimental and novelty songs during wartime nourished the ascendance of the popular vocalists, with audiences responding favorably to their interpretations of such songs as "Praise the Lord and Pass the Ammunition," "Don't Sit under the Apple Tree," "I'll Be Seeing You," and "As Time Goes By." By latching on to this trend during the war, several country music singers rose to levels of prominence that rivaled, and in some cases exceeded, their popular counterparts. The success of three vocalists from Texas—Gene Autry,

Tex Ritter, and Al Dexter, the Texas triumvirate—demonstrates the appeal of the country pop blend.[12]

No singer more skillfully blended the country and pop music idioms during the war years than Gene Autry. Combining a pop vocalist's polish with his own unique subtlety, Autry literally redefined country singing, paving the way for dozens of other performers who more fully embraced pop stylings. Musically, Gene Autry's recordings of the war years similarly coalesced mainstream and regional instrumentation, delicately balancing steel guitar and fiddle with horns and strings. Lyrically, he sidestepped country music's southernness by concentrating on western imagery early in his career and topical and universal themes as the war progressed. Through his appearances in singing cowboy movies and his aggregation of various American musical forms, Autry did more than any other single performer to nationalize the appeal of country music by veiling it in western vestiges.[13]

Whether or not Gene Autry's recordings can be categorized as true country music remains open to debate. Only Frankie Marvin's inconspicuous steel guitar lends any country flavor to them musically. An amalgamation of trumpets, clarinets, violins, accordions, and castanets swirls around Autry's unruffled vocals. The formula of combining pop-flavored, infectious melodies with rustic imagery initially established on Autry's recordings of the mid-thirties (after he abandoned a Jimmie Rodgers–style approach) remained remarkably buoyant well into the 1940s, with "Don't Fence Me In" (released in 1945) representing the apogee of the Autry sound. The aggregation of Cole Porter's western lyrics, Autry's breezy voice, and Art Satherley's sweeping production resulted in one of the greatest moments in American music. The pop-tinged vocals added to country songs "It Makes No Difference Now" and the Academy Award–nominated "Be Honest with Me" softened the edges of the wistful lyrics just enough to attract thousands of Americans to southern-derived music. Douglas B. Green describes the appeal of Autry's vocal approach: "His voice expressed a sincerity and unaffected honesty which created a feeling of immediacy between the singer and his listeners." When applied to lyrics centering on the effects of wartime separation, such as "At Mail Call Today" and "I'll Be Back," Autry's voice encapsulated the apprehensions of a nation at war. Gene Autry was less a country music figure than a symbol of Americana. Nevertheless, his association with country music during the war years, established through song selection, diction, and use of rural imagery, helped to establish the genre as an authentic national phenomenon.[14]

Ironically, Gene Autry, a singer so often identified as a country musician or western singer, fits the standard definition of neither. As noted above, his recordings offered only token allegiance to country music instrumentation; his singing, meanwhile, bore little if any resemblance to frontier vocal styles. Early western recordings offered listeners unadorned self-accompanied vocal presentations of narratives devoid of the romantic elements that characterized most twentieth-century cowboy songs. The music and film industries adroitly supplanted the authentic cowboys' penchant for singing about their work and the unnerving solitude they faced with less austere imagery. For every performer like Gene Autry who convincingly played the cowboy role, however, there were a dozen others who looked absurd singing cowboy songs. One successful country singer of the 1940s, however, managed to bridge the gap between frontier authenticity and Tin Pan Alley romanticism more successfully than any other. While by no means a real cowboy, Tex Ritter helped to reinvigorate interest in authentic cowboy songs when he brought his impressive apprehension of the lost genre to New York in 1936.[15]

Attending the University of Texas, Ritter developed his interest in the music of the American West while studying under J. Frank Dobie and John Lomax, two noted folklorists. After a stint with a traveling musical troupe, he journeyed to New York City, where he became quite popular in the mid-thirties on radio and among folk culture enthusiasts. At his first recording session, with Decca in 1935, he sang four cowboy songs, accompanied only by his guitar, including "Rye Whiskey," a song he reworked several times over the course of his career. In 1936, he left New York for Hollywood, where he appeared in several western movies. Dropped by Decca in 1939, he signed with Johnny Mercer's new Los Angeles–based Capitol label in 1942.[16]

Backed by such country music notables as Johnny Bond, Wesley Tuttle, Merle Travis, and Cliffie Stone, Ritter's Capitol recordings during World War II differed considerably from his first solo performances. While his early Decca releases owed a great deal to the authentic cowboy tradition, the Capitol sides represent the epitome of the western and country blend. Less pop flavored than Autry's releases, Ritter's recordings placed more emphasis on fiddle and guitar solos. As producer of the sides, Johnny Mercer brought his background in popular music to the first session, adding background vocals and accordion to the country-band backing of "Jingle, Jangle, Jingle." Occasionally, he would add a clarinet or strings to the rubric. Ritter's deep, weathered voice, however, squarely places these recordings in the country music fold, as does the straightforwardness of the lyrics written by Jenny Lou Carson, Scotty Wiseman, and Ritter himself. By war's end, Ritter was well established as one of country music's most identifiable and successful performers.

As the third member of the Texas triumvirate that brought country music to Americans through the incorporation of pop sounds, Al Dexter gained national notoriety during the war on the strength of only one song. Many musicologists consider Dexter a honky-tonker because of his infamous use of barroom imagery, but it seems more appropriate to describe him as a novelty singer and songwriter with an incomparable talent for putting gleeful lyrics to catchy tunes. Possessing neither the voice of the pop crooner nor the charisma of the singing cowboys, Dexter momentarily surpassed all his competitors in his ephemeral rise to fame when "Pistol Packin' Mama" burst on the American scene in 1943.

The sharecropper's son turned housepainter from Jacksonville, Texas, made his first recordings in 1936 under the direction of Art Satherley. From the outset, Satherley let Dexter know that he was looking for something different and strongly suggested to the singer that he abandon his penchant for writing gospel and Jimmie Rodgers–like songs in favor of more up-tempo material: "Art Satherley . . . told me to write honky-tonk songs. When I told him I like pretty songs, he said . . . 'My lad, do you want to sing pretty songs or do you want to make money.' I wrote 'Honky-tonk Blues' and 'Jelly Roll Blues' and after that, all they wanted from me was honky-tonk." In the context of the 1930s, *honky-tonk* meant material suitable for dancing, and Dexter proved himself up to the challenge. Using his experiences as a tavern owner during the Texas oil boom, Dexter wrote a series of jazzy tunes depicting life in the southwestern honky-tonks. "Car-Hoppin' Mama," "Honky-tonk Baby," and "Bar Hotel" all make light of inebriate excess. By 1940, with the formula well in place, he recorded "When We Go Honky Tonkin' " backed by a fiddle, electric steel guitar, amplified mandola, and acoustic rhythm guitar. Around 1942, Satherley added an accordion and trumpet (played by Harry Holinger) to the mix to create a unique sound that historian Nick Tosches describes as "an alembic in which bubbled the forces of old-timey blues, western swing, honky tonk, and outright pop." On "Pistol Packin' Mama," Satherley and Dexter perfected the jaunty sound, and the record sold one million copies in the first six months after its release.[17]

The success of "Pistol Packin' Mama" was due in part to the AFM ban instigated by James Petrillo, which left the American public hungry for new material. Art Satherley points out another contributing factor to the song's popularity: "When we made 'Pistol Packin' Mama' with Al Dexter, we had war hysteria, and it was what people of the time wanted." Undeniably infectious, the song blared from jukeboxes coast to coast. With pressings limited by shellac shortages, black market discs of the song sold for as much as $1.25 each. Commenting on the sensation, puzzled editors of *Life* magazine described the song as "naïve, folksy, and almost completely devoid of meaning [with] a melodic line [that] is simple and [a] lyric [that is] rowdy, and, of course, monotonously tautological." In the midst of the recording ban, Dexter's original version cornered the market, and, in the process, generated a national interest in country music. *Billboard* conceded that its success proved that "corn can thrive in any part of the country." In late 1943, Bing Crosby and the Andrew Sisters recorded the song at the first Decca recording session after the AFM ban, but by then, as Dexter explains, his version had already established itself: "See, my record was out about a year before Bing Crosby and the Andrew Sisters could record it. All the recording companies were on strike with the musicians union, so my record got the go on 'em." On the coattails of "Pistol Packin' Mama," Dexter went on to dominate the country music charts in 1944, scoring four of the year's ten biggest hits. In most of their post–"Pistol Packin' Mama" efforts, Dexter and Satherley implemented the same formula, in some cases updating fiddle- and amplified mandola–dominated selections such as "Calico Rag" and "Wine, Women, and Song" with trumpet, accordion, and clarinet backing, with considerable commercial success. Al Dexter's achievements proved that country music could compete with popular music for the nation's attention, and although the playing field at the time was not exactly level due to the AFM ban, country music's proponents could still point to "Pistol Packin' Mama" as partial proof that the genre would remain neither sectionalized nor marginalized for much longer. [18]

"Pistol Packin' Mama" was neither the first country music song to sell nation-wide nor the first country music song covered by popular artists like Bing Crosby. In its ubiquity, however, it proved the most publicized. Contemporary artists Bob Wills and Elton Britt also set precedents for national sales in the early 1940s. Britt's "There's a Star-Spangled Banner Hanging Somewhere" swept the country in 1942 and surpassed the million-seller mark in April 1943. Wills's "New San Antonio Rose," nearly devoid of all country trappings, reached number eleven on *Billboard*'s national sales chart in 1940; Crosby's version reached number seven. Crosby went on to record several popular country songs, such as "You Are My Sunshine," "Walking the Floor over You," and "I'm Thinking Tonight of Blue Eyes," with orchestral backings. The accompaniment of his brother Bob Crosby's Bob Cats on "Walking the Floor" transforms the song into a jazzy, up-tempo rollick, complete with a heavy beat and tenor saxophone backing. Crosby's crossover versions drew even more attention to country music, especially in the music industry. In July 1943, *Billboard*'s country music column, "American Folk Tunes and Tunesters," became a weekly feature, and by early 1944, the genre had its own weekly chart, "Most Played Juke Box Folk Records." [19]

Country music's inherent perspicuity contributed a great deal to the genre's wartime expansion. Music historian Ian Whitcomb points out, "In wartime you get down to fundamentals and hillbilly kept it all close to the earth." Country songs dealing both directly and indirectly with the impact of soldiers' separation from their wives and sweethearts, such as "Each Night at Nine," "Have I Stayed Away Too Long," and "At Mail Call Today," captured the war-torn emotions of millions of Americans. Country musician and songwriter Ted Daffan explains the appeal of a song like "No Letter Today": "This was because during the war, World War II, so many people were separated and even civilians, a lot of the men would go elsewhere to look for work or to work in war plants and housing would not be available for awhile, so everybody was looking for a letter and so I had a million seller."[20]

Country music songwriters also proved themselves capable of writing lyrics that directly dealt with wartime separation and mortality. Wartime fatalities averaged around 1 percent of the adult population of most states in just the first two years of the conflict, and as a result songs like Ernest Tubb's "Soldier's Last Letter" and Tex Ritter's "Gold Star in the Window" appealed to innumerable Americans. Stephen Tucker describes country music during the war as "an emotional salve [with] honest lyrics and simple melodies [that] appealed to men and women who had come face to face with the fact of their own mortality." Countless other Americans responded to the rousing patriotic message in such tunes as "Smoke on the Water," "Stars and Stripes on Iwo Jima," and "Remember Pearl Harbor." In October 1942, *Billboard* noted that "the folk field, far more than the pop field, has come through with war tunes of the type asked for by government officials." Answering the call, southern songwriters steadily provided the American populace with lyrical pieces that crystallized the national wartime zeal. Through its ultranationalism and ability to encapsulate the emotions of war, country music drew in millions of American listeners to its rapidly expanding audience.[21]

Country music served as a soundtrack for a nation at war, and it also became an instrument for politics. Latching on to its grassroots appeal, many politicians soon discovered its electoral appeal, especially in the South. Former mill owner turned radio personality Wilbert Lee O'Daniel successfully won the governorship of Texas in 1938 touring with a campaign band called the Hillbilly Boys. O'Daniel's radio program with the band furthered his cause, as evidenced partially by the fact that he won a plurality of the vote in every county within range of its broadcast. In 1941, he organized another band during a special election for a vacant U.S. Senate seat, beating Lyndon Baines Johnson by 1,300 votes. In September 1941, *Billboard* featured a story on the connection between country music and politics in Texas, which included a survey of Texans' musical preferences. While country music ranked third among various musical genres as Texans' favorite, at least 50 percent of those polled maintained that they at least occasionally liked to listen to country music. Not surprisingly, the percentage of farmers who went so far as to say they liked country music was twice that of large city dwellers. However, one-third of the latter group maintained at least an occasional interest in the music. By no means confined to Texas, country music's appeal served as a public relations medium in the North and other parts of the South. In Arkansas, Colonel T. H. Barton enlisted the help of *Grand Ole Opry* performers Jamup and Honey in his 1944 United States senatorial campaign. Also that year, Governor Green of Illinois featured WLS's Patsy Montana at a campaign rally in Chicago. By the end of the war, many politicians clearly viewed an association with country music with less hostility than they did in the late 1930s.[22]

Jimmie Davis's successful bid for the governorship of Louisiana in 1944 illustrated country music's electoral pulling power, especially in the South. Davis performed the music of the southern folk as a means to catapulting himself into office, but he was not the first southern politician to do so; Tennessee's Bob Taylor and Georgia's Tom Watson used their fiddle-playing skills for political purposes in the late 1800s. Davis, however, was the first commercial country music performer to win a position as notable as a state governorship. Davis began a career in public service in 1930 when he became a criminal court clerk in Shreveport. In 1938, he made a successful bid to become the city's commissioner of public safety. In the absence of an attractive reform-minded candidate, the anti–Huey Long forces convinced Davis to run for the office of governor, and the singer formally announced his decision in the autumn of 1943. Although Davis was initially hesitant to sing at his rallies, he soon formed a band consisting of such country music notables as Moon Mullican and Johnny Gimble to accompany him on the campaign after potential voters began accusing him of haughtiness. Davis's political adroitness and musical talents proved an unbeatable combination, and the singer eventually won the election by 37,000 votes. Davis's victory made him a national celebrity and no doubt influenced the Democratic National Committee's decision to invite him to sing at their Chicago convention in 1944.[23]

Other country music notables tossed their hats into the political ring during and after the war. Roy Acuff began flirting with the idea in early 1944, going so far as to announce his decision to run for the Tennessee governorship before taking himself out of the race several weeks later. In 1948, he made a more determined run at the office, touring with his band on the campaign trail but eventually losing the election. In 1951, the Prohibition party nominated country music singer and songwriter Stuart Hamblen for president, with similar results. Davis, on the other hand, ran another successful campaign for Louisiana governor in 1960. Prior to World War II, such political notions seemed inconceivable given country music's backward image. Largely due to Jimmie Davis's dignified manner and electoral success, however, country music and its performers increasingly became less a target for disparagement among political leaders and the press.[24]

Jimmie Davis's triumph and the general utilization of country music for political purposes drew a great deal of media attention to the genre. Meanwhile, on a more grassroots level, the intermingling of servicemen from various parts of the country brought countless Americans in touch with white southern music for the first time. In a 1968 interview, producer Steve Sholes referred to the population shifts of military personnel and production workers during World War II as "the biggest single factor" in the growth of country music. At PXs around the country, servicemen swapped stories of their youth and their homes. Clarence Merson, stationed in Texas, recalls the cultural exchanges in a letter to his family back in Pennsylvania: "And so on into the night, these countless remembrances of things past. The whole intricate fabric of their lives is rewoven simply, sometimes naively and always without restraint." Many soldiers turned to the PX jukeboxes, which were often filled with country music selections, as a source of inexpensive entertainment. Others stationed in the South heard daily local hillbilly radio programs and, on Saturday night, the barn dances. Jack Stapp recalls the popularity of the Saturday night *Opry* at Fort Jackson, South Carolina: "I'd walk around the camp and no matter where I went I'd never leave the *Opry*. The *Opry* was on every radio in every barracks, and there wasn't any way these kids from New York and New Jersey could get away from it. . . . It had to rub off on 'em." Jim McReynolds (of Jim and Jesse) recalls several nights when soldiers squabbled over station selection on the lone radio in his company's barracks. In the absence of a radio, many soldiers sang country songs to the accompaniment of their own guitars, often to the chagrin of their northern counterparts, who overwhelmingly preferred the music of bands like Harry James and Tommy Dorsey and the voices of Bing Crosby and Frank Sinatra. In Texas, makeshift country bands introduced military bases to two-steps that acquired the name "kicker dances." Countless other semiprofessional country musicians took to performing as well. Veteran performer Jack Penkola recalled his impromptu shows in the South Pacific: "In my fourteen years of constant traveling I've played every state . . . played the best theaters and the worst; now with the camp shows I've seen things that will live with me forever. Shows may be held in a mess hall or even under a tree. One day one was held in a graveyard, another in a church and once on a ship."[25]

Dozens of country music notables served during the war; the amount of time they spent playing music varied considerably: Johnny Gimble recalls that he "didn't get to play a lick during the war"; Hank Thompson picked guitar in the barracks and occasionally on the Armed Forces Network (AFN); Leon McAuliffe formed his own band while serving in the Navy; and Ferlin Husky entertained his merchant marine shipmates with songs he had played at informal gatherings in his youth. Husky remembers, "Some of the most enthusiastic people were those who came from parts of the country where this kind of music was almost unknown." Musicians serving stateside, such as Floyd Tillman, found time to perform at local nightclubs and to make recordings during leaves and furloughs. While stationed in Indianapolis, Bob Atcher joined forces with Hoagy Carmichael to write songs for army shows. Transferred to the Pacific, Atcher joined with a number of other servicemen to organize a traveling music show, *By the Numbers,* which often performed at precarious locations: "We were at the front—quite often, in between the artillery and the infantry, and we were listed as infantry ourselves. So we were in the active spots all the way along." Some country music performers, such as the Bolick Brothers, served in active combat; others, such as Joe Maphis, were assigned to special services to entertain troops. After he enlisted, Grandpa Jones brought his guitar with him on his trip overseas to Europe. In Germany, he organized the Munich Mountaineers, performing one hour each morning for five months on AFN. As Jones recalls, the program generated a considerable amount of mail, both favorable and critical in nature: "We started getting stacks of fan mail from lonely GIs who hadn't been able to hear any real country music since they got overseas; most of the military music was brass bands, and the touring show troops consisted of pop singers like Al Jolson. . . . Of course, we got hold of some people who hadn't heard much country music. Some liked it, some didn't."[26]

The Armed Forces Radio Service (AFRS) deserves a great deal of credit for introducing American GIs stationed overseas to country music. On the air since May 1942, AFRS quickly mushroomed into a major source of entertainment for Allied troops. Over the course of 1943, AFRS increased the number of its outlets from 21 to 306. The network initially broadcast country music shows as a time filler between transcribed network shows from the states, most of which featured popular music and comedy. Gradually, however, AFN began to devote more airtime to programs that featured such popular country music performers as Roy Acuff. Acuff's style, described by D. K. Wilgus as one that "captivated the folk and embarrassed but fascinated others," proved magnetic to AFN listeners. In 1944, Ken Marvin of the *Munich Morning Report* asked listeners to send in letters indicating their preference for either Roy Acuff or Frank Sinatra performances.

When Acuff supporters sent in six hundred more votes, AFN's program directors promptly added two new country music programs to their schedule, Jones's show and a Saturday night feature called the *Hillbilly Jamboree*. They undoubtedly also found use for prerecorded country shows, made available on sixteen-inch transcriptions and twelve-inch V-Discs that featured Acuff himself. A transcribed thirty-minute network portion of the *Grand Ole Opry* satisfied the appetites of many Acuff fans; other strained to hear the early morning live broadcast of the entire program. In a letter to Acuff in April 1944, I. W. Peters, a serviceman stationed in northwest Africa, described the Saturday night ritual: "Conditions are still such that once in awhile we are able to hear the *Grand Ole Opry* direct from the states. It starts coming in over here around two or three in the morning, so we have to make an all night job of it. We usually can hear it until about six or seven A.M. Here and then she fades out. But it's worth the loss of sleep." Peters's comments reflect the *Grand Ole Opry*'s expanded popularity, a phenomenon both indicative of and contributive to country music's nationalization during the war years.[27]

The war years represent the *Grand Ole Opry*'s adolescence, the period between the show's prewar pubescent regionalism and its postwar maturity into country music's paramount barn dance. The *Opry*'s network hookup in 1939 and the coast-to-coast broadcasts begun in July 1940 laid the foundation for the show's wartime growth. In 1943, the network portion of the program reached an audience estimated at 25 million listeners. Behind the scenes, the Stone brothers, Harry and David; network producer Jack Stapp; and stage manager Vito Pellettieri usurped George Hay as the program's primary architects some time in the thirties. Harry Stone established the WSM Artists' Service Bureau because he envisioned the *Opry*'s commercial potential. With promoter J. L. Frank, Stone brought several notable acts to the *Opry* in the late thirties and early forties that contributed to the show's ascendancy. By the end of the war, the star-centered system rebuked in the *Opry*'s early days was firmly in place. In bringing Pee Wee King, Roy Acuff, Bill Monroe, Eddy Arnold, and Ernest Tubb to the show in the late 1930s and early 1940s, the *Opry*'s backstage administrators provided listeners with a peerless cross section of country musical styles that attracted listeners of various backgrounds from all parts of the country. Acuff, the string-band vocalist; Monroe, the progressive instrumentalist; and Arnold, the maturing crooner, represented the present and future of southeastern country music, while King and Tubb symbolized the modernizing forces of the Southwest in their costuming and instrumentation. Together, they liberated the *Grand Ole Opry* from its prewar provincialism and set the program on its course to barn dance preeminence. The impact of Monroe's and Arnold's presence did not fully materialize until after the war, and Acuff's influence peaked in the early forties, but King's and Tubb's popularity produced immediate effects. Pee Wee King was not the first country music performer to wear western regalia, and other acts anteceded Tubb in using electric instrumentation, but in bringing their styles to the *Grand Ole Opry*, they altered the image protracted and sound produced by southeastern country music bands in unprecedented ways. Ironically, the southeastern-based *Grand Ole Opry* received its biggest push toward national popularity by adapting southwestern motifs.[28]

Before Pee Wee King brought his western-attired band to the *Opry* in the late 1930s, Hay's promotion of the burlesque bucolic dominated the show's first decade. The audience was primarily regional, and self-parody seemed as innocuous as it was commercially effective. The progressives struggled to attain respectability, however, and many country music performers donned clothes and costumes de-emphasizing the hillbilly caricature. Bill Malone points out that the singing mountaineer provided one such alternative, conveying the romantic image of a remote land populated by individualistic and ethnically pure Anglo-Saxons with virtuous moral leanings. The Carter Family personified the unsullied mountain image, projecting what Patrick Carr refers to as "the old country values of harmony, tradition, and continuity." Ultimately, however, the mountaineer image proved unsuitable after government reports, Hollywood movies, and photographer's portraits of southern poverty began appearing with uncomfortable regularity. Some acts, such as the Blue Sky Boys, the Delmore Brothers, and Roy Acuff, began wearing suits and sport coats in an effort to impart a sense of dignity and legitimacy to their music. In one sense, this proved effective, particularly in distancing the music from negative connotations, but it failed to present a unique and vital image that could captivate country music fans and beguile potential listeners. The cowboy image, on the other hand, afforded a more suitable alternative to hillbilly and mountaineer stereotypes and all of their undesirable associations.[29]

The widespread national appeal of the cowboy image in the late 1930s and 1940s undoubtedly influenced country musicians' decision to don western garb. Americans first demonstrated an interest in the American cowboy in the late 1800s in their attendance of Buffalo Bill Cody's wild west shows and their purchase of dime-store western novels. Commenting on the literary works of Zane Grey, Peter Field, and others in the western genre, Buck Rainey notes that they "created a sensationalized, glorified, romanticized, distorted, imaginative, and downright inaccurate impression of the American cowboy." The cowboy song anthologies published in the first two decades of the twentieth century further romanticized the western cowhand. Interest in recording western-style tunes developed after Carl Sprague's "When the Work's All Done This Fall" sold nearly one million copies in the mid- to late 1920s. Jimmie Rodgers popularized the western image among a southeastern audience when he recorded several cowboy numbers, while the Prairie Ramblers on WLS's *Barn Dance* introduced a western repertoire to record and radio listeners in the mid- to late 1930s. Meanwhile, out in California, the movie industry discovered the profitability of creating low-budget cowboy musicals. Utterly devoid of realism, the singing cowboy films filled a void in the hearts and minds of millions of Americans in the Depression decade. Douglas B. Green explains, "The singing cowboy . . . embodied a confluence of many of the aspects of the American dream, representing a sense of glamour and of adventure, a sense of the rugged individuality Americans have long prized." Self-reliant and resilient, the mythical cowboy of books, songs, and films offered Americans an image of the past that fostered a sense of national pride while offering absolute truths in a time of economic uncertainty.[30]

Country music performers' espousal of the cowboy image contributed to country music's wartime nationalization in two ways: symbolically, it fostered an association of the musical genre with an American ideal, and more directly, it offered performers a venue in which they could attain national exposure, that is Hollywood films. In regards to the former, Green points out that "no youngster in the thirties and forties ever wanted to grow up to be a hillbilly, but thousands upon thousands wanted to be cowboys." By adopting western regalia and changing its name, a country music act could theoretically transform itself from a hillbilly string band into a cowboy ensemble. Following the prototype established by the Sons of the Pioneers in the 1930s, more and more new groups during and after the war chose names that referred to southwestern geographic locations or traditionally western occupations or imagery, such as Hank Williams's Drifting Cowboys, Hank Snow and the Rainbow Ranch Boys, and Eddy Arnold, the Tennessee Plowboy. Established performers who appeared in singing cowboy movies welcomed the national exposure that the movies offered. Such notables as Bob Wills, Red Foley, Ernest Tubb, and Jimmie Davis made western films in the early forties. A few shared Roy Acuff's reluctance to wear western costuming in his films: "I am very annoyed when someone calls me a cowboy. You can see there is nothing cowboy about me. Only cowboy song I ever sang was 'Home on the Range,' and that's the President's favorite. I only sing country or folk songs. When I was in Hollywood they wanted me to dress like a cowboy for a picture and I refused. I don't intend for the public ever to see me as a cowboy." Acuff reasserted his position in his 1948 gubernatorial campaign: "I *am* a hillbilly fiddler and singer, and if that is a crime, I'll have to plead guilty to it. I'll even go further than that and tell you I am *proud* of it." The vast majority of performers possessed neither Acuff's stature nor his degree of wealth, and they clamored less about the introduction of western stylings into their acts. Green explains, "The singing cowboy gave much to country music . . . in dignity and glamour in a time when country music was seen by outsiders and critics as possessing neither." Long after the singing cowboy faded in popularity in Hollywood films, country musicians retained the western image as a means to furthering their careers. The precedent of donning southwestern regalia established by such *Grand Ole Opry* performers as Pee Wee King and Zeke Clements not only survived the war but flourished in the late 1940s and early 1950s.[31]

Ernest Tubb's contribution to the southwesternization of the *Grand Ole Opry* proved more controversial than that of Pee Wee King and Zeke Clements. In bringing an electric guitar player to the show on a regular basis, Tubb virtually revolutionized the program and helped sculpt the configuration of country music in the Southeast after the war. Ronnie Pugh notes, "Ernest Tubb did more for the *Opry* in his early years there than the *Opry* did for him." Tubb made his debut on the network portion of the program in January 1943. Backed by an electric guitar, Tubb's performance elicited a tremendous response from the audience. As Tubb recalls, however, not everyone seemed pleased with his instrumentation: "Judge Hay didn't like it too well, but I said, 'Judge, I make my records this way,' and he finally said to go ahead." Tubb received inspiration for use of electric guitar backup from a jukebox operator in Fort Worth, who mentioned to Tubb that patrons could not hear his early acoustic sides over the tumults of the nightlife atmosphere. A Jimmie Rodgers devotee, Tubb first recorded with just an acoustic guitar, producing songs that reflected more than a passing resemblance to the Blue Yodeler's singing and playing style. In developing his own sound, Tubb augmented his rhythm acoustic with a lead guitar played acoustically at his first Decca sessions in 1940. When lead guitarist Fay "Smitty" Smith plugged in at a 1941 session, the Tubb sound finally coalesced. "Walking the Floor over You" became Tubb's first big seller and his ticket to the *Grand Ole Opry*. Described by Pugh as "just a straightforward, no frills, drawling and believable baritone, framed only by the insistent, piercing melody line of an electric guitar," the Ernest Tubb sound epitomized the immediate future of country music. In 1945, the *Mountain Broadcast and Prairie Recorder* reported that "Ernest Tubb is the most 'imitated' singer in [country] radio today." Younger performers emulated Tubb's use of single-string, lead electric guitar parts, as well as his voice. In stark contrast to country performers influenced by popular singers more interested in vocal effect than the meaning of lyrics, Tubb used his voice as an instrument for establishing an immediate connection with listeners. Completely natural, Tubb's singing style lent a considerable amount of sincerity to his straightforward lyrics. In the war years, Tubb excelled at exploring the tenuous nature of relationships, and the sparse musical backdrop accented rather than subjugated the vocal performance and lyrical emphasis. The addition of a fiddler and a bassist in the latter war years demonstrated the possibilities of applying conventional country imagery to electric instrumentation, what would soon become known as the honky-tonk sound.[32]

Two other native southwestern country music artists aided in the architecture of the honky-tonk sound and the popularization of electric instrumentation in country music: Ted Daffan and Floyd Tillman. Daffan merged his boyhood interest in electronics with his attraction to Hawaiian music when he purchased his first amplifier equipped with a pickup in 1934. Playing with several Texas bands in the mid-1930s, Daffan fine-tuned his abilities as an electric steel guitarist and developed an interest in writing country songs. In 1939, the success of Cliff Bruner's version of Daffan's "Truck Driver's Blues" garnered him his own recording contract. From the outset, Daffan worked to establish a unique sound with his own band, one that downplayed the jazziness of the western swing bands he played with yet still utilized electric steel guitar parts. Organized in Dallas around 1940, Ted Daffan's Texans went on to produce several of the most successful country music records of the war years. Remarkably astute at writing lyrics that captured the moods of working-class southerners, Daffan scored with such songs as "Worried Mind," "Born to Lose," "No Letter Today," and "Headed down the Wrong Highway." Augmenting his steel guitar with piano, accordion, and lead electric guitar, Daffan created an infectious blend of pop and southwestern sounds that appealed to listeners across the country. His economical steel guitar leads undeniably influenced scores of fledging guitarists.[33]

Even more uninhibited in his musical approach, Floyd Tillman merged his pioneering single-string, amplified guitar leads with an idiosyncratic vocal style that defied categorization. At an early age, the Ryan, Oklahoma, native acquired an appreciation of the importance of volume while playing with his older brother: "I was listening to [his] metal guitar, listening to how weak my mandolin was and I thought, well, I'll never make any money playing on the mandolin." He began performing with his brothers around Post, Texas, where he grew up, before graduating to the east Texas club scene in the mid-1930s. Battling crowd noise, Tillman initially played a metal acoustic guitar equipped with a resonator to amplify his jazzy solos inspired by the trumpet playing of a fellow band member. As Tillman recalls, audiences at dances did not quite know what to make of his amplified solos: "It was quite a sensation, people just standing around watching me play lead on guitar and it was different because you're not supposed to do that." Once in Houston, he enlisted Ted Daffan's assistance in equipping his amplified guitar with a homemade pickup. In addition to playing regularly with western swing bands, he took up songwriting. According to Tillman, one of his songs, "It Makes No Difference Now," covered by Jimmie Davis and Cliff Bruner, became so popular that "one guy in Baytown . . . shot the jukebox out with a shotgun because he was so sick of it." In 1939, Tillman began a solo career backed by several of his western swing comrades, including Bob Dunn, Moon Mullican, and Cliff Bruner. Tillman's early sound reflected his background in Texas string bands, but he also branched out into the country pop field on numbers such as "I'll Come Back to You" and the popular "They Took the Stars out of Heaven." By 1944, he appeared ready to fully embrace pop stylings with such songs as "There's No Use to Try It Anymore" and "Each Night at Nine," which showcased clarinet solos. After 1945, however, Tillman returned to his Texas roots, releasing some of the hardest-hitting honky-tonk songs of the postwar period. Tillman's wartime sides retain their significance as modifications of the Texas string-band sound aimed at a mainstream audience. When considered alongside the contemporary recordings of Ernest Tubb and Ted Daffan, Tillman's recordings indicate the homogenization of regional styles in the first half of the 1940s.[34]

The process of musical interaction that began with the barn dances in the 1930s accelerated during World War II as a result of several factors. Wartime migration introduced southerners to northern music and northerners to southern music. For the first time, country music did not seem as foreign to nonsoutherners. Meanwhile, rural white southerners grew increasingly familiar with urban culture through their own migration to northern and southern cities, thereby modifying their worldview. Folk music parks provided a weekend refuge for many transplanted southerners, as did the traveling country music package shows organized by promoters. Southerners who enlisted in the armed forces clung to their music and their culture in an effort to cope with homesickness and the perils of war. They brought their guitars or listened to the *Grand Ole Opry* whenever they could and, in the process of finding release from their concerns, introduced their northern counterparts to the music of their homeland. As PXs around the world and jukeboxes across the nation reverberated with the sounds of country music, thousands upon thousands of Americans grew increasingly attracted to the genre's earthy and patriotic lyricism. Meeting the American public halfway, many performers adapted popular instrumentation and nonsouthern costuming in an effort to further the country music cause. Aided by movies and the inner struggles of the popular music industry, country music gained tremendous national exposure and established itself as a legitimate American art form. World War II shattered the cultural isolation of the rural white South and its music and in the process brought about the nationalization of both.

Within the world of country music, the rigid boundary between the Southeast and the Southwest grew increasingly inconspicuous. Just as the southeastern progressives borrowed from one another in the 1930s, they adopted the musical stylings and cultural image of their southwestern colleagues in the early 1940s. Gene Autry, Tex Ritter, and Al Dexter demonstrated quite clearly the appeal of pop instrumentation and the cowboy look, and Ernest Tubb, Ted Daffan, and Floyd Tillman revealed the possibilities of incorporating electric instrumentation into the standard acoustic musical matrix. For their own part, southwesterners proceeded in their established pattern of musical experimentation, increasingly leaning toward dance-based music with a beat for entertainment and solace. In time, many country music artists would incorporate the realism so prevalent in southeastern lyrics with the Tubb-Daffan-Tillman musical hybrid, creating a diffuse subgenre currently referred to as honky-tonk. Other artists shunned lyrical realism and all musical constraints, initiating a country music anomaly known as western swing.

3 THE SOUTHWESTERN COMPONENT
TEXAS SWING, WESTERN SWING, AND
URBAN COUNTRY MUSIC

Country music that falls under the umbrella of western swing includes a variety of improvisational musical styles designed for dancing that originated primarily west of the Mississippi River in the 1930s. Unlike prewar country musicians of the Southeast, western swing practitioners demonstrated less interest in lyrical content than they did in the overall musical effect of their performances. Western swing was more urban in both its sound and audience and evinced a worldly sophistication and cosmopolitan outlook divergent from contemporary country music. Isolated from mainstream country music in its incipient years, western swing provided much of the musical framework for country music's postwar modernization by infusing the genre with its heavy beat and modern instrumentation. Western swing vanquished country music's provincial outlook and adherence to conventional instrumentation. In just over ten years, western swing grew from small musical combos performing at Texas house parties to large orchestras playing Los Angeles dance halls. As a result of its antagonism toward southeastern country music and its increasing affiliation with popular music, western swing eventually perished in the early 1950s when Nashville rose to prominence and when country music in general reached its apogee in national appeal. Before its postwar plummet, however, western swing reached a spectacular summit in popularity and influence unmatched by any other subgenre.

Evolutionary and eclectic, western swing in many ways defies definition and description. The term *western swing*, in fact, did not become a common label for the subgenre until after World War II. Prior to the war, record companies labeled early western swing as "Novelty Hot Dance" or "Hot String Band" music. In 1941, the Victor recording company referred to its latest release of Texas and Louisiana country groups as "Texas Swing." In October 1944, *Billboard* made the following announcement, unceremoniously giving the subgenre its common label for the first time in a national publication: "Spade Cooley will put out 25 of his original tunes, together with an album of band numbers and suggestions on arrangements for Western Bands. Book to be titled *Western Swing*." The most straightforward definitions of the subgenre center on its musical characteristics.

Bob Wills describes western swing in this paradigm: "West of the Mississippi River when we played, we played for dancing. East of the Mississippi river they played a show, or they played a schoolhouse, just for people to sit and listen, visual or audible entertainment and not for dancing." Hank Thompson builds on Wills's description of the subgenre, emphasizing the music itself: "The [music of the Southeast] was more the hill country music, banjos and fiddles, where the music of the Southwest was a lot more up—you know, up-tempo and had more life to it, more of a lively type thing." Country music historian Bob Pinson forthrightly refers to western swing as "the Southwest's response to the big dance band." As an amalgam of American popular, jazz, and Texas folk music, the western swing subgenre represents country music's first response to the urban environment. The birth of western swing occurred when guitar-fiddle duets playing at Texas house parties began augmenting their sound with rhythmic instruments, such as piano, banjo, and string bass, in an effort to provide a more danceable beat for listeners. Gradually, as the music moved into dance halls, these bands soon discovered the importance of volume, a problem solved through the electric amplification of a variety of instruments, from Hawaiian steel guitars to mandolins. Growing up in an environment of ethnic diversity and responsive to the popular and jazz music they heard on records and radio, western swing performers thrived on musical improvisation and experimentation. While some experimented with amplification, others augmented their sound with horn sections. Invariably, all western swing bands of the late thirties and forties accentuated the primacy of a rhythmic thrust that kept listeners dancing while providing their musicians with plenty of leeway to showcase their mastery of instruments. Over the course of the period, instrumental emphasis varied among different schools of western swing. In Texas, the fiddle more often than not became the focal point of most country swing bands, particularly in the early period.[1]

Brought over to America in the early colonial period, the fiddle became a mainstay at informal community gatherings, particularly in rural areas. Although frowned on by several religious denominations, the fiddle remained popular among a variety of social classes in the rural South throughout the nineteenth century. In Texas, as in the Southeast, the fiddle became an important fixture at rural house parties and at informal dances, or "frolics," throughout the nineteenth century. Texas fiddlers at these gatherings played everything from Old World tunes to current popular favorites, encompassing a variety of musical styles from waltzes to reels. In addition to playing at dances, fiddlers could also demonstrate their musical abilities at fiddling contests. The popularity of these contests in Texas carried over into the twentieth century and encouraged improvisation among fiddlers in the state. Texas fiddlers preferred a long-bowed style over the short-bowed, rhythmic style of fiddling so popular in the Southeast, because it permitted them to add melodic adornments to familiar tunes. Some long-bowed fiddlers incorporated elements of blues into their playing, imbuing their music with more feeling and less technique, while others embraced jazzy solos termed "take-offs" to demonstrate their musical dexterity. Texas fiddlers also borrowed heavily from the various ethnic groups that inhabited the state. In the process, they established the precedent of musical amalgamation that provided a crucial element in western swing's early development.[2]

Among the first nonnative settlers in Texas were whites from the Southeast, including migrants from the Appalachians who brought with them their fondness of Anglo-American folk songs and their Scotch- and Irish-derived fiddling style. In time, several central European immigrant groups, including Germans and Bohemians, settled in Texas as well, bringing their penchant for polkas, schottisches, and waltzes to the region. Cajuns from Louisiana transported a French cultural element, and Mexicans already in the area introduced Texans to Norteño music popular in northern Mexico. For almost all ethnic groups, dances were highly anticipated social events, with fiddlers generally taking center stage. By the early 1900s, Texas fiddlers demonstrated an appreciation of all of these ethnic elements, as well as an exposure to African American music. As Lawrence Levine explains, black musical idioms proved particularly attractive to performers with improvisational inclinations: "Many of the whites who found jazz and blues stimulating in the 1920s and 1930s did so because these musical forms seemed to promise them greater freedom of expression." The advent of the country music era in the early 1920s allowed for the further intermingling of musical styles. Additionally, Dixieland jazz, Hawaiian music, and popular music all made an impact on Texas musicians. Audience preferences equally influenced the Texas bands' choice of material. In 1940, *Variety* offered the following advice to bandleaders with upcoming dates in Texas: "Be prepared to play 1) Viennese waltzes 2) the schottische 3) the polka 4) the varsovienne. To be perfectly safe, [they] should have 'Get Along Sally,' 'Turkey in the Straw,' 'Little Brown Jug,' and other Ozark items in [their] repertoire." At the point where blues, jazz, and traditional Texas folk music intersect, a hybrid developed that bunched all three musical forms into one danceable package. As a product of over one hundred years of ethnic and musical conglomeration, no one musician invented western swing. Two performers in the 1930s, however, deserve credit for complementing the Texas musical matrix with a danceable rhythm, thereby forging Texas Swing, the precursory sound that would later develop into western swing.[3]

Milton Brown and Bob Wills each made distinct contributions to the Texas string-band sound in the process of creating the western swing anomaly. Brown popularized a much smoother vocal approach than the one used by other Texas string-band vocalists, which were few in number. He also introduced the piano via Fred "Papa" Calhoun and the electric steel guitar through Bob Dunn to Texas country music. Wills took Brown's important innovations one step further, adding horns and more complex arrangements to the mix while never losing sight of the music's rural roots. In Brown's Musical Brownies and Wills's Texas Playboys, the rhythm section provided a heavy beat that enabled other musicians to improvise on their solos. While their musical visions were by no means congruent, both worked in similar ways to expand the sound of the traditional Texas string band for the dance hall atmosphere.

Western swing historian Garna Christian terms Fort Worth, Texas, "the cradle of modern Texas music" because both Wills and Brown began their musical experimentations there in the late twenties and early thirties. Brown arrived in Fort Worth with his family in 1918, singing with his father occasionally at house dances and at other informal gatherings before forming a vocal trio nearly a decade later. From the outset, his vocal style was unique among his Texas peers, owing more to popular and jazz music than to country music vocalists. In 1929, he met Bob Wills and Herman Arnspiger at a house party in Fort Worth. Along with Brown's brother Derwood, they soon formed a band. Together they began appearing regularly at the Eagles Hall Lodge, and the band offered a unique blend of the popular tunes Brown sang with his vocal group and the country music and Texas ethnic conglomeration Wills grew up with. Brown used a megaphone to increase the volume of his voice at these dance events until around 1930, when he began using a public address system. By late 1931, the group, by then known as the Light Crust Doughboys, was appearing on 50,000-watt WBAP with Wilbert Lee O'Daniel, in addition to their regular local performances. Brown clashed with O'Daniel over the latter's opposition to the group's dance appearances. Moving to rival station KTAT, Brown and his new band, the Musical Brownies, consisting of his brother on rhythm guitar, Ocie Stockard on tenor banjo, and Wanna Coffman on string bass, began appearing frequently at the Crystal Springs Dancing Pavilion, about three miles west of Fort Worth. The addition of Fred "Papa" Calhoun to the band in late 1932 advanced the band farther from the traditional Texas string-band sound. Up to that point, the Musical Brownies were limited in their musical improvisation due to their preoccupation with maintaining a strong rhythm for dancing. With the addition of Calhoun's piano, the group found a way to add both volume and improvisation to their danceable rhythm, essentially establishing the foundation of the western swing sound. In the fall of 1934, Brown hired steel guitarist Bob Dunn to the fold. The first country musician to amplify the steel guitar, Dunn provided even more volume, and his trombone-modeled playing style moved the band closer to a jazz sound without forsaking the rhythmic requirement. At the time of Brown's death in 1936, the Musical Brownies were one of the most popular bands, and perhaps the most renowned, in Texas. The Brownies' instrumental makeup virtually revolutionized the Texas string band, heretofore consisting of a fiddle, guitar, and banjo, reconfiguring it for dance hall purposes. Additionally, Brown introduced into the Texas string-band repertoire dozens of popular, jazz, and blues numbers, many of which became western swing standards. Brown essentially took Texas country music to town, urbanizing it and electrifying it in ways previously unimagined. He left a legion of followers in the Southwest.[4]

Bob Wills incorporated into Brown's vision a luminous personality and energy that transformed the innovative Musical Brownies sound into what eventually became known as western swing. While Brown deserves recognition for laying the groundwork for the subgenre, Wills merits the honor of giving it its vivacious style and country character. From his bluesy fiddle playing to his cowboy hat and boots, Wills instilled enough rural ornamentations into the music to preserve its folk lineage without forsaking its urban orientation. In the process, he introduced its progressive sounds to a southern audience that would have otherwise balked at its musical embellishments. Throughout his career, Wills remained more popular west of the Mississippi River than he did in the Southeast, with his audience plainly distinguishable from the customary country crowd. Nevertheless, Wills managed to connect with a variety of regional and economic demographics and in the end bridged the gap between urban and rural, South and West, black and white, and past and present more effectively than any other country performer before or since.

Wills learned to play the fiddle at an early age and began performing in public when he was about ten years old. As a teen, he accompanied his fiddle-playing father at dances, and he worked a variety of jobs during the week. He gained exposure to a variety of musical styles, including blues, Spanish and Mexican, Texas folk, and country music. In the late twenties, he returned from a stint in a medicine show to form the Wills Fiddle Band, and around 1930 he teamed with Milton Brown. Wills remained with O'Daniel after Brown left to form his Musical Brownies, but parted ways with the flour mill owner and politician in 1933, eventually moving to Waco, where he formed his first incarnation of his Texas Playboys. In 1934, an ever-expanding version of the band began appearing on KVOO in Tulsa, Oklahoma, which they maintained as a musical base until 1942.[5]

Once in Tulsa, the distinctive elements of the Bob Wills prewar sound began to fall into place. As the group's emerging lead vocalist, Tommy Duncan possessed one of country music's most versatile voices; he was able to sing everything from Jimmie Rodgers tunes to popular standards in a thoroughly convincing manner. He also possessed a remarkable ability to memorize song lyrics, which proved indispensable given the band's wide spectrum of material; by 1938, they had 3,600 selections in their repertoire. Leon McAuliffe joined the band as steel guitarist in 1935. While enamored with Bob Dunn's revolutionary amplified sound, McAuliffe soon developed his own style, as much based on Hawaiian music as it was jazz. Other integral members of the group included fiddler Jesse Ashlock, jazz pianist Al Stricklin, and drummer Smokey Dacus, all of whom remained with Wills for most of his tenure at KVOO. Dacus's presence indicated the uniqueness of Wills's outfit. Unlike smaller bands that followed the Milton Brown model, Wills's group comprised eighteen musicians by 1940, with a full brass and reed section in addition to the augmented rhythmic component. Dacus's drums offered a sturdy rhythmic pulse that freed up even more instruments for improvisation. Another important addition to the group, guitarist Eldon Shamblin, arrived in 1937. A jazz guitarist with a knowledge of music theory, Shamblin played an important role in arranging songs for the large group, as well as developing the twin-guitar sound (lead standard and steel) with McAuliffe that became one of the band's signatures.[6]

A musician's credentials certainly played into Wills's selection of group members, but a performer's personality and musical versatility dictated his or her duration with the group. Bill Malone points out, "Wills' genius lay in his ability to attract musicians who could play jazz and other forms of music, and in his skill to extract from them every ounce of musicianship they possessed." At dances, Wills required his musicians to be ever ready to take solos when the leader pointed his bow at them. As Eldon Shamblin explains, Wills relished in the extemporaneous efforts of his crew: "The [musical] choruses was every man for himself. Nothing cut and dried, because the old man didn't like it that way." More often than not, the musician rose to the occasion and enjoyed the challenge. For many musicians, entering Bob Wills's Texas Playboys became as much of an endurance test as it was a musical challenge. Al Stricklin recalls words of advice he received from Wills prior to his entering the band in the mid-thirties: "Strick, we work hard. We travel a lot and we don't get much sleep. You can just smell them old bodies getting lathered up and emotional. And then there's the winters. They're just as bad as the summer. Your fingers are going to get cold, and when you hit them old keys they are going to hurt, but you've got to keep smiling. And keep playing." Wills also encouraged his musicians to intermingle with the audience, a process that enabled Wills to discern a crowd's musical tastes and structure the band's performance around them. In smaller towns, he often emphasized strings more, with particular emphasis on fiddling; at larger, urban venues, such as Cain's Academy in Tulsa, he would bring out his larger, big band ensemble. Wills assembled a band capable of playing everything from square dances to sophisticated popular numbers, so he appealed to multiple economic and social strata, from young adults to the elderly, from the rural, working class to urban professionals, with a sound described by Art Satherley as "semi-country, semi-city." Not surprisingly, Bob Wills and his Texas Playboys became the Southwest's most popular band in the late 1930s. As their leader explains: "We give 'em western music . . . but we give 'em rhumbas too. And when there are jitterbuggers in the joint we get 'em so happy they can't stay on the floor. We lay it on like they want it."[7]

More than anything else, Bob Wills understood that when people came to see his band, they came to dance and to revel in his showmanship. His audience appeal was nothing short of spectacular, and listeners were mesmerized by his magnetic personality. Al Stricklin recalls a typical Bob Wills entrance: "I heard the damnedest racket I had ever heard. There was applause, yelling and whistling. People just going wild. Bob Wills had finally arrived. He got up there with us [on stage] and drug his fiddle out of its case. . . . When Bob started, the applause drowned out the music." Eldon Shamblin offers another observation regarding Wills's popularity: "Back in '40, '41, he couldn't even walk down the street. He was hotter than a pistol." A master of showmanship with an infectious zest for life, Wills offered his musicians freedom from all constraint and his listeners deliverance from the prosaic details of everyday life.[8]

Bob Wills and the Texas Playboys backed up their swagger with uncanny musical abilities. While their recorded output of the 1930s and early 1940s does not quite capture the rapture of a Bob Wills dance, it does demonstrate his band's versatility and vivacity. Two selections from their initial session for Columbia Records in 1935, "Osage Stomp" and "Get with It," adequately convey the band's dynamic energy. "Maiden's Prayer" and "Spanish Two-Step" offer glimpses into Wills's rural and Texas folk roots. Wills's penchant for blues material shows up on "Sittin' on Top of the World," a number originally recorded by Mississippi Sheiks and later covered by a black string band in 1930. Wills's horn section, originally objected to by producer Art Satherley, proved quite capable of playing blues ("No Matter How She Done It"), Dixieland Jazz ("Old Fashioned Love in My Heart"), swing ("Oh! You Beautiful Doll"), and big band music ("Lyla Lou"). Leon McAuliffe's innovative electric steel guitar work dominates such numbers as "Steel Guitar Rag" and "Tulsa Stomp." The steel guitar–lead guitar duet sound spun by McAuliffe and Eldon Shamblin moves front and center on "Twin Guitar Special" and "Honey, What You Gonna Do." Shamblin's arrangement of the virtually stringless "Big Beaver" was indicative of the band's inclination toward a big band sound as the thirties progressed. Wills and Satherley frequently disagreed on the former's use of brass at the expense of strings. Satherley explains his objection to Wills's attraction to the big band sound: "A few of the brass section recordings we threw out, or had to cancel, because people were returning them saying they didn't believe this was Bob Wills with brass in his band." Wills's artistic vision stemmed less from his objection to country material than it did a desire to stretch musical boundaries, as drummer Smokey Dacus points out: "Bob Wills would never allow music to be put into a straightjacket. It did not have to conform to anything but human feeling." Part of Wills's secret to success was his sagacious perception of the diffuse relationship between country and popular music. Like Jimmie Rodgers before him, Wills casually mixed the two musical idioms in an effort to reach a wider audience. The spectacular prewar success of "New San Antonio Rose" offered a model for future western swing performers intent on penetrating the pop market. In consistently reverting to his country and southern roots both lyrically, as in "Home in San Antone" and "That's What I Like about the South," and musically, as in "Time Changes Everything" and "Take Me Back to Tulsa," however, Wills sustained his popularity among country music listeners. His adoption of cowboy attire around 1939 further solidified his rural following. In discreetly augmenting his sound with brass and reeds, he tested not only his musicians' abilities but his listeners' preconceived notions as well. In doing so, Wills simultaneously introduced popular music to the country audience and country music to urbanites. Commonplace in later decades, this achievement was rather remarkable in the late 1930s. Wills himself proved an extremely capable musical politician, sharply refuting an association with southeastern country music ("Please don't anybody confuse us with none of them hillbilly outfits") while unfailingly remaining faithful to its folkish roots.[9]

A Texas swing performer who successfully bridged the gap between traditional and progressive sounds on more of a regional basis was Bill Boyd. Boyd was born to a farming family in Fannin County, Texas, in 1910. In 1926, he, his brother Jim, and two neighbors began their radio career. They remained part-time musicians when they moved to Dallas in 1929, where Bill began working at a series of odd jobs while Jim continued his schooling. In 1930, Bill Boyd and two cohorts passed an audition for a spot on Dallas's WFAA. By 1932, Jim entered the fold and the group, now called the Cowboy Ramblers, moved to WRR, where they remained for twenty years. As a four-piece string band consisting of Bill Boyd on guitar, Jim Boyd on bass, Art Davis on fiddle, and Walter Kirkes on banjo, the group made their initial recordings in 1934.[10]

A strong western flavor dominated the group's early pressings, but with the addition of fiddler Jesse Ashlock and electric steel guitarist Wilson "Lefty" Perkins, the group began experimenting with the Texas swing sound. "River Blues," recorded in February 1936, represents a turning point for the band, with Perkins playing Dunn-like solos and Ashlock delivering a bluesy vocal. Such tunes as "Goofus" and "Way out There," also from 1936, showed the band sticking close to its western roots, but "Saturday Night Rag" and "Draggin' It Around (Draggin' the Bow)" demonstrate the band's improvisational abilities, particularly in Ashlock's and newcomer Cecil Brower's fiddling. Centered on Bill Boyd's acoustic guitar, the band's rhythm section offered plenty of room for musical experimentation, and the group gradually increased to eight members by 1938. Due to the sales success of "Under the Double Eagle" (1935) and "New Spanish Two-Step" (1938), the group continued to focus on instrumentals well into the 1940s, and nearly 30 percent of its recorded output between 1939 and 1954 were in this vein.[11]

Before the war, the band recorded several polkas, some instrumental and some with vocals. In "Flower of Texas" the group blends ethnic influences with the twin fiddle style that was increasingly gaining popularity among western swing bands. "Jitterbug Jive" offers an early glimpse of country music's experimentation with the boogie beat, while "I'll Take You Back Again" and "Sweethearts or Strangers" hint at the more mainstream approach Boyd would take after the war. For the most part, however, the prewar sides show Boyd adhering to older, regional styles. "Sunset Trail to Texas" and "My Pony on the Range" harkened back to the band's early western material, while "Down at Polka Joe's," "Xenda Waltz," and "Don't Let the Beer Barrel Go Dry" demonstrate the continual ethnic influence on Boyd's music. Boyd also carries on the early country blues tradition of producing risqué numbers ("You Better Stop That Cattin' Around") as well as shows the influence of Milton Brown ("Hold on to That Thing"). In his steadfastness to older styles, Boyd maintained a loyal, albeit isolated following.

The war altered Boyd's musical perceptions somewhat, moving him closer to mainstream postwar western swing, with all its pop inclinations. During the war, he toured extensively with USO shows on the bond-selling circuit and made several guest appearances on various radio shows throughout the country. Occasionally, he toured conjunctively with units from the *Grand Ole Opry* and *National Barn Dance*. In early 1945, he resumed appearances with the Allied

Theatres Circuit, playing dates in Texas, Pittsburgh, and Beverly Hills all within the span of a month. In June 1945, he recorded his most commercially oriented sides with a New York ensemble led by Frank Novak Jr. His version of "At Mail Call Today," complete with sweeping violins and reeds, was even closer to pop than Autry's rendition. Only a weeping steel guitar and Boyd's plaintive vocal lend any country feel to the sessions. The return of Cecil Brower and the addition of Noel Boggs on steel guitar in 1947 moved Boyd back to instrumental pieces like "New Fort Rag" and "Southern Steel Guitar." In 1949, Boyd's ever-changing lineup included legendary western swing banjoist Marvin Montgomery, who brought an old-time feel to the group, as on "Lone Star Rag." On his last sessions in 1950 and 1951, Boyd dabbled in everything from modern country ("Why Don't You Love Me") to polkas ("Stop"). To the very end of his recording career, Boyd harbored both an appreciation of western swing's roots and a willingness to experiment with newer sounds. [12]

From the start, Boyd's strong suit was always ethnic and western material, and by the mid-fifties both types of music had plummeted in popularity. Additionally, Boyd never really saw his group as a dance outfit, preferring to play show dates and radio appearances instead of the dance hall circuit. As a result, Boyd's brand of western swing never really caught on after the war, despite his radio popularity and his use of some of western swing's finest musicians. Boyd deserves considerable credit, however, for innovatively merging western imagery with southwest swing and for keeping alive the ethnic and Texas string-band tradition that sparked western swing's creation. Additionally, as western swing's leading ambassador in World War II, Boyd helped the subgenre break free of its prewar southwestern regionalism. [13]

While Bill Boyd and Bob Wills continually reaffirmed western swing's folk roots, another group of Texas musicians worked to shed the subgenre's rural and western trappings. Profoundly influenced by Milton Brown's modernistic approach, many members of this school (some former Musical Brownies) applied a more urban approach to western swing, wearing suits instead of cowboy hats and playing more jazz than country blues and traditional folk numbers. Like Wills, they stressed improvisational solos backed by a sturdy rhythm section; unlike Wills, however, they adhered more to Brown's streamlined principle, seldom having more than six members in their groups. They also relied more on amplification to create the full sound needed to reverberate off the walls in the Texas dance halls they so frequently played. The Milton Brown school of western swing never really caught on outside of Texas the way the Bob Wills–inspired groups would after the war, yet it proved influential on both country music's and western swing's postwar development, particularly in its emphasis on lead electric guitar solos.

Milton Brown's followers created a sound more urban in style and content than any other group of country performers in the decade before the end of World War II. Essentially a product of Texas urbanization, the musical style developed by such groups as Bob Dunn's Vagabonds, Leon Selph's Blue Ridge Playboys, and Cliff Bruner's Texas Wanderers matured in an environment bustling with social tumult. In the late 1930s, such towns as Beaumont, Dallas–Fort Worth, and Houston reeled in the oil boom that began around the turn of the century. Historian Daniel Cooper captures the chaos that accompanied the discovery of oil in eastern Texas: "Beaumont set the paradigm for all future oil booms. The city was a blueprint for swindles, gunfire, gambling, mud, sex on the cheap, and leased trades on the basis of rumor and speculation." The first southern state to experience rapid urbanization, Texas witnessed a 41 percent increase in its urban population in the 1920s, with Houston more than doubling in size and Dallas–Fort Worth swelling with migrants. During the oil boom, Dallas experienced a transformation from the cotton and livestock business center of the region to the oil capital of the state. By 1940, nearly one-quarter of all white Texans (as defined by the United States Census Bureau) lived in cities of 50,000 people or more, 8 percent higher than the South as a whole, 20 points higher than the percentage of whites in the metropolitan areas of Arkansas and Mississippi. Exponential urban population increases continued with the coming of World War II; the area around Beaumont witnessed a 59 percent increase in its population between 1940 and 1943. Dallas and Fort Worth, meanwhile, became manufacturing centers, and the number of workers employed in this economic sector rose 184 percent in the city of Dallas between 1940 and 1953, three times the national average. In the midst of economic and social revolution, Texas towns brimmed with refinery workers and war plant employees, some hell-bent on having a good time, others just looking for trouble. For musical background, Larry Willoughby notes, "every tavern from the rail yards of Dalhart to the refineries of Orange had either a live band or a jukebox." For those interested in dancing, ballrooms and dance halls offered an alternative to the tavern atmosphere. [14]

In the late thirties and early forties, western swing performers began appearing across the Southwest in numerous dance halls. Generally, one or two bands dominated the scene in major cities. In Dallas–Fort Worth, Roy Newman and His Boys' blend of blues and New Orleans jazz brought out the crowds, and in San Antonio, Adolph Hofner showcased his blend of Milton Brown swing and thorough knowledge of German and Czech ethnic music. Hofner transformed an interest in Hawaiian, popular, and Jimmie Rodgers music into Texas swing after hearing Milton Brown. Like so many other Brown aficionados, Hofner was attracted to the full sound the Musical Brownies delivered. In Houston, a number of other Milton Brown–influenced groups surfaced, most notably Leon Selph's Blue Ridge Playboys and Cliff Bruner's Texas Wanderers. Although never quite the dance hall town Beaumont would become after the war, Houston became a focal point for innovative Texas musicians.[15]

Ironically, the town where Ted Daffan, Cliff Bruner, Leon Selph, and Floyd Tillman all played at one time or another was initially hostile to Texas string bands. Jerry Irby, leader of the popular Bar-X-Cowboys, recalls that many dance hall owners harbored a skepticism about a country band's ability to bring in crowds. Irby eventually sidestepped the issue by opening his own hall around 1940. Leon Selph recalls the similar reaction he received from owners of large dance venues: "You couldn't book into the dance halls because they didn't want no guitars and fiddles . . . and they had good reason, too. They said that guitars and fiddles just wouldn't be loud enough to entertain the crowd of people that they had. They had four, five, six hundred people in their dance halls." Selph and other performers solved the problem in two ways: first, by renting or buying halls themselves, and second, by amplifying their instruments. Club owners eventually became more receptive to the eclectic string bands after seeing the amazing turnouts for their appearances. Selph recalls that although many urbanites opposed band appearances, others regularly attended: "[Houston] was especially hard-nosed about country music. . . . They didn't want to have nothing to do with the country music but when we gave a dance we had a hall full of people . . . [and] a lot of our crowds were not people that lived in the country." In securing the dance halls, Texas string bands found a way to make a living playing music. The halls drew more patrons in one night than most southeastern bands could play to in a week. Hank Thompson explains: "If you'd go play those schoolhouses . . . you'd have a house full of people and you still didn't come out makin' a whole lot of money. Where at dances, they'd charge like a dollar and four to five hundred people came for that and you'd get sixty to seventy percent off the door." Texas's early urbanization and the repeal of Prohibition opened the dance halls and provided musicians with a unique and possibly lucrative opportunity. In conquering the amplification obstacle and convincing hall owners of their popularity, they opened the door to playing halls with even larger capacities.[16]

No single performer deserves more credit for popularizing amplified guitar in western swing than Bob Dunn. Leon McAuliffe, Floyd Tillman, and Bobby Simons (Al Dexter's guitarist in the mid-thirties) all made important contributions to the subgenre with their popularization of amplified instruments, but none equaled Dunn in stature or influence in the Southwest of the mid- to late 1930s. In stark contrast to his southeastern steel guitar counterparts, Dunn eagerly embraced sophisticated urban sounds and styles to the point that the bands he played with bore little if any semblance to a country ensemble. Steadfast in his desire to transform the steel guitar into a jazz instrument, Dunn eventually drifted into country music obscurity in the postwar years. Between the mid-thirties and early forties, however, as Eldon Shamblin points out, "he was *the* steel guitar player."[17]

Born in Oklahoma in 1908, Bob Dunn began his musical education listening to the traditional breakdown tunes his fiddle-playing father liked to play. As he grew older, however, he became intrigued with both Hawaiian and jazz music, two styles that he eventually blended into the development of his own unique steel guitar playing style. In the late twenties and early thirties he performed with a variety of bands, specializing in everything from western to jazz music. By the time he auditioned for Milton Brown's group in 1934, he had developed a unique sound on his steel guitar, playing the instrument as if it were a horn, emphasizing short bursts as well as improvisational runs. Dunn then constructed a sound system to amplify his steel guitar for the large dance halls that the Musical Brownies began playing. Despite the availability of primitive electric guitars on the market, Dunn opted to amplify his acoustic Gibson model with a pickup attached to an amplifier. Seeking a more brilliant tone, Dunn magnetized the strings as well in an effort to further emulate jazz instruments. Kevin Coffey describes the resultant sound: "[Dunn's] tone and phrasing was very trumpetlike and when he sailed into the upper registers he sounded at moments uncannily like Louis Armstrong replicated on steel; at others, he sounded more like a trombonist." The combination of amplification and improvisational playing established by Dunn became the standard among Texas swing bands shortly after he joined the Musical Brownies. Some musicians, such as Leon McAuliffe, took the two tenets and applied them to a more Hawaiian-based steel guitar playing, while others, such as Floyd Tillman and Leo Raley, incorporated the new style into single-string leads on formerly acoustic guitars and mandolins. Amazingly, Dunn, Tillman, and Raley all gathered in Houston in March 1939 for a series of sessions that showcased the innovative sounds of the Southwest as well as Dunn's prominence and versatility.[18]

In many respects, the March 1939 session marked the apex of Dunn's prominence and the creative zenith of the Milton Brown school of western swing. Following Brown's death in 1936, Texas swing remained dominated by the Brown sound, largely due to the performances of Brownie alumni in the Houston area. Several musicians who worked with Brown at various times fronted their own bands after the leader's death, most notably Cliff Bruner, Leon Selph, and Dunn. The group that recorded as Dunn's Vagabonds at the 1939 session included, among others, Moon Mullican on piano and vocals, Leo Raley on amplified mandolin, and Dunn himself on steel guitar and occasional vocals. Excluding the fiddle and adding drums, Bob Dunn's Vagabonds produced some of the most adventurous string-band sounds of the time, displaying little if any likeness to a country music group. The musical interplay between Mullican's bluesy vocals and piano playing, Raley's amplified single-string leads, and Dunn's jazzy steel guitar bursts created a sound a decade ahead of its time. Somewhere between jazz and blues, the Vagabonds' sound epitomized southwestern musical experimentation. The intended audience was urban and avant-garde. Dunn's group offered everything from blues ("Mean Mistreater") to jazz ("It Must Be Love") to pop ("Blue Skies"). Remarkably, they succeed at all levels. The group shifted to more popular-oriented material on subsequent sessions in September 1939 and the spring of 1940. Only the relentless "Stompin' at the Honky Tonk" bares a glimpse of the group's early dynamism. After serving in the navy in World War II, Dunn returned to the Southwest, appearing with and fronting a number of western swing and pop-oriented jazz bands before drifting into semiretirement around 1950. In the late thirties in general and at the first Vagabonds' recording session in particular, Dunn demonstrated the artistic potential of amplified steel guitar. No instrumentalist ever so conspicuously intertwined the sounds of country music and jazz.[19]

Leon Selph led another group at the March 1939 sessions. Dunn, Raley, and Mullican all appeared as members of the Blue Ridge Playboys. Selph initially formed the group with a different lineup around 1936, when he began appearing regularly on Texas radio. An accomplished violinist and graduate of the Houston Conservatory, Selph drifted into country music after recognizing its economic potential. He first gained an appreciation in his youth, listening to his breakdown-playing uncle. After a stint with W. Lee O'Daniel's Light Crust Doughboys in the early thirties, Selph spent some time in Dallas–Fort Worth, playing with both Bob Wills and Milton Brown. After Wills's departure for Tulsa, Selph moved back to his hometown of Houston and formed the band that became the Blue Ridge Playboys. The incarnation began as a heavily Brown-influenced group with the notable exception of Floyd Tillman's lead-guitar playing. On the 1939 session, Tillman's unique half-spoken, half-singing vocal approach further differentiated the group from the Brown legacy, although Dunn's and fiddler

Cliff Bruner's solos bore the Brownie trademark. Tillman's plaintive singing and songwriting contributions to the 1939 sessions lent a considerable country feel to the recordings, and both Dunn and Mullican were appropriately more restrained in their playing. After the departure of Tillman and Dunn, sometime around 1940, Selph took charge of the band's musical direction. The Brownie-influenced sound remained in the steel guitar and piano parts, but Selph's fiddling demonstrated more emphasis on melody than on improvisation, lending more of a pop than jazz feel to the sessions. The addition of an accordion player and even more emphasis on single-string electric guitar leads in 1941 moved the group further from the Milton Brown sound. Just as Bob Dunn drifted increasingly to jazz, Selph inclined toward more commercial and dance material. The group disbanded at the beginning of World War II, and Selph took a job with the Houston fire department before enlisting in the navy. He continued to play occasionally after the war, but he did not perform regularly until after his retirement from the municipal service in the early 1970s. [20]

Cliff Bruner's Texas Wanderers are a third offshoot of Milton Brown's mid-thirties supergroup. Like Selph and Dunn, Bruner also envisioned a brand of Texas swing more receptive to improvisation than folk music convention. Throughout the late thirties and forties, Bruner consistently challenged members of his group to produce extemporaneous solos that showcased their abilities more than they adhered to a song's melody. Ironically, Bruner, Selph, and Dunn, all musicians known for their impromptu style of playing, recorded for Decca Records' Jack Kapp, a man notorious for his insistence on musicians following melody. He even went so far as to place a statue of a Native American with a sign around his neck reading Where's the Melody? in the Decca lobby to remind musicians of the company's policy. Commenting on Kapp's rule of thumb, *Variety* noted that "this [policy] particularly applies to some of his swing bands who like to get lost in improvisation, arranged or interpolated, instead of playing a tune as written." Kapp soon found out after signing Bruner in 1937 that there was no way of containing the talented fiddler or his band. Virtually unsurpassed in his command of the long-bow fiddling style, Bruner could turn any type of song played at any pace into a fiddling tour de force. He particularly excelled when in the presence of like-minded musicians, such as Dunn, Mullican, and Raley. As the youngest graduate of the Milton Brown school of western swing, Bruner kept its leader's spirit alive long after other stylistic modifications eclipsed the jazz-based configuration in popularity. [21]

Bruner took up fiddling around the age of four, eventually embarking on a career as a musician when his family moved to the Houston area in the early thirties. The allure of traveling and playing proved irresistible to the talented teenager: "[I] started playing the old country dances that we used to have, with the corn meal on the floor. I never did pick cotton or raise watermelon and I found out I could make more playing my fiddle than I could doing that." Performing across the state of Texas with a variety of musicians, Bruner augmented his preference for popular and jazz music with a knowledge of a variety of playing styles. By the time he joined Milton Brown in the summer of 1935 at the age of twenty, he was already one of Texas's most proficient fiddlers. Returning to Houston after Brown's death, Bruner contacted Leo Raley, a musician he encountered during his rambling days. Taking a cue from Dunn and Tillman, Raley soon found a way to amplify his mandolin for the large dance halls by acquiring an electric pickup: "I had a little Vol-U-Tone amplifier. Ted [Daffan] rigged me up a little old pick-up. . . . You couldn't buy them in them days. . . . And the damn thing worked. They heard that! I'd get up there on that bandstand. Everybody stood up and I'd jump around and slap on that 'A' string—make that mandolin go 'zip'!" Carrying on the Brown tradition of having a small band with a big sound, Bruner eventually enlisted, in addition to Raley, pounding pianist Moon Mullican, string bassist Russell Vernon "Hezzie" Bryant, rhythm guitarist and vocalist Dickie McBride, a tenor banjo player, and Dunn for his prewar version of the Texas Wanderers.[22]

The group's first sessions in 1937, without Dunn and Mullican, reflect Bruner still in the shadow of Milton Brown. Amid pop-tinged numbers and Brown covers were Bruner's improvisational flourishes to such songs as "Red Lips—Kiss My Blues Away" and "Truckin' on Down." Raley's newfangled electric mandolin becomes the focus of attention on "I Saw Your Face in the Moon" and especially "Beaumont Rag," and McBride's velvety baritone highlights several numbers as well. The addition of Dunn and Mullican sometime in 1938 shifted the group's focus, with Dunn's improvisational bursts, in particular, adding a jazz feel to the band's musical approach. "Ease My Worried Mind" is somewhat reminiscent of the southeastern country blues sound, but when played at the volume of the Texas Wanderers it becomes peculiarly Texas swing. Never in need of any amplification whatsoever, Mullican's piano playing steers the group in a blues direction, while Bruner and Dunn pull it back to a jazz and blues center. Bruner's fiddling adds a country element missing from the Vagabonds' sessions, although contemporary listeners east of the Mississippi would challenge the notion that anything the Texas Wanderers ever recorded during this period falls into the country category. The group's version of "Star Dust" (September 1939) aptly demonstrates how much closer its sound was to pop and jazz than country. Only

Mullican's barrelhouse playing and down-home vocal reel in the band's urban eclectisism.[23]

Whether through Kapp's encouragement or Bruner's desire to reach a wider audience, the group's recordings from 1944 show a definite shift to a less jazzy, more streamlined sound. The addition of saxophone and drums coupled with the absence of Dunn and Raley move the band closer to contemporary swing bands, as in, for example, "You Always Hurt the One You Love." Mullican's solos also reflect a more toned-down approach. In his postwar recordings, Bruner continued to flirt with pop while allowing himself more room for displaying his multifaceted fiddling capabilities. Bruner's style, in fact, meshes nearly as well with the pop material as it does with his prewar jazz and blues work, an indication of the breadth of his versatility as a fiddler.

Unlike most of the postwar western swing combos, Bruner opted to maintain a small, string-based group without multiple fiddle or brass sections. He also remained in Texas, for both personal and professional reasons, after most groups fled to California. Having moved to Beaumont shortly after forming the Texas Wanderers in 1937, Bruner profited from the city's wartime and postwar expansion. Primarily a working-class area more receptive to dance bands than Houston was, the tri-cities of Beaumont–Port Arthur–Orange, known as the Golden Triangle, offered Bruner the opportunity to stay in one place and still make a fairly lucrative living. Remaining in Texas also afforded Bruner insulation from the musical winds of change blowing from the West Coast that fundamentally altered the branch of string-band swing coming out of Texas.

After the war, practitioners of the country swing sound based in California eclipsed the Milton Brown alumni in musical influence and dance hall drawing power. In doing so, they turned the Golden State into one of the focal points of country music's postwar development, and for a time the state rivaled if not surpassed Nashville in prominence. California country, with all its innovative sounds and magnetic showmanship, offered musicians and listeners an urban alternative to what they continued to perceive as the rustic sounds coming out of the Southeast. In bringing Texas swing to the West Coast and embellishing it with sophisticated touches and glossy instrumentation, California performers moved the subgenre closer to popular music and further from the Wills-Brown country-blues-jazz hybrid. Eventually, they stripped the music of nearly all of its country hallmarks, detaching it from its Texas roots, and in doing so left it to wither in the vacillations of pop music trends. For a time, however, they ruled the West Coast and gave *Grand Ole Opry* performers a run for their money as country music's most prominent figures.[24]

California western swing owed much of its postwar rise in prominence to two irrepressible forces: westward migration and promoter Foreman Phillips. The migration of southerners from Oklahoma, Texas, and Arkansas began in earnest following the dust storms of the early 1930s, but reached phenomenal heights in the late thirties and early forties. Between April 1940 and October 1941, the population of Los Angeles increased by 150,000, with southerners accounting for a good portion of the rise. The war accelerated this trend, as many migrants sought jobs in aircraft plants. Consequently, the population of California rose from seven million in 1940 to nine million in 1945. During this period and after the war, promoters and radio station executives began to recognize the profitability of booking country performers for radio broadcasts and dances. Country songs suddenly appeared on thousands of jukeboxes in the Los Angles area. KXLA began broadcasting an ever-increasing amount of the music, eventually becoming the nation's first twenty-four-hour country station in the late 1940s. Dick Schofield, program director at KXLA, explains the impetus for this phenomenon: "At that time at least eighty-five percent of the population of Los Angeles had migrated there from the Midwest and South. So there was a great demand for this music that we were supplying." Wartime migrants could turn to radio and jukeboxes for country music, but many preferred the social interaction that the dance halls provided. Thousands of workers packed the halls in their off-hours, and on the weekend, crowds literally reached illegal proportions. In Oakland, the fire department forced a ballroom to close its box office after it sold seven thousand tickets to a Bob Wills performance in the summer of 1944. Almost overnight, country music became big business in California. In Los Angeles, one promoter rose above all others in his ability to book country shows that packed the ballrooms.[25]

Foreman Phillips's ascension as southern California's most successful promoter began on June 26, 1942, the night he opened the long vacant Venice Ballroom on Venice Pier for the *Los Angeles County Barn Dance.* At the time, Phillips had several popular programs on Los Angeles's KRKD, including *The Western Hit Parade,* a show gauging the popularity of songs based on listeners' mail. The inaugural *Los Angeles County Barn Dance* brought in a crowd of 4,200; Phillips's booking of Bob Wills the following week drew 6,200. Other popular acts included Texas Jim Lewis, Patsy Montana, and the Sons of the Pioneers. For atmosphere, Phillips reconstructed the ballroom in a western motif, with large blowups of popular western entertainers hanging on the walls and a heavy wooden fence placed in front of the bandstand. Initially, Phillips sold tickets from a stagecoach, but with crowds averaging over six thousand a night, he soon replaced the stagecoach with four ticket windows. On the success of the Venice

Ballroom, Phillips opened three others in the area, in Compton, Baldwin Park, and Culver City. In the mid-1940s, it was not unusual for Phillips's ballrooms to bring in between twenty and thirty thousand patrons on weekends. Because many ticket buyers worked shifts around the clock in the defense industries, Phillips's clubs remained open well into the predawn hours, with such popular acts as Ray Whitley and Al Dexter working from eight in the evening to midnight at one location and midnight to four in the morning at another. Recalling his days as a musician in several groups contracted with Phillips, Merle Travis notes that bands maintained the hectic schedule "cause the people who worked in the factories would get off at midnight and they'd [feel] cheated [if they] had to just go home." Phillips's ballrooms remained a staple on the Los Angeles area scene throughout the forties before his retirement in 1952. At the height of western swing's popularity, Foreman Phillips reigned as western swing's greatest dance hall promoter.[26]

Audiences at Phillips's ballrooms and at western swing dances in general came to forget their everyday worries and to socialize. Describing the nature of western swing, Leon McAuliffe points out that "our music is designed to make you forget about realistic things." Western swing bands accomplished this purpose by focusing on lighthearted lyrics and music that kept dance hall patrons dancing. Because western swing was primarily a dance-oriented phenomenon, performers rarely delved in lyrics of a serious nature. Over half of the recorded output between 1939 and 1954 of western swing's most significant performers dealt with upbeat subject matter, primarily love fulfilled and novelty selections. No other subgenre comes close in its emphasis on instrumentals, with 20 percent of the sampled output falling in this category. The fact that less than 10 percent of Texas and western swing performers' songs centered on sentimental and religious subject matter further accentuates the subgenre's escapist leanings. When addressing the subject of severed relationships, western swing performers usually offset the bluesy self-pity of lyrics with up-tempo beats and, in the case of Bob Wills particularly, vocal interjections and extended musical solos. Taking a cue from contemporary popular music, Texas and western swing offered its war-torn and work-wearied audience temporary relief from their concerns. Western swing performers usually accented the music's liberating purpose with cowboy outfits that further detracted listeners from everyday life. Douglas Green points out, however, that while western swing performers shared the same costuming as their singing cowboy counterparts, they did not serve the same purpose: "While they both offered escape, each one did so in a profoundly different way. One offered romance, the other commonality." In contrast to their southeastern country music counterparts, Texas and western swing bands generally ran roughshod over traditional rural mores, displaying less affection for folkways than modern sensibilities. Blatantly hedonistic in style and urban in character, western swing appealed to transplanted southerners and other California migrants seeking refuge from present uncertainties in communal celebration.[27]

The bands that Foreman Phillips hired to entertain his ballroom patrons not only furnished the necessary rhythms for dancing but also created some of the most adventurous country music ever produced. While working their audiences into frenzies, the California school of western swing also shook the foundation of the Texas music that spawned it. Their rumblings eventually reverberated all the way back to Nashville, and the emerging country music industry adopted many of the innovations popularized in southern California. Together with the country pop and country blues artists located in the Los Angeles area after the war, practitioners of California western swing rivaled, if not surpassed, their southeastern counterparts in popularity and in doing so dramatically altered the course country music would take in the postwar period. In blending Texas fiddling with pop and jazz instrumentation, the California school built on the Milton Brown tradition of opening the music up to urban influences. Three performers in particular, Spade Cooley, Tex Williams, and Hank Penny, successfully challenged conventional musical preconceptions and played a significant role in both western swing's and country music's modernization.

In the mid-forties, Spade Cooley virtually ruled the Los Angeles ballroom circuit as the "King of Western Swing." Though born in Oklahoma, Cooley developed a musical approach that owed less to the Southwest country swing bands than it did to contemporary pop and jazz. Unlike many of his contemporaries from Texas, Cooley insisted on tight musical arrangements, orchestrating everything from band members' solos to his own movements on stage. His musical genius lay in employing three fiddles to create a fuller, more melodic sound and in his liberal use of steel guitar solos, played by some of country music's finest instrumentalists. A string bass–drums–accordion rhythm section propels many of his tunes, most of which keep an up-tempo pace. In song selection, Cooley favored the instrumentals, which comprised nearly 40 percent of his repertoire, and lighthearted subject matter in general. Cooley's band, decked out in elaborate western costumes and weaving songs of lyrical escapism, provided audiences with what they wanted to see and hear: epicurean dance music. As the 1940s progressed, Cooley moved further away from country music and, in doing so, opened himself up to competition from pop acts, but at his height, in the mid-forties, Cooley's immense influence literally redefined the country swing band tradition.[28]

Born in Oklahoma in 1910, Spade Cooley moved with his family to Oregon at an early age. In the Northwest, he studied classical cello and violin prior to his family's move to Modesto, California, in 1930. By the mid-thirties, Cooley's dislike for farmwork took him to Los Angeles, where he gradually earned a reputation as a talented fiddler in various western country bands, playing both live and in the studio. Working with Jimmy Wakely in the late thirties, Cooley began an association with Foreman Phillips, and when Phillips and Wakely parted ways in 1942, Cooley stepped up to front a band at the Venice Ballroom. To his eight-piece band, which consisted of four guitarists, a pianist, an accordionist, a female vocalist, and himself on fiddle, Cooley soon added vocalist and bassist Tex Williams. For nearly a year and a half, Cooley's band remained the featured attraction at the Venice Ballroom until a disagreement with Phillips (allegedly over his hiring of Bob Wills) prompted Cooley to lease the Riverside Rancho ballroom, where he enjoyed continued success. In September 1943, he signed with Columbia Records, scoring a major hit with his first single, "Shame on You," the second most popular country song of 1945. In March 1946, Cooley made the cover of *Billboard;* an accompanying story reported his drawing over twelve thousand patrons a weekend at the Rancho. Later that month, he moved his act to the even larger Western Palisades, also known as the Santa Monica Ballroom, where he stayed for the remainder of the 1940s and into the 1950s.[29]

Cooley's success owed a great deal to the distinctive sound he developed with arranger and accordionist Pedro DePaul and the vocal style of Tex Williams. Cooley and DePaul supplied the sophisticated sound that appealed to urbanites while Williams's plaintive vocals attracted the country crowd. *Billboard* described the Cooley sound in this context: "With plenty of toe-teasing incentive to his pert Western rhythms, with fiddles and electric guitar strums in the lead, the music [of] Spade Cooley's large band holds enough dance appeal for the city folk as well." With a harp, an accordion, and drums, the Spade Cooley sound could not pass for country music east of the Mississippi in the early 1940s, but the three-fiddle combo, steel guitar work of Joaquin Murphy, and Williams's presence all lent a considerable earthiness to Cooley's Columbia recordings. Essentially a large-sized string band, Cooley's mid-forties group proved capable of everything from straight pop ("I Guess I've Been Dreaming Again") to contemporary country ("Forgive Me One More Time") to adventurous jazz ("Spadella") to road-house boogie ("Oklahoma Stomp"). On most occasions, the group's playing overshadows Williams's singing, as members trade solos back and forth. Williams's vocals, however, were an essential ingredient to Cooley's success, as they anchored the group from drifting into jazzy excess and established its place in the country market. His departure from the band in June 1946 left a void that Cooley never successfully filled. Disenchanted with Cooley's megalomaniac tendencies, most of the band followed the lead singer to Capitol Records after his dismissal. Switching to RCA-Victor, Cooley retained the three-fiddle sound and the services of Noel Boggs on steel guitar and Jimmy Wyble on electric lead, but he opted to augment his band with three horn players and four reed instrumentalists. The band eventually increased to twenty-three pieces, and Williams was replaced by pop-oriented vocalists Becky Warfield, Ginny Jackson, and Les Anderson. Jackson and Anderson helped turn country numbers "Honky Tonkin' " and "Hillbilly Fever" into pop swing tunes, which had the horn section essentially drowning out the barely audible fiddle and steel guitar. Even closer to straight pop, "I Miss You Already," "Don't Call Me Sweetheart Anymore," and "Someone Left the Golden Gate Open" demonstrate Cooley's desire to reach a wider market. Evidently, Cooley's recording company encouraged this musical direction; *Billboard* reported in 1949 that "RCA is grooming Spade Cooley away from the strict Western-hillbilly style in favor of the trend to corn-flavored pop material." Regardless of its pop inclinations, Cooley's band produced some extraordinary western swing during the RCA years, particularly on instrumental numbers "Bogg's Boogie," "Minuet in Swing," and "Texas Star." In the midst of the square dance craze around 1950, Cooley also released a series of old-time tunes, but his strong suit remained pop-flavored songs with punchy horns and hot guitar solos, such as "Tailor-Made Baby" and "Mountain Boys Have Fun with Mountain Girls."[30]

Meanwhile, Cooley's career in another medium began to take off. In June 1948, a television program broadcast from the Santa Monica Ballroom that was eventually titled *The Spade Cooley Show* became a huge hit in Los Angeles. For a brief period in the summer of 1951, the show was broadcast coast to coast over the CBS network. The program remained a huge success in the Los Angeles area in the early fifties, and Cooley's ballroom performances continued to draw huge crowds as well. *Billboard* estimated Cooley's gross earnings in 1953 at $220,000.[31]

Switching to Decca in early 1951, Cooley temporarily dropped the brass for a more streamlined, nine-piece group, while continuing with the same base formula. Only "Horse Hair Boogie" and a revamped version of "Swingin' the Devil's Dream," the latter of which utilized horns to great effect, resembled the vibrancy of his earlier work, however, and the record company eventually dropped him from the label in 1955. Competition from TV programs such as *The Lawrence Welk Show* and *I Love Lucy* diminished record sales, and poor health eventually forced Cooley into semiretirement in the late 1950s. In the 1960s, Cooley's life ended on a tragic note. Plagued by personal and professional problems, Cooley brutally murdered his wife, Ella Mae Morse, one of western swing's first female singers, in a fit of jealous rage in March 1961. Cooley remained imprisoned for the remainder of his life, dying of a heart attack in November 1969, three months before a scheduled parole.[32]

Cooley's career will forever be marred by a senseless act of violence, but its musical legacy remains quite distinguishable. Spade Cooley successfully brought an aura of urban sophistication to country music and helped establish the genre in the large dance halls of the West Coast. In doing so, he increased its audience and popularized several musical innovations, including multiple fiddle ensembles, the electric steel guitar, and the use of drums. More a dance band than a country band, Spade Cooley's orchestra nonetheless made an impact on the southeastern country music scene.

Equipped with most of Cooley's band, Tex Williams in the postwar era carried on many of the innovations popularized by Cooley in the early forties. Williams also adopted a brass sound, albeit more tentatively than Cooley. Williams, however, placed considerably more emphasis on vocals, and in doing he so brought western swing closer to mainstream country music than Cooley ever could. He also helped establish western swing as a vehicle for comedy; over one-third of his recorded output from 1939 to 1954 fell in the novelty category. Backed by one of country music's most creative bands, Tex Williams mixed humor and musical innovation to produce a brand of western swing as entertaining as it was energetic.

Born in Fayette County, Illinois, in 1917, Tex Williams took up the banjo at the age of five and made his radio debut in 1930. The Depression sidetracked his hopes of becoming a professional performer, when he and his brothers moved to Washington state in 1934 to work as apple pickers. Although Williams appeared in several country music acts in the 1930s as a part-time musician, his career did not really begin until he joined Cliff Goddard and his Reno Racketeers in 1940 for a tour of several states and Canada. Following the tour and a short stint with Walt Shrum's band, Williams met up with Spade Cooley in southern California.[33]

In mid-1946, Capitol Records representative Cliffie Stone offered Williams a contract on the strength of his performances with Cooley. Unable to work out an arrangement with Cooley, Williams branched out on his own, and several disgruntled members of Cooley's band joined him. In the summer of 1946, the renamed Western Caravan debuted at Los Angeles' Redondo Barn, and within a few months, it moved to the Palace Barn, near Glendale. Almost immediately, Williams began to integrate a good deal of comedy and showmanship into the act; as he explains: "Time was when Western dance fans were satisfied to go to a dance just to dance, but now they want to be entertained. On an average dance night of, say four actual playing hours, we give about two hours of dance music and two hours of entertainment. Most nights it leans heavier toward the entertainment. Every musician . . . has to be a showman. He must be able to either sing, clown, or do some solo work on his particular instrument." Williams's emphasis on showmanship and comedy provided the framework for his recorded output of the late forties and early fifties. "Smoke, Smoke, Smoke (That Cigarette)," an up-tempo tune written by Merle Travis, became Capitol Records' first million seller and spawned several musical sequels. Augmenting the Spade Cooley sound with trumpet and more background vocals, Williams created an eclectic and bouncy jazz and pop mix, perfectly suited for the group's lighthearted offerings, such as "Never Trust a Woman" and "Suspicion." The band also recorded several innovative instrumentals, ranging from the traditional ("Rakes of Mallow") to the experimental ("Artistry in Western Swing"). Fine solo work pervades nearly all of the Western Caravan's Capitol work, including several standout performances by guitarist Johnny Weis and accordionist Pedro DePaul. Guest appearances by guitarists Jimmy Bryant ("Wild Card") and Joaquin Murphy ("I Lost My Gal from Memphis") also mesh well with Williams's emphasis on showmanship. The Western Caravan proved adroit at playing nearly every type of music, from slow ballads ("Castle of My Dreams," "Leaf of Love") to polkas ("Capitol Polka," "California Polka"), but up-tempo western swing remained their forte ("Crocodile Tears," "I Got Texas in My Soul").[34]

Moving to RCA-Victor in 1951 and to Decca in 1953, Williams began introducing a fuller brass segment into the Western Caravan sound. "Money" and "Hey, Mister Cotton Picker" from the Decca years illustrate the relationship between western swing and rock and roll, with a crashing steel guitar and saxophone exchanging musical barbs; "Don't Call My Name" is virtually indistinguishable from early rock recordings. "Sinful" from the RCA years accurately captures the western swing mindset in its tale of dancers attempting to have a good time despite warnings of the sinfulness of their lively steps. Throughout the late forties and early fifties, Williams provided his listeners with danceable sounds and predominantly frivolous lyrics, all designed to entertain and keep audiences moving. Williams's success demonstrated the profitability of mixing comedy with musical prowess on the West Coast. Another California western swing performer, Hank Penny, struck a similar balance, with equally astonishing musical results.[35]

Hank Penny grew up in Alabama, where, after learning to play banjo at an early age, he began appearing on Birmingham's WAPI at the age of fifteen. In the mid-thirties, he left for New Orleans and began working at WWL. While in New Orleans, Penny heard the sounds of Milton Brown and Bob Wills coming out of the Southwest, and he immediately became infatuated with Texas swing. Recognizing the novelty of the music, Penny returned to Alabama with hopes of introducing the new sound to the Deep South while avoiding the competition in Texas and Oklahoma. The prewar version of his Radio Cowboys differed slightly from the Texas swing bands in that piano was excluded, but he willingly adopted their jazzy up-tempo pace and carefree swagger. Penny explains the musical approach of his early bands: "Me and the Radio Cowboys were trying to do something similar to Bob Wills. We were the only ones in the Southeast that were doing this. . . . We were different because most of the others were playing strictly hillbilly music, and I, for one, never liked hillbilly music, per se. . . . When we did a hillbilly song, we would make it swing." In 1939, Penny took his sound to Atlanta's WSB, where he hired steel guitarist Noel Boggs and began fine-tuning the sound.[36]

After their confrontational encounter with *Grand Ole Opry* management (see chapter 1), Penny's group moved to Cincinnati. Then near the end of the war, upon Merle Travis's urging, they moved to California, where Penny started appearing on Foreman Phillips's ballroom circuit. Ever the uncompromising renegade, Penny eventually split with Phillips and soon began a very successful career on Los Angeles television, working with the likes of Spade Cooley and Cliffie Stone before starring in his own show. While in California, he continued to record western swing material, gradually adopting more of the California sounds. Although many promoters regarded Penny a temperamental rebel, no one could ever question his musical talents and enthusiasm for music. Over the years, he produced some of the most spirited country music ever recorded with several notable musicians.[37]

Penny's first recordings with an early version of the Radio Cowboys took place in 1938. From the outset, Penny made clear his musical intentions: "We didn't mind sounding a little like Milton Brown or Bob Wills. We just didn't want a Nashville sound." Centered on his propulsive acoustic guitar work, Penny's early session moved along with a vigor that became a trademark of the Hank Penny sound. In developing his own style Penny borrowed heavily from such Texas swing stalwarts as Bill Boyd as well as Brown and Wills. The Bill Boyd string-based sound pervades on "Blue Melody" and "Yankee Doodle," while the Milton Brown influence clearly appears on such numbers as "Hesitation Blues" and "She's Just That Kind." Two of Penny's early steel guitarists, Sammy Forsmark and Eddie Duncan, based their style on Bob Dunn's hornlike bursts, while Noel Boggs, who worked with Penny in 1939 and again after the war, incorporated a faster chord-style of playing. A jazz influence emerges in Sheldon Bennett's fiddling, which at times sounds remarkably like a clarinet, as in "Back Up a Little Bit."

Penny also worked with the classically trained fiddler Boudleux Bryant in the prewar years, who gave the session an even more sophisticated sound.[38]

After the war, Penny opened up the band's sound, incorporating an accordion, trumpet, and occasional clarinet into the mix. Working with Merle Travis, Noel Boggs, and fiddler Harold Hensley, Penny recorded several sides in mid-1945 that in many ways represent the pinnacle of his musical career. Penny proudly recalls these recordings as the most commercial of his career, but they also represent an artistic zenith. "Steel Guitar Stomp" may very well be the crowning achievement of both Travis and Boggs; both guitarists rise to the challenge the other presents. Travis's and Hensley's exceptional solos on "Two Time Mama" and Boggs's work on "When You Cry, You Cry Alone" lend credence to the session's significance. For his part, Penny offers some fine vocal performances as well as his incomparable rhythmic work. Recorded in mid-1945, the session remains an important benchmark in the development of postwar western swing, a changing of the guard in western swing's preeminence from the Texas swing band sound to the California eclectic hybrid.[39]

Penny went on to record several other significant numbers for the King label, gradually incorporating more orchestral instruments. However, the steel guitar, as played by such musicians as Wesley W. "Speedy" West ("Hillbilly Bebop"), Herb Remington ("Remington Ride"), and on the RCA label, Joaquin Murphy ("Tater Pie"), remained the centerpiece of his sound. Penny reluctantly became typecast as a singer of comic and novelty numbers in the late forties, partly due to his role of comedian on the Spade Cooley television show, but he remained uncompromising in his preference for recording with some of southern California's finest musicians, and in doing so, he continued to produce vibrant western swing well into the 1950s. With a recalcitrant will and an invigorative spirit, Penny deserves recognition for his part in postwar configuration of Texas and California styles.[40]

Ironically, western swing became an endangered subgenre on the West Coast soon after the California school took its identifiable form. Two discernible trends inevitably led to the demise of California western swing: the end of the big band era and the beginning of the age of television. While not directly interconnected, these two phenomena occurred during the same period, in the late 1940s and early 1950s. Several western swing bands survived the former development by downsizing and amplifying several of their remaining stringed instruments, but television's catastrophic impact proved unavoidable to all groups who counted on ballroom attendance for a significant portion of their incomes. Many performers and promoters, including Cooley, Williams, Penny, and Phillips, embraced the new medium in an effort to ride the wave of its success, but the communal dance hall atmosphere did not translate well over the airwaves into people's living rooms, and they could not compete against the network shows that grew in popularity in the mid-1950s. In the end, simple economics determined the fate of western swing in the postwar period.

The advent of television produced immediate discernible changes in the characteristics of the western swing band and audience. Like their popular music counterparts, western swing acts measured their success in dance crowd turnout and, to a lesser extent, record sales. Simply put, the bigger the crowds, the bigger the band could be. By the end of the war, however, bands grew increasingly difficult to maintain, both logistically and economically. Many band members joined in the war effort, and those who remained secured larger salaries due to their demand. In July 1944, *Billboard* reported a substantial reduction in the number of new bands formed in 1943 and pointed toward rising costs as the culprit. After the war, the trend continued, with many bands experiencing downsizing or disbanding as a result. Simultaneously, the American public grew increasingly disenchanted with jazz-oriented big bands, and the number of hit records produced by these groups fell 50 percent in the period between 1942 and 1948. As the popularity of the dance bands decreased, the average age of their followers began to rise. Like many Americans in the postwar period, western swing fans began to settle down and start families, and many chose to stay home on weekend nights. The void that may have existed in their source of entertainment was quickly filled by the emerging television industry, which offered an inexpensive, comfortable alternative to going out to a dance.[41]

Television made a revolutionary impact on American society in general and western swing in particular. Charles Townsend explains: "Television trained [younger Americans] to sit passively before it and consequently before music. The pre-fifties generation was active and creative in entertainment; that generation danced. The post-1950 generation was generally passive in entertainment." Bob Wills's guitarist Eldon Shamblin makes a similar observation: "Back in the days when we were going strong, TV played very little part and people had to get up and do somethin', so a lot of 'em chose to go to dances. When TV came in it changed the pattern because the dance business became smaller." The astounding rise of television that Shamblin referred to occurred between 1949 and 1951, when sales of sets skyrocketed, partially due to a drop in prices. During that period, the industry went from a $25 million loss to a $41 million profit. In mid-1947, over half of television viewers were concentrated in the New York area, but by late 1948 Chicago and Los Angeles also became major markets. Fortunately for western swing bands in California, Los Angeles stations had yet to become affiliated with the ABC, CBS, and NBC networks; programming remained local. Ever the entrepreneur, Foreman Phillips appeared on Los Angeles television six days a week, six hours on weekdays and one hour on Sunday; western swing performers followed suit. Commenting on the trend, Johnny Bond, a member of one of Foreman Phillips's contracted bands, notes that "a performer who ignored the new tube, with its grainy reception, risked certain obscurity."[42]

Western swing performers found themselves between a rock and a hard place: they recognized that television was cutting in on their crowds but they were unable to change it. *Billboard* suggested in early 1949 that television increased the number of nights set owners in the Los Angeles area spent at home by 68 percent. The onset of the Korean War further diminished dance hall crowds. Facing extinction, western swing bands reacted in various ways. Some mixed contemporary pop sounds with steel guitars, seeking to expand their record sales. Those who chose this route eventually fell victim to becoming indistinguishable from their popular counterparts, not twangy enough for the country fans and too folkish for urbanites. Others downsized their bands and began exploring ways to hold on to their core audience. Leading the way, Bob Wills determined that western swing would not go down without a fight.[43]

The first stage of Bob Wills's career effectively ended shortly after the onset of World War II. His large band scattered in various directions, many joining the armed forces or taking defense jobs. Thirty-eight years old, Wills found himself conscripted in the U.S. Army in December 1942. The mismatch of the free-spirited entertainer and the stoic army soon became apparent, leading to Wills's discharge the following summer. Later in 1943 and early in 1944, Wills put together a twenty-two-piece orchestra in California. In Oakland, he outgrossed big band icons like Harry James, the Dorseys, and Benny Goodman at the city's Civic Auditorium. In all parts of the state he drew enormous crowds, often breaking attendance records. A journalist in the Fresno area captured the atmosphere of a Bob Wills appearance in Tulare:

> Bob played until almost 1:30 A.M. The crowd applauded, screamed and cheered all evening. When he finally stopped the music, at least 1,500 people [of an esti-mated 2,300] were still on hand, cheering and applauding. . . . Entire families lis-tened to Bob Wills and the lads. Little boys and girls, old men and women, young folks—they were dancing, cavorting, shouting, yelling, enjoying every minute. Mothers carried babies in their arms. I never in my life saw such happy people at a public dance.

Understating the obvious, *Billboard* noted that "Bob Wills has caught on" in a favorable review of a Playboys performance at the Aragon Ballroom in Ocean Park.[44]

Despite all the success, Wills was unable to keep his large, brass-fronted band. When the laws of supply and demand eventually caught up to him, it became economically infeasible to retain twenty or so musicians. He also realized that a large segment of his crowds preferred a more string-based approach. Sometime in late 1944 or early 1945, he downsized to nine band members. The addition of Noel Boggs and electric guitarist Jimmy Wyble helped to fill the void somewhat because both musicians were capable of producing the full sound necessary to fill the large dance halls. In January 1945, the group entered Columbia's Hollywood studios for a series of sessions that featured its new string-based sound. In the absence of a full brass and reed section, Wills's band sounded more country than it did before the war, creating sophisticated folk music, a blend of blues, jazz, and country. The group fused the genres effortlessly, particularly on such numbers as "Texas Playboy Rag" and "Roly Poly." Boggs's full-bodied solo on "Smoke on the Water" marked the beginning of a new era in steel guitar playing, one dominated in the immediate postwar years by the aggressive West Coast style. The group continued the sophisticated folk formula at two sessions in September and October of 1946. By this time, two stringed sections fronted the band, one consisting of Bob Wills, Jesse Ashlock, and Joe Holley on fiddles, and a guitar trio made up of Herb Remington on steel, Lester "Junior" Barnard on electric lead, and Tiny Moore on electric mandolin. The addition of Moore cemented the Wills postwar sound, which was increasingly centered on amplified guitar solos. Many of the Playboys of this period displayed an affinity for jazz music in their playing, but Bob Wills never let his band drift too far from the folk and blues music that he grew up with in Texas. Lyrically, Wills embraced his country roots in such songs as "Sugar Moon" and "Can't Get Enough of Texas," both replete with rural imagery. The addition of Barnard and Moore reestablished the bluesy side of the band. Barnard's work on "Brain Cloudy Blues" resembles postwar African American blues more than it does jazz, as does Moore's electric mandolin work on several other numbers.[45]

In 1946, the group relocated to Fresno and began making transcriptions for the Tiffany Music Corporation. The Tiffany transcriptions, recorded between March 1946 and December 1947, offer a glimpse of the Texas Playboys at their finest, performing in a live, spontaneous atmosphere. Anyone doubting that western swing provided the spirit for rock and roll need only listen to these recordings to be convinced otherwise. With a combustible chemistry, the band piles through its vast repertoire of folk, blues, and jazz material, and Wills provides the fuel for the fire, encouraging band members with his patented vocal interjections and determining the song list often on the spot. Fiddler Joe Holley explains, "[The Tiffany transcriptions] were unique because Bob did not rehearse the band. We simply set up and played as if it was a dance. Everything was spontaneous—in Bob's words, 'not cut and dried.' " The Playboys reach a dizzying peak on such ferocious numbers as "My Window Faces the South," "Nobody's Sweetheart Now," "I'm a Ding-Dong Daddy," and "Fat Boy Rag." They also produce some outstanding blues numbers, such as "Blackout Blues," "Milkcow Blues," and "Cotton Patch Blues," and revamp several traditional numbers, including "Sally Gooden" and "Get along Home Cindy," in modern arrangements. Wills also demonstrates his new string-based group's ability to play hot jazz on rework-ings of "Jumpin' at the Woodside" and "Take the 'A' Train." The Tiffany trans-criptions show Bob Wills and the Texas Playboys at their finest, funneling their individual talents into one dynamic whole. Unable to swing with horns, Wills chose to tremble with strings. Along with many of Wills's prewar recordings, the Tiffany transcriptions cast him as one of American music's most creative forces. [46]

In the process of recording for the Tiffany Company, the Playboys relocated their home base to Sacramento in 1947, transmitting over 50,000-watt KFBK. Growing tired of touring, Wills purchased a ballroom site, renamed it Wills Point, and established a resort, complete with a dance hall, swimming pool, and amusement park. In the meantime, Wills signed with MGM Records, and the Texas Playboys recorded their first sides for the label in the fall of 1947. Much of the spirit of the Tiffany transcriptions carried over into these sessions, albeit a bit more contrived in the semiformal studio setting. The first number recorded at the session, an instrumental entitled "Silver Lake Blues," resembled the tran-scriptions' freewheeling style. With "Dog House Blues" and "Blues for Dixie," the band produced some fine blues; "Playboy Chimes" and "Papa's Jumpin' " featured Eldon Shamblin, who rejoined the group, working with Remington and Moore to play jazz-tinged numbers. Shamblin's return as musician and arranger tightened up the group's sound, and multiple fiddle and guitar parts were fea-tured on solos. The real star of the session, however, was vocalist Tommy Duncan, who reached his peak around this time period as country music's most versatile singer ("Still Water Runs Deepest," "Blues for Dixie"). Unfortunately, just as the Playboys were reaching a creative summit they began to disintegrate. [47]

Hampered by personal problems, Wills missed several tour dates, much to the chagrin of band members, who often faced disappointed crowds. In September 1948, Duncan and Wills parted ways after sixteen years together. Coupled with the rise of television, this event rang the death knell for western swing's influence on country music. From the outset, the Texas Playboys were always more about chemistry than musical talent, with Duncan and Wills providing the country ground for the group's jazzy adventurousness. Duncan's unassuming vocal style and Wills's uninhibited personality complemented one another, producing just the right amount of restrained enthusiasm that made the band's musical energy all the more inflammable yet never immoderate. Replacement vocalists in the band possessed neither Wills and Duncan's shared appreciation for Texas folk music nor the former lead singer's effortlessly convincing manner. The addition of Johnny Gimble and his bluesy amplified fiddle style matched with Wills's tired, yet relentless spirit helped save the group from the freefall that awaited many western swing bands in the early 1950s, but the spark that ignited the band's music gradually disappeared. The Texas Playboys continued to make great music in the late forties and early fifties, particularly on numbers "End of the Line," "Texas Blues," and a reworking of "Sittin' on Top of the World," but the group's roots to traditional folk sources eroded, which was no doubt partially attributable to the onslaught of honky-tonk and, later, rock music. After Duncan's departure, Wills returned to the Southwest, first to Oklahoma City in 1949 and then to Dallas in 1950, before beginning a series of moves back and forth from the West Coast to Texas in the mid-fifties. In the Southwest, Bob Wills's notoriety remained undaunted in the late 1940s and early 1950s, but the crowds that came out to see his band gradually became smaller.[48]

On his own, Tommy Duncan encountered similar problems. Duncan formed most of his musical identity with Wills, whom he worked with since his early twenties. As a youngster growing up in west Texas, Duncan developed an affection for country music and Jimmie Rodgers records, gradually becoming interested in dance music and the pop warblings of Bing Crosby. Wills hired Duncan in August 1933 as both a singer and piano player, but Duncan's talents clearly lay in the former pursuit, and when Wills hired pianist Al Stricklin in 1935, Duncan soon became the featured lead vocalist of the band. With Wills, Duncan recorded numerous memorable vocal performances in a variety of musical settings. Adapting to Wills's chameleonic musical nature, Duncan sang hot swing ("Get with It," "Oozlin' Daddy Blues"), pop ("I Found a Dream, "Waltz You Saved for Me"), and old-time country ("Ida Red," "Lil' Liza Jane"), but he excelled at bluesy material ("I Ain't Got Nobody," "Empty Bed Blues") and Jimmie Rodgers's covers ("Mississippi Delta Blues," "Mean Mama Blues"). Duncan could yodel, croon, lilt, or bellow, depending on the musical mood, exhibiting a vocal dexterity unrivaled among his contemporary country peers. As his voice matured, it became even more evocative, developing a weathered texture that gave his performances an enhanced aura of authenticity. In a subgenre dominated by musicians, Duncan established the human voice as one of its most versatile instruments.[49]

When Duncan and Wills split in 1948, the singer soon formed his own band, made up of refugees from the Texas Playboys and Spade Cooley's orchestra. With Noel Boggs, Cameron Hill, and Jimmy Wyble as guitarists, Ocie Stockard and Joe Holley as fiddlers, and Millard Kelso on piano, Duncan appropriately named the group the Western All-Stars. Songs like "You Put Me on My Feet (When You Took Her off My Hands)" featured some great instrumental work, but from the start, the band revolved around Duncan's vocals. In "Gambling Polka Dot Blues," "In the Jailhouse Now," and "Never No More Blues," Duncan delivered some extraordinary vocal performances, but the musical chemistry never developed. Eventually, the Spade Cooley defectors returned to their old boss, and in 1950, sagging record sales led to Capitol Records' dismissal of Duncan. Signing with Intro Records in 1951, Duncan formed a new band and adopted a more mainstream approach, experimenting with background singers and a steel guitar–less lineup. "Wrong Road Blues" and "Mississippi Delta Blues" demonstrated just how great a blues singer Duncan could be, while "Relax and Take It Easy" and "Move a Little Bit Closer" illustrated Duncan's flair with up-tempo numbers. One of his finest vocal appearances came in January 1953, when he recorded four bluesy numbers with a makeshift band. Duncan switched record labels again around 1954, moving to Coral, but only "Walkin' in the Shadow of the Blues" rivaled his earlier performances. Eventually, Wills and Duncan teamed up again briefly in the early 1960s with a new version of the Texas Playboys. The reunion proved short-lived, however, and Duncan once again toured as a solo act before succumbing to a heart attack in 1967. As western swing's most accomplished singer, Tommy Duncan set the precedent of versatility for all vocalists who followed in the subgenre.

Nearly as influential on western swing was instrumentalist Leon McAuliffe, Bob Wills's steel guitarist in the 1930s and early 1940s. Along with Bob Dunn, McAuliffe introduced the steel guitar to thousands of impressionable young musicians. Born in the Houston area in 1917, McAuliffe learned to play guitar at an early age, first playing a standard flattop but soon switching to a model with a metal resonator that produced more volume. As a teenager, he played on the radio and at root beer stands and parties around the Houston area. He soon became intrigued with the Milton Brown sound and traveled to Fort Worth occasionally to see the band. McAuliffe established a rapport with Dunn, and the legendary steel guitarist eventually let the youngster sit in for him when he took breaks. In

1933, at the age of sixteen, he joined the Light Crust Doughboys after Bob Wills left the group. In 1935, Wills found himself without a steel guitarist and invited the young McAuliffe to join his band in Tulsa. Fascinated with the Bob Dunn amplified sound, McAuliffe convinced Wills to invest in an electronic setup similar to Dunn's. McAuliffe's guitar eventually became an integral part of the Bob Wills sound, particularly after the release of "Steel Guitar Rag" in late 1936. McAuliffe turned the instrumental piece, which was derived from a Hawaiian tune, into country music's first steel guitar standard. He also emerged as a capable vocalist, featured on some of the group's up-tempo pop numbers, such as "Lyla Lou" and "Oh! You Pretty Woman," but it was McAuliffe's steel guitar playing that established his fame in country music. According to Al Stricklin, McAuliffe's instrument was the most popular among dance crowds who came out to see the Playboys. As his playing style matured, McAuliffe began using volume controls to produce a swelling "doo-wah" effect later adopted by many prominent steel guitarists in the forties. Upon the coming of World War II, McAuliffe left Wills to join the navy, and upon returning, he decided to embark on a solo career. [50]

McAuliffe initially organized a modern dance band after returning to Tulsa, a large twelve-piece outfit, but the group's emphasis on popular numbers failed to impress southwesterners well aware of McAuliffe's musical background. He then downsized the band to eight, converted it to a western swing outfit, and began playing on 50,000-watt KVOO, advertising his dance hall appearances. McAuliffe soon developed a huge following in the area, and crowds responded favorably to a sound centered on his steel guitar playing, twin fiddles, and a small horn section. Picking up Eldon Shamblin for a time in 1946, the Cimarron Boys signed with Majestic Records. [51]

The group's Majestic releases reflected McAuliffe's fondness for experimentation. He recalls, "We were playing dance music. We were playing . . . with horns, we were playing with drums . . . we were changing keys. We were playing with vocal backgrounds. . . . I don't think there's a thing in modern music that we weren't playing." With an eagerness to improvise, McAuliffe added bluesy saxophone solos to "Steel Guitar Rag" and "A Plain Talking Man from the West" and flirted with boogie rhythms on "T-U-L-S-A Straight Ahead" and "The Covered Wagon Rolled Right Along." A high point of his tenure with Majestic, "Twin Guitar Boogie" offered some great instrumental work from McAuliffe and Shamblin, but the sound had not yet coalesced. In February 1949, McAuliffe, now without Shamblin, signed with Columbia, recording several numbers that mixed pop and western sounds to great effect. Not surprisingly, the band excelled on tunes centered on McAuliffe's steel guitar playing, including the popular "Panhandle

Rag" and "Blue Guitar Stomp." The band also excelled at bluesy numbers that featured the guitar work of Robert Kiser and the Cimarron Boys' horn section, such as "I've Never Lived in Tennessee" and "Somebody Else Is Beating My Time." In the early 1950s, legendary fiddler Cecil Brower joined the group, injecting a dose of jazz into such numbers as "Hear Me Now" and "Redskin Rag." Gradually, however, the Cimarron Boys drifted closer to popular music and mainstream country. The group remained quite capable of producing great music, particularly on instrumentals such as "Mr. Steel Guitar" (1954), but they were becoming increasingly less improvisational in their approach. Undoubtedly, this reflected the downslide in dance hall attendance that forced McAuliffe to pay more attention to record sales. For several years after the war, however, McAuliffe and his Cimarron Boys produced some innovative western swing, daringly releasing several jazz- and blues-tinged numbers in defiance of country music's shift toward honky-tonk and pop material.[52]

By the early 1950s, all signs pointed to the extinction of western swing: the Texas Playboys and Bob Wills–derived groups were feeling the economic pinch of dwindling dance crowds and sagging record sales, and California swing bands were embracing the sounds of popular music. Developments in Nashville signaled the rise of the city as the country music center, further isolating western swing as a regional phenomenon. From the outset, the eclecticism of western swing entertainers clashed with the conservatism of the *Grand Ole Opry,* but this mattered little to performers playing to packed dance halls thousands of miles away. Primarily dance music, western swing's success owed little to record sales or even to radio. The bread and butter of its performers remained dance hall grosses well into the 1950s. Some regionally based acts survived in pockets, as in west Texas, where the Miller Brothers Band and groups led by Hoyle Nix and Billy Briggs (among others) continued to draw crowds. Most major western swing acts died a slow death, constantly on the move playing to increasingly smaller audiences. Musically, many of the subgenre's acts began to sound alike, turning more toward popular music for inspiration. Aside from Bob Wills, only one major western swing performer sought out new ways to expand his audience within the parameters of country music instrumentation. Hank Thompson essentially turned western swing inside out in his quest to survive as a country music artist without having to rely on Nashville for support. Ironically, his remarkable success marked the pinnacle of western swing's acceptance east of the Mississippi River. By relying on his own songwriting talent and holding steadfast to a smooth, full-bodied string approach, Hank Thompson survived the honky-tonk, country pop, and rock eras by providing listeners with a unique alternative to mainstream country.[53]

Born in 1925, Hank Thompson grew up around Waco, Texas, where as a youngster, he performed at theater matinees playing the current country hits. After winning several local contests, he began appearing on Waco radio during his high school years. Stationed on the West Coast during World War II, Thompson gained exposure to the western swing sounds of Bob Wills and Spade Cooley and developed a keen interest in the music of Ernest Tubb, who also occasionally performed in the area. After his discharge, he returned to west Texas, attended college, and returned to radio. He organized a band, the Brazos Valley Boys, and began appearing at schoolhouses, gradually building a following. Through a local contact, he signed with a local independent label and made his first recordings in August 1946. A self-penned number, "Whoa Sailor," drew the attention of radio mogul Hal Horton of Dallas, and an acetate of "Humpty Dumpty Heart" landed him a major contract (facilitated by Tex Ritter) with Capitol Records.[54]

A rudimentary sound and an Ernest Tubb vocal approach characterize Thompson's pre-Capitol recordings. Gradually, his vocal style became more assured and individualistic, developing a softer tone and reversing Tubb's emphasis on low notes and tentativeness on higher ones. At his first session for Capitol in October 1947, Thompson's distinctive sound, characterized by his new vocal approach and the use of multiple fiddle and guitar parts, began to coalesce, and "Humpty Dumpty Heart" became a major hit. As Thompson explains, he knew that in order to succeed he needed to come up with a fresh approach: "Back then, you looked for a style, an identifying thing that was gonna make you sound different from somebody else." Thompson's unique style cross-pollinated western swing's use of twin fiddles and electric guitars with postwar popular music's emphasis on smooth vocals and novelty lyrics. Unlike many of his western swing and pop contemporaries, he eschewed the use of horns to give the music a distinct country feel, but he retained a danceable rhythm. Thompson astutely realized that it was western swing's wall of sound that turned off so many traditional country music listeners, and by toning down its jazziness he drew an audience both east and west of the Mississippi River. Stripping western swing of its musical omnipresence, Thompson drew more attention to lyrical detail, an unprecedented development in the subgenre's history. His vocal style offered the perfect balance between western swing's cool detachment and country music's intimacy, and his self-penned lyrics were frivolous enough for dance crowds and earthy enough for the folk audience. Most of his pre-1955 repertoire (nearly 50 percent) centers on failed relationships, but he effectively disguises the forlornness in songs such as "Waiting in the Lobby of Your Heart" and "Hangover Heart" with clever wordplay. On "The Wild Side of Life" he strikes a balance between interregional musical styles, melding a smooth vocal approach and carefully arranged sound with a traditional country tune. Possessing one of country music's most underrated voices, Thompson could convey remarkable emotiveness ("Breakin' the Rules") or careless abandon ("New Rovin' Gambler") with equal effectiveness.[55]

Musically, the Brazos Valley Boys sound revolved around twin fiddles, steel guitar, drums, and after 1952, Merle Travis's lead guitar. Thompson worked with several steel guitar players, most notably Ralph "Lefty" Nason and Wayma K. "Pee Wee" Whitewing. Nason's unique tuning and playing style set the standard for subsequent Thompson steel guitarists, and Whitewing's use of a foot pedal to adjust both volume and tone further contributed to the development of the Hank Thompson trademark sound. In mid-1953, Travis joined the group as lead guitarist and consultant, offering valuable advice on arrangements as well as supplying several memorable solos. The band's astonishing rendition of "Wildwood Flower" with Travis symbolized the group's eclecticism as much as it did their musical capabilities.[56]

Thompson's use of drums contrasted with mainstream country music sounds coming out of Nashville. Earlier in the decade, Bob Wills created quite a stir when he came to the *Grand Ole Opry* in late December 1944 insisting that the show's management allow his drummer to play on stage in front of the curtain. Thompson made a number of guest appearances on the *Opry* in the latter half of 1948, before he began using drums, rejecting a regular spot on the show mainly for financial reasons: the *Opry* paid a minimal salary and required artists to appear every Saturday night. Thompson quickly realized that remaining in Nashville would restrict him both artistically and financially: "I just didn't feel at home on the Nashville music scene . . . I didn't feel that I could have developed my music there." Thompson returned to the Southwest, drawing crowds around Texas and Oklahoma, and occasionally made trips to the West Coast. Upon the success of "Wake Up Irene," Thompson came back to the *Opry*, and the show's management allowed him to bring his drummer along (a rare acquiescence on the *Opry*'s part). Thompson remained based in the Southwest throughout the rest of his career, enjoying the creative freedom of remaining outside the *Opry* orbit. His influence on mainstream country music was considerable, however, because he legitimized many of the musical innovations of the Texas string bands and western swing pioneers.[57]

Hank Thompson produced a brand of western swing as appealing to listen to as it was to dance to. He recognized that in order to survive in the country market of the early 1950s with a western swing band he needed to stimulate listeners with appealing lyrics as well as good musicianship. During the war years, country music embraced newer sounds in an effort to attract a wider audience and in the process became infatuated with pop and western swing instrumentation. In the late forties, the pendulum swung back to the primacy of lyrics and decreased emphasis on effervescent musical frills. Country music in the Southeast espoused the amplified standard and steel guitar sounds of the Southwest but retained its prewar preference for sentimental and realistic lyrical subject matter. The balance of power between the West Coast and the Southeast teetered in the postwar period, but western swing increasingly played a diminished role in the battle as country blues artists located on the West Coast stepped forward. The urban middle-class audience that the wartime Texas triumvirate and western swing drew to country music turned to these artists in the late forties and early fifties for flashy amplified sounds and lighthearted lyrics. Meanwhile, the rural southerners that made up the majority of the prewar audience began to reassert their influence on the genre's creative development. The war changed their lives considerably, with many moving to urban areas and taking nonfarm jobs. Along with the rest of America, they put their nickels in jukeboxes and chose selections that cut through the noise of the cafés and taverns they frequented. They liked the full-bodied sounds of western swing but cared little for its frivolous merriment. Most remained rural in mindset and working class in economic status, with many feeling uncomfortable in their new urban surroundings. They wanted to hear the music they grew up with played in a new way, with lyrics and music applicable to their current situation. Southerners who remained in or returned to rural areas preferred the older sounds, but as their number decreased, so too did their impact on country music trends. Nationalization indelibly changed the identity of country music and the American South. Both underwent a modernizing process in the postwar era; there was no turning back for either.

PART

TWO

THE MODERNIZATION OF COUNTRY MUSIC

4 | ALTERNATIVE STRING BANDS AND OLD-TIME REVIVALISTS
THE POSTWAR TRADITIONALISTS

After World War II, country music underwent a transformation in both musical composition and audience demographics that reflected changes in southern
society and fluctuations in performance styles. In distancing themselves from
country's rough-hewn roots, the progressives, wartime singers, and western swing
acts gave the genre a respectability it did not have before the war. The progressives
generally worked within the parameters of southern music, utilizing harmonies,
emphasizing vocals, or softening their approach in order to domesticate country
music, while continuing to choose lyrical material and instruments that reflected
the music's rural, southern upbringing. Wartime performers such as Gene Autry
and Tex Ritter displayed more of an interest in expanding their audience beyond
its Southeast and barn dance radio base. They do not coalesce enough to form
a subgenre and in some instances cannot accurately be described as country
music performers, but their importance as traditional figures in country music's
modernization is worth noting. Many dressed in cowboy attire and sang songs
about the Old West and American patriotism to attract listeners who previously
associated country music with hillbilly imagery. In adopting more popular instrumentation, they distanced themselves even further from derogatory stereotypes.
Eclectic western swing performers and early proponents of electric instrumentation offered listeners an urban alternative to the rustic rhythms of prewar country
music, and in doing so completely reconfigured the genre's musical parameters.
Together, the progressives, wartime acts, and western swing performers effectively
nationalized country music, simultaneously diffusing it across the nation while
reconciling it with America's popular music trends. Many country music performers after the war worked within the nationalization model, fusing country music
with other musical genres to promote its commercial viability. Concurrently, two
subgenres developed that reaffirmed country music's southernness in the wake of
its wartime dilution, honky-tonk and postwar traditionalism. Generally, honky-
tonk appealed to transplanted rural southerners in rapidly expanding urban areas
while postwar traditionalism gained popularity among rural folk hesitant to accept
the progressive sounds that accompanied country music's nationalization. The

postwar traditionalists survived without the benefit of radio airplay or aggressive record company marketing in rural pockets throughout the Southeast. Their success in light of postwar industry trends demonstrated that the old-time/prewar sound and lyrical emphasis retained a substantial following long after their descent from commercial dominance.

The postwar traditionalists offered a diversity of sounds and lyrical subject matter for listeners. They can essentially be broken down into three groups: the old-time revivalists, postwar duets, and alternative string bands. Little if anything distinguished the revivalists from their old-time and prewar progressive counterparts. Grandpa Jones made a career out of playing banjo in an old-time style; some acts, such as the Bailes Brothers and Molly O'Day, spoke to the postwar apprehensions of thousands of southerners with their religious lyrics, usually sung in rough singing styles. The postwar duet acts carried on the harmonic traditions of the Blue Sky Boys and other brother acts of the 1930s, some incorporating modern instrumentation. A third group, the alternative string bands, embraced the jazzy improvisational leanings of western swing sans the electric instrumentation and hedonistic impulse. They forged a sound that became known as bluegrass, a term that did not come into widespread usage until well into the 1950s. Before it had a name, however, listeners simply regarded it as old-time music played in a new way.[1]

Alternative string-band music stemmed from the prewar sounds of Bill Monroe, the Carlisle Brothers, and other groups of the thirties that emphasized musical showmanship. Groups in this new mold resembled old-time string bands in their utilization of acoustic instruments and rural-derived lyrical repertoire, but differed greatly in their performing style. Bluegrass bands tended to play their songs at a faster pace, and their instrumental solos owed more to jazz impulses than they did to melodic constraints. From the prewar progressives, they borrowed an emphasis on vocal harmonies, but their singing style tended to be high-pitched and bluesier, with more emphasis on multiple vocal parts. The guitar and fiddle played a diminished role, and innovative mandolin and banjo playing began taking more lead parts. Ultimately, their music evinced more seriousness than prewar country acts; performers were more interested in demonstrating their musical dexterity than in entertaining audiences through humor. Alternative string-band music was innovative in its modification of prewar musical tenets and alternative in its rejection of contemporary country's use of electric instrumentation and pop stylings. Bluegrass provided a refuge for musicians and listeners seeking dynamic country music with an old-time sound. Described by Alan Lomax as "folk music in overdrive with a silvery, rippling, pinging sound," bluegrass rejuvenated prewar country music and in the process kept the old-time traditions alive long after they disappeared from country's commercial mainstream. In modernizing the Southeast string-band sound, bluegrass groups maintained its impact on contemporary and future musicians and ensured its survival in the winds of change.[2]

No single performer deserves more credit for the development of the alternative string-band sound than Bill Monroe. Defying contemporary trends within country music, Monroe set out to create a variation of the acoustically based string-band sound in the postwar years. The new sound combined the velocity of his early rendition of "Mulcskinner Blues" with a syncopated rhythmic background and instrumental embellishments. Additionally, a strong blues element permeated through high-pitched singing and expressive fiddling. Lyrically, Monroe's songs presented an idyllic view of the rural past and included elements of religion, mournfulness, and tragedy. Monroe maintains that he intended the music for folks in the hinterland, and that was why he incorporated strong rural components: "I thought bluegrass would never get no further than the farmer; I designed it the way I thought he would like it, because that was where I was raised." Monroe's vision of the alternative string-band sound centered on several key components: "Bluegrass—it's a high pitched music when you come to singing. And it's got a touch of blues in it. It's got a little touch of jazz in it. And it's got bagpipes in it. And it's got hymn singing in it. And it's got a wonderful drive, a good beat." In his prewar recordings, Monroe constructed the framework for the music, particularly with his propulsive mandolin playing and wailing vocals. Aside from these important distinctions, however, Monroe's band resembled many other acts of the period. But after the war, the alternative string-band sound began to coalesce, first when Monroe hired vocalist and guitarist Lester Flatt in the spring of 1945 and later when he added banjoist Earl Scruggs the following autumn.[3]

Lester Flatt began playing guitar for tips on the streets of Liberty, Tennessee, as a youngster. As a teenager, he worked in the textile mills, first in Tennessee and later in Virginia. He continued to harbor thoughts of becoming a full-time musician, and in 1939, at the age of twenty-five, he joined a group on Roanoke radio. He worked briefly with Clyde Moody in North Carolina before returning to Tennessee in 1942 in search of more stable employment. He drifted in and out of the music business during the war, touring for a time with Charlie Monroe's Kentucky Pardners, before joining Bill Monroe in 1945. An appreciator of old-time music, Flatt played rhythm guitar in a two-pick style, brushing chords by alternating bass notes and downstrokes. He also brought to the Blue Grass Boys a soft, mournful voice perfectly suited for the group's repertoire.[4]

Earl Scruggs's admission to the band in September 1945 marked a turning point in country music history. At the time, as Bill Monroe points out, "[the banjo] was on its way out," largely due to the ascendance of southwestern and popular music sounds in the war years and the progressives' downplay of the instrument in favor of guitar and mandolin parts. The novel three-finger banjo-playing style that Scruggs introduced to the *Grand Ole Opry* audience when he began appearing on the show with Monroe captivated listeners and reawakened interest in the instrument. Scruggs grew up in western North Carolina, a region where the distinctive style flourished in the 1930s. Unlike the frailing technique used by most banjoists in the Southeast, the three-finger method of playing placed less emphasis on rhythm than on single-note picking, allowing nimble-fingered musicians to strike a remarkable number of notes when playing at a fast pace. As a youngster, Scruggs tried to play the clawhammer frailing style but found it too uncomfortable. Upon hearing the three-finger method, he adopted it: "There were several people around North Carolina, Smiths Hammet, [a] blind man [named] Mac Woolbright, DeWitt ["Snuffy"] Jenkins. Those people inspired me and I wanted to pick like them. Before then, I was picking with just a finger and a thumb." Before the war, while still a teenager, Scruggs worked with local groups like the Carolina Wildcats and the Morris Brothers. After a stint in a textile mill during the war, Scruggs embarked on a full-time career in music, joining a band led by Lost John Miller. The group's trips to Nashville eventually led to an audition with Bill Monroe, with Scruggs accepting the position in September 1945 after Miller decided to stop touring.[5]

The final crucial piece of the Blue Grass Boys' developing sound fell into place soon thereafter, when fiddler Chubby Wise rejoined the group. Wise initially played in an old-time style, but while working with Monroe he developed a hard-driving, bluesy method of playing in accommodation with the leader's vision: "[When I first joined him,] I was a country fiddle player. Bill Monroe taught me the long blue notes. Many a day, in motels and hotels—him with that mandolin and I'd have my fiddle—he taught me to play bluegrass music." As all elements came together, Monroe began to prepare his group for upcoming appearances on the *Grand Ole Opry*. Scruggs's breakneck solos elicited an enthusiastic response from *Opry* management and the listening audience. Judge Hay began calling him "the boy from North Carolina who makes the banjo talk," and the *Opry* crowd cheered him on with each solo. The band as a whole rolled along like a perfectly tuned v-8 driven by Monroe's forceful mandolin playing. The stirring effect of their performances mesmerized audiences accustomed to subtler *Grand Ole Opry* acts.[6]

On record, the band proved no less invigorating. At their first session together in September 1946, they introduced their sound on "Heavy Traffic Ahead," a mid-tempo piece about life on the road. Wise's bluesy fiddle playing shines particularly and Scruggs offers two relatively conservative solos. "Toy Heart," an up-tempo number, gives the young banjoist more of an opportunity to flash his skills as well as showcases the remarkable vocal interplay between Flatt and Monroe; meanwhile the group's rendition of "Blue Yodel #4" demonstrates Monroe's affinity for both the blues and Jimmie Rodgers songs. The following autumn the group reassembled for two final sessions that interwove such ferociously paced numbers as "I'm Going Back to Old Kentucky" and "It's Mighty Dark to Travel" with sentimental and religious tunes. On such gospel-tinged songs as "Shine Hallelujah Shine" and "I'm Travelin' On," Monroe uses a close-harmony group singing style (which first appeared on his 1940 rendition of "Cryin' Holy unto My Lord") that subsequently became standard for bluegrass bands tackling religious material. Rural imagery pervades nearly every song, and Monroe's penchant for sentimentally depicted southern folklife appears predominantly on "Little Cabin on the Hill," a number that demonstrates why many view Lester Flatt as bluegrass's greatest singer. Complementing Flatt's singing, Monroe's equally impressive mandolin solos reflect his ability to balance soulfulness and skill effortlessly. "Bluegrass Breakdown" marks a musical highpoint for the group. Like most Blue Grass Boys songs, it centers on Monroe's mandolin playing, but it also features outstanding instrumental work from Scruggs and Wise. With its breakneck pace, innovative instrumental solos, and shadowy resemblance to old-time music, it is the definitive example of the alternative string-band sound, as envisioned by Bill Monroe. The departure of Flatt and Scruggs in 1948 presented Monroe with the challenge to duplicate once again the sound he worked so long and so hard to perfect.[7]

The retention of Chubby Wise offered some continuity to Monroe's immediate post–Flatt and Scruggs Columbia recordings, done in October 1949. Noticeably, however, Monroe's music became increasingly less democratic: less emphasis was placed on banjo solos, despite the replacement of Scruggs with the thoroughly capable Rudy Lyle. Bluegrass bands began popping up across the South, and Monroe's competitive juices started flowing; he went so far as to leave Columbia in 1949 after the label signed the Stanley Brothers. Moving to Decca in 1950, Monroe rose to the musical challenge, recording several fine numbers with Lyle, guitarist and vocalist Jimmy Martin, and fiddler Vassar Clements. Reaffirming his role as progenitor of the alternative string-band sound, Monroe began the fifties with "Blue Grass Ramble," an instrumental that exhibited his preference for the mandolin as the centerpiece of bluegrass. Lyrically, Monroe delved even deeper into rural imagery for all types of songs, from celebrations of love ("My Little Georgia Rose") to nostalgic recollections of the past ("I'm on My Way to the Old Home"). In "Uncle Pen," Monroe tips his hat to one of his prime musical influences while demonstrating his underrated storytelling abilities. He also recorded several Jimmie Rodgers covers that accent his aforementioned fondness for blues-flavored material. Recognizing the need to move forward, Monroe experimented with such novel approaches as three-part singing on secular numbers (used to nice effect on "On and On") and multiple fiddle ensembles (showcased on "White Horses"). Remarkably, Monroe never lost his footing, surviving the country rock and Nashville Sound periods through as much stubbornness as perseverance. Bill Monroe and bluegrass became inextricably associated with one another as time wore on, largely due to Monroe's fortitude in preserving his musical vision. In the realms of country music history, he remains one the genre's most recognized figures.[8]

When Lester Flatt and Earl Scruggs left Bill Monroe in 1948, bluegrass as a musical form began to branch out from the Monroe source in different directions. Flatt and Scruggs possessed their own musical vision of the alternative string-band sound, one characterized less by frenetic mandolin solos than by rolling banjo passages. Lyrically, their recording output resembled Monroe's in their nearly identical emphasis on lost love themes and serious subject matter, which made up around 30 percent of their pre-1955 selections. Musically, however, they lowered the singing pitch and slowed the tempo somewhat, creating a relaxed atmosphere that belied Flatt's sorrowful lyrics and Scruggs's taut, note-filled solos. Flatt and Scruggs created a bluegrass sound as expressive as it was impressive, drawing listeners into songs instead of distancing them with abstract musicianship. In this, they remained more musically grounded in the prewar country duets than in the string-band or jazz traditions that shaped Monroe's musical approach.

Flatt and Scruggs did not leave Monroe with the intention of forming their own group; inevitably, however, they teamed up and began appearing on Virginia radio in March 1948. From there, they began a tour of stations in the mid-South and the Carolinas. They made their first postwar recordings, accompanied by a second guitarist, fiddler, and string bassist, in the autumn of 1948 after signing with Mercury Records. During their two-year tenure with the label, they recorded several gospel selections on which Scruggs played guitar, but on secular numbers, Scruggs's banjo playing clearly becomes the group's focal point. Mandolinist Curly Seckler joined the fold in 1949, occasionally playing solos on some of the band's recordings, but his input and that of fiddler Benny Sims remained secondary to Scruggs's banjo. In the band's first recorded numbers that featured a banjo ("We'll Meet Again Sweetheart," "My Cabin in Caroline"), the mandolin is noticeably absent; instead, Scruggs is playing circles around Flatt's vocals. The easygoing feel of songs like "Down the Road" portended the direction the group would take in the coming years. "Foggy Mountain Breakdown," from 1949, symbolized Flatt and Scruggs's musical declaration of independence from Monroe, and rolled along with a breeziness and carefree abandon that contrasted with Monroe's high-compressed arrangements.[9]

With the move to Columbia Records in 1950, the band's sound reached maturity; Flatt came into his own as a singer-songwriter on such selections as "I'm Waiting to Hear You Call Me Darling" and "The Old Home Town." Flatt's subtle inflections of his voice accentuate a song's lyrical imagery, lending a sorrowful feel to slower numbers and a somber tone to religious numbers. Scruggs's playful banjo style on such instrumentals as "Dear Old Dixie" and "Flint Hill Special" offsets the group's otherwise somber repertoire. On lighthearted lyrical numbers, such as "Don't Get above Your Raising," Scruggs experiments with different banjo sounds that appropriately accent Flatt's casual singing. The addition of Benny Martin on fiddle in 1952 furthered this trend. Like Chubby Wise, Martin played in a style that owed a great deal to the blues, but he also accentuated his solos with jazz flourishes that complemented Scruggs's improvisations ("Flint Hill Special," "Your Love Is Like a Flower"). The band supplemented other touches to the sound as well: Louis Innis's percussive acoustic guitar provided a heavier beat, and Burkett H. "Buck" Graves's Dobro (after 1955) added yet another dimension. Experiments with pop-flavored material ("'Tis Sweet to Be Remembered," "Till the End of the World Rolls 'Round") signaled Flatt and Scruggs's ability to smoothly bridge the gap between artistry and commercialism. Given the band's musical accessibility, it is not surprising that they enjoyed considerable commercial success, particularly in the sixties during the folk music revival. A long association with Martha White Flour led to a series of popular radio and television shows featuring the duo. Flatt and Scruggs's openness to new sounds allowed them to breach the barrier between alternative string-band and mainstream country music. Remarkably, they succeeded without ever compromising their musical integrity.[10]

The western North Carolina region that spawned the three-finger banjo-picking style that Earl Scruggs popularized also produced Don Reno, early bluegrass's most accomplished musician. Reno possessed a fine tenor voice as well, and when he teamed with Red Smiley in the early 1950s, they produced several close-harmony vocal duets reminiscent of the Blue Sky Boys and the Delmore

Brothers. In addition to being one of the first groups to mix close harmony with the alternative string-band sound, Don Reno, Red Smiley, and the Tennessee Cut-Ups recorded some of the most innovative bluegrass of the period, featuring Reno's arsenal of playing styles as well as electric instrumentation and a rhythmic and harmonic structure borrowed from western swing. Years ahead of their time, Reno and Smiley at once demonstrated an appreciation for tradition and a musical foresight that lifted them above their contemporaries.

Don Reno grew up in the Carolinas, where he learned to play both guitar and banjo by the time he reached his teens. As it did with so many other young musicians in the area, the three-finger picking style found its way into his banjo playing, but he also credits the Delmore Brothers as an influence. Reno joined the Morris Brothers in 1940 and eventually formed his own band in 1943. Hearing Reno in Spartanburg, South Carolina, Bill Monroe invited the young musician to join the Blue Grass Boys, but the military draft precluded the arrangement. After the war, Reno returned to South Carolina, and upon learning of Earl Scruggs's departure, teamed with Monroe briefly before joining a band led by Tommy Magness that included a vocalist named Red Smiley. A native of Asheville, North Carolina, Smiley grew up entrenched in folk music, mainly through his father's association with Bascom Lamar Lunsford, founder of the Asheville Folk Festival. By the late 1930s, he was working on Knoxville radio. After their brief tenure with Magness, Reno and Smiley eventually formed their own band in 1951, signing with King Records the following year. [11]

At the behest of King executive Syd Nathan, Reno and Smiley centered their first King session on gospel material. Reno played mandolin on several of these numbers, but "I'm Using My Bible for a Roadmap," which featured his double-string banjo work, became the session's big seller. Several other selections featured his banjo playing as well: "Tennessee Cut-Up Breakdown" displayed his high-velocity picking, while "Crazy Finger Blues" and "There's Another Baby Waiting for Me down the Line" showed him experimenting with different tunings. For the most part, however, the session demonstrated the band's musical roots, with the aforementioned "There's Another Baby Waiting for Me down the Line" sounding more like a Callahan Brothers number and "A Pretty Wreath for Mother's Grave" squarely in the Blue Sky Boys tradition. The tributary feel extended into their second session for King, in early 1953 ("My Mother's Bible," "I Could Cry"), but in their utilization of electric bass and snare drums they showed their experimental inclinations and, with "Emotions," their willingness to try pop-flavored material. The real standouts of these sessions were the instrumentals: "Dixie Breakdown" and "Tennessee Breakdown" showcase Reno's ability to maneuver the banjo neck at a lightning pace. "Limestone Blues" is a sterling example of Reno's mastery of the instrument, with alternating chordal passages and single-note runs. The group's revival of the old popular tune became a bluegrass standard. Reno explains his reasons for incorporating older songs into the group's repertoire: "If it was a hit on Tin Pan Alley, then everybody in the world could hum a few bars. If it had been in the movies, like 'Limestone Blues'—the tune always kind of haunted me. . . . People would say you can't play that on the banjo. I'd say if you can play it on one instrument you can play it on another." On the band's November 1954 session, Reno demonstrated his pyrotechnical skills on "Charlotte Breakdown," and the group adopted a twin fiddle approach on several other numbers. Two slower-paced numbers, "Double Banjo Blues" and "Banjo Riff," illustrate the musical chemistry of Reno and fiddler Mack Magaha, who also provides a third part in Reno and Smiley's mellifluous harmony. "Jesus Is Waiting" and "Get behind Me Satan" reveal Reno's command of the standard acoustic guitar, and his flat-picking solo on the latter is one of the many musical highlights of his career. In 1955, after years of being part of a studio band, Reno and Smiley organized a touring version of the Tennessee Cut-Ups. Moving to Virginia, the band became a staple on the *Old Dominion Barn Dance* in the 1950s and early 1960s. Several bluegrass groups in the 1960s and beyond adopted many of their innovations, and many young banjoists took their cue from Reno's instrumental work.[12]

Although producing some outstanding lead vocal and harmony work, such groups as Reno and Smiley, Bill Monroe's Blue Grass Boys, and Flatt and Scruggs more often than not emphasized the instrumental side of the alternative string-band sound. For the most part, they derived this style from the musical tradition of the mid-South and western North Carolina. The Stanley Brothers, on the other hand, emphasized their Appalachian roots in both their musical approach and lyricism and in the process produced some of country music's most haunting harmonies and gothic lyrical imagery. Almost 25 percent of their recorded output before 1955 centered on death, most often of a violent or tragic nature. They equally excelled at songs that dissected the emotional tribulations of heartache and human suffering. Like the Delmore Brothers and Hank Williams, they used the southern rural landscape to great effect in fashioning lyrical imagery that portrayed afflictions of the spirit. As time wore on, they tempered their lyrical approach with increased emphasis on their considerable musical talents, but in the late forties and early fifties few acts could match their ability to produce atmospheric country music with a decidedly melancholy slant.

As a product of deep Appalachia, the Stanley Brothers owed much of their lyrical worldview to the mindset of the mountain folk. Historian Jack Kirby describes the subregion as "a different South . . . hidden behind a mountain fastness, serenely beyond the modern world, primitive, clannish, violent, and beautiful." A 1942 sociological study of an area near the Stanleys' birthplace described a culturally isolated community with no cars, electricity, or telephones and a value system (termed "traditionalism") designed to protect the social structure from modernizing influences. Strong family ties, a Puritan worldview of absolute rights and wrongs, and a religious vision of an omnipotent, austere God shaped the values of its inhabitants. Aesthetically pleasing with lush, rolling hills, the southern Appalachians were also rugged and forbidding. [13]

The Stanleys grew up in Dickenson County, in southwest Virginia, an area steeped in mountain folkways and reeling from the effects of the Depression. Romanticized in the nineteenth century as one of the last bastions of preindustrial society, southern Appalachia in the 1930s found itself wrapped up in the economic downturn of a coal-mining industry that came to the region in the early 1900s. Ralph Stanley witnessed firsthand the pernicious nature of mountain life, which was wracked by labor strife and mining disasters: "There's always been a lot of murder, a lot of death and heartache in these mountains. Life was very, very hard here. It was all you could do to get through it. The old songs I do are all about that, about the hardness of life and the hope for something better beyond." Like many other mountain families, the Stanleys turned to music for recreational escape and to the church for fortitude. In the local church, the Stanley Brothers learned the basics of a cappella singing as well as the tenets of their religion. At home, their father sang old-time ballads and their mother picked the five-string banjo, eventually teaching both of her sons how to play the instrument. In 1936, their musical education continued when their family purchased a battery-powered radio that brought the sounds of the Carter Family, Mainer's Mountaineers, and the *Grand Ole Opry* into their home. As time wore on, the brothers began playing at school events and pie suppers, eventually making their debut on radio in the early 1940s in Bristol. After serving in World War II, the brothers came home to face the choice of whether or not to attempt careers as professional musicians. Ralph Stanley explains the rationale behind their eventual decision: "We come to think we could make a career out of playing. We knew we didn't want farm work and we darn sure didn't want the mines." After appearing briefly in late 1946 on radio in Norton, Virginia, the brothers, along with mandolinist and singer Darrell "Pee Wee" Lambert, moved to Bristol, Tennessee's WCYB. [14]

While in Bristol, the Stanley Brothers recorded several sides for the Johnson City–based Rich-R-Tone label in 1947. Less responsive to contemporary country trends than to local styles, these early recordings reflect the traditional sounds of the mountains. Ralph Stanley recalls, "We were interested in the old-time sound right from the start." Accordingly, such songs as "Little Maggie" and "Mother No Longer Awaits Me at Home" hearken back to older styles. Pee Wee Lambert's tenor vocals and mandolin playing reflect the influence of Bill Monroe ("Rambler's Blues"), but the group's choice of darker lyrical material and mountain harmonies set them apart from contemporary bluegrass groups. In particular, "Death Is Only a Dream" and "Jealous Love" distinguish the band and portend its future. [15]

The group amassed a loyal following in Bristol, but eventually moved to Raleigh's WPTF, where they drew the attention of Columbia Records' Art Satherley. After signing with Columbia in 1949, the band recorded several breathtaking numbers during their two-year tenure with the label. Although the Monroe influence reemerged on a couple of selections, the band clearly was developing its own unique sound, one characterized by haunting three-part harmonies and bluesy fiddle work. While the Stanley Brothers worked with Flatt and Scruggs on WCYB's *Farm and Fun Time,* Ralph Stanley's banjo playing began to resemble more contemporary styles, but, as he explains, the group's musical approach remained rooted in Appalachian tradition: "It's got a different sound than any other bluegrass, it's more of a down-to-earth, more of a mountain sound." Lambert's mandolin work and Ralph Stanley's three-finger banjo playing add great effect to the recordings, but the vocals and lyrical material distinguish them more than anything else. Sorrow and death pervade nearly every number, but the pastoral imagery transforms the simple tales of destitution into poetic reflections on the anguish of unrequited love and the grievous loss of loved ones. In "White Dove" and "Angels Are Singing in Heaven Tonight," the singer somberly recounts the death of family members and envisions their passage into a brighter hereafter. In "The Fields Have Turned Brown," a young man leaves his birthplace and parents behind to ramble, only to return after their death to find the home desolate and the land barren. In "Little Glass of Wine," a variation of an old mountain tune, a jealous lover poisons a woman after suspecting her of an impropriety, then reveals to her at the end that he has taken the poison as well. In their tales of lost love, the Stanleys utilize descriptions of the mountain landscape to capture the breadth of the languishment ("The Lonesome River," "We'll Be Sweethearts in Heaven"). In "Life of Sorrow," the group's effective use of three-part harmony does as much to convey the sorrow of the lyric as the words themselves. Throughout most of these tunes, the Stanleys downplay musicianship in favor of vocal effect and lyrical imagery. In this, they distanced themselves from Monroe's looming shadow. The Columbia releases of the Stanley Brothers mark a high point in postwar traditional lyricism; they captured more poignantly the trials and tribulations of the southern rural folk than any other contemporary recordings.[16]

Surprisingly, the Stanley Brothers disbanded in 1950; Ralph left the music business and Carter teamed with Bill Monroe's outfit. Near the end of 1951, they regrouped, eventually signing with Mercury Records in 1953. In the interim, the band members embraced many aspects of the alternative string-band sound, integrating Monroe's energy with Flatt and Scruggs's focus on the banjo. On their Mercury records, the group plays and sings with more assuredness, and, after adding George Shuffler on string bass, with considerably more drive. Lyrically, they produced several memorable numbers. "I'm Longing to See the Old Folks," replete with rural images, tells of a rambler returning to the refuge of his childhood home; "The Weary Heart You Stole Away" offers a mature glimpse of marriage strained by love in doubt; and "Memories of Mother" recounts a young mother's death and the void it leaves in her children's lives. Musically, the group plays more aggressively: Shuffler's thumping bass pushes the group to new musical heights, and Ralph Stanley comes into his own as a top-notch banjoist in the three-finger picking style. The group also moves more toward musical experimentation, evidenced particularly on "Blue Moon of Kentucky," which bears more than a passing resemblance to Elvis Presley's version. As time wore on, the Stanleys aligned themselves more with the bluegrass sound, moving ever so slowly away from their base in old-time music. Today, many view them as bluegrass icons.[17]

Several other groups began to emulate and expand on the bluegrass sound in the late 1940s and early 1950s. Many old-time sounding bands became bluegrass groups. Mac Wiseman, who worked briefly with Flatt and Scruggs and Bill Monroe in the late forties, became one of the most successful bluegrass acts of the 1950s on the strength of his impressive guitar playing, unique voice, and distinct twin-fiddle sound. Jimmy Martin, who worked with Bill Monroe in the early fifties, carried on the hard-driving tradition established by Monroe, augmenting it with more humorous subject matter. A third major bluegrass act that emerged in the 1950s, the Osborne Brothers, added drums and later electric guitar to the alternative string-band sound while reversing the established pattern of the high vocal harmony, with Bobby Osborne's tenor providing the melody. These and other groups expanded on Bill Monroe's musical vision of the postwar period and worked to ensure its survival in the rock era. With the folk music revival of the 1960s, they re-established the bluegrass sound and introduced it to a more sophisticated, middle-class audience. Ironically, a substantial portion of bluegrass listeners today reside in urban areas.[18]

As a branch of the postwar traditional movement, the alternative string bands found an audience among listeners seeking old-time music played in a novel way. For the most part, this audience remained isolated in the Appalachian mountain and rural areas of the mid-South. Record companies were slow to respond to the musical preferences of this demographic group, realizing instead the profitability of gearing their product for more urban listeners. Consequently, several independent labels appeared that took advantage of this oversight. Among them, Jim Stanton's Rich-R-Tone label, operating out of Johnson City, Tennessee, emerged as the principal beneficiary in the Appalachian region. Stanton established the label in the fall of 1946, using the studios of a radio station in nearby Bristol to record the artists he signed. He recognized the trend in the country music industry toward smoother sounds and sensed the Appalachian region's preference for older styles. He began by selling records out of the trunk of his car, eventually expanding by hiring distributors and posting mail-order ads. As the only independent label in southern Appalachia during the first few years of his operation, he tapped into the region's vast reservoir of local talent. Most notably, he signed the Stanley Brothers, Wilma Lee and Stoney Cooper, and the Bailey Brothers. Stanton had no problem peddling the releases of the Stanley Brothers and other artists in surrounding communities, but sold few outside the area. Nevertheless, by filling the void created by the majors' neglect of local preferences, Stanton netted a profit. Other Appalachian-based labels emerged in the late forties and early fifties, but few reached the degree of success enjoyed by Stanton.[19]

Rich-R-Tone and other independent labels offered postwar traditional performers a commercial outlet for their music. They took chances on acts deemed old-fashioned by late forties country music standards. Many of these seemingly obsolete groups included banjo pickers; others featured female vocalists. In general, the immediate postwar period was a time when women struggled to reestablish their place in country music. In the 1930s, radio and the domestication of country music helped their cause considerably, but after the war the male-dominated recording industry and traditional southern mores concerning female performers hindered their progress and negated many of their achievements. This trend relegated women to independent labels and effectively blocked their advancement. The postwar traditional field, with its radio and rural folk base, initially offered women the best opportunity for a career in country music. As an outgrowth of the string-band tradition, bluegrass remained a man's domain, but female performers in the Southeast could still find work on radio, playing old-time ballads and other songs in the Carter Family tradition. Many sang with their husbands; male-female radio duets continued to flourish in the late forties.

In the postwar traditional subgenre, Wilma Lee and Stoney Cooper emerged as one of the most successful acts in this vein.

The two met in the early 1940s when Stoney Cooper joined the touring Leary Family Singers, an act that comprised Wilma Lee, her mother, father, and three sisters. After the war, the two, by then married, embarked on their own, eventually landing on Wheeling, West Virginia, radio in 1947. That same year they secured a recording contract with Rich-R-Tone; the next year they obtained a major label contract with Columbia. With their group, the Clinch Mountain Clan, Wilma Lee and Stoney Cooper remained a popular fixture on Wheeling radio for a decade, entertaining their audience with their old-time style and repertoire. Undoubtedly influenced by Roy Acuff, Wilma Lee describes herself as a product of Appalachian tradition: "I'm a country singer with [a] mountain twang." In her duets with Stoney and her solo singing, Wilma Lee Cooper became one of the most respected female singers of the postwar era.[20]

The most towering female figure in the postwar traditional subgenre remains Molly O'Day. While Bill Monroe and other bluegrass musicians redefined the string-band sound, O'Day reawakened interest in the emotional, heartfelt singing style made famous by Roy Acuff. Few country singers of her time could match the fervor she put into her vocal performances. Specializing in gospel songs and numbers laced with tragedy, O'Day appealed to thousands of rural southerners in the Appalachian region, who were attracted to the sincerity and warmth of her voice. Working with her husband, Lynn Davis, and a band of traditionally minded musicians, the Cumberland Mountain Folks, O'Day reproduced the Acuff sound and applied it to the postwar setting. With a heartfelt determination to retain country music's moral purpose, O'Day worked to keep alive the gospel tradition. Both her singing style and fortitude served as a model for dozens of major female performers of the 1950s and beyond.

Born LaVerne Williamson in Pike County, Kentucky, the future Molly O'Day grew up listening to female performers on the *National Barn Dance* and the *Grand Ole Opry* (of whom Lula Belle Wiseman remained her favorite). She began performing locally with her brothers as a youngster and eventually embarked on a radio career in West Virginia in 1939, predominantly singing comic and cowboy numbers. After the group dissolved in 1940, she contacted a performer named Lynn Davis about a position with the Cumberland Mountain Folks, a band based out of Kentucky. In the spring of 1941, she and Davis married and subsequently embarked on a tour of stations, including one in Montgomery, Alabama, where they met a young musician named Hank Williams who introduced them to a song called "Tramp on the Street," which they soon incorporated into their repertoire. Over the course of the war, Williamson, now known as Molly O'Day, and the group began focusing on more gospel-tinged material. After World War II, they settled in east Tennessee, where publisher Fred Rose heard them sing "Tramp on the Street" over WNOX and arranged a meeting with Columbia's Art Satherley about the possibility of recording the group. Released in the summer of 1947, "Tramp on the Street" brought O'Day and Davis increased popularity, particularly in the Appalachian region. Over the next few years, they drifted in and out of the music business, eventually leaving it entirely in the early 1950s for more religious pursuits. The records they made for Columbia in the late 1940s with the Cumberland Mountain Folks remain some of the most emotionally expressive of the postwar period.[21]

The group's first sessions, in December 1946 and December 1947, musically revolve around George "Speedy" Krise's Dobro playing and old-time fiddling. Davis provides a duet vocal on several numbers, most effectively on "Why Do You Weep Dear Willow?" and "Too Late Too Late," but O'Day is clearly the centerpiece of the proceedings. She delivers three emotionally filled interpretations of Hank Williams's compositions that show her debt to Roy Acuff's singing style. She excels at mournful and tragic songs, such as "Tramp on the Street" and "I Heard My Mother Weeping," and shows her prowess with gospel material on "Matthew Twenty-four" as well. Collectively, it is a stunning series of vocal performances. Returning to the studio in 1948 with even more determination and assuredness in her voice, she produced one of country music's finest gospel vocal performances of "Coming down from God," which was accented by her own clawhammer banjo picking, and continued her mastery of songs filled with tragedy on "Teardops Falling on the Snow," an emotion-packed number about a mother's loss of her soldier son. Jimmie Selph's Dobro-modeled electric steel guitar playing updates the sound somewhat, but the music is clearly roots-oriented. At their first session in 1950 and 1951, O'Day and the Cumberland Mountain Folks focus even more on gospel material, with "When My Time Comes to Go" and "When We See Our Redeemer's Face" providing chilling high points. No female country singer ever sang religious material with more conviction, and few could match her vocal sincerity on somber numbers. Along with Hank Williams, Molly O'Day kept alive a singing style that would otherwise have withered in the postwar zeal to expand country music's markets with smoother approaches. She provides proof of country music's emotive capabilities and domestic heritage.[22]

Not all country music produced by the postwar traditionalists was as somber in lyrical tone as that produced by Molly O'Day and the Stanley Brothers or as complex in musical arrangement as the alternative string-band sound. Country music has deep comedic roots as well, dating back to the traveling minstrel show and carried on in the genre's early period by performers like Uncle Dave Macon. In the late 1940s, Grandpa Jones emerged as the torchbearer of country comedy in the postwar traditional field. With an engaging personality and keen wit, Jones combined a mastery of old-time banjo with a self-deprecating humor to create a style that jokingly commented on the South's folk roots and the region's stumble into the modern period. In the process, he demonstrated the appeal of humorous lyrics and older banjo-playing techniques in the postwar period.

The son of a Kentucky sharecropper, Louis Marshall "Grandpa" Jones grew up listening to the WLS *Barn Dance* and the Jimmie Rodgers recordings his brothers collected. He began playing at local dances at age eleven, and in his later teens commenced a radio career that eventually teamed him with Bradley Kincaid in the mid-thirties. From his association with Kincaid, Jones learned a great deal of traditional material and gained professional experience in touring. The veteran folk singer also gave Jones the idea for the "Grandpa" persona he later adopted, a moniker indicative of both his preference for older song material and his raspy yet resonating voice. Parting ways with Kincaid in 1937, Jones embarked on a solo career that took him to several West Virginia radio stations, where he played predominantly Jimmie Rodgers– and Bradley Kincaid–type songs to the accompaniment of his own acoustic guitar playing. In Wheeling, he learned to play banjo in the old frailing style as a means of customizing his instrumentation to mountain-audience preferences. During the war years, he moved to Cincinnati, appearing on the *Boone County Jamboree* and recording his first sides with Merle Travis for record shop owner Syd Nathan's new King label before enlisting in the army. Stationed in Europe, Jones continued to play music over the Armed Forces Network as part of the Munich Mountaineers. The show drew a great deal of fan mail from soldiers wanting to hear country material, and Jones took note of the appeal of his old-time banjo playing. After the war, he returned to Cincinnati and made his debut on the *Grand Ole Opry* in March 1946. In the late 1940s, he appeared on both the *Opry* and on Richmond's *Old Dominion Barn Dance,* eventually becoming a permanent fixture on the WSM program in the late 1950s.[23]

Grandpa Jones deserves a great deal of credit for sustaining interest in old-time banjo playing at a time when the three-finger style was ascending in popularity. Interest in the banjo plummeted in the late 1930s with the proliferation of progressive duets that emphasized mandolin playing. Uncle Dave Macon and Carolina banjo pickers Wade Mainer and Snuffy Jenkins maintained the instrument's presence on the country music scene, but its future remained uncertain. After the war, the alternative string bands rescued the instrument from obscurity with their novel playing technique but in the process rendered the frailing method of playing anachronistic. Merging his natural comedic abilities with his "Grandpa" persona and enthusiastic performing style, Jones demonstrated the appeal of the older style of playing when applied to up-tempo humorous numbers, including reinterpretations of traditional material. In the process, he made a career for himself as a reversional act appealing to rural southerners attracted to his old-time sounds and folkish humor as well as neourbanites seeking an alternative to contemporary country sounds. [24]

Jones began his recording career in 1943, when he and Merle Travis (as the Sheppard Brothers) recorded the King label's inaugural pressings. The first releases under his own name also featured Travis on guitar, who added a bluesy flavor to a number of songs about failed relationships. From the start, however, Jones seemed much more at ease with more earthy subject matter, turning in two fine vocal performances on a prison lament ("It's Raining Here This Morning") and a rounder tune ("I've Been All around This World"). The two returned to the studio in March 1946 for another session, replicating the rhythm-acoustic and lead-electric guitar sound; "Eight More Miles to Louisville" marked a high point of their collaborative efforts. At that same session, Travis and Jones recorded two religious sides with the Delmore Brothers as the Brown's Ferry Four, which would become one of country music's most popular gospel groups (with Travis and Red Foley alternating as the fourth member). While Jones's solo sides sold respectably, he did not have a big seller until he recorded "Mountain Dew" in March 1947 with a group that included the multitalented team of Henry "Homer" Haynes on guitar and Kenneth "Jethro" Burns on mandolin. Both "Mountain Dew" and "Going down the Country," another song from the session, prominently featured Jones on banjo, the first time he recorded with the instrument. Jones explains his reasons for experimenting with this new approach:

> The greats who played old-time banjo, like Uncle Dave Macon, couldn't get recorded during those years—the sound wasn't "modern" enough. But I knew from my mail and from my fans at shows that they did like my old-time frailing banjo style, especially on fast numbers. . . . About that same time Earl Scruggs had been playing his new bluegrass banjo with Bill Monroe, and they were going over well on the Opry and on records, so I thought that I might try recording a little old-time banjo playing.

"Mountain Dew" became his biggest seller up to that point and convinced him and Nathan that a market existed for this type of sound. According to Jones, "After that, I started using my banjo more and more, and doing more up-tempo songs with an old-time flavor." A follow-up single in the same up-tempo, humorous vein ("Old Rattler") sold even better, cementing Jones's association with the banjo as well as the "Grandpa" persona.[25]

For the remainder of his time with King Records (until late 1951), Jones produced several up-tempo, banjo-centered numbers, including "I'm My Own Grandpa," "Uncle Eph's Got the Coon," and "My Little Nagging Wife," with the last number noticeably demonstrating the Uncle Dave Macon, old-time influence. Jones obviously excelled at humorous and novelty pieces, but he also possessed an ability to carry religious numbers ("Jonah and the Whale") as well as traditional tunes ("Jesse James") in a thoroughly convincing fashion.

Switching to RCA-Victor in 1952, Jones recorded a series of topical and novelty numbers with Chet Atkins and several other notable Nashville musicians, including fiddler Tommy Jackson and steel guitarist Jerry Byrd. According to Jones, RCA producer Steve Sholes encouraged the movement toward topical material, with mixed results. "You Ain't Seen Nothin' Yet," which offers a humorous glimpse into the future, and "TV Blues," which comments on the impact of television, stand out as effective satirical pieces. Jones is clearly more comfortable, however, with older sounding tunes such as the self-penned "The Closer to the Bone (The Sweeter Is the Meat)" and traditional numbers such as "Old Dan Tucker." Several selections from the RCA years feature the musical interplay between Jones and Atkins, most notably on "Sass-a-Frass," as well as the continued integration of old-time sounds with newer electric ones. Regardless of the musical setting, Jones emerges as the focal point of the proceedings, drawing listeners in with his magnetic personality and high-spirited playing. A stalwart of the old-time sound, Grandpa Jones refuted the contemporary belief that music needed to evolve in order to remain vibrant. Jones's sense of humor and infectious banjo-playing remain timeless in their appeal to country music listeners.[26]

While Jones kept alive elements of the musical spirit of country music's pioneers, several duet harmony groups in the late 1940s and early 1950s built on the vocal and instrumental innovations of the progressives. They retained the mandolin and Dobro but also displayed a willingness to incorporate the bluegrass banjo style and other popular postwar sounds into their repertoire. As time wore on, these younger acts drifted closer to either mainstream country or the alternative string-band sound as their prewar musical influences became viewed as passé. In their modernization of prewar vocal and musical styles, they endeavored to secure a foothold in the country music industry without having to abandon the old-time sounds and lyrical themes they heard as youths. Their success demonstrated that wartime nationalization and the ascension of western swing instrumentation did not obliterate the rural tradition in country music, but rather placed it in a state of occultation. Disguising their rural roots in modern arrangements, three harmony-based acts of the postwar period, Johnnie and Jack, Jim and Jesse, and the Louvin Brothers, reconciled the folk tradition with contemporary trends.

Of the three aforementioned duet-based groups, Johnnie Wright and Jack Anglin enjoyed the greatest degree of commercial success in the decade after World War II, scoring five top-ten singles in the period. Instrumentally backed by the Dobro work of Harold B. "Shot" Jackson and the fiddling of Paul Warren or Benny Martin, the Johnnie and Jack sound clearly owes more to prewar than postwar musical trends. Their clever application of gospel-based harmony to secular lyrical material and employment of Latin American percussive effects gave their music a modern feel, both unique and appealing. Johnnie and Jack were also among the first country music acts to cover rhythm and blues material. Although other tunesmiths furnished them with the song material that became their biggest hits, Wright and Anglin were gifted songwriters, particularly adroit at composing songs that combined clever wordplay with infectious melodies. Their unique vocal style allowed them to shift from religious to secular material with relative ease and equal effectiveness. The consolidation of these attributes enhanced their popularity among a cross-section of listeners: rural folk were attracted to their acoustic sound and old-time harmonies, and urbanites were drawn in by their novel musical arrangements.

Although Johnnie Wright and Jack Anglin met and worked with one another in the late 1930s, they did not begin their long-term collaboration until after World War II. Jack Anglin grew up in Athens, Alabama, in the same area where the Delmore Brothers lived for a time. Working with his two brothers, Anglin began his radio career in 1935 in Nashville. The Anglin Brothers produced several notable records before separating in 1940, but they never achieved the commercial success of many other harmony-based groups of the time. After he and his brothers went their separate ways, Jack Anglin moved to Nashville with his wife, where they teamed up with his brother-in-law, Johnnie Wright, and a group of musicians soon to be named the Tennessee Hillbillies. Born in Wilson County, Tennessee, just east of Nashville, Wright grew up listening to the old-time music played by his relatives and the musicians on the *Grand Ole Opry*. Wright also began his radio career in the mid-thirties in Nashville, working with Muriel Deason, also known as Kitty Wells, and her cousin under the name Johnnie Wright and the Harmony Girls. Both Wright and Deason, who married in 1937, held other jobs in addition to their part-time radio work. After the breakup of the Anglin Brothers,

Wright and Anglin began flirting with the idea of teaming up professionally, initially making several unsuccessful attempts to appear on WSM. In late 1940, the Wrights, Anglins, and the Tennessee Hillbillies relocated to Greensboro, North Carolina, and later to West Virginia in search of a sustaining program on a large station. Wartime gas rationing halted their progress, however, and they returned to Nashville, where Wright obtained a job at a defense plant and Anglin joined Roy Acuff's band before entering the army in mid-1943. Late in the war, the Wrights moved to Knoxville and later Raleigh trying to energize their musical career. After the war, Wright and Anglin reunited in Raleigh before returning to Nashville, where they formed a new group, the Tennessee Mountain Boys, and began appearing daily on WSM, eventually procuring a spot on the *Grand Ole Opry*. Around 1947, they signed with Apollo Records and began their recording career.[27]

Johnnie and Jack's first recordings with the Tennessee Mountain Boys place them squarely in the prewar duet tradition in vocal style, musical approach, and lyrical repertoire. Mandolinist Paul Buskirk and fiddler Paul Warren both lend an old-time feel to such sentimental numbers as "Lord, Watch over My Daddy" and "Paper Boy." After recording several gospel numbers as the King Sacred Quartet for King Records in 1947, the band signed with RCA-Victor, making their first recordings for the label in early 1949. They continued in the old-time vein at their first RCA session, aside from the electric steel guitar work of Shot Jackson, whom they picked up while working on the *Louisiana Hayride*. Around this time, however, the group began experimenting with novel techniques in search of a sound, as Johnnie Wright explains: "We hadn't created for ourselves our own style . . . we weren't plowing new ground. We were in truth singing like a lot of other people. It takes something different." The three-part vocal chorus on "For Old Times Sake" signaled the group's increasing willingness to blend gospel harmonies with secular lyrical material. In March 1950, they recorded several interesting contemporary religious numbers, including "Too Much Sinning" and "Jesus Hits like an Atom Bomb," as well as their first sizable hit, "Poison Love." At the suggestion of bass player Ernie Newton, the group added maracas, which were strapped to Newton's hand, in an effort to create a unique and marketable sound. The maracas gave their songs a Latin American feel, soon to become a trademark of the Tennessee Mountain Boys.[28]

In the early 1950s, Johnnie and Jack recorded several numbers that featured the group's gospel-like harmony and Latin American percussion, as well as some outstanding instrumental work from Paul Warren and Shot Jackson, who switched from electric steel to Dobro. Selections "Ashes of Love" and "Slow Poison" demonstrate the group's newfound approach, in which old-time sounds converge with novel vocal and musical arrangements. Lyrically, Jim Anglin, Jack's brother, penned some of the most cunning country music songs of the period for the group. In "Heart Trouble," "Love Trap," and several others, Anglin demonstrates his keen (and largely unrecognized) ability to blend clever wordplay with country themes, a lyrical device that became a fixture in modern country music. The group continued its music expansion in 1954, adding Buddy Harmon on drums and bass singer Culley Holt, who had been working with the famed Jordanaires vocal group. Holt lent a decidedly pop sound to Johnnie and Jack's country harmonies, undoubtedly contributing to the chart success of "Kiss Crazy Baby," "(Oh Baby Mine) I Get So Lonely," and "Goodnight, Sweetheart, Goodnight." These last two numbers were actually rhythm and blues hits that Johnnie and Jack covered as country songs, with Shot Jackson's Dobro work and Paul Warren's fiddling representing the group's continued adherence to traditional sounds. Working with Holt and various incarnations of the Tennessee Mountain Boys, Johnnie and Jack resuscitated the duet tradition through their liberal vocal and music approach: innovative yet never compromising.[29]

While Johnnie and Jack incorporated elements of pop, ethnic, mainstream country, and gospel music into their sound, other duets, such as Jim and Jesse, explored the possibilities of merging the progressive vocal approach of the Blue Sky Boys and the Delmore Brothers with the alternative string-band sound. Jim and Jesse McReynolds succeeded as a country music act through arduous practice and sheer persistence in the face of overwhelming obstacles. They grew up in southwestern Virginia, where their father worked in the coal mines in addition to tending to the family's sixty-acre farm. Jim McReynolds entered work in the mines as a young teenager but quit after a mining accident nearly took the life of his father. The brothers grew up surrounded by music, with several members of their family playing instruments. As Jim McReynolds recalls, the relatives gathered frequently, and music usually was a mainstay at the get-togethers: "[Our father] played banjo and fiddle and all of our uncles played too. Whenever they would come to visit, instead of just talking, they would take out the instruments and pick away." The brothers also grew up listening to the *Grand Ole Opry*, WNOX, and the records of the Monroe Brothers, the Carter Family, and the Delmore Brothers. Although they began playing together locally, they did not give much thought to pursuing a professional career until Jim returned from army service in 1947. Over the next two years, they made several unsuccessful attempts at establishing themselves on the personal appearance circuit. As Jim McReynolds explains, an unstable Appalachian economy rendered the odds of their success tenuous: "We were working in coal-mining country in the early days. If the miners were working, it was great. But if they got into a labor dispute with the owners and went on strike, it could be pretty difficult. Entertainment was the first thing to go. They had no money to spare." In 1949, they joined WGAC in Augusta, Georgia, where they began working with Hoke Jenkins, nephew of Snuffy Jenkins, the influential three-finger banjo picker. Jesse began developing a method of playing called cross-picking, in which he single-picked at a rapid speed to simulate the western North Carolina banjo style. Jim McReynolds explains the impetus behind his brother's diligence in mastering the difficult method of playing: "In the early days, so many of the groups would try to copy Monroe or do the same thing. But to me, you'd always be putting yourself in second place. What's sacred to being successful in the music business is you've got to create a sound that your fans will identify you with." Following their stint in Georgia, the duo embarked on another tour of stations, starting out in Kentucky and then moving on to the Plains states, where they played western-flavored music, before returning to Kentucky in 1950. In 1951, they recorded several gospel numbers with Larry Roll as the Virginia Trio for an independent label, many of which showcased Jesse's unique mandolin-playing style. The following year they signed a major label contract with Capitol Records and augmented their acoustic mandolin–string bass instrumental background with banjo and fiddle; their new sound introduced them as a product of both the alternative string-band and progressive duet traditions.[30]

Jim and Jesse recorded two sessions with Capitol Records before 1955, producing five singles. With the exception of the predominantly instrumental "Air Mail Special," these records focus mainly on the close harmony of the brothers. At this stage in their career, the group resembled less a bluegrass entourage than a brother duet team of the late 1930s. Jesse McReynolds's impressive and innovative mandolin playing, featured on "I'll Wash Your Love from My Heart," "Are You Missing Me," and "Waiting for a Message," and the three-finger banjo picking of either Hoke or Owen Jenkins distinguish the band from its prewar counterparts, but the emphasis on the complicated vocal interplay between the McReynolds brothers hearkens back to the innovations of the Blue Sky Boys. The act builds on the harmony tradition as well. In "Just Wondering Why," "Waiting for a Message," and several other numbers, the brothers interweave their voices around minor and sharp chords in a way that portends the Everly Brothers' similar vocal approach. Like the Stanley Brothers, Jim and Jesse emphasize vocals more than instrumentation, but unlike their Virginia neighbors, they aim for a higher, softer, and less dramatic singing style that produces a more aesthetic, less haunting quality. Part of this stems from their relative downplay of lyrical imagery in favor of an accentuation of vocal effect. With considerable shortsightedness, the record companies shunned Jim and Jesse in the mid-1950s, after the rock era began. Executives at labels with country divisions failed to see the appeal of the McReynolds brothers' cool vocal blend, most likely due to their identification with the bluegrass sound, which was viewed as retrogressive. Eventually, with the folk music revival of the 1960s, Jim and Jesse gained the attention they so rightly deserved for their modernization of the prewar progressive vocal and instrumental approach.[31]

The Korean War halted the career of the McReynolds brothers in the early 1950s: the army drafted Jesse in 1952. While in Korea, McReynolds teamed up with another musician transferred to the army's Twenty-fourth Division, Charlie Louvin. After forming a five-piece band, Louvin and McReynolds began touring officers' clubs and hospitals as members of Army Special Services in the Korean theater. After the war, the two went their separate ways, both returning to the brother acts they established in the late forties. Along with Jim and Jesse, the Louvin Brothers modernized the duet sound in early 1950s, and they too faced a hostile recording industry in their quest to market their sound. The opposition the Louvins faced, however, stemmed less from their affiliation with bluegrass than their designation as a gospel act. Displaying a willingness to customize their sound with mainstream country instrumentation, the Louvins went on to become one of the most successful country acts of the latter half of the 1950s. In doing so, they and the Everly Brothers popularized country music harmonies among a widespread audience in ways previously unfathomable.[32]

Charlie and Ira Louvin (né Loudermilk) grew up in northeastern Alabama, the same region that produced the Delmore Brothers. Their father played the old clawhammer style of banjo, and their mother sang old ballads and sentimental pieces around the house, but, according to Charlie Louvin, it was their mother's affiliation with church singing that made the most lasting impact on the brothers: "We were raised on religious music. Our mother was what they called a four-note sacred harp singer." As youngsters, they also became entranced with the sounds of the Blue Sky Boys, Delmore Brothers, and Bill and Charlie Monroe. Tellingly, they showed little interest in the records of Jimmie Rodgers. As they grew older and mustered up the courage to sing in public, they began performing at numerous community events. Meanwhile, Ira taught himself to play the mandolin by listening to Monroe Brothers records. In 1942, they obtained their first radio spot on a small station in Chattanooga and juggled a daily show and personal appearances with their jobs at a local cotton mill. The duo drifted in and out of the business for the next two years before beginning their professional career in earnest in 1947 with a move to Knoxville. There they adopted their stage name and met a musician named Eddie Hill, who helped them secure a job on Memphis's WMPS. During their stay in Memphis, their songwriting talent drew the attention of publisher Fred Rose, who helped land them a recording contract. While they remained a popular radio act, their recording career did not show much promise until they signed with Capitol in 1952.[33]

The Louvins' pre-Capitol sides reflected their radio repertoire, which interspersed secular songs with their popular gospel material. Instrumentally, they augmented their guitar and mandolin base with more contemporary electric guitar and fiddle, creating a half-modern, half-traditional sound. As Charlie Louvin recollects, this tentativeness pushed them even further toward religious material: "We didn't have the instrumentation to do the modern-day songs with all the rhythms, so we did the kind of songs that we thought would sound good with the instrumentation that we had to give 'em. And it just happened that they were either folk songs . . . or they were gospel songs." After they switched to Capitol, their lyrical repertoire became almost completely religious-oriented, with a sentimental piece or topical number occasionally thrown in. Some of Nashville's finest musicians, including Chet Atkins and Tommy Jackson, provided the musical backdrop for their early Capitol sides, which featured Ira Louvin's mandolin solos as well as electric guitar and fiddle interludes. Vocally, many of their recordings from this time period reflected the influence of the Blue Sky Boys, such as "No One to Sing for Me" and "Robe of White." The biblical fundamentalism pervasive in such songs as "Broad-Minded" and "The Family That Prays (Shall Not Part)" demonstrates the Louvins' lyrical debt to the Bolicks. In several cases, they apply this traditional religious approach to the contemporary social scene; "Broad-Minded" stands as a variation of "I'm S-A-V-E-D," popularized by Karl and Harty and the Blue Sky Boys, updated in a postwar setting. In "The Great Atomic Power," the Louvins offer one of the most effective country gospel songs of the postwar period, utilizing the ubiquitous threat of nuclear destruction to impress upon listeners the imperative of reconciling with God. Historian James C. Cobb explains, "[It] was the musical equivalent of the camp meeting evangelist's last-ditch effort to employ fear of 'this man's invention that it called atomic power' as the instrument of salvation." Despite the effectiveness of their religious tunes, however, the Louvins realized that their career would never progress as long as they remained a gospel-centered act. An additional hindrance to commercial success was their use of string instruments, which limited their acceptance in the gospel field. Charlie Louvin describes the brothers' musical predicament: "We were caught in the middle. Gospel musicians shied away from us because we played mandolin and guitar. Country didn't want us because we had sung so much gospel." In 1955, the brothers brazenly gambled their future by abandoning their emphasis on religious material in favor of secular material. The decision turned out to be a wise one, as they scored several top-ten hits in the late 1950s with songs that fused their high harmonies with more mainstream instrumentation. Just as Jim and Jesse brought the Delmore Brothers' and Blue Sky Boys' harmonic technique to bluegrass, the Louvins helped integrate the vocal style into modern country music. [34]

In many ways, the rise of the postwar duets symbolized the passing of the torch from a prewar generation of singers popularizing rural southern singing styles through the use of radio technology to a postwar group integrating folk traditions with contemporary music trends. Both groups appealed predominantly to rural white southerners with an affection for familiar instrumentation and relatable lyrical subject matter. The postwar duets and alternative string bands furnished rural listeners with sounds and lyrical expressions that appealed to their traditional musical interests without sounding particularly old-fashioned. In general, the bluegrass bands focused on musical innovation within the parameters of acoustic instrumentation, and the duet-based groups applied more novel musical and progressive vocal techniques to rural lyrical imagery. Lyrically, most of these acts focused on devout themes that reflected the importance of religion in southern life and were a sign of the times.

The religious impulse of rural southerners in the mid-twentieth century stemmed predominantly from two centuries of Protestant upheavals. The awakenings of the eighteenth and nineteenth centuries effectively democratized American religion, and in the South, the Great Revival of the early 1800s roused rural southerners to the vision of universal salvation preached by the Methodist and Baptist sects. Evangelical movements of the 1800s instilled in southern religion an emotional power as well, which was heightened by the Pentecostal surge late in the century. Music and religion increasingly intertwined in the South, particularly after the gospel movement made its way to the region in the late 1800s. As with so many other aspects of American culture adopted by the South, the southern version of the evangelical and gospel movements took on distinctly regional qualities. W. J. Cash describes the manifestation of the divinity that developed in the southern environment: "The God demanded was an anthropomorphic God . . . a God who might be seen, a God who *had* been seen. A passionate, whimsical tyrant, to be trembled before, but whose favor was the sweeter for that." Songwriters within the southern gospel movement espoused this vision with the emotional urgency of evangelical revivalism, stressing self-reproachment, reconciliation, and the promise of a glorious afterlife. Nationwide, the religious fervor that dominated in the nineteenth century abated somewhat in the first decade of the twentieth century, with church membership increasing only slightly, from 43 to 48 percent between 1910 and 1940. Between 1940 and 1950, however, this figure rose to 55 percent, with the millennial and Pentecostal sects showing particularly substantial growth. Historian William G. McLoughlin Jr. attributes this surge to a series of historical shocks, beginning with the Depression and culminating in the social upheavals and elusive peace of World War II. Not surprisingly, the threat of nuclear war loomed large, and many evangelists, such as Arkansas native Asa A. Allen, ominously pointed to the time when "a great black cloud in the form of a skeleton reaches its tentacle arms toward America to embrace her in the embrace of death." Radio listeners in the South demonstrated a decided preference for religious programs in the mid- to late 1940s, and postwar traditional acts responded by including numerous religious and gospel selections in their radio and recording repertoires. [35]

Songs with religious overtones never came close to dominating the charts, but they did make up around 30 percent of the recorded output of the postwar traditionalists in the late forties and early fifties. Many country music performers grew up listening to gospel groups at home and in church. Some, like Johnny Cash, attended Pentecostal services that mixed fire and brimstone eschatology with musical interludes: "I learned to sit through the scary sermon just to hear the music: mandolins, fiddles, bass, banjo, and flat top guitars. Hell might be on the horizon, but the wonderful gospel-spiritual songs carried me above it." The Pentecostal bent made its way into several country songs of the period, many apocalyptic in nature, using the atomic bomb metaphor. One country group more than any other, however, captured the images of southern religion described by both W. J. and Johnny Cash. In combining Pentecostal proselytizing with a Roy Acuff singing style and progressive instrumentation, the Bailes Brothers put to words and music the postwar apprehensions of thousands of southerners. [36]

Johnnie, Walter, Homer, and Kyle Bailes grew up near Charleston, West Virginia, in the 1920s and 1930s. The brothers began performing on radio with other musicians and in various sibling combinations in the mid-1930s, but they did not gain notoriety in the region until Johnnie and Walter moved to WSAZ in Huntington in 1942, with Homer and Kyle appearing with them occasionally. Johnnie and Walter remained there during the war, until 1944, when Roy Acuff came to the region. Impressed with the duo's talent, he arranged their move to WSM, where they played an early morning show in addition to performing on the *Opry*. Homer rejoined the group in Nashville after his discharge from the army, and Kyle became the brothers' manager and agent. They also added mandolinist Ernest Ferguson and steel guitarist Shot Jackson to the fold during this period. They relocated again in 1946, this time to Shreveport, where they became charter performers on the *Louisiana Hayride,* which soon became a major barn dance program in the late 1940s. The Bailes Brothers became very popular in the Texas-Arkansas-Louisiana region even as they went through various personnel changes, including the departure of Walter in 1947 and Homer in 1949, who both left to join the church. When Homer left, Walter returned to work with Johnnie as a gospel duet in the early 1950s, until the Bailes Brothers disbanded as an active performing group in 1956.[37]

In musical style, the Bailes Brothers' first recordings, in February 1945, resemble the sound of the prewar progressives. Recorded before they added electric steel guitarist Shot Jackson to the group, these early sides predominantly feature the duet vocals of Johnnie and Walter, the mandolin playing of Ernest Ferguson, and the old-time fiddling of Del Heck. The brothers' singing, open throated and emotionally charged, owes a great deal of influence to Roy Acuff, particularly on "As Long as I Live." Acuff made a distinct impression on Walter Bailes the first time Walter heard him: "He was telling me exactly how I was feelin'." Lyrically, little distinguishes the secular numbers of the session from contemporary country. The brothers' own individual lyrical style begins to surface on religious numbers, as on "The Drunkard's Grave" and especially on "Dust on the Bible," songs that center on man's sinfulness and a perceived lapse of religious conviction in society. Due to the Bailes Brothers' old-time musical feel and preachy lyrics, Columbia Records hesitantly released the singles, which were a departure from the popular records of the time. A *Billboard* review of "Dust on the Bible" and "I've Got a One-Way Ticket to the Sky" probably reinforced their ambivalence: "The two Bailes boys, getting string band accomps, sing in backwoods gospel style for both of these religious folk tunes. . . . Swell for the rocking chair brigade, but they don't spend nickels." After switching to the King label and adding Jackson to the fold, the group crafted sounds simultaneously old-timey and modern. Encouraged by King executive Syd Nathan, Jackson played steel guitar solos that added considerable punch to sessions revolving around gospel material. "He'll Strike You Down," "Building on the Sand," and "We're Living in the Last Days Now" offer chilling interpretations of postwar society's wayward stride and the ultimate price that must be paid. Such secular numbers as "Broken Marriage Vows" and "Everybody Knew the Truth But Me" pale in comparison to the vocal intensity displayed on a religious number such as "Daniel's Prayer." The Pentecostal fervor carried over to their 1947 recordings for Columbia. "Do You Expect a Reward from

God" is one of their most effective sermonlike songs, and "Come to the Savior" offers a haunting interpretation of an old Blue Sky Boys' tune. In the background, Jackson and Ferguson exchange solos in a musical tug-of-war between older and newer sounds while Homer Bailes's eerie fiddling accentuates the apocalyptic feel of the proceedings. After the group fragmented in the late 1940s, Johnnie and Walter reunited in 1953 for a series of gospel sides for King. What these last records lack in musical intensity they make up for in lyrical quality and vocal sincerity, most notably on "Goodbye, Hallelujah, I'm Gone." In their prime, the Bailes Brothers offered a unique perspective on postwar social developments, free of the restrictions imposed by mainstream trends toward more lighthearted lyrical material. Their sole musical concession to contemporary sounds, Jackson's steel guitar, only reinforced the fervor of their performances. The fact that the Bailes Brothers' popularity extended from the backwoods of Virginia to the cities of the Southwest offers testament to the widespread apprehensions felt by members of a postwar southern society in flux.[38]

The changes in southern society precipitated by World War II filled its rural inhabitants with a forbidding sense of their future. As C. Vann Woodward points out: "The traditionalist who . . . watched the Bulldozer Revolution plow under cherished old values of individualism, localism, family, clan, and rural folk culture . . . felt helpless and frustrated against the mighty and imponderable agents of change." Many who found work in cities or served in the armed forces knew deep in their hearts that they could never return to their prewar ways of life. In some cases, they simply did not wish to, and in others, they could not even if they wanted to. World War II made the world a radically different place for many Americans, but for rural southerners in particular. Before the war, they lived in communal hamlets, relatively isolated from the cultural impositions of urban and American society. During the war, many left the countryside, both involuntarily and by choice, to join in the national crusade or to try to better their lives. As historian Jack Kirby points out, those moving to cities experienced a transition from a sense of community to a sense of alienation, from interpersonal to impersonal relationships. Many constructed support systems in cities and maintained contacts with family members back home. Transplanted southerners in northern cities and the armed forces obstinately clung to their culture in the face of social upheaval. They would adapt but not succumb to a foreign way of life that they viewed as aberrant. Country music served as one of the primary weapons in their struggle to maintain their southern identity. Country music, however, was also changing. Over the course of its nationalizing process, it increasingly drifted away from its southern and rural roots. Western swing and the wartime Texas triumvirate of Autry, Ritter, and Dexter symbolized the shift in country music's creative nucleus to the urban Southwest. As a result, mainstream country music at the end of World War II no longer appealed to many rural southerners lyrically or musically.[39]

The postwar traditionalists emerged in the mid-forties to fill the void created by country music's nationalization. Part reactionary and part innovative, the postwar traditional impulse offered an old-world view in a fresh musical setting. It celebrated country folk traditions but recognized their musical obsolescence. The alternative string bands blended improvisational instrumental techniques into their rudimentary country band sound, infusing it with a vigor and soulfulness tantamount to western swing's high-spiritedness. Mournful, religious, and pastoral lyrics, together with a steadfast adherence to acoustic instrumentation, affirmed bluegrass groups' association with the countryside. Other performers, such as Molly O'Day and Grandpa Jones, entrenched themselves in Appalachian traditions, finding both humor and tragedy in mountain and folk culture. Playing old-time music in an old-time style, they appealed to listeners whose tastes had not changed over the course of the war. Finally, a generation of duet-based acts emerged that built on the progressive tradition, subtly augmenting their vocal harmonies with novel instrumentation. They too used rural lyrical imagery to lend an unpretentious feel to their recordings, occasionally adding a familial and religious piety that tended to reinforce rural, communal norms. Together, the postwar traditionalists offered cultural continuity to a generation of rural southerners dealing with social dislocation and a foreboding future.[40]

Although the postwar traditionalists maintained a loyal following, they essentially remained an underground movement in the eyes of the country music industry. Acts that readily incorporated elements of popular music and electric instrumentation during the war continued their domination of the country music charts in the latter half of the 1940s. Many transplanted rural southerners and new country listeners across the United States embraced the new sounds. Though some attended the increasing number of folk music parks in the Northeast and Roy Acuff's newly constructed Dunbar Cave in Clarksville, Tennessee, as a means to reacquaint themselves with their rural past, most accepted their urban lot and the new sounds coming from radios and jukeboxes. The country music acts that appealed to these predominantly urban listeners, however, splintered over the implementation of electric instruments in country music and the degree that they wanted to adopt elements of other musical genres. Generally speaking, those artists most enchanted by the western swing innovation mixed southwestern instrumentation with a bluesy beat for dancing; other musicians followed in the footsteps of the country and pop fusion popularized during World War II to create a softer, more listener-oriented music; and a third faction accepted southwesterners' use of the electric steel guitar but chose to retain much of the rural feel of prewar country music. The records of this third group appealed to neourbanites seeking a music that reflected the southern folk tradition but recast it for the urban environment. In time, this type of music acquired the "honky-tonk" appellation.[41]

Roy Acuff, progressive country music performer. Courtesy of Country Music Hall of Fame and Museum.

The Delmore Brothers, progressive and country blues performers. Courtesy of Country Music Hall of Fame and Museum.

Tommy Duncan, western swing performer. Courtesy of Country Music Hall of Fame and Museum.

Ernest Tubb, honky-tonk performer. Courtesy of Country Music Hall of Fame and Museum.

Kitty Wells, honky-tonk performer. Courtesy of Country Music Hall of Fame and Museum.

Eddy Arnold, country pop performer. Courtesy of Country Music Hall of Fame and Museum.

Merle Travis, country blues performer. Courtesy of Country Music Hall of Fame and Museum.

Elvis Presley, country blues perfomer. Photo © Alfred Wertheimer. All rights reserved. Courtesy of Country Music Hall of Fame and Museum.

5 | COUNTRY MUSIC AT THE DAWN OF THE SUNBELT ERA
HONKY-TONK AND THE PROMOTIONAL BLITZ

The urbanizing forces of World War II filled rural southerners with both hope and apprehension. Many joined the 15.3 million American civilians moving to cities during the war in search of defense industry jobs. This marked the beginning of the South's Sunbelt era, a period characterized by rapid population and economic growth. The lure of a steady paycheck and escape from the agricultural quagmire proved especially enticing to younger southerners attracted to urban amenities and the promise of a brighter future. Those returning from military service also had good reason to believe that cities offered economic advancement and social mobility. Some migrants displayed an eagerness to assimilate into urban culture, while others clung to the culture of their youth, one grounded in folkways and a provincial worldview. Jack Kirby points out that in Ohio, natives distinguished between "southerners," well-dressed migrants who used regional colloquialisms sparingly, and "briars," who dressed and spoke in a decidedly rural, southern fashion. Regardless of the degree to which they wanted to acclimate to their new surroundings, southern migrants faced similar challenges. All who traveled to northern urban areas struggled with hillbilly and hayseed stereotypes. On the Near West Side of Chicago, southern migrants constructed a social enclave to combat native prejudices. As noted in chapter 2, southern folk moving to urban areas within their own region faced similar cultural intolerance.[1]

As a rule, the new urban order presented southern migrants with a variety of economic and social obstacles. For one thing, the nature of both work and interpersonal relationships changed, and migrants had to grow accustomed to time clocks and peculiar anonymity; for another, the new urban existence often clashed with the tenets of their rural-oriented faith. City life pushed and pulled against traditional mores, and migrants were left to reap the whirlwind of the South's catapult into modernity. Commenting on the region's phenomenal wartime expansion, a contemporary observer noted: "The South . . . will emerge from [the] war with more social change and more unfinished business than any other section of the country."[2]

In the mid- to late 1940s, southern cities bustled with economic activity as local chambers of commerce in the South focused on cementing the gains made possible by outside investments during the war. Industry soon came to rival agriculture as the South's primary business pursuit. When industrial production workers began to outnumber farmers late in the decade, the region's rural ethos suffered a symbolic defeat. As an exponent of southern folk culture, country music soon adapted to its listeners' transplantation to urban areas.[3]

When country music moved to the city, it initially retained much of its lyrical realism while adapting to the new urban environment. As such, country music songwriters replaced pastoral imagery with portraits of the new social landscape. As the postwar traditionalists clung to their rural past, country music performers who spoke for the displaced persons entering the cities examined the psychological effects of the rural/urban dichotomy. Most of the time they did so without directly commenting on urbanization, but rather on its emotional aftermath. In the cities, many former rural dwellers congregated at taverns, termed "honky-tonks," where they sought solace from the traumas induced by their separation from their folk roots. Honky-tonk performers addressed the realities encountered by country music listeners facing the alienating repercussions of postwar urbanization and industrialization. Their songs were "real" in the sense that they captured the dissolution of the prewar lives of returning veterans and neourbanites. Additionally, they tapped into the personal strains of urban newcomers who found true love and personal contentment elusive. Ironically, honky-tonkers donned western attire when singing about the effects of urban alienation; they did so primarily as a means to give their transplanted hillbilly music more respectability and enhance its entertainment value. Most often, they sang about severed relationships; lovelorn and breakup selections accounted for nearly half of their lyrical repertoire in the postwar decade. In this, they resembled the progressive performers, but in their manner of approaching the subject, they differed considerably. Honky-tonk love laments display less pleading for reconciliation than they do pensive soul-searching on the emotional ramifications of a breakup. More than any other subgenre, honky-tonk explores feelings of guilt over infidelity and other moral trespasses. Unlike the postwar traditionalists, honky-tonk performers resign themselves to life in an urban-industrial society however incompatible it may seem with their rural upbringing. Their resignation often fosters self-pity, occasionally reflected in songs about drinking and general disillusionment, but more often expressed through tales of estranged love. As time wore on, a new generation of performers emerged that concentrated less on self-meditation than on transfusing lighthearted material into what later became known as the honky-tonk sound.[4]

Like other country subgenres, honky-tonk is distinguishable by certain vocal and musical criteria. The progressives built on the string-band and domestic traditions, and the postwar traditionalists concentrated on fusing these musical conventions with novel instrumentation; the honky-tonkers applied the vocal style of such progressives as Roy Acuff and Jimmie Davis to a restrained version of the western swing musical motif. Honky-tonk performers embraced the electric steel guitar and the single-string solos of Floyd Tillman and early Ernest Tubb guitarists as well as the expressiveness of Texas fiddling. They also occasionally adopted western swing's twin-fiddle sound and heavy, danceable beat. Honky-tonk groups, however, differed considerably from their western swing counterparts in their implementation of these musical techniques. Primarily, they played country music in a style much closer to blues than jazz or American popular music, and as a result, their solo passages were more economical and evocative in nature. Secondly, they transposed western swing's emphasis on instrumentation and downplay on vocal. In honky-tonk, musicians accent but never overshadow the singer. Singers, meanwhile, express lyrics in a more emotional style, creating a sense of intimacy between performer and audience similar in fashion to the Delmores and the Stanley Brothers. In sum, honky-tonk lies somewhere between a string band's adaptation to an urban environment and a western swing group's acculturation to a tavern setting. It arose from the need to reconcile country music's folk traditions with its urban inclinations, and it symbolized the accession of the club over the schoolhouse as the primary haunt for country music's dislocated audience in the postwar period.[5]

At first sight, the honky-tonk appeal seemed curious to some, magnetic to others. Bill Porterfield's description of a typical east Texas honky-tonk in the 1940s depicts the establishment's milieu:

As you entered, the front part of the building had a bar on the right side and on the left, tables and chairs and a couple of pool tables and marble machines and a shuffleboard. If you were hungry, you could get cold cuts and hot links at the bar, which only served beer and pop. If you wanted to dance, you had to walk through a gate in a little wooden fence that cut off the dance floor from the front. During the day there was no cover and you could dance to the jukebox as long as you had the nickels and quarters. At night, if the house band was playing you paid a dollar to get in. . . . Honky-tonks were cheap places frequented by [working]-class . . .

customers. They were not particularly dangerous places, although some were. If a fight broke out, the best bet was to keep dancing.

Members of the white southern working class frequented honky-tonks for a variety of reasons. A study conducted between 1947 and 1949 on southern migrants in the North described patronage of "hillbilly taverns" in Chicago as "a form of voluntary segregation," a means to reaffirming identity in an urban environment characterized by impersonal and anonymous relationships. Whether in the North or the South, country music listeners went to clubs for a variety of other reasons as well, as John Morthland explains: "Honky-tonks provided a gathering spot, a community center. . . . Men went there to decompress after a hard day at a demanding job: to drink and celebrate, to drink and commiserate, to find a woman, to dance, to swap lies, to get in fights, to cut up in general." For music, club owners initially booked bands that played for tips or for a portion of beer sales. In the early days of the Texas honky-tonks, these groups, sometimes consisting of just a fiddler and guitarist, played acoustically, but many soon discovered the need to adopt vocal and instrumental electric amplification in order to be heard above the natural sounds of socializing. By the mid-1940s, as Bill Malone points out, "most of the bands featured the rhythm guitar played in a percussive, closed-chord style, an electric steel guitar, an electric lead, . . . a fiddle, a bass [both acoustic and electric,] and often a piano." As an alternative to hiring a band, economically minded owners of small clubs simply installed a jukebox to provide musical background; they too found selections with a heavier beat to be more popular among the nightlife crowd. In the decade after World War II, the popularity of jukeboxes and honky-tonks grew hand in glove; coin machine operators became the country music industry's biggest consumers and suppliers of music.[6]

Bands and jukeboxes provided the pounding heartbeat for honky-tonks, but the souls of the cavernous establishments were endowed by the club patrons. Customers could be jovial one moment and cantankerous the next. Some turned to violence for recreation, others to vent their frustrations. Huey Meaux, who played the nightspots with George Jones in the late forties, points out that many patrons "honky-tonked" to escape the drudgeries of everyday life: "In them days, all you did was went to dancehalls and drank beer and fought all night, 'cause there was no other sports to do in them days. And that was the name of the game: who was the best fighter." Not surprisingly, honky-tonks soon acquired a reputation as places for upstanding citizens to avoid. In the early 1940s, Senator George Moffett of Texas sponsored a bill that called for the revocation of liquor licenses at places that allowed "conduct lewd, immoral or offensive to public decency." Moffett aimed the bill at clubs officially labeled honky-tonks, places that permitted the following social practices:

The use of or permitting the use of loud and vociferous or obscene, vulgar or indecent language. The exposure of person or permitting any person to expose his person. Rudely displaying or permitting any person rudely to display a pistol or any other deadly weapon in a manner calculated to disturb the inhabitants of such place. Solicitation of any person for coins to operate musical instruments or other devices. Solicitation of any person to buy drinks or beverages for consumption by the retailer or his employees. Intoxication on licensed premises [licensed to sell alcoholic beverages] or permitting any intoxicated person to remain on such premises. Permitting entertainment performances, shows or acts that are lewd or vulgar. Permitting solicitations of persons for immoral or sexual purposes or relations.

Many taverns and dance halls fit at least one of all of these criteria, but it seems likely that the bill, which was signed into law by Governor Coke Stevenson in 1943, was intended as a means to close some of the more dangerous establishments.[7]

Musicians who played the rougher honky-tonks considered themselves lucky if they made it through a night unscathed. Carl Perkins describes his experience in these establishments: "I'm talking about rough places, where half the people went there to fight. . . . And a lot of these places had chicken wire around the jukebox and us to keep the bottles from hitting—these guys actually had axe handles behind the bar and about four or five inches on the big end of the axe handle was bored out and poured full of hot lead." Floyd Tillman similarly recalls playing the rough spots in east Texas, "where you had to dodge beer bottles, and when the fights broke out you were supposed to speed it up and play the music real fast." Not all honky-tonks were quite this rough, of course, and many employed bouncers to maintain a certain degree of tranquility. Floyd Tillman remembers at least one time, however, when this setup provided him with a false sense of security:

When [a World War II vet and amputee put his head down on a table], the auxiliary police who worked the place went to take him out. I said, "Hey, leave that guy alone, he's not hurting anybody," but that didn't stop 'em at all. They just hauled him out. That really burned me up, so [I dedicated a song to him]. That didn't stop 'em either. In fact, it made them so mad that they threw the guy out and then came back for *me*—lifted me off the bandstand and threw me out! And I was the guy putting on the dance! I'd rented the hall and hired those cops!

From the schoolhouse to the barroom proved a jolty trek for country music and its performers. Like the country music audience that journeyed from the countryside to urban areas, musicians who made the transition into the honky-tonks faced certain perils in their pursuit of economic opportunity. Honky-tonk performers' success paralleled the South's unyielding pull toward urbanization. As the musical equivalent of the rural/urban dichotomy, honky-tonk flourished in the postwar period.[8]

The honky-tonk era symbolically began in February 1946, when Floyd Tillman recorded a Jerry Irby song entitled "Drivin' Nails in My Coffin." Tillman's interpretation of Irby's tale of a man driven to alcohol by lost love marked a turning point in country music as a modernization of an earlier honky-tonk hybrid developed in the late thirties and early forties. In the prewar period, producers and musicians considered "honky-tonk songs" music for dancing; accordingly, Al Dexter made light of the barroom experience in such up-tempo tunes as "Bar Hotel," "Honky Tonk Blues," and "When We Go Honky-tonkin'." During the war, Ted Daffan and Ernest Tubb blended brooding elements of traditional country lyricism with novel electric instrumentation to reconstruct the definition of a honky-tonk song, and the jukebox popularity of their recordings indicate a changing of the guard. When Tubb began augmenting his rhythm guitar–lead guitar approach with a fiddle and steel guitar in the latter war years, the modern honky-tonk genre began to take shape. Tillman's recording merged the lyrical starkness of a Ted Daffan tune, such as "Headin' down the Wrong Highway," with the dark rumination of an Ernest Tubb song, such as "It Just Don't Matter Now," and set it to a fuller, western swing–like instrumental backdrop characterized by seering twin fiddles, Leo Raley's bluesy mandolin work, the pounding piano of Ralph Smith, and Tillman's own half-spoken vocal drawl. Musically, it marked a substantial turnabout for Tillman, who began as a western swing performer in the mid-thirties and moved closer to pop during the war years, and set the tone for his postwar portfolio. With its free-spirited instrumentation, "Drivin' Nails in My Coffin" represents less an archetypal honky-tonk recording than it does a manifestation of the western swing–Daffan–Tubb nexus that brought the subgenre to fruition. Nevertheless, Tillman deserves the credit for capturing the lyrical and musical spirit of honky-tonk on his February 1946 recording.[9]

Many people associate honky-tonk with songs about drinking and infidelity. Less than 10 percent of all songs released by classic honky-tonk performers, however, deal with this subject matter. Floyd Tillman is the only performer in the honky-tonk subgenre with a plurality of songs of this type. No other honky-tonk performer addressed more forthrightly or explicitly the actual honky-tonk atmosphere. Characters in Floyd Tillman songs live lonely, desperate lives: most turn to alcohol to cope with their forlorn existence; others seek sexual companionship; and some are consumed with self-pity. Tillman spins these tales in his unique half-spoken manner, skillfully using vocal inflections to convey the destitution of his characters. In "Sign on the Dotted Line" and "It's a Cruel, Cruel World for Me," husbands watch as their marriages fade away, ultimately ended by their wives' unfaithfulness. In "Take My Love with You," a wife leaves her husband for another man, taking the couple's baby as well. "This Cold War with You" stands as one of the most insightful portraits of a marriage besieged by mistrust, and "Slipping Around" and its sequel "I'll Never Slip around Again" deal frankly with the consequences of marital infidelity. Characters in "Some Other World," "I'm Leaving This Old World Someday," and "You Made Me Live, Love, and Die" stand on the brink of suicide or suffer interminably from broken hearts. "I Gotta Have My Baby Back" and "I Almost Lost My Mind" delve deep into the blues, the latter featuring some particularly evocative guitar work from both Tillman and steel guitarist Herb Remington. Ultimately, Tillman's characters turn to alcohol for solace, only to find no escape from haunting memories of abandoned love. In "A Small Little Town," a man's loneliness is compounded by the fact that the taverns close early, leaving him little hope for finding a woman to share his troubles with or a bottle to sink himself into. The subject of "It's Got Me Down" relinquishes all hope for finding a "nice girl" to settle down with, displaying a tinge of class consciousness in his contempt for the attraction of wealth. In the absence of lasting love, characters in "Gotta Have Somethin'," "I'll Be Playing the Field," and "I'll Take What I Can Get" search for ephemeral, physical relationships. Taken together, Tillman's songs paint a picture of honky tonk culture unparalleled in country music. Tillman was truly one of the genre's first "outlaws," electing to stay in the Houston area after the war instead of pursuing a more lucrative career in Nashville and continually writing songs that dealt with applicable, yet unspeakable issues. When "Slipping Around" appeared, some stations refused to play it, and the *Lucky Star Hit Parade* censored it. Tillman's unnerving snapshots of honky-tonk life may have made some listeners uncomfortable, but they endeared him to a generation of displaced southerners haunting the taverns and dance halls in search of an elusive contentment.[10]

While Floyd Tillman focused on the honky-tonk experience, Ernest Tubb concentrated on the harsh realities of everyday life, often voicing the hopes and anxieties of a wartorn and emotionally disoriented country music audience. Tubb possessed neither a superlative voice nor a knack for lyrical imagery, but few performers could match his vocal sincerity and his uncanny ability to write and record songs that defined common apprehensions in a plainspoken manner. More than anything else, Tubb realized the importance of authenticity in the presentation and selection of songs: "If those of us in this field are not sincere, the audience seems to sense it immediately. . . . If I don't feel a certain way about a song, I will not sing it." Unpretentious and identifiable, Tubb's singing style paved the way to his success as a country music performer. Bill Porterfield grew up listening to Tubb and explains the singer's instantaneous appeal: "He can't sing any better than you and me. . . . To hear Ernest was to hear your uncle, the one that lost his farm to the bankers and lost his heart to a good-looking mama who treated him like dirt. It wasn't pretty singing, but Lord, it was real. Out of the old rock." Commenting on Tubb's singing style and lyrical repertoire, historian Ronnie Pugh points out the underlying reason for Tubb's magnetism: "His concerns were their concerns, voiced without frill, without metaphor, without simile, in a sparse, rough-hewn, down-to-earth style. . . . Listeners knew what he was singing about and identified with his viewpoint."[11]

Born in Crisp, Texas, south of Dallas, in 1914, Ernest Tubb developed an interest in becoming a country music performer in his early teens, after hearing a Jimmie Rodgers recording. Tubb patterned his singing style after his idol's and began playing publicly at local square dances and parties in the early 1930s before landing a spot on a small San Antonio radio station in 1933. With the assistance of the widow of Jimmie Rodgers, Tubb secured his first recording contract with RCA-Victor, the late singer's label, in the mid-thirties, but his career did not begin to flourish until he later signed with Decca in 1940. In November of that year, Tubb became a full-time performer when he moved to 5,000-watt KGKO in Fort Worth, where he developed a strong regional following. He soon secured a sponsor, Gold Chain Flour, and on the strength of "Walking the Floor over You," a spot on the *Grand Ole Opry* in early 1943. As a result of a string of several successful singles, including "Time after Time," "I Wonder Why You Said Goodbye," "You Nearly Lose Your Mind," and "It's Been So Long Darling," and his popular tours and *Opry* appearances, Tubb, nicknamed the "Texas Troubadour," became a household name throughout the South by the end of World War II.[12]

Ernest Tubb's last wartime sessions set the tone for his postwar output. The day before V-J Day, he recorded two songs that succinctly captured the ambivalent feelings of returning veterans: "It's Been So Long Darling" and "Should I Come Back Home to You?" In the former, a soldier expresses the hope that his wife will be waiting for him when he returns; in the latter, a soldier acknowledges the possibility that his wife has been unfaithful in his absence and ponders his response. The session marked the first time Tubb utilized the steel guitar on a full-time basis. Earlier attempts, such as "Our Baby's Book" and "You May Have Your Picture," produced mixed results, but during the recording ban of 1944, Tubb worked out the new sound on several transcriptions he produced for the World Broadcasting System with steel guitarist Ray Head. At Tubb's first session of the honky-tonk period on February 13, 1946, Head's guitar work complements Tubb's trademark vocals nicely, particularly on "I'm Free at Last," and lead guitarist Jimmie Short's economical, high-gain solos are another distinct aspect of Tubb's postwar sound, one carried on by Tommy Paige and Billy Byrd in the late forties and early fifties. For the most part, Tubb retained the simple instrumentation that characterized the early postwar sides, but he occasionally added piano, percussive "sock" rhythm guitar, and even subtle drumming. As with his war sides, however, his honky-tonk era songs revolve primarily around electric lead guitar solos and his own singing. [13]

Lyrically, Tubb's most impressive songs of the postwar period focus on failed relationships, many taking place in a topical setting. The self-penned "Those Tears in Your Eyes (Were Not for Me)" continues in the same vein as "Should I Come Back Home to You?" with a soldier returning to find his wife in love with another man. It was Tubb's rendition of the Carlisle Brothers' "Rainbow at Midnight," however, that established him as the country music spokesman for returning veterans. The song tells the story of a soldier on a ship returning home and focuses on his idyllic postwar dreams: a wife, children, and a home in the country. Historian George Lipsitz compares it with Perry Como's "Till the End of Time" as a song that "laid claim to patriarchal promises," describing it as a "distinctively male fantasy." Many listeners related to the aspirations expressed in the song and found Tubb's interpretation of it genuinely appealing. Not surprisingly, the record sold around half a million copies. [14]

In spite of his limited vocal abilities, Ernest Tubb carried a wide range of material convincingly. He excelled at mid-tempo pieces about failed relationships, but he also proved himself a very capable balladeer ("I Love You Because") and sentimentalist ("Give Me a Little Old-Fashioned Love"). For his honky-tonk following, Tubb offered up such songs as "I'm with a Crowd But So Alone," "Driftwood on the River," and two Cindy Walker selections, "Warm Red Wine" and "Two Glasses, Joe." Tubb's acute interpretative abilities surfaced throughout the postwar period, lending a plaintive intimacy to Hank Thompson's "A Lonely Heart Knows" and adding weight to several Jimmie Rodgers covers, including "Mother, Queen of My Heart" and "Why Should I Be Lonely." The Texas Troubadour astutely maintained his distinctive musical style throughout most of the postwar era, but he occasionally experimented with different sounds as well. In one of the most unlikely vocal collaborations in American music history, Tubb and the Andrew Sisters recorded together in early 1949 with surprisingly successful results. The vast majority of the Texas singer's duets with Red Foley proved less fruitful, mainly due to trite lyrical material, but "Don't Be Ashamed of Your Age" worked well and confirmed Tubb's adeptness at humorous material. Always attuned to his audience's lyrical tastes, Tubb focused on recording songs about failed relationships directly after the war and then moved to more lighthearted material in the early 1950s. Tubb succeeded by lyrically identifying himself with his audience and musically maintaining his own individual style. With a unique sound and a universal appeal, Ernest Tubb demonstrated more than any other performer the importance of connecting with an audience and accommodating listeners' changing tastes. Few could match the authenticity of his vocal performances and the charm of his musical simplicity.[15]

Honky-tonk performers such as Ernest Tubb and Floyd Tillman attained the most success when they addressed the concerns of rural southern migrants trying to reconcile their traditional values with their rapidly modernizing environment. Hank Williams achieved great acclaim as well through his ability to express this inner struggle in his performances. Williams brought to plain view the torments of southerners at odds with the twin blades of urbanization and industrialization. Wracked by inner demons and the enervating consequences of his own success, Williams ultimately lost his personal battle with the debilitating forces of the Bulldozer Revolution. In his public search for peace, some viewed him as a hero, but others saw him as a tragic figure doomed from the start. Sanctified by avid fans and anatomized by historians and sociologists, Hank Williams reasserted country music's rural, southern roots at a time when urban and western influences were pulling it in a different direction. No other country music performer contributed more to the genre's stylistic development in the period of its modernization.

Born in rural southern Alabama in 1923, Hank Williams grew up in an environment of economic hardship. His father, a World War I veteran and locomotive engineer, suffered from the debilitating effects of the war and entered a veterans' hospital around the time his son turned seven, effectively leaving Lillie Williams, a church organist, to raise their child alone. Lillie and Hank traveled to Greenville, where Hank worked a series of odd jobs, including selling peanuts and shining shoes, to augment the family's meager income. While in Greenville, the youngster also took the opportunity to learn the rudiments of guitar playing from a black street musician named Rufus Payne, who was also known as "Tee-Tot." Under Payne's instruction, Williams added bluesy rhythms to his appreciation of country music and familiarity with religious material. In 1937, the Williams family moved to Montgomery, where Hank began fine-tuning his public performance skills and appearing on local radio. From mid-1941 to mid-1942, listeners in the area heard Williams over Montgomery's WSFA singing Roy Acuff songs and other country music standards. The lure of the better-paying war industries led him to Portland, Oregon, briefly before he settled in Mobile for two years working for a shipbuilding company. Returning to Montgomery in late 1944, Williams began to earnestly pursue a career in country music, appearing at schoolhouses and beer joints in the area. Spurred by the success of his personal appearances and popularity of his radio show, Williams journeyed to Nashville in September 1946 to audition for Fred Rose, cofounder of Acuff-Rose Publications. Sufficiently impressed, Rose helped Williams secure a recording contract with Sterling Records. On the strength of Williams's first recordings, Rose landed him a contract with a major label, M-G-M, in early 1947. Williams remained on WSFA until mid-1948, when Rose convinced the management of the *Louisiana Hayride* on 50,000-watt KWKH to take a chance on the young musician with the wild reputation. The conservative *Opry* avoided Williams like the plague even after the singer topped the charts with his remake of "Lovesick Blues" in the spring of 1949, but a few months later *Opry* management acquiesced, beginning a stormy three-year relationship with Williams. Riddled by a chronic drinking problem and other personal woes, Williams lost his job with WSM in August 1952. He returned to the *Louisiana Hayride,* but continued to experience difficulty booking large shows, a development that relegated one of 1952's best-selling artists to the honky-tonk circuit. With a tragic inevitability, Williams died soon thereafter, on January 1, 1953.[16]

Hank Williams's first recordings for the Sterling label, with a western band named the Oklahoma Wranglers, demonstrate the young singer's debt to Roy Acuff, in both vocal style and lyrical makeup. On his first session, in December 1946, Williams sings three religious songs in the heartfelt Acuff style backed by a sound centered on old-time fiddles and accordion rhythm, the steel guitar noticeably absent. Williams's last session for Sterling introduced the steel as well as the percussive ("sock") rhythm electric guitar to Williams's sound, particularly on "Honky Tonkin'." Merle Travis dates the percussive guitar style back to banjo players in Dixieland bands who used it to provide loud rhythm in the days before microphones. Chet Atkins, who played with Williams later in his career, explains the way guitarists of the forties created the effect: "In this technique, one turns up the electric guitar to a very high volume and plays rhythm on the last four strings, while muting it at the bridge with the hand. The resulting sound is something like a plucking banjo." Lyrically, the session produced two more Acuffesque numbers, a "Wabash Cannonball" clone called "Pan American" and the lovelorn "I Don't

Care (If Tomorrow Never Comes)." With its carefree abandon and employment of electric instrumentation, "Honky Tonkin'," however, helped Williams distinguish himself from Acuff. [17]

At Williams's first session with M-G-M Records in April 1947, Fred Rose had him record with several musicians from Red Foley's band. In terms of the lineage between country and rock, "Move It on Over" is one of the most important country music recordings of the 1940s. In particular, Ernie Newton's aggressive, thumping bass presages Bill Black's work with Elvis Presley. Williams borrows an old blues melody to spin a humorous tale of a man sent away by his wife after a late night out, presumably honky-tonking. Other songs from the session owe more allegiance to Williams's rustic roots: "I Saw the Light," characterized by gospel lyrics and Tommy Jackson's sawing fiddle, reflects Williams's rural religious background, and "Six More Miles" has a decidedly country feel to it as well. [18]

Williams continued to integrate country with blues, gospel, and other rural-based genres throughout the remainder of his career with his own band, the Drifting Cowboys. He particularly excelled at blues-tinged numbers, such as "My Sweet Love Ain't Around," "Lost Highway," "Ramblin' Man," and "Long Gone Lonesome Blues." Few singers could immerse themselves in a song the way Hank Williams could, and fewer still could convey the emotional torture of such numbers as "I'm So Lonesome I Could Cry" and "Cold Cold Heart" with as much vocal intimacy. Williams worked with a number of notable musicians, but their playing nearly always assumed a secondary role to the leader's singing. In fiddler Jerry Rivers and steel guitarist Don Helms, Hank Williams found skilled musicians who complemented his singing without distracting listeners from the lyrical emphasis of his songs. With their subtle musical touches, the Drifting Cowboys helped transform their leader's individual blues into communal honky-tonk laments. [19]

Lyrically, Hank Williams concentrated predominantly on songs about failed relationships, occasionally with a tinge of anger ("I Just Don't Like This Kind of Living"), but more often with a sense of despair ("I Can't Help It [If I'm Still in Love with You]"). Characters in Hank Williams's songs are often grief-stricken and imprisoned in their loneliness ("I Can't Escape from You," "Take These Chains from My Heart"); lost love haunts them, particularly at night, and they yearn for a resolution that never materializes; breakups leave them emotionally scarred with little hope of recovery ("You Win Again"). Under the pseudonym Luke the Drifter, Williams recorded several recitations that delved into more sentimental and moralistic material. "Help Me Understand" deals more forthrightly with the consequences of divorce than most country songs of the period, and "Men with Broken Hearts" provides an eerie glimpse into the hearts and minds of wandering souls. On up-tempo numbers, meanwhile, Williams's characters live life without fear of social judgment ("Settin' the Woods on Fire" and "Hey Good Lookin' "). There is little if any ambiguity in Williams's songs; the overwhelming majority of them leave little room for doubt as to the mindset of their characters. As Williams explains, most of his songs aim at encapsulating emotional experiences: "I listen to people and try to understand how they feel about things. Feelings about things, that's what songs should be about." Williams's unpretentious, heart-on-sleeve writing and singing approach contributed more to his popularity than anything else. His songs and his life paralleled in many ways; both were characterized by an emotional roller coaster that left many wondering where the next turn would lead him. The country music audience listened to Williams, identified with him, rooted for him, and ultimately grieved for him as if he were a member of their own family. Jimmie Rodgers is the only other country music artist who could sustain such a personal and intimate relationship with an audience. One of Williams's closest friends, Ray Price, sums up the singer's timeless attraction: "The man had it. He had the magic. He had the touch. . . . [He and Jimmie Rodgers] had the heart."[20]

In the wake of Hank Williams's death, country music fans and the country music industry moved to consecrate the late singer. Disc jockeys who curtailed their broadcasts of Hank Williams's records in the months before his death suddenly began devoting two-hour segments to him. Sales of Williams's discs skyrocketed and a multitude of tributes appeared venerating the singer's contribution to country music. In Montgomery, 20,000 gathered at his funeral, among them Roy Acuff, Ernest Tubb, and Webb Pierce. Red Foley sang "Peace in the Valley," and a who's who of country music performers joined together in a rendition of "I Saw the Light." In September 1954, Tubb, Acuff, Jimmie Davis, and a throng of other artists returned to Montgomery for Hank Williams Memorial Day, along with 200 disc jockeys and thousands of fans. At the climax of what became a two-day event, a crowd of 8,500 watched the unveiling of a huge marble memorial monument that officially transformed Hank Williams into a country music icon. The presence of Tennessee governor Frank Clement, as one of the principal speakers, symbolized Williams's widespread popularity and indicated mainstream southern society's recognition of the music of its white, working-class citizenry. In death, Hank Williams redeemed the slights against country music and the southern folk culture that gave birth to it.[21]

In the last five years of Hank Williams's life, his music followed its listeners from the rural routes to the city streets by splicing the South's folk cultural tradition within the exigencies of urban life. Williams's musical style emerged from the churches, the fields, the front-porch swings, and the back roads of the rural South to become the sound of a society in transition. The southern working class identified with Williams because he drew on their common experience and expressed feelings in a way that made individual problems seem less peculiar. Williams did not evoke a class consciousness so much as he raised awareness of the universality of emotional afflictions. He encrusted country music with rural adornments at a time when it seemed overrun with urban embellishments. A honky-tonk singer with a hillbilly heart, Hank Williams demonstrated that country music could adapt to city life without succumbing to urban culture.[22]

Hank Williams's success spawned a number of country music performers who continued to work within the honky-tonk paradigm, that is, the process of adapting prewar country music to its new urban setting. In the aftermath of Williams's death, Ray Price emerged as the torchbearer of the rough-hewn, rural-derived honky-tonk sound pioneered by Ernest Tubb and perfected by Hank Williams. In time, Price would merge that sound with western swing to create a distinct honky-tonk style as danceable as it was barroom compatible.

Ray Price spent his early years on a farm in east Texas, where he grew up listening to Jimmie Rodgers and Gene Autry records. In 1937, when he was around eleven years old, his parents divorced, and he moved to Dallas with his mother. While in high school, Price began performing in public, but he gave little thought to a career in music, enrolling in a veterinary college instead. The war interrupted his studies, but he returned to the school in 1946, after spending two and a half years in the Marine Corps. Price remained interested in music, however, and in 1948 began appearing on Abilene radio. In 1949, after securing a regular spot on Dallas's *Big D Jamboree,* he decided to become a full-time musician. A demo of a friend's song that Price recorded brought the singer to the attention of producer Jim Beck, who secured the release of his first single on Bullet Records. Despite unimpressive sales, Price found an ally in Troy Martin, a talent scout of sorts for Columbia Records and the *Grand Ole Opry.* Price signed with Columbia in 1951, the same year he met Hank Williams, who invited him on a tour with the Drifting Cowboys. In early 1952, Price moved to Nashville and began appearing on the *Opry.* He continued to tour and record with the Drifting Cowboys after Williams's death, but in 1954 he formed his own band, the Cherokee Cowboys, with whom he worked out a unique style, characterized by multiple fiddles (played in single-string style), duet vocals, drums, a walking bass line, and a shuffling beat. He went on to become one of the most successful country music acts of the 1950s and 1960s.[23]

Ray Price's only release for Bullet Records gave no indication of his honky-tonk future. In "Jealous Lies," he sounds more like a crooner, with the sweeping steel guitar in the background lending a definite country pop touch to the record. At his first sessions with Columbia, a year later, Price continued in this vein, although "I Saw My Castles Fall Today" and "Until Death Do Us Part" have more a blues feel and "If You're Ever Lonely Darling" demonstrates the honky-tonk influence of Lefty Frizzell. After meeting Hank Williams, Price moved closer to his mentor's sound, evident especially on a version of Williams's "Weary Blues (from Waitin')." When Price relocated to Nashville from Dallas in 1952, the Drifting Cowboys began backing him on his recordings. On "Talk to Your Heart," Price sings with more assuredness; on "Move on in and Stay" and "Don't Let the Stars Get in Your Eyes," Price demonstrates his willingness to experiment with western swing fiddling and honky-tonk piano, two elements not characteristic of Hank Williams's recordings. After Williams died, Price continued to record numbers with the Drifting Cowboys; "You Always Get By" is his most accurate imitation of the late singer. In late 1953, however, Price declared his independence with two numbers, "Release Me" and "I'll Be There." For continuity, Price retained several members of the Drifting Cowboys, but he augmented the sound with a drummer and a second fiddler and for the first time flirted with the shuffling tempo he would later completely adopt on "Crazy Arms," a huge hit in 1955. He also began using the full force of his strong tenor, allowing it to rise above the band's more voluminous sound and cut through the honky-tonk smoke. At his last sessions in Nashville before returning to Texas, Price cemented his honky-tonk–western swing synthesis on "I Could Love You No More" and "If You Don't, Somebody Else Will." By August, Price replaced the Drifting Cowboys with the Cherokee Cowboys, a Texas band with a decidedly southwestern feel. Tommy Hill, with Price during the transition, recalls how audiences east of the Mississippi River reacted to the new, fuller sound: "The first date that we played with the two fiddles and the whole big band with the suits and western hats and so forth was Roanoke, and we had a packed house. . . . And we had eight, nine pieces, the band scared the hell out of [the audience]. They just sat and looked like we were monkeys in a cage." With the addition of Clifton Howard Vandevender, who was also known as Van Howard, on vocal harmony in late 1954 and fiddler Tommy Jackson in 1955, the Cherokee Cowboys sound coalesced. With his new band and honky-tonk–western swing hybrid, Price discovered a way to survive the rock and roll onslaught of the mid-fifties. Just as Thompson kept western swing alive by adding elements of honky-tonk, Price remained a redoubtable honky-tonk force by embracing western swing.[24]

Honky-tonk singers enjoyed widespread popularity in the postwar era principally because they captured the mood and ambivalence of country music's male listeners. They spoke to an audience of members who migrated to cities during the war and struggled with the transition to urban life and of returning veterans who faced a barrage of new problems. In addition to tussling with the mental adjustment of civilian life and an uncertain atomic peace, many American men returned to find the "Rainbow at Midnight" patriarchal vision delusive. Nationwide, 1.5 million servicemen married during the war, with the dramatic upsurge in weddings beginning shortly after the passage of the Selective Service Act. While men went off to war, women entered the workforce, encouraged by the government and the media to contribute to the war effort. Consequently, many women entered previously male-dominated professions, both blue- and white-collar. Over 5 million women entered the labor force during the war, an increase from one-quarter to over one-third. Nearly half of all women found employment at some point during national mobilization; three-quarters of those who did expressed an interest in remaining in the workforce after the war. Many women discovered economic independence and novel employment opportunities and exhibited a reluctance to relinquish the advancements they made during the war. In the South, female workers in Bessemer, Alabama, protested the Tennessee Coal and Iron Company's dismissal of 430 women (on the grounds that they were "inclined to marry") by staging a demonstration. In entering and winning several stock car races in 1946, Louise Smith symbolized southern women's challenge of traditional gender roles. [25]

Hasty marriages, wartime separation, and the redefinition of gender roles gave impetus to a wave of divorces in the postwar period. In 1945, one in three couples divorced, resulting in over half a million marriage dissolutions. In early 1946, 200,000 veterans were involved in divorce proceedings, and the number of American divorces rose to 600,000 by the end of the year. The issue of wartime infidelity weighed heavy on millions of wartime wives and returning servicemen. A 1943 survey indicated that nearly one-half of young married women doubted the fidelity of their husbands. Men, meanwhile, returned to marriages and families dramatically altered by the war. Steven Mintz and Susan Kellogg explain, "After worrying for years about defeating the Axis, now they worried about the fidelity of their wives, their unfamiliarity with their children, their economic prospects, and finding a niche in the post-war world." [26]

The rapid transformation of American society precipitated by World War II, the upsurge in divorces in the postwar period, and the onset of the Cold War left millions of Americans reeling in the uncertainties of the times. In the South, transplanted rural dwellers and returning veterans filled the honky-tonks in search of some escape from alienation and disillusionment. Ernest Tubb, Floyd Tillman, and Hank Williams spoke to their concerns and gave voice to their confusion. These and other honky-tonk singers directly addressed previously veiled issues of divorce, infidelity, and alcohol abuse with vocal and musical styles that accentuated their listeners' mindset and accommodated their newfound urban environment. As a subgenre, honky-tonk reasserted the male domination of country music that radio curtailed in the prewar years; in the process, honky-tonk alienated many of country's recently emancipated female listeners. Just as postwar American society pointed the scepter of blame for the nation's social ills at women, honky-tonk offered a one-sided account of male suffering that often distorted the realities of male-female relationships in the mid- to late forties. Reacting to early honky-tonk's male-dominant views, a number of female country singers emerged in the postwar period who challenged prevailing claims of woman's culpability for failed marriages and the breakdown of the American family. Using honky-tonk instrumentation as a musical backdrop, these women combated traditional female country music stereotypes and broke through the industry's male bulwark. [27]

Southern women found an unlikely spokeswoman in Kitty Wells. Born Muriel Deason in Nashville, Tennessee, the "Queen of Country Music" grew up listening to the *Grand Ole Opry*, singing hymns in church, and attending the square dances her guitar-playing father played at. In 1936, while still a teenager, she began appearing on Nashville's WSIX with her cousin as the Deason Sisters. After marrying Johnnie Wright in 1937, she continued to work part-time in radio, moving with her husband to a variety of stations in the Southeast in the late thirties and early forties. As Wright recalls, Wells's occasional appearances on his show with Eddie Hill in Knoxville elicited quite a listener response: "She had that little tremor to her voice, and I think that's what sold her. Anyway, she started to draw more mail than any other person on the show." When Wright and Jack Anglin moved to Shreveport's *Louisiana Hayride* after the war, Wells began appearing more regularly with the group, both on record and on radio. In 1949, with the help of Chet Atkins, Wells recorded her first sides for RCA-Victor, backed by Wright, Anglin, and the Smokey Mountain Boys. [28]

On her eight sides released on the RCA label in 1949 and 1950, Wells appears backed by traditional instrumentation. "Gathering Flowers for the Master's Bouquet," "My Mother," and "Don't Wait Till the Last Minute to Pray" all have an old-time feel, both in musical and lyrical approach. With its temperance message, "Death at the Bar" hints at Wells's later commentaries on honky-tonk life, but "Love or Hate," written by Jack Anglin, stands out as the sessions' most notable cut. The song tells the story of a strong woman who ultimately leaves her husband when he fails to keep his "promise" to her. In "I'll Be All Smiles Tonight," Wells's character shows more vulnerability, uncertain of how long the man she loves will stay with her, but willing to take the chance to be with him in fleeting moments. Promoted half-heartedly by RCA-Victor, the records failed to sell substantially. As Chet Atkins explains, part of the reason for this lack of interest stemmed from established industry standards: "It wasn't because [the record companies] had any prejudice against women, they just didn't think they could make any money off them. No one ever had in the past and in those days women were confined by conformity." As Wright recalls, WSM executives similarly responded to Wells's presence in the Johnnie and Jack entourage: "Jim Denny . . . said the *Opry* didn't need a girl singer, so Kitty didn't work the *Opry* with us in that time period."[29]

In 1952, Johnnie Wright convinced Decca's Paul Cohen to record his wife. Wells recalls, however, that she had little reason to be optimistic: "In 1949, about the time Johnnie started recording with RCA, I sang gospel songs for them. But that was before a girl [any girl] had really got started in the recording field. . . . After I left RCA and signed with Decca . . . I really thought it would be the same all over again." At Wells's first Decca session, in May 1952, she once again appeared with Johnnie and Jack's backup band, at the time consisting of rhythm guitarist Eddie Hill, steel guitarist Shot Jackson, and fiddler Paul Warren. Upon Cohen's suggestion, the band recorded an answer song to Hank Thompson's "Wild Side of Life" entitled "It Wasn't God Who Made Honky Tonk Angels"; it offered a strong indictment of men's honky-tonk ways and forthrightly pointed out men's role in facilitating adulterous relationships. Banned by NBC and *Opry* management, the song still managed to spring to the top of the charts in August and immediately bolstered Wells's career. Robert Oermann points out, "The immense popularity of 'Honky Tonk Angels' transformed the teetotaling, nonsmoking, church-going Wells into a honky tonk heroine." Mary Bufwack notes that the success of the song also made an immediate impact on country music: "The popularity of Wells' lament about male victimization of women indicates a conscious acknowledgment of women's discontent in postwar America and an interest within the country audience in a dialogue about male-female behavior."[30]

Not surprisingly, Wells recorded several other numbers in the early 1950s that explored the feminine side of the honky-tonk equation. In "Paying for the Back Street Affair," another answer song, to Webb Pierce's "Back Street Affair," a woman finds out that the man she loves is actually married; in "After Dark," she tries to make her lover realize the scandalous consequences she faces in being the other woman. In both cases, men deceive their mistresses into thinking they are not married or that they will soon leave their wives. In "I Heard the Jukebox Playing," "Divided by Two," and "I'm a Stranger in My Home," Wells portrays wives with cheating husbands left alone with babies to care for and broken hearts that never mend. In "Honky Tonk Waltz" and "You're Not Easy to Forget," lost love drives heartbroken women to the tavern, where they listen to country music and drink with other lovelorn souls, finding only temporal relief in brief encounters with men. The character in "I Don't Claim to Be an Angel" expresses doubt that her husband will ever trust her because of her (presumably) honky-tonk past and lies awake at night in her uncertainty. In a duet with Red Foley entitled "One by One," both husband and wife admit their mistakes and part ways knowing that they can never trust one another. Wells is most effective in the role of a strong woman who refuses to take a cheating husband back, most effectively depicted in "A Wedding Ring Ago" and "Cheatin's a Sin." The interplay of Paul Warren's old-time, breakdown style fiddling and Shot Jackson's Dobrolike crying steel guitar accentuate Wells's smooth yet searing vocals to create an unmistakably honky-tonk sound that simultaneously retains a rural feel. In breaking through the honky-tonk barricade with her tales of feminine valiance and vulnerability, Kitty Wells ensured that country music would not slight women's perspective on the transformation of postwar southern society.[31]

The success of Kitty Wells opened the door for a number of other female country music performers. In the honky-tonk field, Texas Ruby, Charline Arthur, and Jean Shepard emerged as other popular performers within the subgenre. Ruby Agnes Owens, better known as Texas Ruby, recorded several innovative and outspoken numbers from 1945 to 1947 that dealt candidly with infidelity and spousal recrimination, including "If You Don't Want Me, Set Me Free" and "You've Been Cheating on Me." In "Soldier's Return," she addresses the issue of relationships broken up by the war. Charline Arthur was country music's most irrepressible female artist in the late forties and early fifties. With a free-spirited stage presence and an attraction to brutally honest song material, Arthur never fit the mold of a female country singer or an *Opry* performer. She endured a rather stormy relationship with the Nashville establishment before returning to her native Texas in the mid-1950s. Before RCA-Victor dropped her, she recorded several historically important songs, including "Heartbreak Ahead," "The Good and the Bad," and "Kiss the Baby Goodnight." On the latter two numbers, her singing exudes a sexuality uncommon in contemporary country circles. The publication of Alfred Kinsey's *Sexual Behavior in the Human Female* (1953) affirmed the realistic quality of Arthur's repertoire. The report declared that half of all women surveyed had sex before marriage and that one-quarter of married women committed infidelity. Jean Shepard approached the issues of female sexuality and infidelity as well. In "Please Don't Divorce Me," she portrays a wife who storms out of the house after an argument with her husband; her "weakness" leads her into the arms of an old flame. In "Twice the Lovin', Half the Time," an unfulfilled woman turns to a stranger for sexual gratification without emotional baggage. "Don't Fall in Love with a Married Man" warns women of unfaithful married men's deceitfulness, and "Two Hoops and a Holler" accurately captures the double standard between men's and women's behavior in an outspoken call for female solidarity in the battle of the sexes.[32]

Shepard, Arthur, Owens, and Wells were vanguards in the struggle for women's recognition in postwar country music. Although their degree of commercial success varied, their very presence indicated the change that loomed on the country music horizon. Lyrically, they spoke out about the problems in women's lives and the male/female dichotomies that surfaced in the late forties and early fifties. Their honky-tonk instrumentation symbolized their determination to have their side of the story heard within the male domain.

While female performers shifted the focus of honky-tonk away from its myopic lyrical perspective, another group of singers based in the Southwest chiseled away at the subgenre's vocal rusticity. Ernest Tubb, Hank Williams, Kitty Wells, and the other honky-tonk realists effectively used their voices to convey the stark authenticity of their lyrics. The Southwest vocalists who emerged in the postwar period concentrated more on employing the human voice as an emotional transmitter. Both groups of performers embraced the treble sound of the old-time fiddle and electric steel guitar that permeated the urban establishments equipped with jukeboxes, but the Southwest vocalists used a wider variety of singing techniques, from whispering to wailing, that accentuated atmosphere over lyrical context. Their success contributed greatly to the ascension of Texas as the honky-tonk recording center in the decade after World War II.

As the area where western swing originated, the Southwest possessed a thriving music scene even before World War II. After the Texas swing bands moved west, honky-tonk emerged as the primary musical export of the state. In cities, such as Houston and Dallas, western swing and honky-tonk acts enjoyed a peaceful coexistence, as there was enough interest in both to fill both dance halls and honky-tonks. As records gained in popularity after the war, many of these performers strove to get contracts with major labels. Unfortunately, the majors continued to focus their efforts on established performers, leaving many acts dependent on club appearances for their income. Invariably, independent labels and studios arose that sought out popular regional performers. These entrepreneurial operations concentrated on local preferences and operated on a grassroots level, similar in organization to Jim Stanton's Rich-R-Tone operation. In Houston, Bill Quinn's Gold Star label emerged as the first semisuccessful independent in the Southwest when it released Harry Choates's "Jole Blon" in 1946. Another entrepreneur, Jim Beck, also recognized the lack of supply to meet demand, and set up a recording studio in Dallas. Through his association with KRLD (as an announcer), he developed an awareness of the popularity of country music acts on the *Big D Jamboree* and began gearing his recording efforts in this direction. On the strength of his demo pressings and recordings for such independents as Bullet in Nashville and Cincinnati's King label, Beck soon developed a relationship with the majors as well. As sales slumped in its country music division, Columbia grew particularly interested in Beck's recordings in the early fifties. Don Law, in the time before as well as after he stepped up as director of Columbia's country division following Art Satherley's retirement in the spring of 1952, worked closely with Beck in an effort to secure much-needed new talent for the label. Through his association with Beck and with the help of Troy Martin, Law signed Ray Price and Lefty Frizzell, among others. In Frizzell, Beck and Law found honky-tonk's next superstar and the most notable of the southwestern vocalists.[33]

Lefty Frizzell rivals Hank Williams for the distinction of country music's most influential male singer of the modernization period. Certainly, no country singer ever used his vocal abilities to greater effect. Frizzell experimented with all types of vocal inflections and phrasing, slurring words and bending notes to give new meanings to familiar diction. He could turn the simplest lyrics into complex expressions with a curve of his voice or a slant in his phrasing. The directness of his lyrics only intensified the subtle power of his performances, instantaneously forging a bond with listeners drawn to his amicable voice. Merle Haggard describes the immediate effect of his performances: "He delivered every line in a song like Henry Fonda . . . absolutely believable. . . . Every breath was authentic." Frizzell particularly excelled on mid-tempo numbers and ballads that left plenty of room for improvisation, but he could deliver up-tempo novelty numbers with equal effectiveness. By adapting a soft singing style to the honky-tonk sound, he became the consummate singer to two generations of young performers from George Jones and Merle Haggard to George Strait and Randy Travis. Frizzell revolutionized honky-tonk singing and in the process helped it acquire more widespread acceptance and popularity.[34]

The son of an itinerant oil field worker, William Orville Frizzell (1928–75) grew up in a succession of oil boomtowns in the Southwest. As a youngster, he listened to the *Grand Ole Opry* and, if radio waves permitted, the Texas Playboys on KVOO,

Tulsa. Like so many other youngsters in the area, he idolized Jimmie Rodgers, and he decided quite early in life that he wanted to follow in the Singing Brakeman's footsteps: "I knew when I was twelve years old what I was gonna do. I was gonna sing. Jimmie Rodgers, absolutely, just his voice, the guitar, and the yodel shaped my part in life." Shortly after his self-revelation, Frizzell began appearing on radio, playing Jimmie Rodgers and oft-requested Ernest Tubb tunes, and performing at dances. In the mid-forties, he entered the honky-tonk circuit, playing a number of Southwest clubs before returning to Texas in 1948. After a brief stint in the oil fields, he made an unsuccessful attempt at acquiring a spot on the *Louisiana Hayride*. Despite the disappointment, Frizzell persevered, fine-tuning his singing style and adopting honky-tonk instrumentation. In early 1950, he traveled to Dallas for a prearranged meeting with Jim Beck, who recorded a Frizzell demo of a song called "If You've Got the Money, I've Got the Time" that drew the attention of Don Law. Signing with Columbia in June, Frizzell sold half a million copies of his re-recorded version of the demo in the span of two months. In December, he made his first *Opry* appearance, and in early 1951 he commenced a year of tremendously successful touring, including a brief pairing with Hank Williams. As it turns out, 1951 marked the year that Lefty Frizzell truly reigned as country music's king; he spent nearly six months at the number one position on the *Billboard* charts with three different singles. Frizzell's whirlwind of success continued into 1952 before coming to an abrupt halt mid-year when he and his manager, Jack Starnes, parted ways. Near the end of the year, he quit the *Opry* and relocated to California, where he became a popular performer on Los Angeles's *Town Hall Party*. Like so many other honky-tonk singers, Frizzell suffered a stall in his success during the heyday of rock and roll, but he managed to rebuild his career in the sixties and early seventies before succumbing to a heart attack in 1975. With their accolades and tributes, Willie Nelson and Merle Haggard revitalized Frizzell's forgotten legacy soon thereafter, leading to his posthumous induction into the Country Music Hall of Fame in 1982.[35]

Lefty Frizzell established his musical and vocal style at the outset of his recording career, in July 1950, when he recorded "If You've Got the Money, I've Got the Time" and "I Love You Mostly," among others. The tinkling piano of Madge Suttee placed Frizzell's sound in the honky-tonk vein, and the musical effect was duplicated by succeeding pianists. Vocally, Frizzell introduced his innovative approach, most noticeably on "I Love You a Thousand Ways," a plaintive ballad that demonstrated his gifted songwriting abilities as well. The playful "Shine Shave Shower" and the subsequent "Give Me More, More, More (of Your Kisses)" and "I'm an Old, Old Man (Tryin' to Live While I Can)," meanwhile, revealed

Frizzell's humorous side. Nearly one-third of Frizzell's repertoire before 1955 consisted of happy love songs, most of them ballads. On slower tunes, Frizzell used his voice to the greatest effect, particularly on "I Want to Be with You Always" and "Forever (and Always)." As a songwriter, he proved equally adept at sentimental pieces and songs about failed relationships. "Look What Thoughts Will Do" is a fine example of how he blends clever phrasing with vocal flexibility. Like Tommy Duncan, Frizzell built on his affection for Jimmie Rodgers's singing style, adapting it to his voice to make it his own. Two Rodgers covers, "Travellin' Blues" and "My Rough and Rowdy Ways," illustrate the point. As the fifties progressed, Frizzell augmented his honky-tonk piano–old-time fiddle–steel guitar sound with harmonica, drums, and mandolin, with mixed results. Such musical embellishments detracted a bit from the intimacy of Frizzell's compelling vocal presence. Through it all, however, Frizzell's voice shone through, weaving its way around the musical backdrop straight to the audience. Up to and including his last recordings in the seventies, Lefty Frizzell never lost the ability to entrance listeners with his vocal ambience.

Hank Locklin is another southwestern performer whose distinctive vocal style became the centerpiece of his recordings. The native of McLellan, Florida, began his radio career in Pensacola around the age of twenty. During the war, he moved to Mobile and began touring as lead guitarist with a group on the Alabama-Florida coast. In the fall of 1946, the band relocated to Shreveport, where Locklin stepped up as one of the group's vocalists. Within two years, he and his band, the Rocky Mountain Boys, were in Houston on radio and playing in the city's thriving dance halls. While there, the group made its first recordings for the local Gold Star label. Soon thereafter, the band broke up, and Locklin moved to Dallas, where he teamed with Bill Callahan for a tour of north Texas. Locklin's recording career did not begin in earnest until he returned to Houston in 1949 and signed with the Four-Star label. On the strength of several regional hits, he began to attract the attention of Nashville executives and the *Grand Ole Opry*, which he appeared on in late 1953. He continued to reside in Houston in the mid-fifties, however, commuting to Dallas for his regular performances on KRLD's *Big D Jamboree* before finally joining the *Opry* in 1960.[36]

Locklin's legacy to country music revolves around his mellifluous vocal style and his aptitude at writing heartfelt ballads. Before he began recording in Nashville near the start of 1952, he used a variety of Houston session musicians for instrumental backing on his Gold Star and Four-Star releases. These deft musicians generally provided sparse instrumentation to Locklin's commanding tenor. After a number of tentative vocal performances on his first recordings, Locklin began singing with more assertiveness on "The Same Sweet Girl," a lovely ballad from 1949 that also debuted his penchant for writing ballads that celebrated marital fidelity. "The Same Sweet Girl" and another self-penned love song, entitled "Send Me the Pillow You Dream On," established Locklin as a popular regional performer in the Southwest. He went on to record a number of other similarly constructed songs, including the poignant "Our Love Will Show the Way" and the sanguine "The Place and the Time." Locklin possessed a pleasant voice, full-bodied but not piercing, with just enough country twang to appeal to honky-tonk crowds. When Locklin stretches his singing powers to the limit, as he does on "No One Is Sweeter Than You" and "Let Me Be the One," he also pulls listeners in with his vocal adventurousness. Locklin was the ultimate honky-tonk crooner, with an exuberant, pop-tinged vocal style that convincingly translated the dreamy imagery of his lyrics without appearing saccharine. It comes as no surprise that he survived the rock and roll massacre and emerged as a popular mainstream country singer in the 1960s.[37]

Of all honky-tonk singers of the postwar period, none possessed a more robust voice than Webb Pierce. Regardless of subject matter, Pierce brazenly sang full force in an effort to fill the clamorous nightspots with his powerful voice. Musically and vocally, he unabashedly embraced the unvarnished roots of honky-tonk at a time when the subgenre was beginning to soften its rough edges. Lyrically, he masterfully mixed brutal honesty with portraits of his characters' vulnerability to capture the nature of postwar concerns about fidelity and trust. The combination of his sturdy voice, musical approach, and lyrical forthrightness ensured his broad popularity among country music listeners and contributed greatly to honky-tonk's domination of the charts in the early 1950s.

As a youngster growing up in Monroe, Louisiana, Webb Pierce developed an interest in playing country music from listening to Jimmie Rodgers records and watching Gene Autry films. As a teenager, he started performing on local radio before joining the army in World War II. After his discharge, he and his wife traveled to Shreveport in 1944, where they began performing together on Hal Burns's *Hillbilly Hit Parade.* For several years, Pierce maintained a day job and remained a part-time performer, but his prospects improved when he signed with Four-Star Records in 1949. The following year, he secured a spot on the popular *Louisiana Hayride,* which offered him much-needed exposure. In 1951, he signed with Decca and by the end of the summer had his first number one hit with "Wondering." In late 1952, he moved to Nashville and joined the *Grand Ole Opry.* Currying the favor of disc jockeys and jukebox operators and making himself accessible to fans, Pierce emerged as the most successful honky-tonk performer after Hank Williams's death, spending twenty weeks at the number one position in 1953 and producing four of the top ten country singles of 1954, a feat heretofore surpassed only by Eddy Arnold in 1948. The rise of rockabilly and his estranged relationship with the *Opry* tempered his success in the mid- to late fifties, yet he continued to produce a number of top-ten singles well into the 1960s.[38]

Pierce's first recordings for Four-Star reveal an artist in search of a distinctive sound. Backed primarily by just a steel guitar and his own rhythm acoustic, Pierce offers a couple of sturdy vocal performances on "New Panhandle Rag" and "Georgia Rag" and dabbles in crooning on "I've Loved You Forever It Seems." On several numbers recorded for the Pacemaker label in 1950 and early 1951, Pierce builds on his initial sound by adding a heavier beat (provided by an upright bass and "sock" electric guitar), most noticeably on "In the Jailhouse Now." He also begins to reveal his vocal assuredness on "The Last Waltz" when he takes his tenor into the high register. The Webb Pierce sound fully coalesced when he switched to Decca; his voice rings out above a band that augmented the Pacemaker sound with a fiddler, pianist, and drummer. "Drifting Texas Sand" established the precedent of Pierce altering old songs to fit the honky-tonk mold, more often than not with successful results. His version of an old Cajun tune, "Wondering," established his presence on the country music scene, and twelve other number ones followed in the 1950s. A searing fiddle (over time played in unison with the electric lead guitar), tinkling piano, and accentuating steel guitar squarely placed Pierce's songs in the honky-tonk mode, as did his piercing vocals. On "Slowly," Bud Isaac's revolutionary use of pedal steel guitar, which altered the pitch of the instrument and produced innovative chords, set a new industry standard in the mid-fifties.[39]

Lyrically, Pierce concentrated on failed relationships, and his sad stories were often set to up-tempo musical background, as in "It's Been So Long," "You Can't Be True," and "Even Tho'." Many of his songs broached the dicey subject matter of adulterous relationships and failed marriages. In "I Haven't Got the Heart," Pierce spins the tale of a husband trapped in a loveless marriage; in "That Heart Belongs to Me," a husband pleads with his wife to ignore rumors of his infidelity and resigns himself to fighting for her. "Don't Throw Your Life Away" explores a couple's struggle to overcome a woman's past indiscretions, with the man trying to convince her to look more toward the future. In one of country music's most unique love songs, "Back Street Affair," a man married to an adulterous wife finds love with another woman but has to struggle with the shame he has brought on her in deceiving her about his marital status. Such unspeakable subject matter undoubtedly raised the eyebrows of many listeners, but did not deter Pierce, who explains the criteria of his song selection and force behind his strident singing style: "It's the sincerity of the song, but yet you must perform it right by putting your heart and soul into it. . . . It tells a story about life, the way it is. I always tried to sing about something that all people have done, but never talked about, but when they heard the song, that became an emotional outlet. They would think, 'that is my life.'" This philosophy led Pierce to the center of controversy when he released "There Stands the Glass" (1953), a song about finding solace in alcohol. Some radio stations banned it; nevertheless, it reached number one. Pierce did not hesitate in his decision to record it: "Both Jim Denny of the *Grand Ole Opry* and Fred Rose said recording it would ruin my career because it tolerated drinking. I went ahead and put it out anyway, and [it became] one of my most requested songs." Pierce's daring attracted fans and helped him survive the rock and roll onslaught. Unlike many other singers, he resisted full embracement of newer sounds: "I just never would want to be a rock and roll singer. I don't have the heart for it. My heart is with country music." No one could ever confuse Webb Pierce with a rock singer; his voice was pure country, and the lyrical subject matter he chose evidenced his appreciation of country music listeners' concerns. Disconcerting to some, Pierce's vocal and music style endeared him to the honky-tonk audience that continually pushed him to the top of the charts.[40]

As the distinctions between the honky-tonk realists and Southwest vocalists indicate, different schools within the subgenre approached their music in various ways, emphasizing vocals, lyrics, or a distinct musical ambiance. One common factor united nearly all of them: a deep appreciation of Jimmie Rodgers. Lefty Frizzell fondly recalls listening to the Singing Brakeman in his youth: "I loved his voice and I'd yodel and harmonize with him and it gave me peace. I can truly say he was the biggest influence on my life." Webb Pierce enjoyed listening to his mother's Jimmie Rodgers records as a youth, with "In the Jailhouse Now" being his particular favorite. While many viewed Pierce's 1954 version of the song as sacrilege, Pierce himself probably intended it as a salutary gesture. Ernest Tubb remembers Hank Williams as a Rodgers fan as well. No honky-tonk performer publicly esteemed Rodgers more than Tubb himself, who frequently reminded the country music industry and audience of the singer's legacy. In the notes accompanying an album reissue of Rodgers recordings, Tubb wrote: "The great contributions this man made to what we now refer to as country and western music has directly or indirectly affected more performers in this field than anyone I can think of. Jimmie Rodgers had more impact than any other single individual, past or present." Despite his legion of fans and lingering spirit, Rodgers was on his way to becoming a faint memory by World War II; RCA-Victor listed only one of his records in its 1941 catalog. A reissue of his records later in the decade produced only moderate sales. By the early fifties, Rodgers was largely forgotten, but the honky-tonkers and several other country music artists moved to revitalize the late singer's legend.[41]

Sometime around 1951, Ernest Tubb raised the idea of a Jimmie Rodgers Memorial to another Rodgers admirer, Hank Snow. Working with city officials and the chamber of commerce of Meridian, Mississippi (Rodgers's birthplace), Snow and Tubb arranged a daylong celebration marking the twentieth anniversary of Rodgers's death. Shortly after the festival began, Justin Tubb and Jimmie Rodgers Snow, sons of the event's organizers, unveiled a white marble statue of the Singing Brakeman, and short speeches were made by such notable guests as Jimmie Davis, Governor Frank Clement (of Tennessee), and Rodgers's widow. In the evening, the celebration moved to a local junior college stadium, where at least twenty thousand gathered for what one reporter described as "the greatest assemblage of hillbilly talent ever seen in one show." The following list represents only a fraction of the performers who participated in what Hank Snow described as "one big giant jam session": Roy Acuff, Hank Snow, Little Jimmy Dickens, Carl Smith, Webb Pierce, Bill Monroe, the Carter Family, Minnie Pearl, Charlie Monroe, Billy Walker, Jim Reeves, Tommy Duncan, Jimmie Davis, Slim Willet, and the Texas Troubadours. In hindsight, the Jimmie Rodgers celebration stands as one of the most significant moments in country music's history. In addition to representing Rodgers's redemption and symbolizing country music's collective spirit, it validated the genre's presence in southern society by demonstrating its respectability and reverence for tradition. On May 26, 1953, "hillbilly" music became "country" music in the eyes of its beholders.[42]

The coordinated effort to change the name of the music predominantly produced by white rural southerners actually began early in the postwar period, when its nationalization stimulated the movement to replace *hillbilly* with a less depreciative term. Some performers found it offensive; others simply viewed it as a contradiction of business principles, as Ted Daffan explains: "As a result of [the hillbilly] label, many people who would have liked the music would not buy it." Floyd Tillman makes a similar observation: "When it was 'hillbilly,' there would be people who'd look around to see if anybody was watching before they bought a hillbilly record." Ernest Tubb loathed the term, cautioning those who used it: "Smile when you call me a hillbilly." Hank Williams and others preferred the term "folk" music, a label affixed to the genre in the early forties by the trade papers.

Fred Rose, Williams's producer and manager, wrote an impassioned letter to *Billboard* in 1946 that vehemently defended "folklore" and chided its detractors: "We call it 'hillbilly' music, and sometimes we're ashamed to call it music. I think, if we took the time to check up on it, we would find that all the wrong and bad is in our conception of 'folklore,' not in 'folklore' itself." While Rose attacked the pejorative term from one angle, Ernest Tubb approached it from another, pointing out the folly of it to industry executives: "[Hillbilly] had kind of a mocking tone to it. . . . So I started telling the record companies, 'Don't let's call it "hillbilly,"' let's call it something else.' So I thought, 'why not "country,"' since we all come from the country?' After awhile, the name stuck." Eventually, Tubb and Decca's Dave Kapp agreed on the more elastic "country and western" tag, which encompassed some of the more pop-oriented acts, and *Billboard* adopted the phrase in its jukebox charts in June 1949.[43]

Ernest Tubb contributed to country music's respectability in other ways as well. In 1947, he led a troupe of *Grand Ole Opry* performers in a successful appearance at New York's Carnegie Hall. While the entourage's appearance was not the first of its kind at the prestigious theater, its success ensured that it would certainly not be the last. A *Billboard* reviewer commented that the show's $12,000 gross revealed three things: country music's drawing power, the loyalty of its audience, and its increasing profitability. In 1952, the opening of the Hayloft, an all-country nightclub in the heart of downtown Chicago, further illustrated country music's appeal in northern cities. The opening of Ernest Tubb's Record Shop in Nashville in 1947 established the precedent of country performers becoming record retailers in large urban areas. Soon thereafter, similar stores appeared in Los Angeles, Cincinnati, Washington, D.C., Dallas, Hollywood, Wheeling, Knoxville, New York, and Louisville, further making country music listeners' presence felt.[44]

In the South, politicians fell in line with country music's growing presence and popularity. In early 1953, Mississippi representative William Arthur Winstead sponsored a bill three months before the dedication of the Jimmie Rodgers Memorial to designate the date National Hillbilly Music Day. The following year he extended an open invitation to leading political figures to attend the second annual Jimmie Rodgers celebration. Unfortunately for country music fans and Rodgers's devotees, Adlai Stevenson took Winstead up on his offer, delivering a forty-five minute political speech that rained on the spirit of an already drizzly day. Another southern politician, Howard H. Baker of Tennessee, called on Congress to issue a joint resolution declaring June 30–July 5, 1954, National Hillbilly Homecoming Week; festivities were patterned on a regional country celebration in Maryville, Tennessee, and were to take place all over the nation.

Politicians realized that sponsorships and appearances at such country music gatherings not only garnered them votes, but also pumped money into local economies. [45]

By 1954, country music was a $70 million a year business, with most earnings ($40 million) coming from personal appearances east of the Mississippi. Big-name artists, such as Roy Acuff, earned from $1,500 to over $2,000 for concert appearances, while other major acts, such as Webb Pierce and Hank Snow, brought in between $1,000 and $1,500 for their services. As the country music audience expanded and the industry burgeoned after the war, the nature of the personal appearance changed dramatically. Promoters who booked country music acts at folk music parks in the early forties expanded their efforts to other venues, such as stadiums, drive-ins, and minor league baseball parks (when home teams were out of town), as well as indoor municipal auditoriums. On Sundays, country music artists played the folk music parks, usually for a flat performance fee, but during the week they concentrated on the other locales, either for a flat fee or a percentage of the proceeds. Folk park owners charged sixty cents to a dollar for admission and spent around $2,000 for performers. The Sunday shows ran all day and into the night, normally from 1:00 P.M. to midnight, with featured acts performing three half-hour segments. Because the touring season ran from Easter through October, it was not unusual for popular performers to make upwards of $20,000 from the Sunday shows alone. In the early fifties, many of these acts continued to book themselves, particularly at smaller billings, but professional promoters, radio station artists' service bureaus, record companies, and even disc jockeys generally placed artists in larger venues. Promoters Oscar Davis, Connie Gay, and Tom Parker scheduled their individual acts at indoor stadiums and municipal auditoriums for shows that ran approximately two hours and opened with local acts. In between, time was set aside for the selling of songbooks and commemorative items. Parker helped RCA-Victor organize its "Country Caravan," an entourage that included Eddy Arnold, Johnnie and Jack, Charline Arthur, and Chet Atkins and that played ten cities in a fifteen-day period. Fans could obtain tickets for the shows at retail record shops, and at a reduced price if they purchased an RCA-Victor recording by a country artist. Promoters often organized these group bookings, or package shows, on their own as well. Oscar Davis, for instance, promoted the Carnegie Hall concert in 1947. In the summer of 1951, 43,000 people jammed the Cotton Bowl in Dallas for a one-night show featuring Bill Monroe, Minnie Pearl, and a group of popular regional performers. An Ernest Tubb–Hank Williams–Minnie Pearl conglomeration at the Kansas City Auditorium grossed $17,000. In towns of over 100,000 people, where television use soared, promoters found it necessary to increase the number of big names in the package shows, from two to four, in order to draw people out of their homes. Country music promotion in the postwar period revolutionized the country music industry, accounting for well over half of its profits and helping transform it into big business.[46]

Under these conditions, performers without connections to promoters and large stations fell by the wayside. As Bill Bolick recalls, this put considerable pressure on prewar acts, such as the Blue Sky Boys, to fall in line with contemporary trends or perish: "Most groups had booking agents or managers, and were combining groups of at least three or four different acts for one date. We had seldom played with other acts or used more than three people. We were constantly harassed to use more modern material in our songs . . . most recording directors did not understand or appreciate old-time music. They simply let true, authentic folk music wither on the stalk." Many traditionally oriented acts continued to work on regionally popular barn dances, such as the *Renfro Valley* show, that discouraged the star system and instrumental modernization. They retained core listeners and continued to draw crowds to their tours, but their economic grosses paled in comparison to acts booked by big-name promoters and agencies. Large-wattage stations, such as WLW (Cincinnati) and WLS (Chicago), maintained promotional divisions to set up barn dance performers' tours, but were considerably less aggressive in their efforts than the WSM Artists' Service Bureau and hence lost many of their most popular performers to the *Grand Ole Opry*. Longtime WLS performer Bob Atcher describes the situation: "WSM was doing a tremendous job of keeping just the cream of their old talent and constantly turning over and looking for new faces, new names. . . . Then, on top of that, the star system was always practiced on the *Grand Ole Opry*, as against the family type thing [on WLS]." Atcher and several other performers left the *National Barn Dance* after the war, leaving only a handful of big-name draws. The program's inability to retain network affiliation after the war and the failure of a television version of the show symbolized WLS's fall from competitive status.[47]

Although the *National Barn Dance*'s attempted move to television signaled changing times, radio's popularity continued to soar on a national level in the late 1940s, with nearly 95 percent of all American homes reporting at least one receiver in 1950. In the South, the number jumped from 62 percent in 1940 to 91 percent in 1950. An increase in the number of stations (doubling between 1945 and 1950) accompanied the rise in radio sets. Of the approximately 2,000 stations broadcasting in 1950, 650 featured country music shows. Though television penetrated into larger markets, persons in rural areas continued to depend on radio for entertainment well into the 1950s. As a result, several of the regional barn dances that appeared in the 1930s and early 1940s continued to thrive in the late forties alongside several others that debuted in the postwar period, such as the *Big D Jamboree* (KRLD, Dallas) in 1945, the *Old Dominion Barn Dance* (WRVA, Richmond) in 1946, the *Hometown Jamboree* (KXLA, Los Angeles) in 1947, the *Virginia Barn Dance* (WDVA, Danville) in 1949, and the *Saturday Night Shindig* (WFAA, Dallas) in 1952. Most maintained an affiliation with national networks, but only one, the *Louisiana Hayride,* came to rival the *Grand Ole Opry* in stature. [48]

W. K. Henderson's Shreveport, Louisiana, station broadcast country music as early as 1925. In the mid-thirties, it launched a weekly country variety show that featured the Shelton Brothers that continued on as *The Saturday Night Round-Up* in the early 1940s. Discontinued during the war, the show re-emerged as the *Louisiana Hayride* in the postwar period. Essentially the collective brainchild of KWKH's Henry Clay, Horace Logan, Dean Upson, and the Bailes Brothers, the *Hayride* premiered in early April 1948 as a three-hour program broadcast from the 3,800-seat capacity Municipal Auditorium. Attracting such up-and-coming performers as Hank Williams, Webb Pierce, Johnnie and Jack, and others, the show gained notoriety as the "Cradle of the Stars." As the appellation suggests, most performers left the program after gaining enough popularity—usually through a hit record—to transfer to the *Grand Ole Opry.* [49]

Louisiana Hayride performers left the show to join the *Grand Ole Opry* because the latter offered three things that the former did not: network affiliation, star status, and an aggressive promotion and booking agency. After its network hookup in 1939, the *Grand Ole Opry* soon became a nationally popular show. By August 1947, it ranked seventh in popularity among all shows that featured some type of music. By 1949, the program was providing WSM with two-thirds of its advertising revenue. Not surprisingly, both station owners and the show's network sponsor, R. J. Reynolds, developed a keen interest in the program after the war. According to David Cobb, a popular announcer at WSM since the mid-thirties, R. J. Reynolds and the Esty agency in New York had an enormous impact on station policy, even influencing the decision to hire Red Foley as a replacement for Roy Acuff in 1946: "I think the *Opry* was just a bit too country for the agency people up in New York. . . . Red Foley, his style was not typical *Opry* style. He was . . . from the Chicago scene, and his songs . . . came closer to the pop ballad thing." Accordingly, when Acuff returned to WSM in 1947, Foley retained his position as host of the network portion of the program. Jimmy Wakely tellingly terms Foley "the big changer of the *Grand Ole Opry*"; his hiring not only brought an aura of sophistication to the show but also demonstrated the station management's resolve to build a stalwart cast of barn-dance all-stars.[50]

Ironically, the displaced Roy Acuff deserves the credit for turning the *Grand Ole Opry* into a star-centered program in the first place. Before his ascension, the show, like so many other barn dances, frowned on individual showmanship that detracted from its folk and amateurish feel. Acuff's success undoubtedly opened the minds of the show's sponsors and hastened the program's emphatic shift toward star-stalking during and after the war. When the *Louisiana Hayride* appeared, it adopted a different format from the *Opry*'s, de-emphasizing featured acts and presenting instead a multitude of performers. The *Hayride* imposed time constraints on its acts and maintained a large roster of singers in an effort to breed a competitive atmosphere, thus forestalling complacency and keeping the program fresh. In this, the management underestimated the powerful attraction of star status and hence lost popular performers who recognized the financial opportunities that the *Opry* offered.[51]

Broadcast with 50,000 watts, the *Louisiana Hayride* certainly provided plenty of national exposure and even some star status, but in the late 1940s, the name of the game was personal appearance revenues. Country music tours grossed substantial profits, and the key to success centered on promotion. KWKH did not maintain a structured booking agency, and therefore failed to systematically promote the appearances of *Hayride* performers. WSM, on the other hand, consistently demonstrated its commitment to this pursuit, beginning in 1934 with Harry Stone's establishment of the Artists' Service Bureau and continuing on in the late 1940s and early 1950s under the principal direction of James R. "Jim" Denny, who increased *Grand Ole Opry* tour billings 50 percent within four years after assuming the position of bureau manager. Denny helped organize package shows, booked *Opry* members into large-capacity venues, and set up a system of civic and business contacts to ensure *Opry* members (and the bureau) a steady flow of income. A 1953 list of performers promoted by the bureau reads like a who's who of country performers, including, among others, Roy Acuff, Bill Monroe, Ernest Tubb, Hank Snow, George Morgan, Carl Smith, Moon Mullican, Ray Price, Webb Pierce, George Jones, and Red Foley. Artists on *Grand Ole Opry* tours in 1954 accounted for more than one-half of all country music records sold that year. Not surprisingly, many young performers in the late forties and early fifties, like Charlie Louvin, viewed establishment in Nashville as the key to their success: "We felt that Nashville was where it was at. If you weren't in Nashville, you were just almost next to being out of the business." With its promotional tentacles, network exposure, and status, the *Grand Ole Opry* attracted acts that otherwise would have balked at the nominal salary they received for performing on the program. Likewise, *Opry* members waived potentially lucrative Saturday night booking to retain their affiliation with the show. As Ernest Tubb points out, "You had to be back in Nashville every Saturday night, come hell or high water, for the *Opry*." With shrewd business sense, Jim Denny and WSM management helped institutionalize the *Grand Ole Opry* and in the process contributed to the establishment of Nashville as the hub of country music.[52]

Country music's emergence as big business and its move toward respectability and acceptance inevitably led to an effort to sanitize the honky-tonk sound. On jukeboxes across the South, honky-tonk reigned in the early fifties, as Ernest Tubb, Hank Williams, and Kitty Wells continued to rack up hits alongside the somewhat less serrated southwestern vocalists. In the late forties and early fifties, the honky-tonk subgenre grew steadily in popularity, eventually dethroning country pop from its wartime and postwar dominance. Concurrently, country music expanded ever further beyond its prewar working-class, rural, southern base. Many younger country music listeners and newcomers to the genre found honky-tonk's stark lyrical realism and nasal, shrilling singing styles unbecoming even as they readily accepted its blend of old-time fiddling and scathing steel guitar. As a result, primal honky-tonk (Ernest Tubb, Floyd Tillman, Kitty Wells, and Hank Williams) and transitional honky-tonk (Lefty Frizzell, Webb Pierce, Ray Price, and Hank Locklin) enjoyed popularity side by side with a more toned-down approach to the subgenre. Soft honky-tonk emerged in the early 1950s as an alternative to the sound born in the taverns of the South. Members of this group sang with less emotional intensity and delved less frequently into issues of infidelity and internal suffering. Not surprisingly, this more sophisticated approach to honky-tonk took shape in Nashville, a city ever-increasingly populated by industry movers and shakers with a pulse on country music's commercial possibilities and designs on its cosmopolitan future. In Carl Smith and Faron Young, country music found two talented candidates for this new honky-tonk style.

Born in 1927, Carl Smith grew up in Union County, Tennessee, north of Knoxville. As a youngster, he enjoyed listening to Roy Acuff, Bill Monroe, and Ernest Tubb on the *Grand Ole Opry*. After learning to play the guitar, he began performing at several informal local events before journeying to Knoxville to start on radio in 1944. After a stint with the United States Navy, he returned to east Tennessee in 1946 to begin his career in earnest. Over the next three years, he worked at several radio stations in the region, performing on daily shows and scheduling personal appearances. Eventually, he returned to Knoxville radio, where a demo he recorded for a fellow band member attracted the attention of

Troy Martin, who brought up the young singer's name to Columbia's Don Law and the *Opry*'s Jack Stapp. After some initial misgivings, Stapp agreed to give Smith a spot on the *Grand Ole Opry,* and soon thereafter, in the spring of 1950, Law signed the young singer to a contract. Smith benefited from the tutelage of Ernest Tubb and others, and his recording career and radio popularity soon blossomed, with his first top-ten hit, "Let's Live a Little," and first number one song, "Let Old Mother Nature Have Her Way," both coming in 1951. Between mid-1951 and late 1954, he scored twenty top-ten hits en route to becoming one of the most popular country music performers of the early 1950s.[53]

Carl Smith combined strong, confident vocals with sparse instrumentation to create an exuberant honky-tonk sound that defied the subgenre's rueful roots. Between 1950 and 1955, he did not use a fiddler on his recordings, opting instead to emphasize steel guitar and lead guitar parts to complement the emotions of a lyric. As time wore on, he added drums to create a heavier beat that added even more spirit to his up-tempo repertoire. Many of his mid-fifties pieces bore more than a passing resemblance to rockabilly, a country and rhythm and blues hybrid, but Smith never became a rocker. He possessed neither the demeanor nor the inclination to do so. The secret of Smith's success lay in the restrained passion he and his band brought to their recordings, always teetering on exultation but never letting loose like a rockabilly performer. Somewhere between a crooner's glibness and a blues singer's swagger, Smith's vocals epitomized just the right mixture of confidence and self-composure to carry his predominantly lighthearted repertoire to the brink of honky-tonk's parameters without overstepping its bounds. As the "Gentleman Honky-tonker," Carl Smith respected the honky-tonk tradition even as he worked to modernize the subgenre.

Smith's first recordings, from 1950, reveal the characteristics of his early fifties output. "Guilty Conscience" exhibits the primacy of his vocals, "Washin' My Dreams in Tears" demonstrates his preference for up-tempo material, and "I Betcha My Heart I Love You" sets the optimistic tone of his song selection. Over 45 percent of the songs he recorded before 1955 center around fulfilled love and lighthearted lyrical material. Such songs as "(When You Feel Like You're in Love) Don't Just Stand There" and "It's a Lovely, Lovely World" brim with positivism, while "Trademark" and "Just Wait Till I Get You Alone" flow along with an assurance that defies honky-tonk's melancholy nature. Smith generally avoids such scabrous subject matter as infidelity; when he does address the topic, as in "This Orchid Means Goodbye," the character ends up breaking off the extramarital relationship and returning to his wife. While other honky-tonkers invite their sweethearts out to the working-class dance halls and taverns, Smith dresses in a suit and tie to take his wife out dancing ("Let's Live a Little"). Smith excels at up-beat pieces, such as "Let Old Mother Nature Have Her Way," but he could also sing laments, such as "If Teardrops Were Pennies" and "Are You Teasing Me?" with equal cogency. The addition of steel guitarist Johnny Sibert, lead guitarist Sammy Pruett, and drummer Farris Coursey lends considerable punch to such lively songs as "Back up Buddy" and "Go Boy Go." The musical character of the latter number illustrates a point Smith makes about his group's mid-fifties approach: "It was between rock 'n' roll and western swing, really. We knew what we were doin'. I done all things during that period. I used to do 'Shake, Rattle, and Roll' on the stage and songs like that before Elvis started really clickin'. The audiences got a kick out of it—It was pretty rockin'." *Grand Ole Opry* management did not object to Sibert's Dobrolike electric steel guitar playing, but as Smith recalls, his use of drums proved more controversial: "Ernest [Tubb] told me I'd go broke, and Acuff wanted to get me fired off the *Opry*. It caused a lot of confusion, and I never did get 'em on the *Opry*." Smith eventually left the program in 1956 to join Red Foley's *Ozark Jubilee*. He continued to perform regularly on a variety of shows before retiring to his ranch in 1977. Unjustly overlooked by many country music historians, Carl Smith deserves recognition for his innovations to the honky-tonk genre and his foresight into country music's future.[54]

Like Carl Smith, Faron Young (1932–96) brought a great deal of lyrical positivism to honky-tonk, and just as some of Smith's songs heralded rock, many of Young's records served as precursors to the pop flavorings of the Nashville Sound. The Shreveport native's first musical influences were Nat King Cole and Frank Sinatra, and when he started singing in public as a teenager, he sang such popular numbers as "The Object of My Affection" and "Stay as Sweet as You Are." Young developed an interest in country music after seeing and hearing Hank Williams: "Well somebody took me to the *Louisiana Hayride* one night to see Hank. And I saw him encore nine times. And I said, well, he gets a little more applause than these pop songs I've been singing and I just got to listening to it and one thing led to another." After attending college for a year, Young decided to pursue a career in country music and, around early 1951, began appearing with Webb Pierce on Shreveport radio. Pierce helped Young obtain his first recording contract and secured him a spot on the *Louisiana Hayride*. His performances on KWKH brought him to the attention of Capitol's Ken Nelson, who signed the young singer to Capitol in early 1952. Young made his first appearances on the *Grand Ole Opry* in mid-1952 and soon relocated to Nashville. A month after recording two songs destined for the *Billboard* top ten, Young was drafted into the army, in November 1952. His singing and musical talent landed him on a stateside radio recruiting program, *Town and Country Time,* that gave him considerable exposure during his two years in the service. The army also allowed him to make occasional *Opry* appearances and to record. After leaving the army, he returned to Nashville and the *Grand Ole Opry,* enjoying a prosperous two years before rock and roll began taking its toll on the honky-tonker's career. Young made the transition well to country pop and the Nashville Sound, however, and went on to become quite successful in the sixties and early seventies, scoring twenty-three top-ten hits in the period.[55]

Young's first recordings, which were released on Gotham, show him searching for a style and sound. Combining pop-tinged vocals and southwestern instrumentation, "Just Imagination" and an early version of "Have I Waited Too Long?" indicate Young's vocal strengths and point to the musical direction that he took after signing with Capitol. Both "Tattle Tale Tears" and "Have I Waited Too Long?," from his first Capitol session, focus on Young's considerable vocal prowess, showcasing his ability to swoon like a crooner while still retaining a country edge in his singing. "I Knew You When," from May 1952, demonstrates Young's pop background; he almost sounds like a country Bing Crosby. In "Going Steady" and "I Can't Wait (for the Sun to Go Down)," Young begins singing like Hank Williams and moves to more forthright honky-tonk instrumentation. Both songs are positive love songs about courtship, and both reached the top ten. Lyrically, Young found his niche in songs of this type, with a voice perfectly suited for the optimism in "Just Married" and "That's What I'd Do for You." Gradually, Young stepped out of Hank Williams's shadow to create a unique blend of honky-tonk instrumentation and full-bodied, distinctively pop-tinged singing. In outstanding interpretations of two Tommy Collins songs, "If That's the Fashion" and "If You Ain't Lovin', You Ain't Livin'," Young sings with an engrossing assuredness. Over the next two years, he successfully recorded everything from honky-tonk struts ("Live Fast, Love Hard, Die Young") to country pop ballads ("Sweet Dreams"). His rendition of "In the Chapel in the Moonlight," from mid-1954, serves as a precursor to the Nashville Sound and reveals why his transition to the new country music style proved so smooth. Possessing one of honky-tonk's most versatile voices, Faron Young helped keep the subgenre alive by choosing and writing songs that appealed to younger listeners as well as the established audience.[56]

The confident optimism evident in the recordings of Faron Young and Carl Smith represents a shift in the lyrical focus and vocal styles of honky-tonk performers. In the early postwar period, the hard-edged approach of the honky-tonk realists dominated the subgenre before the transitional southwestern vocalists emerged in the early 1950s with their moderate alternative. Smith and Young took the process one step further, lyrically moving further away from the bleakness of the realists and musically adopting more up-tempo rhythms and pop stylings. The entire subgenre was a blend of intraregional distinctions, but the soft honky-tonk style indicated the merger of country and American popular music.

The cross-pollination of the two musical genres had roots in World War II, when Americans discovered the music of the Texas triumvirate and when country began adopting pop music instrumentation. After the war, American popular music endured an identity crisis precipitated by the demise of the big bands and the archaic nature of Tin Pan Alley triteness in the atomic age. Between 1947 and 1949, the burgeoning record industry suddenly took a downturn, and sales fell 17 percent in 1948 and another 8 percent in 1949. New York songwriters could still write catchy tunes, but as historian Lawrence Levine points out, they seemed incapable of grasping the postwar mood: "In a period when divorce rates were rising, family stability declining, pastoral lifestyles disappearing, bureaucratic impersonality and organization increasing, popular music constructed a universe in which adolescent innocence and naivete became a permanent state." While the idyllic vision of pop music proved incongruous with contemporary realities, the realism of the honky-tonkers seemed to capture the postwar situation perfectly. In contrast to Tin Pan Alley tunesmiths who resided in New York, honky-tonk artists lived in the trenches and were more attuned to the impact of sociocultural developments and the tribulations of modern life. As Ted Daffan explains, country music in general seemed more authentic and accessible to American listeners and hence began to draw their attention: "Pop music was very flowery and sentimental. And a lot of the words and phrases were not natural, were more poetic than natural everyday talk. And country writers, me included, would tell it in straight, simple language, like it was. And this appealed to a great number of people because it sounded much more real." Just as country performers in the early forties appealed to Americans' sense of patriotism and wartime sentimentalities, the lyrics of the honky-tonkers spoke to their postwar concerns.[57]

In their search for a way to reverse the downward spiral of record sales in the late forties, executives in the pop music industry soon discovered the appeal of country music lyrics. Knowing that the American public would balk at the harsh instrumentation of the honky-tonkers, they opted to have popular singers record versions of country songs. Several country music songwriters, Floyd Tillman for example, had their songs reach the pop charts in revamped versions in the late 1940s, but Hank Williams emerged as the pop industry's favorite source of alternative material. The deluge began in 1951, when Tony Bennett reluctantly recorded "Cold Cold Heart" at the behest of Columbia Records' Mitch Miller. After the success of several other Hank Williams covers, *Billboard* reported in August 1952 that "pop a and r men will be anxiously awaiting the release of . . . new Williams' disks." As the polisher of many of Hank Williams's songs, producer and publisher Fred Rose deserves a great deal of credit for this development as well. Although country music did not exactly save the pop music industry, it did give it a much-needed boost in the late forties and early fifties, with honky-tonk songwriters leading the way.[58]

Honky-tonk injected a dose of realism into popular music, and it made a considerable impact on country music's postwar development as well. Like the postwar traditionalists, the honky-tonkers reasserted country music's southern identity at a time when nationalization downplayed it. With sawing fiddles, weeping steel guitar, and plaintive singing, honky-tonk merged southwestern instrumentation with southeastern vocal styles to create a sound for the country music audience's new urban environment. Lyrically, honky-tonk in its early years stressed angst and alienation to become the sound of southern working-class misfits struggling to adjust to the radical lifestyle changes in a new sociocultural environment. While the postwar traditionalists emphasized fortitude through religious and traditional values, early honky-tonkers indirectly suggested that listeners find strength in the recognition of their collective plight. With honky-tonk songs crossing over to the pop charts and country music gaining legitimacy as both a musical genre and a prosperous business, however, industry executives began to view the rough-hewn sounds of the honky-tonk realists as obsolete. The emergence of the southwestern vocalists and soft honky-tonk of Carl Smith and Faron Young rectified the situation by offering a more positive outlook with a less abrasive sound. As a result of these developments, honky-tonk became less discernible as a subgenre, a process accelerated by widespread adaptation of honky-tonk instrumentation throughout the genre.

As its early fifties heyday indicates, honky-tonk, in its new, modified form, dominated country music in the period preceding the rock explosion. When the youth movement struck, honky-tonk, as the music of the urban hillbilly, suddenly became expendable. Honky-tonk performers' cowboy attire turned into an eyesore, and their instrumentation seemed antiquated. Floyd Tillman terms the years 1955–60 the "Hillbilly Depression" because of the disappearance of steel guitars and fiddles from country music during the period. Badly wounded by the onset of the rockabilly, honky-tonk reemerged in the sixties as the Bakersfield Sound, in the seventies as the Outlaw movement, and in the eighties as the music of the New Traditionalists. What began as a lyrical expression of working-class alienation eventually became a musical vehicle for middle-class contentment half a century later. Largely forgotten today, honky-tonk's pioneers established a sound in the forties and early fifties that provided the musical framework for modern country. Their impact on country music before 1955 was considerable as well: steel guitars and fiddles became the norm throughout the genre during the postwar decade. As the country music audience expanded and many honky-tonk listeners moved into the middle class, however, several performers modified the sound, including Faron Young and Carl Smith. Young and Smith stayed within the parameters of honky-tonk in their styles and instrumentation, but others began adding elements of pop and blues music into the musical matrix. The country pop and country blues subgenres developed as a result and took country music in the last two directions it would take in the era of its postwar modernization. One way set the stage for the rockabilly movement, while the other served as a precursor to the Nashville Sound.[59]

6 | THE SOPHISTICATION OF COUNTRY MUSIC
THE RISE OF COUNTRY POP IN THE POSTWAR DECADE

When country music burst on the American scene in the late thirties and early forties, it began a transformation in style and character that brought it more in congruence with both urban and national culture. Expanding from an audience composed primarily of white, working-class, rural southerners to one made up of a cross section of regional and demographic groups, country music emerged in the decade after World War II as a genre with genuine national appeal. Many of the southern songwriters and performers who continued to dominate country music after its wartime nationalization directed their efforts at the genre's core audience even after they gained national exposure. The postwar traditionalists and early honky-tonk artists in particular strove to produce songs and sounds that appealed to southern working-class listeners in rural and urban settings, respectively. Southern society underwent a radical transformation as a result of the war, and country music selections generated by performers within these two subgenres often dealt with contemporary misgivings about the sociocultural effects of modernization. The honky-tonkers' ingenuous portraits of failed relationships and social vicissitudes attracted the attention of other Americans as well, who generally preferred to hear popular entertainers sing them in a more polished style. As time went on and country music became big business, the genre began experimenting with other ways to cross the hillbilly barrier, to reach American audiences directly. As participants in an alternative movement, the postwar traditionalists demonstrated little interest in the dilution of country music's rural southernness, preferring to build on the musical foundation laid by the prewar progressives with lyrical respect to the southern vernacular. The honky-tonk realists adapted urban instrumentation but retained a plaintiveness in both their singing style and lyrical worldview. The southwestern vocalists mollified the realists' lyrical discontent somewhat, but it was not until the development of the soft honky-tonk sound that the subgenre began to fuse with American popular music. By that time, many members of the honky-tonk audience were entering the middle class, finding the contentment that seemed elusive in the immediate postwar period.

Concurrent with these developments, two groups of performers emerged in the postwar decade that resolved to liberate country music from its rural, southern past in a more decisive fashion. Country blues artists took the energy and eclectic instrumentation of western swing and merged it with African American blues to create an intoxicating blend of country music that appealed to urbanites and younger listeners seeking a more aggressive sound with less conservative lyrics. Country pop performers directed their mix of euphonic vocals and conventional lyrical imagery at the urban bourgeoisie and listeners seeking a more aesthetically pleasing strain of country music. Members of both groups similarly sought to distance themselves from the genre's hillbilly trappings but moved in distinct directions, one toward American popular music, the other in the direction of urban blues. Country pop represented country music's future (the Nashville Sound), while country blues soon transformed itself into the genre's nemesis (rockabilly). Country music executives increasingly based in Nashville endorsed country pop because it reconciled the genre's adult orientation with their efforts to expand its audience. In taming the honky-tonkers, isolating the postwar traditionalists, and distancing themselves from country blues liberalism, the country music industry in Nashville overcame the hillbilly obstacle and eventually survived the onslaught of rock and roll. Country pop became their primary weapon in the fight for country music's respectability and economic survival.

Three principal factors contributed to the rise of country pop in the late forties and early fifties: the postwar urbanization and sophistication of the American South; the support of the *Grand Ole Opry;* and the subgenre's affiliation with national musical trends. Between 1940 and 1950, the South underwent a dramatic demographic shift; the population of southern urban areas increased by approximately 6,000,000 (up 13.5 percent). Large metropolitan areas added 2,400,000 whites (up 4.5 percent), while southern rural areas lost 1,100,000 (down 12.5 percent). In 1950, over 50 percent of the white South still resided in the countryside, but the days of the agrarian South were numbered. Many rural white southerners who traveled to southern cities for defense jobs in World War II remained in the region's production force. In 1955, sociologist Rupert Vance reported that of the 3,300,000 southern workers, black and white, only 12.7 percent remained employed in agriculture. Noting the increase of southerners in production and professional jobs, he went on to conclude: "The dominant psychology of the South is no longer agrarian, it is Chamber of Commerce." Comparing the Southeast's population and total per capita income growth in the period between 1939 and 1954 with national figures, Carl Abbott notes a below average increase in the former and above average rise in the latter. Residents in both the southern countryside and southern urban areas began living with more amenities. In 1940, less than one-quarter of dwellings occupied by rural white southerners were equipped with indoor plumbing. In urban areas, nine of ten white southern homes reported working indoor plumbing in 1950. In 1940, one in six southern farms had electricity; five years later, one in three did. In large southern cities, residents already supplied with electricity and indoor plumbing began spending more money on luxuries. In Nashville, the number of automobiles in the city rose from 39,000 in 1945 to 85,000 in 1952, and telephone ownership increased from 59,000 to 105,000 between 1945 and 1951. Many southerners remained rural in outlook and peculiarly southern in cultural attributes, even as they entered urban environments and moved up in economic status, but few longed to return to their prewar existence. Rural migrants struggling with urban alienation and culture shock turned to honky-tonk music for solace, and those who experienced a more pleasant transition viewed country pop as a sophisticated alternative. [1]

Postwar prosperity furnished country pop with an audience, and the *Grand Ole Opry* provided a boost to the subgenre with increased exposure. When they hired the Vagabonds and Pee Wee King's groups in the mid-thirties, Harry and David Stone set the show's precedent for giving smoother sounding acts more airtime. Old Joe Clark points out that when the Stone Brothers supplanted George Hay as the show's architects, they immediately moved to distance themselves from hillbilly stereotypes: "They were seein' the things that were oncoming and kindly helped steered it off." The R. J. Reynolds Tobacco Company, sponsor of the *Grand Ole Opry*'s half-hour network segment, and their advertising agency in New York, William Esty Company, both encouraged the shift to programming that appealed to listeners beyond the rural, southern base. To this end, the Esty ad agency handpicked Red Foley to replace Roy Acuff as host of the network segment after the latter stepped down in early 1946 to do more touring. The *Opry*'s financial supporters viewed Acuff's departure with ambivalence; they regretted losing a singer with national popularity but welcomed the opportunity to replace him with a more cosmopolitan figure. David Cobb explains the circumstances behind Foley's hiring: "I think the *Opry* was just a bit too country for the agency people in New York. . . . Red Foley, his style was not typical *Opry* style. He was . . . from the Chicago scene and his songs like 'Old Shep' and [others] came closer to the pop ballad type thing." Foley took over the network portion in April 1946 and retained the position as host even after Acuff returned. The network portion offered a variety of additional entertainers who appealed to a cross section of listeners. In presenting a diverse array of folk talent, *Grand Ole Opry* management consciously directed the program toward a wider audience and, in the process, obtained more sophisticated sounding acts.[2]

Country pop performers also benefited from developments in the music industry and, to a lesser extent, postwar societal trends that broadened their potential audience. Frank Sinatra's ascendance in World War II and the mid-forties demise of the big bands ushered in a surge of vocalists on the American music scene that concentrated on song interpretation as a means to attracting listeners. Sinatra explained the new approach to singing and its appeal: "I get an audience involved because I'm involved myself. . . . I cry out the loneliness. . . . Sentimentality, after all, is an emotion common to all humanity." As a vocal-oriented subgenre, country pop latched on to this trend and profited from the phenomenal rise of the recording industry that accompanied postwar prosperity. When listener-oriented music gained in popularity, country music became more accessible, a process begun in World War II. Commenting on the genre's continued nationalization after the war, *Billboard* columnist Johnny Sippel made the following observation in late 1949: "The promotion given country talent on records, in music publishing, television, radio, theaters, folk music parks, and motion pictures has brought this peculiarly American form of music and talent to the attention of a huge number of urban dwellers." After gaining the attention of urbanites, country pop performers developed a following by offering listeners lighthearted and sentimental pieces that affirmed traditional values and captured the postwar mood. While the honky-tonk acts preferred candor and realism, country pop singers offered nostalgia and emotionalism. With the nationwide urbanization that accompanied the war boom, many Americans developed an interest in retro music, a phenomenon that manifested itself in a waltz and square dance craze late in the decade. Within country music, the waltz fad began with Bill Monroe's "Kentucky Waltz" in 1946 and reached its peak in the early 1950s with a tune called "The Tennessee Waltz," which, in various recording incarnations, sold nearly 5 million copies by mid-1951. Written by Pee Wee King and Redd Stewart, "The Tennessee Waltz" authenticated country music's national acceptance and firmly established the genre in the American musical vernacular.[3]

Appropriately, the creative force behind "The Tennessee Waltz" was a man who helped build up the respectability of both the *Grand Ole Opry* and country music in the late 1930s and early 1940s. Continuing a tradition begun by Vernon Dalhart and Jimmie Rodgers and carried on by Clayton McMichen and the Texas triumvirate, Pee Wee King and his Golden West Cowboys helped bring country pop to maturity. From the moment they stepped on the *Grand Ole Opry* stage with their odd assortment of instruments (by country standards) and western garb to the introduction of "The Tennessee Waltz" and several other mainstream hits, Pee Wee King and his Golden West Cowboys was a band ahead of its time in both attitude and musical approach.[4]

Born in Abrams, Wisconsin, in 1914, Pee Wee King (né Julius Frank Anthony Kuczynski) acquired an affection for playing music at a very young age, principally from his father, who played fiddle in an old-time ethnic band. King first taught himself how to play harmonica, then, with his father's encouragement, learned to play the fiddle/violin from formal lessons; soon thereafter, he joined his father's band. Hearing his sister play piano and accordion, however, he decided to take a somewhat different course than his father's: "The accordion fascinated me because I thought there was so much more music to it than [the fiddle]." In high school, he formed his own band and began performing at parties and other local events, eventually landing a radio job in Racine, Wisconsin, playing polkas, waltzes, and other old-time ethnic music. He listened to the *National Barn Dance,* and he soon incorporated elements of western music into his act: "There was Bradley Kincaid, we took a lot of his songs . . . and there was a group, Louise Massey and the Westerners . . . and we started patterning ourselves after them, because they had smooth singing, fine accordion music, and fine arrangements." While on a tour of the Midwest, Gene Autry and promoter J. L. Frank heard King's radio show and asked the accordion player to join them on their tour. After the tour, King traveled with Autry to Louisville, broadcasting over 50,000-watt WHAS. Working with Autry, King learned more western material and acquainted himself with the ways of the music business. When Autry left for Hollywood, around 1935, King stayed in Louisville with a band called the Log Cabin Boys before leaving to form his first incarnation of the Golden West Cowboys. Later King moved to Nashville, where Frank teamed him up with Roy Acuff for a series of successful personal appearances. Gaining a reputation as a professional, smooth-sounding band, the Golden West Cowboys drew the attention of David and Harry Stone, who invited them to join the *Opry* in 1937.[5]

From the outset, Pee Wee King's Golden West Cowboys was one of the *Opry*'s most innovative bands. Along with Zeke Clements, they introduced western attire and songs to the show's audience; in time, they would also become one of the first *Opry* acts to play electric instruments (via James Clell Summey) and drums (via Harold "Sticks" MacDonald). Additionally, they brought with them a professional mindset and business savvy, as Pee Wee King recalls: "I was used to playing vaudeville theaters, and [other *Opry* acts] were playing schoolhouses— this was something new to me, we would never play schoolhouses, no—play theaters." Over the years, many notable vocalists worked with the group, including

Eddy Arnold, Cowboy Copas, and Redd Stewart. After several successful years with the *Grand Ole Opry,* on stage and on tour, King and his band left the show in 1947 to return to Louisville, where he began a daily radio show while maintaining a weekly local television program. By the early 1950s, he had weekly television shows in Chicago, Cleveland, and Cincinnati as well. Following the popularity of "The Tennessee Waltz," the Golden West Cowboys became a fixture in the country top ten in the early 1950s. The rock and roll phenomenon took its toll on their success, however, and King eventually disbanded the group in 1959.[6]

Despite their popularity on the *Opry* and on the road, Pee Wee King and his Golden West Cowboys did not appear on record until after the war. Following two tentative recordings released on the Bullet label in 1946, King's group signed with RCA. With eight musicians, including a drummer, the Golden West Cowboys more closely resembled a western swing band than a standard *Opry* act. Musically, the band offered tight arrangements and generally up-tempo songs on their early pressings. "Steel Guitar Rag" and "I Hear You Knockin' " allow plenty of room for the band to showcase their talents, and "Keep Those Cold Icy Fingers off of Me" and "Ten Gallon Boogie" hint at King's penchant for novelty material. Their cover version of "Kentucky Waltz," however, represented the future of the group. The band remained in western swing mode until December 1947, when they recorded "The Tennessee Waltz." With twin fiddles, Parisian accordion playing by King, and a smooth vocal by Redd Stewart, "Tennessee Waltz" clicked with country music's more sophisticated listeners and, in the hands of Patti Page, went to number one on the pop charts in 1950. Publisher Wesley Rose commented on the song's significance: "It had the effect of breaking down all the barriers. . . . It was a case of the people just couldn't kid themselves about country music anymore." The success of the song encouraged King to record a number of waltzes in the late forties, many virtual clones of the original. Adding a pianist to the group on "When They Played That Old Missouri Waltz" in 1949, King began moving ever closer to a pop sound.[7]

Vocalist Redd Stewart emerged as the most valuable member of the band in the early fifties. With a crooning singing style reminiscent of Bing Crosby, Stewart masterfully handles the vocals on mid-tempo pieces ("Tennessee Tears," "River Road Two-Step") and ballads ("If and When," "Changing Partners"). Stewart's vocals bore little if any resemblance to other country singers, emphasizing a tremolo effect and exhibiting no twang whatsoever. "Within My Heart," from 1950, is an unabashed attempt at pop in which Stewart shows off his considerable range in an arrangement devoid of country instrumentation. King also experimented with other pop vocal approaches, including trio leads ("What, Where,

When") as well as female background singing reminiscent of the Andrew Sisters ("Railroad Boogie").[8]

As a country artist interested in incorporating pop elements into his repertoire in an effort to reach a wider audience, Pee Wee King avoids rural imagery in his lyrics. Most of his songs revolved around lighthearted material, often escapist, sometimes humorous, and occasionally trite. With "Slow Poke," he turned his fondness for novelty material into a huge country seller and a pop crossover smash. "Silver and Gold," with its hand-clapping and percussive effects, provided him with another number one hit. Two other hits, "Changing Partners" and "Backward, Turn Backward," were clearly designed for an uptown crowd and point toward country soft sell in the late fifties. As early as 1944, *Billboard* labeled the Golden West Cowboys "one of the smoothest units of its kind"; ten years later, the trade paper commented: "King's music isn't the rootin', tootin', hell-raising kind of western stuff, [but rather] country music at its sweetest." From his early days on the *Grand Ole Opry* to his popular television broadcasts in the Midwest, Pee Wee King stressed modern arrangements and professional appearance and, in the process, helped carry country music over the hillbilly hump.[9]

Pee Wee King helped lay the groundwork for country music's shift toward sophistication; Eddy Arnold accelerated the process with a manner and singing style that commanded the respect of the American public and the popular music industry. Major country music figures, such as Roy Acuff, Bob Wills, and Ernest Tubb, deserve considerable credit for bringing the genre closer to national acceptance, but in penetrating the urban and pop markets, Arnold directly introduced country music to more Americans than any other contemporary performer. In doing so, he revolutionized country music, opening it up to a middle-class audience and effectuating the Nashville Sound. Sidestepping the boisterousness of western swing and the stridence of honky-tonk, Eddy Arnold became country music's leading ambassador in the late 1940s and early 1950s.

Born in Chester County, Tennessee, in 1918, Eddy Arnold grew up surrounded by music played in church and at local gatherings. He developed an interest in playing music at an early age and by his mid-teens was performing regularly at picnics, parties, dances, and church suppers. Although he liked to listen to Jimmie Rodgers and Carter Family records, he patterned his singing after Gene Autry and Bing Crosby, opting for a softer and smoother vocal approach. Arnold made his radio debut in 1934 with a guest appearance on WTJS in Jackson, but did not pursue a career in the medium until early 1937, when he returned to the station and began appearing daily. A year later, he and a fellow musician named Howard "Speedy" McNatt journeyed to Saint Louis, where they broadcast over a small station by day and played the honky-tonks at night. Arnold soon grew tired of the honky-tonks, however, and upon learning of the departure of the lead singer of Pee Wee King's band over at WSM, wrote to the bandleader inquiring about the position. After hearing a recording by Arnold, King and J. L. Frank invited the young singer to Nashville to join the group in 1940. Over the next few years, Arnold accompanied the Golden West Cowboys on numerous bookings, including the Camel Caravan, all the while improving his vocal delivery and learning the ways of the music business. By early 1943, with a family to support, Arnold decided to pursue a solo career and approached WSM's Harry Stone about a spot on the station. In addition to an early morning show, Arnold also began appearing on the *Opry*, eventually securing a fifteen-minute segment on a non-network portion of the Saturday night program. He soon put together a band for personal appearances, built around Ivan LeRoy "Little Roy" Wiggins's Dobro-influenced steel guitar playing. Near the end of the war, he forged a relationship with promoter Tom Parker and record company RCA-Victor that soon set his career in motion. [10]

Arnold and his band signed with RCA-Victor in late 1943 and made their first recordings a year later, after the American Federation of Musicians ban was lifted. At their first session, Arnold's group recorded two sentimental pieces, "Mother's Prayer" and "Mommy, Please Stay Home with Me," that owed a great deal to pre-war country music. Commenting on the old-time feel of the recordings, *Billboard* noted that there was "nothing light-hearted in either side to make for jukebox favor." Perhaps taking note of reviews and unimpressive record sales, Arnold and producer Steve Sholes picked up the tempo after the war and incorporated more-lively fiddling as in "I Couldn't Believe It Was True." The band's sound and Arnold's increasingly confident vocals really began to gel in early 1947, when they recorded several upbeat and up-tempo numbers. With its emphasis on Wiggins's effervescent steel guitar playing and Arnold's buoyant vocal, "That's How Much I Love You" provided the band with a signature sound. When Arnold reaches down to sing "baby," he reveals his affection for Bing Crosby's vocal approach, yet he retains just enough plaintiveness to distinguish his singing as rooted in southern folk music. The title of "Just a Little More Lovin'" hints at the lyrical subject matter of most Eddy Arnold songs of the period, and "(In the) Hills of Tomorrow" exhibits the optimism that became his trademark. Several songs from 1947 and 1948 brim with an infectious positive feel: "Easy Rockin' Chair," "There's Not a Thing I Wouldn't Do for You," and "Anytime" all offer affirmations of life and love backed by breezy musical arrangements. Arnold's full repertoire balanced between lighthearted songs, tales of failed relationships, and sentimental numbers, but his biggest hits in the postwar period either centered on lighthearted lyrical material or presented tales of failed love with a lively beat. These types of arrangements appealed to the urban middle class as lyrical expressions of postwar contentment and pleasing musical pieces. Lyrically, Arnold also displayed a social conservatism that attracted southerners across the board. "The Nearest Thing to Heaven" and "Little Angel with the Dirty Face" are celebrations of parenthood, and "Momma and Daddy Broke My Heart" and "Don't Rob Another Man's Castle" examine the consequences of divorce and infidelity. Additionally, Arnold recorded several religious and sentimental numbers that never made the charts but endeared him to thousands of rural listeners and urban migrants. He also proved capable of converting songs from other subgenres and traditional material into the country pop mold. On a remarkable cover of Will Hays's "Molly Darling," Arnold transforms the old folk standard into a modern country classic highlighted by his subtle tremolo and Little Roy Wiggins's effective playing. Arnold virtually reigned over the country charts in the late forties with his blend of musical idioms that appealed to a variety of listeners. In 1948, he reached his apogee, holding onto the number one slot for over forty weeks and recording five of the year's ten biggest hits. Even after the rise of honky-tonk, Arnold remained a fixture on the *Billboard* weekly charts. [11]

With a fully matured self-assurance, Arnold began to venture farther into country pop in the late forties with "The Echo of Your Footsteps," "This Is the Thanks I Get (for Loving You)," and "I'm Throwing Rice (at the Girl I Love)," indicating the softer tone to come. On all three numbers, Benjamin "Buck" Lambert's fiddle is barely audible. Increasingly, Arnold's recordings took on a more sophisticated approach, adding piano, background vocals, twin fiddles, and other effects to create a more marketable sound. Seven crossover hits in 1948 helped spur this tendency; several other developments nurtured the trend. In October 1947, Arnold headlined two sold-out country shows at Washington's austere Constitution Hall. Also around the time, Arnold had a regular slot on the Mutual Network, and, after leaving the *Opry* in 1948, became a featured act on CBS's *Hometown Reunion,* another Saturday night network program. In March 1950, *Billboard* named him the eleventh most popular male singer on the nation's jukeboxes (Frank Sinatra came in tenth). Once recognized as a legitimate vocalist, Arnold began making guest appearances on several television shows with Bob Hope, Milton Berle, Perry Como, and others, eventually obtaining his own video program in early 1955. In 1950, *Billboard* estimated his total record sales to that point at 12 million; five years later, their estimate rose to 30 million. With increased exposure via radio and television, acceptance by mainstream record buyers, and huge turnouts at his concerts, Arnold naturally viewed a shift toward popular music as an opportunity to build on his success and foster country music's respectability. Arnold comments on the reasoning behind his decision: "I never wanted to desert the country side, I just wanted to broaden my thing. I thought there was an audience out there that I could get if I just reached for them a little bit." On another occasion, he defended country pop as a vehicle for helping country music shed its regional provincialism: "It gives it recognition and exposure to the whole of the world that it never had before, and would not have had had this not come about." With twenty-nine top-ten country singles, including thirteen number ones, charted by the end of 1949, Eddy Arnold began the fifties with a certitude that he could expand on the country pop formula and reach a wider audience without losing the support of his customary fans.[12]

Most of Eddy Arnold's recordings from the early 1950s maintain a country feel, principally through the retention of Roy Wiggins's steel guitar. With the addition of Vic Willis on piano in 1950, however, Sholes and Arnold began a determined trek toward pop music. Characterized by twin vocals and tinkling piano, "Enclosed, One Broken Heart" represents a definite turning point; in 1952, Arnold began working more frequently with New York musicians, and "You Always Hurt the One I Love" and "Moonlight and Roses" came very close to straight pop. Future Nashville-Sound stalwart Hank Garland lends an element of jazz to several numbers from the period, complementing Arnold's vocal playfulness on "I'm Gonna Lock My Heart (and Throw away the Key)" and "I've Been Thinking." On "Eddy's Song," a self-parody of the band's earlier approach, Wiggins returns to the forefront, but increasingly Sholes and Arnold chose to record without steel guitars or fiddles. On "I Really Don't Want to Know," Arnold delivers perhaps his finest vocal performance in a sparse arrangement of piano and acoustic guitars. In early 1955, he teamed with orchestra leader Hugo Winterhalter for a reworking of "The Cattle Call" that marked the beginning of the Nashville Sound brought to fruition later in the decade. Rock and roll halted Arnold's progress in the mid-fifties, but he returned triumphantly in the 1960s for another series of top-ten hits. As country music's most respected figure in the late forties and early fifties, Eddy Arnold indurated its national acceptance and extended its appeal to urban, middle-class southerners. From his Stetson hat, starched white shirts, and dress slacks to his varnished vocal and brisk positivism, Eddy Arnold symbolized country music's move uptown. His success cleared the way for a multitude of country pop vocalists who repudiated honky-tonk's harshness and built on Arnold's stylistic fusion in an effort to further broaden country music's audience.[13]

After Eddy Arnold left the *Opry* in 1948, George Morgan emerged as his Nashville-based successor. Although often compared to Arnold, Morgan developed a vocal approach closer to pop and a band sound more firmly rooted in country. Morgan did not reach Arnold's level of national success, but he remains a key figure in the development of country music's urban expansion as a result of producing records that merged sentimental lyrics with a sophisticated, low-key sound.

Though born in central Tennessee, George Morgan grew up in eastern Ohio, where his family moved in the late 1920s. The Morgans enjoyed listening to the *Grand Ole Opry* on Saturday nights, and George developed a liking for the smooth-sounding Vagabonds at an early age. As a teenager, he also developed an appreciation for Montana Slim, who became his idol, and the Blue Sky Boys. In the early to mid-forties, he worked at a variety of jobs after receiving a medical discharge from the army, eventually putting to use the informal music instructions that his mother and father gave him when he began appearing with a band on WWST in Worster around 1947. The other members of the group gave up the idea of a career in music, but Morgan stayed on the air, playing guitar and singing songs in a style patterned after Eddy Arnold. He eventually developed a following in the area and, on the strength of a composition called "Candy Kisses," moved to high-wattage WWVA in Wheeling. He soon returned to Ohio; before he left, however, he sent a demo of "Candy Kisses" to Nashville. Morgan recalled that Arnold's departure from the *Opry* gave him the break he was looking for: "I wondered who would be replacing Eddy Arnold, and on Monday morning I got a call from WSM asking me to audition." In late 1948, he began appearing on the *Opry* and soon secured a contract with Columbia Records. Eddy Arnold ruled the charts, so Columbia directed Morgan toward potential crossover material, with mixed success. Morgan's real strength lay in singing slow and mid-tempo ballads with a country flavor, and he scored several hits in the late forties and early fifties in this vein. Although he left the *Opry* twice, in 1949 and 1956, he remained a fixture on the Nashville scene throughout his career as a staunch supporter of the country pop blend he helped bring to perfection.[14]

At Morgan's first session for Columbia, in January 1949, he recorded "Candy Kisses" and three other chart-making songs with a group of studio musicians. Noticeably, Tommy Jackson's barely audible fiddle sounds more like a violin, in keeping with the record company's crossover plans for the singer. At his next session, Morgan recorded with steel guitarist Don Davis, who became a fixture in his band, the Candy Kids, and whose economical playing soon developed into the cornerstone of its sound. Davis usually played casual, conservative solos that adhered to melody and rarely displayed jazz flourishes. Bill Drake, Floyd Robinson, and other lead guitarists similarly offered economical solos that complemented Morgan's easy-going style. With the addition of Marvin Hughes on piano and organ in 1950, the band added its final crucial component in the development of its sophisticated country sound. Morgan delivers several outstanding vocal performances, particularly on "You Win the Bride," "Almost," "No One Knows It Better Than Me," and other mid-tempo pieces about failed relationships. Art Satherley and Don Law made several attempts at having Morgan record up-tempo numbers, but his strength always remained in ballads and melancholy pieces. Novelty numbers, such as "Somebody Robbed My Beehive" and "You're a Little Doll," reflect the Arnold influence and demonstrate Morgan's suitability to more sentimental material. On numerous occasions, Columbia paired him with different female vocalists, including Rosemary Clooney and Dinah Shore, as well as added group vocals to the mix. Many of these recordings point toward country music's future but failed to catch on at the time of their release. The song "One-Woman Man" seems more appropriate in a country club setting than a honky-tonk. Morgan weathered the storm of both honky-tonk and rockabilly, however, and found a niche on the country music scene in the Nashville-Sound era. Although his contributions to country pop are often overlooked, Morgan merits acknowledgment as a true pioneer in the subgenre's development and one of country music's first cosmopolitan figures. [15]

George Morgan, Eddy Arnold, and Pee Wee King all played key roles in polishing country music's image, meeting nontraditional listeners halfway in their acceptance of the genre. While honky-tonk performers reached the American public with their songs, country pop artists attracted them directly with their performances. The American public in general and urban listeners in particular unquestionably preferred the records of such popular artists as Perry Como, Frankie Laine, and Nat King Cole over country offerings, but grew increasingly receptive to original country pop records, such as "Slow Poke" and "Anytime." In the postwar era, American culture and the national music industry drifted closer to homogenization; regional distinctions were obscured by the movement toward consensus and conformity. Country pop artists reacted to this trend by adopting a smooth vocal approach and pleasant instrumental backing as a means to integrate into the mainstream of American popular music. Some, like Slim Whitman, actually began recording pop songs, a development that further obfuscated the line between white southern and national music. It did not take long for the country music industry to recognize country pop as their deliverance from the hillbilly quagmire and their key to financial success. [16]

Country pop's rise as the primary vehicle for expanding country music beyond its southern folk base correlated with the emergence of Nashville as the industry's hub in the late forties and early fifties. The establishment of the WSM Artists' Service Bureau in the mid-thirties and the Acuff-Rose publishing house during the war helped provide the framework for Nashville's ascendance by setting up a financial infrastructure for country music writers and performers located in the city. As noted in chapter 5, the Artists' Service Bureau contributed greatly to the *Grand Ole Opry*'s barn dance preeminence after the war by offering *Opry* acts economic opportunities through its promotional activities. An increasing number of country music's most prominent acts based themselves in middle Tennessee, and Nashville soon became a recording center as well. Early attempts at field recordings in Nashville produced mixed results; the major labels in the 1930s preferred other southern cities, such as Atlanta, Dallas, and Charlotte, if they recorded in the South at all. This situation began to change late in the war, beginning in December 1944, when Eddy Arnold recorded his first selections in the WSM studio. Around this same period, three WSM engineers, Aaron Shelton, Carl Jenkins, and George Reynolds Sr., set up the Castle Recording Company, using the station's facilities to produce transcriptions and commercials as well as records. With Decca's Paul Cohen leading the way, executives at major labels began using the Castle facility, which relocated to the Tulane Hotel in 1947, to record their country artists. In 1952, Decca built its own studio in Nashville, and RCA-Victor announced similar plans in 1954. Nashville still had some competition in the early 1950s as country music's recording center, but with every passing year it seemed to draw more musicians, writers, promoters, and industry executives into its orbit. Commenting on the migration to middle Tennessee, *Time* magazine in 1951 termed Nashville "Tin Pan Valley." Around the same time, *Opry* announcer David Cobb coined its more permanent label, "Music City, U.S.A."[17]

The gradual concentration of the country music industry in Nashville had an enormous impact on the genre's stylistic development in the early 1950s. Principally, it accelerated its fusion with mainstream popular music that began during the war and furthered the dilution of subregional styles taking place in the late forties. While executives behind the scenes of the *Grand Ole Opry* encouraged more sophisticated sounds, producers in Nashville worked to create a more commercially viable product. To this end, they took a greater interest in the songs artists chose to record and encouraged the use of professional musicians on sessions. Decca's Paul Cohen, for instance, began using session musicians Hank Garland, Ernie Newton, and Tommy Jackson with more frequency in the early

1950s. Versatile guitarists, such as Billy Byrd and Chet Atkins, appeared on the recordings of artists affiliated with several different labels, further homogenizing the Nashville product. The end result of these developments was professionally produced recordings that adhered to music industry standards and appealed to a cross section of listeners. Nashville executives found it necessary to filter honky-tonk; country pop offered few complications. They recognized country pop as the wave of the future and banked on its success. At the same time, they recognized that the base of the country music audience still consisted primarily of rural and transplanted southerners and wisely kept one foot in the genre's folk past. They accomplished this by supporting acts like Little Jimmy Dickens, who offered several humorous observations on southern rural life in a modern instrumental setting. Dickens's willingness to mix rural humor with electric instrumentation brought him considerable success and helped legitimize novel sounds among traditionally minded rural listeners. Tellingly, Appalachian performers in the postwar traditional vein who retained acoustic instrumentation and preferences for more serious subject matter faced a cooler reception in Nashville. In Hank Snow, however, the *Grand Ole Opry* and the country music industry found the key transitional figure in their quest to bridge the gap between past and present.[18]

Hank Snow is country music's most indefinable figure. Were it not for his conspicuous use of the electric steel guitar, he would easily fit into the category of postwar traditionalism. If his nasal baritone was a bit more strident, he might deserve classification among the honky-tonkers. At first glance, his blend of Jimmie Rodgers blues, rural imagery, and energetic rhythms seems out of time in an era when sentimental country pop and realistic honky-tonk reigned over the country scene. Snow managed to rise above these obstacles, however, and reach listeners with his refurbishment of old-time music. Of all the subgenres, country pop comes closest to describing his work because of the listenability of his recordings and the widespread appeal of his approach. Snow defied the odds and found a niche on the Nashville scene; in the process, he led old-time country music's last stand in the postwar era.

Clarence Eugene "Hank" Snow grew up on the coast of Nova Scotia, Canada, where he endured poverty and the physical abuse of his stepfather before leaving for sea at the age of twelve. Upon returning four years later, his supportive mother introduced him to the recordings of Vernon Dalhart and Jimmie Rodgers, and the latter performer soon became Snow's idol. Taking up guitar, Snow patterned his singing after Rodgers's style and, around the time he turned eighteen, successfully auditioned for a Halifax radio station. He gained a following through his broadcasts and his touring in the mid-thirties and eventually secured a spot on the *Canadian Farm Hour,* a coast-to-coast program. His first recordings for RCA-Victor in the mid-thirties, which were released only in Canada, demonstrated enough promise to keep him with the label while he perfected his skills on the Canadian theater circuit. In 1944, Snow drove down to the United States, and in early 1945, he began appearing on WWVA in Wheeling, West Virginia. Over the next three years, he made several attempts to establish himself in the States, including three unsuccessful ventures to Hollywood. In 1948, his career took an upturn when he traveled to Dallas, where some of his Canadian releases were receiving airplay. Later that year, he met fellow Jimmie Rodgers admirer Ernest Tubb, who convinced *Opry* management to give Snow a guest spot on the program. In the meantime, RCA-Victor began releasing Hank Snow selections in the States, and "Marriage Vow" became his first American hit. Snow recalls that the *Opry* crowd responded coolly to his performances at first, until the release of a song entitled "I'm Movin' On": "Audiences changed overnight. It was like magic. They were completely indifferent one week and the next week they were wildly enthusiastic." "I'm Movin' On" went on to become the number one country record of 1950 and led to numerous top-ten singles over the next five years. Although taken aback by the rock and roll surge, Snow retained his poise and returned to the charts in the 1960s with several other hits, all the while remaining ensconced on the *Grand Ole Opry.*[19]

Snow began his recording career as the "Yodeling Ranger," singing cowboy songs and Jimmie Rodgers–like pieces for RCA's Canadian division. Over the years, he incorporated several sentimental and story songs into his repertoire; after his voice deepened, he took on the title of the "Singing Ranger." His first postwar recordings released in the States, "Within This Broken Heart of Mine" and "My Two-Timin' Mama," show both the old-time and Jimmie Rodgers influences; instrumentally, these performances showcase Snow's acoustic guitar backed simply by an electric guitar and bass. On his first recordings in the States, in March 1949, he retains the sparse accompaniment and sentimental approach, evident most clearly on "Nobody's Child." Vocally, Snow offers smooth and articulate singing, one of the trademarks of his recordings throughout his career. When he moved to Nashville in early 1950, Snow sought out a steel guitarist who could play in a simple, old-time way, eventually hiring Joe Talbot, a law student at Vanderbilt University. Talbot grew up in the Nashville area, where he listened to and attended the *Grand Ole Opry* regularly. As an adolescent, he modeled his Hawaiian guitar playing on Pete Kirby's, learning riffs from Roy Acuff's Dobro player while sitting in the front row of the *Opry.* After the war, the sound of Little Roy Wiggins's steel guitar led Talbot to purchase a laptop guitar and amplifier.

He soon began playing around the Nashville area in honky-tonks, experimenting with different sounds and developing his own distinct style, one both old-timey in its Hawaiian and Dobro basics and modern in its electrification. As Talbot explains, Snow was immediately attracted to the subtlety of his style: "He had just come to Nashville and he was having a little difficulty finding the type of steel guitar player he wanted because he preferred more the basic style and at that time everbody'd discovered eight strings and double-necks and all these things. They were gettin' pretty fancy." Snow also found a local fiddler named Tommy Vaden who played in the old-time, bluesy manner that he sought.[20]

At their first session for RCA Victor, the group persuaded Steve Sholes to let them record "I'm Movin' On," an up-tempo number that mixed lyrical train imagery with enthusiastic instrumental backing. The success of the song led to several others in the same vein, most notably "Golden Rocket" and "One More Ride." On "The Wreck of the Old 97," a childhood favorite of both Talbot's and Snow's, the group perfects its style, producing a remarkable cover version that effortlessly mixes old-time country, smooth singing, and vigorous playing to create a sound both modern and reverent. Snow's deep respect for Jimmie Rodgers surfaces on several reworkings of the Blue Yodeler's songs. They also reveal his prowess as a flat-picking acoustic guitarist, a talent that Snow uses to great effect on a variety of other song types as well, from the novelty numbers "Lady's Man" and "Music Makin' Mama from Memphis" to the straight country pop songs "For Now and Always" and "I Don't Hurt Anymore." A guitar duet with Chet Atkins ("Silver Bell") reveals the exceptional skills of both players, one in the electric style, the other in the acoustic tradition. For his own part, Snow never used any type of pickup or amplifier when he played guitar, remaining steadfast in his appreciation of the hollow, acoustic sound: "On sessions I play my guitar in front of a microphone and onstage I do the same thing. Pickups clamp steel onto the wood of the guitar, which alters the guitar's original pure sound." Snow's solos on blues-tinged numbers, such as "Moanin' " and "Confused with the Blues," offer proof of Snow's superior flat-picking abilities and illustrate yet another facet of his musical personality.[21]

Snow's exceptional guitar playing often overshadows his considerable vocal talent. Like his idol, Jimmie Rodgers, Snow could sing everything from rounder blues to sentimental pieces with equal effectiveness. "Bluebird Island" demonstrates his harmonic ability, while "I Went to Your Wedding" and "Let Me Go Lover" reveal him as an adroit pop singer. On "A Fool Such as I," he delivers his finest vocal performance, an impressive fusion of country twang and pop vibrato that deservedly rose to the top of the charts. Although it took his record company some time to realize it, Hank Snow offered many country music listeners in the early 1950s exactly what they wanted to hear: a simple, updated version of the old-time sound with just enough pop-flavorings to satisfy their gradually increasing sophisticated tastes. Just as urban listeners accepted Eddy Arnold's positive message, Pee Wee King's novelty numbers, and George Morgan's crooning, they embraced Hank Snow's musical amalgamation of past and present as the soundtrack of their own transition from southern folk to middle-class Americans. The Nashville country music industry viewed Snow and the other country pop artists as godsends, performers modern enough to draw in new listeners and folksy enough to retain the traditional crowd.

In their quest to free country music from its provincial roots, Nashville music executives enthusiastically promoted artists with widespread appeal, particularly through appearances on the *Grand Old Opry*. In Red Foley, the *Opry* received not only country music's most accomplished singer but the program's emancipator from regionalism as well. In body and spirit, Foley replaced Roy Acuff as the *Opry*'s central figure and became its torchbearer into the modern period. Surrounding himself with Nashville's finest musicians, he produced the most professional-sounding recordings of the postwar decade, all bearing the brand of his full-bodied voice. Possessing an incomparable ability to sing blues, country, and gospel with universal mastery, Foley towered above his peers as country music's most versatile singer. He submerged himself into every song in search of its meaning, a process that allowed him to deliver novelty material, blues numbers, and religious pieces with equal conviction. With a cosmopolitan look, a down-home manner, and a remarkable voice, Foley dispelled country music's hillbilly stereotype, replacing it with the image of an amiable and courteous southerner.

Born in Blue Lick, Kentucky, Clyde "Red" Foley first demonstrated his appreciation for music as a young boy, playing harmonica around his father's country store. When his father accepted a guitar as payment on an account one day around 1920, Foley learned the basics of that instrument as well. In high school, a music teacher took note of his vocal talent and prodded him into entering a local singing competition, the beginning of a process that led to a scholarship from Georgetown College, where he concentrated his study in voice and music. When a talent scout from WLS offered him a radio job making sixty dollars a week, Foley quit school and left for Chicago. Along with Karl Davis, Harty Taylor, and others, he became a charter member of the Cumberland Ridge Runners, specializing in comedy as well as singing. He remained in Chicago until the late 1930s, when he left with John Lair to inaugurate the *Renfro Valley Barn Dance*. After a brief period in Cincinnati, he returned to Chicago around 1940, where he teamed with Red Skelton on NBC's *Avalon Time* and reappeared on the *National Barn Dance*. After making several records with the Cumberland Ridge Runners, he signed his first individual contract with Decca in late 1941. During the war, he made several appearances at the Great Lakes Naval Training Station and opened a dude ranch near Peoria. His popularity skyrocketed during this time, especially in Chicago, where he played to 210,000 people at the Chicago Rodeo in 1944. By the end of the war, "Ramblin' Red Foley" was appearing on three network shows, WLS's *National Barn Dance, Avalon Time,* and *Plantation Party,* and receiving favorable reviews from the trade papers. In 1945, he made some recordings with Lawrence Welk and his orchestra and earned a new nickname: "Sweet Singer of Songs of the Hills and Plains." Foley's national popularity and attractive image made him the perfect candidate to replace Roy Acuff as headliner of the network portion of the *Grand Ole Opry*.[22]

Not surprisingly, the *Grand Ole Opry* crowd reacted tentatively to the smooth singer from Chicago with ties to Lawrence Welk. Foley recalled his own trepidations: "I guess I never was more scared than I was the night I replaced Roy Acuff on the network part of the *Opry*. . . . [The audience] thought I was a Chicago slicker who had come down to pass himself off as a country boy and bump Roy out of his job. It took me about a year to get adjusted." After an initial period of uneasiness, both the host and the crowd became more comfortable with the arrangement; Foley's heartfelt interpretation of sentimental and religious pieces were particularly instrumental in winning over the audience. Foley's career as a country music performer soared after his return to the South, and he recorded forty-nine top-ten hits in the postwar decade. With *Opry* exposure, he retained his popularity throughout the nation, scoring four separate million-selling records in the early 1950s (three gospel numbers and "Chattanoogie Shoe Shine Boy"). Released in late 1949, "Chattanoogie Shoe Shine Boy" went to the top of both the pop and country charts, and Foley's version outsold versions by Frank Sinatra and Bing Crosby. In 1950, *Billboard* acknowledged that "few records in the history of the business have sold with comparable speed and scope." Despite all the success, Foley remained on the *Opry* and toured with package shows promoted by the WSM Artists' Service Bureau. A string of shows in 1949 with Ernest Tubb and Little Jimmy Dickens grossed $48,000 in five days. In 1953, Marty Landau, the *Opry* promoter on the West Coast, set up a seven-day tour that brought in over $31,000. By that time, the singer commanded $2,000 a performance. Foley finally stepped down as host of the *Opry* in the spring of 1953; the following year he signed with RadiOzark Enterprises as host of the *Ozark Jubilee,* broadcast from Springfield, Missouri. ABC initially broadcast twenty-five minutes of the two-hour radio show over its network in 1954; early the next year, it brought a one-hour video version of the Saturday night program to prime-time television. In 1957, the *Wall Street Journal* estimated that 4.4 million American homes tuned into the show weekly. Although Foley had few country hits after 1955's "Satisfied Mind," he retained his national popularity well into the 1960s. [23]

An examination of Red Foley's recorded output of the postwar decade illustrates the true breadth of his singing abilities and indicates the reasons for his phenomenal popularity. After the war, Foley continued to make records in the western pop style, with full vocals accompanied by accordion, clarinet, and other pop music instrumentation. On "Foggy River" and "Lay down Your Soul," however, he reveals his appreciation for blues and gospel. With "Freight Train Boogie" and "Rockin' Chair Money," he begins the switch to more up-tempo country material. In 1946, he formed the Cumberland Valley Boys, a group of talented musicians that included at one time or another Zeke and Zeb Turner on electric guitars, Tommy Jackson on fiddle, Smokey Lohman or Jerry Byrd on steel, and Louis Innis on rhythm guitar. Noticeably, the fiddle rarely makes a prominent appearance on Red Foley's early postwar records, lending the group somewhat of a pop sound. Foley's leanings toward the blues and gospel material and Jerry Byrd's work, however, tend to keep the group grounded in the country genre. When Turner, Innis, and Byrd left for Cincinnati's WLW in late 1948, Foley began working with two talented young guitarists, Hank Garland and Grady Martin, both of whom adapted well to Foley's style. Garland's playing on such hits as "Tennessee Saturday Night" and "Sugarfoot Rag" soon became a characteristic of Foley's early fifties sound. In Martin, Foley secured another versatile guitarist who added jazz and blues touches to a number of recordings. Foley recorded a number of impressive blues numbers with these guitarists, most notably "Open up That Door," "Midnight," "Stranded in Deep Water," and the appropriately titled "Deep Blues." "Midnight" proved so authentic that it began selling well in locations where rhythm and blues records proliferated. Foley's greatest vocal talent lay in gospel numbers with blues overtones. After working with the Delmore Brothers and Grandpa Jones as the Brown's Ferry Four on King Records, Foley began a fertile association with the Jordanaires, another top-notch male vocal group. "Milky White Way," "It Is No Secret (What God Can Do)," "(There'll Be) Peace in the Valley (for Me)," "The Last Mile of the Way," and many others established Foley as country music's most expressive male gospel singer. [24]

In addition to excelling at the blues and gospel idioms, Foley breathed considerable life into up-tempo novelty and pop material. On many occasions, the lyrics make little sense, but Foley manages to convincingly sell such lighthearted pieces as "M-I-S-S-I-S-S-I-P-P-I," "Birmingham Bounce," and "Sugar Foot Rag" with the help of his talented group of musicians. Vocally, Decca teamed him up with a number of female singers, including the Andrew Sisters, Roberta Lee, and Judy Martin. With Lee, Foley turns "Night Train to Memphis" into a boogie-woogie tour de force, and the presence of the Andrew Sisters on "Hang Your Head in Shame" helps transform one of his wartime hits into an effective con-temporary pop piece. For good measure, Decca also paired him with Kitty Wells for several honky-tonk pieces, and the success of "One by One" demonstrated the soundness of their judgment and the evocative abilities of the two singers. In the mid-fifties, Foley continued to record gospel ("Someone to Care"), blues ("Walkin' in the Cold, Cold Rain"), and pop ("Thank You for Calling") without ever losing his footing. With the Anita Kerr Singers, he recorded "Hearts of Stone," a number that indicates Foley's potential in the rock field as well. Just as Foley never fully embraced pop, though, he rejected an affiliation with the more youth-oriented musical phenomenon. Red Foley's most magnetic features were his unpretentiousness and quiet dignity, two characteristics that clashed with the flamboyance of rock. Whether in Chicago, Nashville, or Springfield, Missouri, Foley remained a country boy at heart, even as he applied his sophisticated vocal training to the music of his youth. Foley succeeded by embracing his roots and surrounding himself with like-minded musicians. Topping the charts with "Chattanoogie Shoe Shine Boy," he disproved the industry's misgivings about country artists' marketability and lent an air of professionalism to music produced in the South. In remaining on the *Opry* as its genial host even after he chalked up a series of million-selling records, Foley helped establish both the program and the city of Nashville as the focal point of country music. Despite the magnitude of these accomplishments, Foley's greatest legacy remains the impressive collection of recordings he produced in the postwar period. No other country singer ever demonstrated more versatility in his singing abilities and few appealed to a wider array of listeners.

All of the aforementioned country pop acts maintained a semipermanent affil-iation with the *Grand Ole Opry* at one time or another in the postwar decade. On the West Coast, a country music scene continued to thrive, even as the nucleus of country pop moved eastward. Of the remaining country pop artists located there, only one achieved a measure of success in reaching an interregional audience that rivaled those based in the South after the war. Adding various portions of pop, western, honky-tonk, and western swing to a country stock, Jimmy Wakely concocted a musical recipe that appealed to listeners from coast to coast and estab-lished him as a major figure in country music's move toward national legitimacy.

Born near Mineola, Arkansas, in 1914, Jimmy Wakely spent most of his early years in Oklahoma, where his family moved when he was four. As a youngster, he enjoyed listening to early country artists Carson Robison, Vernon Dalhart, and Jimmie Rodgers; after his father bought him a guitar, he began learning Rodgers's songs. In his teens, he also became interested in gospel (through singing schools he attended), popular music (through his appreciation of Bing Crosby), and western swing (through Bob Wills and the Texas Playboys). In 1937, he made his radio debut on Oklahoma City's WKY, eventually building a group called the Bell Boys with Johnny Bond and Dick Rhinehardt. Wakely remained in Oklahoma City until 1940, when Gene Autry invited him to California as a regular on *Melody Ranch* and a member of his touring group. Eventually, Jimmy Wakely formed his own band and began appearing around California at fairs, rodeos, and theaters as well as on the Foreman Phillips ballroom circuit. Additionally, Wakely found time to make several motion pictures in the singing cowboy vein and produce several hits for Decca during the war, most notably "Too Late" and "I'm Sending You Red Roses." In late 1946 he signed with Capitol Records, releasing a number of enormously successful duets with pop singer Margaret Whiting in addition to solo offerings with his country band. In 1949, *Billboard* named him the third most popular singer on the nation's jukeboxes. Wakely rode the wave of success into the early fifties, touring with Bob Hope and making several guest appearances on the network portion of the *Grand Ole Opry* and a variety of television programs throughout the country. In 1953, Wakely switched to Coral Records, where he produced his own records as well as served as head of the label's country music division. He never completely abandoned country music, but he increasingly recorded with orchestras and toured with large ensembles. Wakely consistently walked a fine line between pop and country; to his credit, he retained a following among listeners in both genres.[25]

Wakely's recordings of the postwar decade reveal his considerable versatility as a singer as well as his foresight into country pop's potential. On his early pressings for Capitol, he used accordion, clarinets, steel guitar, and fiddles interchangeably in a variety of musical settings. In "Easy to Please," "Milkcow Blues," and "Mine All Mine," he keeps the arrangements simple and bluesy, leaving plenty of room for outstanding guitar work from Jack Rivers (on lead) and Pete Martinez (on steel). On "Someday You'll Call My Name" and "I Wish I Had a Nickel" he offers his strongest country performances, while "Dust" and "I Love You So Much It Hurts" serve as excellent examples of his pop potential. On a reworking of Floyd Tillman's "One Has My Name (the Other Has My Heart)," he perfects the country pop approach, blending steel guitar, clarinet, and harmonica sounds with hard-edged lyrics sung in a vibrato style. Wakely explains the arrangement of the song and offers an explanation of its considerable success:

> I saw that Tillman had something going there, so I decided to do it. And I used clarinets and a harmonica in harmony. And I used a Gordon Jenkins's type one-finger piano. In other words, it was the pop sounds of that day to give it a pop western sound. Floyd Tillman had two fiddles, strictly what we called a string band. Well mine went on up to the top of the charts and passed Floyd's because mine had a wider appeal and would get on jukeboxes in the better restaurants, if you will, that wouldn't put on string bands. There was some discrimination in those days and they would put on mine because it had a modern sound so I got away with it.

Despite being banned by the CBS and NBC networks for its adulterous implications, "One Has My Name (the Other Has My Heart)" achieved phenomenal success and firmly established Jimmy Wakely on the country scene. In 1949, he recorded his first duet with songstress Margaret Whiting, a pop singer with the Capitol label since the early 1940s. Wakely maintains that he taught Whiting how to slur her singing to make it sound country; judging from the success of their first duets, "Slipping Around"/"Wedding Bells," he succeeded. Later that year, the duo's appearance at the Ryman drew a crowd of over 4,000; additionally, they made the cover of *Billboard*. Not surprisingly, the success of their debut single led to several other Wakely/Whiting pairings, including "I'll Never Slip around Again," "Let's Go to Church Next Sunday Morning," and "I Don't Want to Be Free." In between recordings with Whiting, Wakely released an array of straight country ("Solid South"), western swing ("Won't You Ride in My Little Red Wagon"), and pop ("Rainbow at Midnight"). Wakely also demonstrated that he was not gun-shy about recording with full orchestras and explains his purpose for doing so: "It's always been my contention that country music should be sold to the, call it the upper echelon, or what have you, [so] I started early in my career using orchestras, large bands like Nelson Riddle . . . and Les Baxter." At the same time, he rarely played straight pop for fear of losing his country base. In 1951, he turned down a potentially lucrative New York engagement because his western dates consistently brought bigger grosses. Switching to Coral Records, he continued on with the eclectic approach, sometimes recording without any country instrumentation ("You Can't Break the Chains of Love") and at other times inserting a crashing steel guitar solo right in the middle of an otherwise straight pop song ("I've Had My Share of Sorrow"). In the early fifties, Wakely chose to remain on the West Coast, enjoying the autonomy that the Coral deal involved. In remaining steadfast to his country course, Wakely continued to produce some of the most interesting country recordings of the mid-fifties. Carrying on the western pop tradition established in the early 1940s, Jimmy Wakely kept the smooth sounds of the California coast alive while making his own contribution to the country genre with his unique musical vision.[26]

The crossover success of artists Jimmy Wakely, Red Foley, and Eddy Arnold in the late forties and early fifties indicated to many observers that the national acceptance country music enjoyed during World War II was neither temporal nor incidental. Country pop artists in general worked to solidify the achievements of wartime singers Al Dexter and Tex Ritter by offering listeners a soft-edged version of country music that belied the hillbilly stereotype. The sophisticated sound of country pop attracted northerners seeking an alternative to bland pop and southerners not particularly receptive to honky-tonk. It initiated a major breakthrough for country music into the American middle class, and Nashville became the primary beneficiary of the development. Ironically, country pop initially arose in Hollywood; Wakely, Ritter, Gene Autry, Elton Britt, and the Sons of the Pioneers all made important contributions to the subgenre's vocal and instrumental development before 1946 with their peculiar mixture of western and popular idioms. Although these artists continued to produce hits after the war, the focus of country pop shifted east after Arnold and Foley brought the subgenre to fruition with their blend of smooth singing, professional musicianship, and nonwestern lyrics. As Nashville became the home of country pop, artists who remained in California focused their attention on creating music for the West Coast audience. Taking a cue from western swing, they embraced danceable rhythms and novelty lyrics on the way to reviving the blues tradition in country music. Their success spawned a country blues renaissance and set the stage for a showdown within the industry for creative control.

7 | ACROSS THE GREAT DIVIDE
COUNTRY BLUES RENAISSANCE AND THE
CENTRALIZATION OF COUNTRY MUSIC

In the late forties, the Nashville and California country music scenes vied for the honor of country music's nucleus. Building on the success of cowboy singers and western swing performers, California remained a hotspot for country music throughout the forties, mainly due to its flourishing dance halls and the multitude of country music listeners located on the West Coast. In the early 1950s, country music performers continued to make frequent treks there for personal appearances. Nashville did not rise to its level of predominance until the mid-fifties. In the mid- to late forties and even into the early fifties, California continued to rival Nashville as "Hillbilly H.Q."[1]

Three factors contributed to southern California's thriving country music scene in the postwar period: the sharp increase in the number of potential listeners there, the television industry's receptiveness to the genre, and the success of Los Angeles–based Capitol Records. Although the *Grand Ole Opry* offered prestige to country music performers, southern California provided greater opportunities for exposure and personal appearance revenue. Before Jim Denny and the WSM Artists' Service Bureau built up a head of steam in the early 1950s, country music artists viewed Los Angeles as the premier touring area of the country. Between 1940 and 1952, the city increased its population to over 2 million (a 36 percent increase), with metropolitan Los Angeles witnessing a 58 percent increase in residents and the city's suburbs growing by 81 percent in the same period. By 1952, 6.5 million people lived in southern California, many with money in their pockets and an affinity for country music. The proliferation of country radio shows and western swing dance halls that emerged in World War II continued to draw crowds after the war. In late 1946, 20,000 to 30,000 people filled the ballrooms on Saturday nights in Los Angeles alone. The coming of television in the late forties put a dent in these figures and hurt many dance-oriented western swing acts, but many other country music performers made the transition to the new medium and took advantage of opportunities it offered.[2]

Several country music shows debuted in southern California in the late forties and early fifties. In 1952, fifteen such programs appeared on Los Angeles television every week. While Spade Cooley's show deserves the honor of Los Angeles's first regular country and western television program, two other series emerged in the late forties and early fifties that eclipsed Cooley in stature and network exposure: *Hometown Jamboree* and *Town Hall Party*. Cliffie Stone was the creative force behind *Hometown Jamboree*, which debuted on local Los Angeles television in 1949. A native of southern California, Stone first appeared on radio as a musician and comedian in the mid-thirties. During the war, he emerged as a major figure on the California music scene, hosting an early-morning radio show, *Wake Up Ranch*, and establishing himself as a noted bassist, producer, and talent scout for Capitol Records. Sometime in the mid-forties, he inaugurated the *Dinner Bell Round-Up*, a noontime program broadcast over KXLA. Stone also appeared on the *Hollywood Barn Dance* in the mid- to late forties before opening his own dance hall in Placentia. Eventually he moved to 2,600-capacity Legion Stadium in El Monte, where he began broadcasting Cliffie Stone's *Hometown Jamboree* over KLAC-TV, opposite Cooley's show before both appeared back-to-back on KLAC-TV. *Hometown Jamboree* offered listeners an eclectic blend of country and pop music with an outstanding house band that sounded anything but hillbilly. With a who's who of southern California performers that included Tennessee Ernie Ford, Harold Hensley, Eddie Kirk, Speedy West, and Jimmy Bryant, *Hometown Jamboree* soon became a fixture on Los Angeles television.[3]

Broadcast from Compton, California, with a cast that included at various times such notables as Tex Ritter, Johnny Bond, Merle Travis, and Lefty Frizzell, *Town Hall Party* offered viewers another Los Angeles–based country television show in the mid-1950s. Put together by promoter William Wagnon, the show debuted on local radio in 1952; soon thereafter, it acquired a network affiliate as well as a spot on local television. Although the program showcased West Coast–based acts, it also welcomed popular country music performers from Nashville. Not surprisingly, some competitive antagonism brewed between Los Angeles and Nashville in the 1950s, as Cliffie Stone pointed out: "The West Coast resented the hell out of Nashville [for] saying they were the home of country music, because they really weren't, you know, but they were smart." The success of Los Angeles–based country television programs and others, such as WLW's *Midwestern Hayride* (broadcast Sundays on NBC-TV for a time), contrasted with Nashville's sluggishness to embrace television. Part of Nashville's hesitation resulted from the limitations of its market potential. An early country music show on Nashville's WSM-TV in 1950, *Tennessee Jamboree*, reached listeners only as far as the Kentucky border. *Opry* management tolerated the California programs but moved to create a video version of the *Grand Ole Opry* for national broadcast when

Red Foley relocated to Springfield and ABC announced its plans to broadcast a television version of the *Ozark Jubilee*. To this end, they commenced filming of *The Country Show: With Stars of the Grand Ole Opry* in late 1954, which debuted on network television the following January. Television versions of *Town Hall Party,* the *Ozark Jubilee,* and *Midwestern Hayride* all outlasted the *Opry*'s *Country Show,* which remained on the air for only two years. In the mid-1950s, the Nashville country music industry accepted defeat in the video medium and concentrated its efforts on promotion, recording, and, of course, the radio program *Grand Ole Opry*.[4]

California migration gave West Coast country acts an audience, television provided them with exposure, and Capitol Records afforded them distribution of their pressings. Established in 1942 by Glenn Wallichs and Johnny Mercer, Capitol emerged as the primary outlet for West Coast country music recordings in the postwar period. California country music and Capitol matured hand-in-hand; artists Tex Williams, Tex Ritter, and Jimmy Wakely all contributed to the label's astonishing growth in sales figures, from $200,000 in 1942 to over $13 million in 1951. Behind the scenes, A and R men, promoters and agents such as Cliffie Stone, Lee Gillette, and Ken Nelson, secured and recorded the finest country music singers and musicians that southern California had to offer, while Capitol's first representative in Nashville, W. D. "Dee" Kilpatrick, concentrated on landing *Grand Ole Opry* talent. Capitol Records opened its doors to all types of country music performers from different parts of the country, but their greatest success after the war came with eclectic, California-based acts, such as Hank Thompson, Merle Travis, Tennessee Ernie Ford, Tex Williams, and Jimmy Wakely. These artists surrounded themselves with musicians willing to experiment with different sounds and styles in an effort to create music that appealed to a variety of listeners. California country recorded by Capitol often bore little resemblance to country music produced east of the continental divide; instead, it more readily bore the imprints of sophistication and musical experimentation and less emphasis on lyrical quality and evocative vocals. Closer to mainstream pop and western swing than to honky-tonk or the music of the progressives, postwar California country was more lighthearted and spirited than heavy-headed and spiritual. Capitol Records offered a polished and professional product for urban listeners initially drawn to Al Dexter's novelty records and the energetic version of western swing envisioned by Spade Cooley. Capitol Records did not hold a monopoly on country music talent in California, but it soon became a stronghold for West Coast performers seeking to distance themselves from hillbilly music, honky-tonk, and even the roots-based country pop produced by southern-bred acts.[5]

Wartime western pop singers affiliated with Capitol, such as Tex Ritter and Wesley Tuttle, along with other California-based performers, such as Gene Autry, helped lay the foundation for the development of the country pop subgenre in the mid- to late forties, which was later fully realized by Eddy Arnold, Red Foley, and other southeastern acts. The country blues subgenre, on the other hand, had roots in the South but matured in California. Despite Jimmy Wakely's success, most successful California country acts did not veer toward the country pop fusion. Dance halls were jumping and migrants still coming, so California performers tended to lean toward more propulsive music suitable for the ballroom milieu and the West Coast state of mind. They liked the energy of western swing but cared little for the sound of the fiddle; they favored the polish and escapism of western pop, but felt averse to its blandness. Mixing the jazz and blues of western swing with the gloss of western pop, they produced a western blues hybrid, the first of three types of country blues produced in the postwar period. Unlike the African American–derived blues produced by artists affiliated with the King record label and youth-oriented rockabilly, western blues was aimed at urban, middle-class adults, attracting them with humorous lyrics and danceable sound. Backed by high-caliber musicians, Merle Travis, Tennessee Ernie Ford, and Rose Maddox fronted the three premier western blues bands based in California after World War II. Each mixed country and blues in a different way, but all shared a penchant for upbeat melodies and novelty lyrics. Their emphasis on lighthearted lyrical fare soon became an identifying characteristic of western blues and an indicator of trends in country music at large.

Beginning with "Pistol Packin' Mama" and continuing on after the war with Tex Williams's "Smoke! Smoke! Smoke! (That Cigarette)," country artists found novelty numbers the best way to reach urban (and suburban) American listeners. In 1954, Steve Sholes noted the development of the novelty song as one of the principal reasons for country music's postwar surge. The percentage of novelty songs on the charts dramatically increased after 1945. Songs of this type maintained a plurality on the charts in every year during the postwar decade except 1949. Even honky-tonkers jumped on the novelty bandwagon; in fact, honky-tonk's rise to prominence in the early 1950s directly coincided with its embrace of more lighthearted song material as well as the rise of a softer vocal approach to the subgenre. As the nation entered the fifties, both country and pop listeners demonstrated a decided preference for novelty and upbeat lyrics. Country music performers of all types recognized this trend; country blues acts, in particular, and especially those located on the West Coast, emphasized humorous subject matter as a means to attracting the postwar urban audience.[6]

Of the aforementioned western blues acts, Merle Travis proved the most deft at writing clever and humorous lyrics. Additionally, Travis was an accomplished musician and the most influential standard guitarist of the postwar period. Few performers could match his wit in writing and mastery of the fingerpicking guitar style. Born in Muhlenberg County, Kentucky, Merle Travis first learned to play the five-string banjo from his father around the age of eight. A few years later, after one of his older brothers built him a guitar, he began absorbing the fingerpicking style indigenous to the area. Rich Kienzle traces the unique playing method back to the early part of the century and notes the contribution of two black guitarists, Sylvester Weaver and Arnold Shultz, to its development. Gradually, through interaction in the coal mines and general musical diffusion, white guitarists in the area, such as Kennedy Jones, Lester "Plucker" English, Mose Rager, and Ike Everly, picked up on the technique and added their own embellishments. Travis heard Rager and Everly playing at local parties and soon adapted the style. Over the years, Travis referred to the technique as "thumb picking": "That's a style of playing with your thumb. You more or less play what a piano player plays with his left hand—the accompaniment—and you play your melody with your finger or fingers, in my case, I just use one finger."[7]

Not receptive to the idea of working in the coal mines, Travis joined the Civilian Conservation Corps (CCC) around 1935, staying only until he saved enough money to purchase a new Gretch guitar. In 1936, while visiting one of his brothers in Evansville, Indiana, Travis joined a local band called the Tennessee Tomcats and began appearing on radio. The next year he toured with Clayton McMichen's Georgia Wildcats before settling in at Cincinnati's WLW in 1938 as a member of a western band called the Drifting Pioneers. Over the course of the next two years, Travis introduced thousands of young guitarists to the Kentucky thumb-picking style through his shows on 50,000-watt WLW, among them, Chet Atkins and Joe Maphis. Years later, Travis commented on the significance of the WLW broadcasts, all the while acknowledging his teachers: "I was probably the first thumb-picker, finger-style player on radio, but I give them all the credit because that's where I learned it, from Mose Rager and Ike Everly." The war broke up the band, but Travis remained on WLW as a member of the *Boone County Jamboree*. After striking up a friendship and professional relationship, Travis and Grandpa Jones met Syd Nathan at a local record store while shopping for some gospel material for their radio show. With Jones, Travis made his first recordings on Nathan's King label in late 1943, just before joining the marines. Discharged early the next year, Travis relocated to California, joined Ray Whitley's popular western swing band, and acted as King's West Coast A and R man briefly. In the California dance halls, Travis learned the importance of a full-bodied, lively sound. Years later, he reflected on the changes precipitated by the war: "[In] the first groups I played with, we played very few dances because we didn't have amplified instruments . . . but after the war, in order to eat, I learned that people liked to get together and dance and hear upbeat tunes." He eventually designed his own solid-body electric guitar, which inventor Paul Bigsby built for him in 1948. Travis recalled the impetus behind his design: "I kept wondering why steel guitars would sustain the sound so long, when a hollow body electric guitar like mine would fade out real quick. I came to the conclusion it was all because the steel guitar was solid." Once on the California music scene, Travis gained a reputation for his jovial spirit, innovative playing at dances, and stellar session work. In 1946, he signed with Capitol Records.[8]

Ironically, Merle Travis played very little guitar at his first Capitol sessions; Cliffie Stone and Lee Gillette encouraged a bouncy trumpet and accordion-dominated sound. Judging from the success of jaunty songs "Cincinnati Lou," "No Vacancy," and "What a Shame," the formula worked perfectly. However, much of the success of these songs and others, such as "Divorce Me C.O.D.," "Sweet Temptation," and "So Round, So Firm, So Fully Packed," must be credited to Travis's superior songwriting skills. Rich Kienzle points out, "Merle wrote colloquial lyrics, spiced with American slang that helped his songs gain instant public acceptance." Travis possessed a keen ability to find humor in the mundane and looked to pop culture and news headlines for material. The songwriter explains the creative process behind the song "Divorce Me C.O.D.": "I came up with an idea and I went to Cliffie Stone and said, 'Hey, I've got an idea to make a record with a word that has never been used on record. I bet people would play this on the jukeboxes when they're out drinking beer.' He said, 'What is it?' I said, 'Divorce.' He said, 'Oh Lord! Wow! I don't think they'd ever allow you to record a song about divorce.' I said, 'Well, I'll make it kind of funny and fast.' He said, 'Well, see what you can do.'" Released in 1946, the song became one the year's biggest hits, despite a ban placed on it by two networks. In 1947, he wrote the number one country song of the year, "Smoke! Smoke! Smoke! (That Cigarette)," for Tex Williams. Over the next few years, he wrote and recorded several other lighthearted hits for the label, including "Fat Gal," "Merle's Boogie Woogie," and "Crazy Boogie."[9]

Merle Travis achieved his greatest commercial success with novelty numbers, but his artistic legacy grew out of his appreciation of blues and folk material. In 1946, he recorded a number of "folk" songs at the behest of Capitol management that appeared on an album entitled *Songs of the Coal Mines*. Backed by Cliffie

Stone's incomparable bass playing and his own acoustic guitar, the songs "Dark as a Dungeon" and "Sixteen Tons" reveal Travis's incisive storytelling abilities. His guitar playing and singing on traditional numbers "John Henry," "Nine-Pound Hammer," and "I Am a Pilgrim" (a song he learned from Mose Rager) were evocative and flawless. As the forties progressed, Travis drifted away from the accordion and trumpet approach and began delving deeper into the blues. On "I Got a Mean Old Woman," and "Start Even," Travis lowers the pitch of his voice and offers some remarkable blues licks on his guitar. Recorded with a vocal and instrumental group called the Whippoorwills, the penetrating blues of "Trouble, Trouble" amalgamates folk and pop music effortlessly. The semiautobiographical "Guitar Rag" offers a humorous glimpse into the life of a popular Kentucky guitar picker and his effect on a small, rural community. Travis periodically returned to straight pop in the early fifties as well, most effectively on "Deep South" and "Let's Settle Down (to Runnin' around Together)." Gradually, he moved closer to all-instrumental work, beginning with a remarkable cover of Gus Kahn's "I'll See You in My Dreams" and continuing on through the mid-fifties with such numbers as "Blue Smoke" and "Walking the Strings." In 1955, his songwriting talents resulted in another million-seller when Tennessee Ernie Ford recorded "Sixteen Tons"; that same year, he began touring with Hank Thompson. Eventually, poor health and personal problems forced him into semiretirement, but he continued to record into the 1980s. Along with a handful of other performers, he remains one of the towering figures in post–World War II country music. Merle Travis revolutionized country music with his guitar-playing style and lyrical devices, and by disguising the blues in western and pop settings, he reawakened country music performers' interest in the genre by demonstrating the musical freedom it provided.[10]

Tennessee Ernie Ford was another West Coast–based performer who explored the possibilities of mixing blues and country. Rural blues provided the framework for Travis's musical exploits, but Ford looked to contemporary rhythm and blues for inspiration. Backed by the most flamboyant country musicians on the West Coast, Ford produced a high-octane version of western blues guaranteed to keep dancers moving and listeners smiling. A natural comic and a gifted singer, he could shout the blues, play the hillbilly rube, and sing sophisticated pop with equal dexterity. As time wore on, he shed himself of the hillbilly caricature and renounced the aggressive sound and style that initially brought him fame and so clearly portended the rock movement. In the postwar decade, however, few country acts could match the energy and drive he and his band put into their performances.

Ernest Jennings Ford grew up in Bristol, Tennessee, surrounded by music. As Ford recalled in his autobiography: "We sang at home, we sang at church, and we sang at weddings and funerals and at prisons or wherever there happened to be a need for it. Not for money, mind you—we never got paid. We just enjoyed singing. . . . It was part of our religion, part of our way of life." Growing up two blocks away from a neighborhood predominantly populated by African Americans, Ford undoubtedly first gained exposure to black folk music in his youth. Additionally, as a result of his family being active Methodist church members, he also came to appreciate gospel music. Harboring dreams of becoming a professional singer, Ford left Bristol after two years as an announcer on WOPI to attend the Cincinnati Conservatory of Music in the fall of 1939. The lure of radio (and the promise of a steady paycheck) led him back into announcing positions at stations in Atlanta and Knoxville before World War II broke out. After serving as an officer in the Army Air Corps during the conflict, Ford returned to Bristol briefly before leaving for San Bernardino, California, to accept a job as radio announcer on KFXM. In California, he initiated an early morning country show entitled *Dude Ranch Party* (later changed to *Bar Nothin' Round-Up Time*), offering rural comedy and spinning (and singing along with) the latest country hits as "Tennessee Ernie." In 1947, he moved to KXLA in Los Angeles and gained popularity for his disc jockey show and his appearances on Cliffie Stone's noontime *Dinner Bell Round-Up*. When Stone's *Hometown Jamboree* debuted in 1949, Ford joined the cast as backup singer and comedian. Additionally, he signed with Capitol Records, charting several hits in his first two years with the label. In the fall of 1950, a duet with Kay Starr entitled "I'll Never Be Free" made its way into the pop and country top five. Gradually, Ford moved away from his hayseed "Tennessee Ernie" image, recording sophisticated big band numbers as well as making concert appearances at such elegant establishments as the Thunderbird Hotel in Las Vegas, the Copacabana in New York, and the London Palladium. In 1956, *The Ford Show* debuted on prime-time television and remained a popular program for the remainder of the fifties. In the late fifties he recorded three successful gospel albums, and, in the early sixties, hosted another variety show on ABC-TV. He remained a popular fixture on television into the 1980s, before declining health forced him into retirement.[11]

Many people associate Ford with his popular gospel material, but the singer actually began his recording career as a country comedy act. His first single for Capitol, "Milk 'em in the Morning Blues," was basically an extension of his *Bar Nothin'* program; Ford laid on an exaggerated accent, cracked jokes between verses, and sang comedic lyrics. An advertisement for the single in *Billboard* pictured Ford in overalls and a straw hat looking every bit the country rube. On Ford's second session with Capitol, he began to move in another direction, closer to the boogie idiom so popular in the forties. A derivative of African American blues, boogie music burst on the Los Angeles scene during the war, with the release of Porky Freeman's "Porky's Boogie Woogie on the Strings." The Delmore Brothers became the first country band to fully embrace the musical style, releasing a series of popular boogie singles after the war, effervescent numbers with an eight-to-the-bar beat and heavy emphasis on bass percussion. With "Country Junction," Ford began to experiment with the motif, backed by Moon Mullican, Merle Travis, Cliffie Stone, and a group of other renowned California musicians. On "Smoky Mountain Boogie," Travis offers a stinging guitar solo while Ford's full-bodied singing adds the appropriate vocal punch. Sometime around 1950, lead guitarist Jimmy Bryant joined Ford's band, which also included Bill Liebert on piano, Speedy West on pedal steel guitar, Harold Hensley on fiddle, Eddie Kirk on rhythm guitar, Cliffie Stone on bass, and Roy Harte on drums. One of country music's most vivacious ensembles, Ford's band played with a drive perfectly suited for the West Coast dance scene. Stone, Kirk, and Harte provide a propulsive, heavy beat, while Liebert and Hensley add jazz and country flourishes to West's and Bryant's electric guitar work. A fan of jazz guitarist Barney Kessel, Jimmy Bryant helped popularize Leo Fender's solid body Broadcaster/Telecaster model, which later became the centerpiece of the Bakersfield Sound. Speedy West gained a reputation on the West Coast soon after arriving from Missouri in 1946. Developing a unique style characterized by crashing chords, fluctuations in volume, and rapid movement of the bar up and down the steel guitar's frets, West soon became a highly sought session musician. In the early 1950s, he recorded 6,000 records with 177 different singers. In 1948, he purchased the first pedal steel manufactured by Paul Bigsby, and the next year, he joined Ford's band. By 1950, Bryant and West had developed a musical rapport that gave all of their recordings together a distinct and professional sound. Recorded in November 1950, Ford's "Shotgun Boogie" is one of the band's many musical highlights. The lyrics made little sense and Capitol executives remained hesitant about releasing the single for several months, but when it finally made its way into the market it went straight to the top of the charts, where it stayed for ten weeks. Ford's spirited vocal and the outrageous musical atmosphere of the recording proved contagious. Perhaps because few of the musicians ever expected the song to find release, the recording has a no-holds-barred feel to it that unchains the bands free-spiritedness. Not surprisingly, several boogie songs followed, along with several other fast-paced numbers ("Hey, Mr. Cotton

Picker," "You're My Sugar," and "Ain't Nobody's Business") that rolled along with infectious carefree abandon. [12]

Ford's boogie hits had roots in blues and jazz and were clearly escapist numbers, long on musical punch and short on meaning. Ford, however, could also sing quite expressively, particularly when the band slowed down the pace and when he tackled more substantive lyrical material. On "You'll Find Her Name Written There," he demonstrates the full power of his voice in a pop setting, and on two covers of songs brought to the pop charts by Frankie Laine, "Mule Train" and "Cry of the Wild Goose," he rivals if not surpasses the popular vocalist's interpretive abilities. When Capitol finally began gearing him to the pop market in the mid-fifties, Ford delivered sturdy vocal performances on "River of No Return" and "There Is Beauty in Everything." Ford's postwar-era legacy, however, will remain his blues and boogie numbers. Paired with jazz and pop vocalist Kay Starr, Ford delves deep into the blues for "I'll Never Be Free," a major hit on both the pop and country charts. On "Sweet Temptation," he transforms Merle Travis's novelty song into a stomping rhythm and blues number backed by a heavy rhythm section, Billy May's big band orchestra, and stellar guitar work from Jimmy Bryant and West. Overcome with enthusiasm, Ford growls out an ecstatic yell right before a huge horn section and West begin trading high-powered musical barbs. On "Blackberry Boogie," Ford and his band pull out all the stops, running full-throttle all the way to rock with pounding drums, dynamic guitar solos, and roadhouse piano playing. On "I Don't Know," he gives contemporary blues shouters a run for their money on a song originally recorded by Willie Mabon on Chicago's Chess label. In early 1953, Ford and his band rocked the London Palladium, playing such up-tempo numbers as "Shot Gun Boogie," "Blackberry Boogie," "Kissin' Bug Boogie," "Stack-O-Lee," and "I Don't Know" as well as slower songs such as "Kentucky Waltz" and Gershwin's "Summertime." Two years later, he moved closer to mainstream country and pop with a smooth reworking of Merle Travis's "Sixteen Tons" and the debut of his cosmopolitan television show. In the late fifties and sixties, he distanced himself from the blues-shouting hillbilly image he projected as "Tennessee Ernie." At their rollicking peak, however, Ford and his band recorded some of the wildest and most uninhibited country music of the postwar era. [13]

The Maddox Brothers and Rose were the only group on the West Coast in the late forties that could match the furious enthusiasm of Ford's band. A motley aggregation with more attitude than inherent talent, the Maddoxes built up a huge following in the California dance halls with their unbridled blend of blues, honky-tonk, and western swing. Rose Maddox stood at the front of the band as their flamboyant and charismatic lead singer. Together with Kitty Wells and Molly O'Day, Maddox helped establish a place for women in country music at a time when men overwhelmingly dominated the genre. After the war, the most successful women in country music were female pop singers who had crossover hits. Some, such as Kay Starr, began their careers in country music before becoming big band vocalists, while others, such as Jo Stafford and Margaret Whiting, initially made names for themselves in the pop idiom. Patti Page, originally from Oklahoma, surpassed all the crossover women with her monster hit, "Tennessee Waltz," in 1950. Women's chances of succeeding within the parameters of country music appeared slim at best in the late forties and early fifties.

The West Coast scene offered the greatest opportunities for women country artists. Some female performers, such as Mary Ford and Rose Lee Maphis, managed to break through the male barrier while working with their husbands, multi-talented guitarists Les Paul and Joe Maphis. Maddox, Wells, and O'Day, however, pushed the envelope just a little farther by fronting unequivocally country bands that more often than not focused attention on their singing. Maddox differed from the other two in her determination to make a full-time career in country music and in her willingness to step out of the demure country woman stereotype. Like the rockabilly women she undoubtedly influenced, Maddox threw herself into the spirit of the music and projected a strong image, all the while never overstepping the boundaries of sexual propriety or appearing morally decadent. Beyond their important contributions to woman's place in country music, the Maddox Brothers and Rose created incredibly invigorating and progressive music a decade ahead of its time. Fittingly, they appeared regularly at Marty Landau's Riverside Rancho, one of the West Coast's biggest dance halls, alongside such dynamic performers as Tennessee Ernie Ford, Merle Travis, Tex Williams, and others. The Rancho was a hedonistic paradise frequented by barflies and migrants looking for escape from their daily worries. From their colorful costumes to their propulsive music, the Maddox Brothers and Rose gave Rancho patrons just what they wanted to see and hear and left an imprint on many young country musicians, who transformed their music into the Bakersfield Sound. [14]

The Maddox family left central Alabama for California at the height of the Depression, in March 1933, in search of employment. Soon after their arrival, they joined the many migratory crop pickers in the fertile San Joaquin Valley working for paltry wages and moving with the crop seasons. Despite their poverty, the young Maddox brothers always found time to play music, carrying on a family tradition established back in the South. In 1937, Fred Maddox, eighteen at the time, grew tired of crop picking and approached a Modesto businessman about the possibility of sponsoring a country show featuring the family. The man agreed to the arrangement but stipulated that a female singer appear with the group. Though only eleven at the time, Rose Maddox took on the job, backed by her brothers Fred (on bass), Cal and Cliff (on guitar), and Don (on fiddle); in time, Henry also joined the band on mandolin. The radio offered a starting point, but the brothers continued to work regular jobs during the daytime, augmenting their income by playing at rodeos on weekends and barrooms at night. In 1939, the group won first prize in the country band competition at the Sacramento State Fair, a one-year contract with a Sacramento station that reached Arizona, Oregon, and Washington, as well as all parts of California. The war halted the group's progress, but the brothers returned in 1945 with a fixed determination to make it in the music business. Mixing comedy with a versatile musical repertoire, the Maddox Brothers and Rose focused their attention on dance hall audiences' preferences for diversionary material. Rose Maddox points out the difference between the pre- and postwar outlook of the band: "Prior to the war we worked for tips, mostly. Then after the war we started getting paid for doing dances and stuff. So we had to change our style some, to really *entertain*." Taking a cue from western swing bands, the brothers plugged in their instruments and hired a lead guitarist (Jimmy Winkle) and a steel guitar player (Bud Duncan). Fred Maddox explains the reasoning behind the decision to enlarge the band and amplify its instruments: "The louder you get, and the more power you put behind it, it puts it in the people's feet and in their bodies, see? . . . And it made us feel it when we played, and it made us do a show." An eclectic mix of comedy, rhythm and blues covers, gospel, honky-tonk, and traditional country favorites, the band's repertoire offered something for everyone. When they began dressing themselves in elaborate western costumes, a trademark that earned them the honor of "America's Most Colorful Hillbilly Band," their popularity soared. Through their records for the Four-Star label, their X-station radio transcriptions, and their exciting performances at clubs such as the Riverside Rancho, the Maddox Brothers and Rose became a highly sought show band west of the Mississippi. On the heels of the success of a gospel-tinged number entitled "Flowers for the Master's Bouquet," they made a guest appearance on the *Grand Ole Opry* in early 1949 and began touring extensively in the East. In the early fifties, they appeared on both the *Hometown Jamboree* and *Town Hall Party* television programs in California and joined the *Louisiana Hayride*. In 1953, they secured a major label contract with Columbia Records and continued to ride the wave of their popularity before television and the rock phenomenon finally took a heavy toll. In the mid-fifties, Rose Maddox embarked on a part-time solo career, and eventually quit the family band in 1956. Ultimately, the Maddox Brothers disbanded in the late fifties. [15]

Though no sound recording could capture the full effect of the group's road-house performances, the Maddoxes' Four-Star releases come remarkably close to capturing the full breadth of the band's eclecticism and musical repertoire. Tackling country, gospel, blues, boogies, western songs, and sentimental numbers, the Maddox Brothers and Rose approach every song with a confidence and enthusiasm that lends a listenable quality to nearly every one of their recordings. When they play it straight, as they do on sentimental tunes ("Careless Driver") and on straightforward love songs ("Sunset Trail Waltz"), they sound like an old-time or western pop band, with subtle instrumentation and sincere singing. On faster numbers, however, the group comes alive with a kinetic energy and carefree spontaneity more indicative of its attitude and musical approach. As the band's unofficial leader, Fred Maddox kept things rolling along with his on-record wisecracks and enthusiastic bass playing. Neither Fred nor any of the other Maddox brothers possessed superlative playing abilities, but what they lacked in talent they more than made up for in self-assurance. Commenting on the group's ability to overcome its limited musical skills, Fred Maddox sums up the brothers' musical approach: "None of us could read music; we were not accomplished musicians. We didn't do music this way, that way, or any other way. We just did what we felt and what came natural." [16]

Fred's pounding upright bass; Henry's loud, staccato, amplified mandolin solos; Don's uninhibited fiddling; and Cal's energetic rhythm guitar and bluesy harmonica playing produced a sound unlike any other contemporary country band. Although they often played at a speed akin to bluegrass, their use of amplifiers and steel guitar preclude a comparison with the alternative string-band sound. Despite their heavy emphasis on bass rhythms and unbridled solos, their downplay of fiddle and steel guitar parts in favor of hot electric guitar runs places them beyond the scope of western swing and closer to rhythm and blues. Hiring seventeen-year-old Roy Nichols as lead guitarist in 1949, the band moved further away from country and closer to the western-blues hybrid. An early Fender Telecaster enthusiast, Nichols combined Eldon Shamblin bass runs and stinging chords with high-gain bursts in a way that portended both rocka-billy and the Bakersfield Sound. Nichols's exciting work on "Water Baby Blues (Boogie)," "(New) Step It Up and Go," and "South," in particular, contributes greatly to the band's recognition as one of the most innovative country groups of the 1940s. Henry Maddox's high-volume electric mandolin solos on "Georgia's Playhouse Boogie" and "Mean and Wicked Boogie" give the listener an idea of how he helped to keep audiences moving at the group's dance hall performances. "Shimmy Shakin' Daddy" and "Sally, Let Your Bangs Hang Down," with their lascivious lyrics and brawling instrumental solos, offer prime examples of the Maddoxes' good-time emphasis. Although Fred Maddox took the lead vocal on the group's more salacious numbers, Rose often joined in on choruses, or in the case of "Whoa Sailor," provided the female side of a story with the duet vocal. Rose Maddox proved quite capable of singing in a variety of musical settings. On "Honky Tonkin' " and "Move It on Over" she sings primal honky-tonk, and "Beautiful Bouquet" and "Forever Yours," both from the group's tenure with Columbia Records, reveal her as a smooth pop singer. One of the most assertive female singers of the 1940s, Maddox could evoke disenchantment ("[Pay Me] Alimony Blues," "Eight Thirty Blues," and "Baby, You Should Live So Long") or aggressiveness ("It's Only Human Nature" and "I'll Make Sweet Love to You") in her portrayals of strong women. "I Can't Stop Loving You" indicates the country pop direction she took upon embarking on a solo career in the mid-fifties. After signing with Columbia in 1952, the band, by edict, became more inhibited. Fred Maddox recalls the origins of the rocky relationship the group had with the major label: "Columbia didn't want us like we was . . . they wanted it a certain way, but Four-Star wanted it like we had it. Still, they had the contract. There was nothin' we could do about it." Though "No Help Wanted" showed signs of spontaneity, most of the Columbia recordings present the band playing more straightforward honky-tonk or country pop. In their kaleidoscopic prime, however, the Maddox Brothers and Rose disregarded all musical boundaries and conventions; in doing so, they created some of the most rousing country music of the postwar period.[17]

The creative freedom given to the Maddoxes by the independent Four-Star label indicates a nationwide trend in the music industry of the late forties and early fifties. Generally, most majors frowned on music that transgressed the parameters of what they viewed as a marketable product. Within the realms of country music, West Coast–based Capitol represented the only large record company willing to booster an eclectic musical form like country blues. With western swing on the decline, the majors looked to country pop and honky-tonk for their big sellers in the country field. Even more so than postwar traditionalism, country blues represented an aberrant musical form and was viewed as a deviation from the direction country music seemed to be going. Despite receiving minimal support from the major labels, however, country blues steadily attracted listeners to its vitality and liberal music message. Its lyrical emphasis on humor and intemperance appealed to a minority group of country music listeners primarily located in urban areas disenchanted with honky-tonk's lyrical commiseration and mainstream country's increasing affiliation with conservative pop music.

As noted above, country blues took several forms; the California version evolved out of western swing and tended to emphasize dance music and escapist lyrics. A large market of western swing devotees and dance hall patrons existed in California, so Capitol sanctioned western blues with reasonable assurance that it would sell well on the booming West Coast. East of the Mississippi, postwar country blues took on a different form, one rooted in African American musical styles and rural lyrical imagery. Syd Nathan emerged as the biggest booster of country blues in the eastern United States after World War II; his Cincinnati-based King label released a slew of records of this type. Upon incorporating King in 1944, Nathan focused on marketing a product attractive to urban southern migrants, both black and white. To this end, he sought out African American blues shouters like Roy Brown and Wynonie Harris as well as dynamic country acts like the Delmore Brothers and Moon Mullican. Although Nathan maintained a roster of roots- and pop-oriented country performers, his greatest commercial success came with acts that favored an energetic approach. Like the other independents that arose after World War II, King Records specialized in a musical style overlooked by the Big Six record labels. For Nathan, country blues, a subgenre frowned on by conservatives in Nashville, provided an inroad on the market.[18]

After the domestication of country music in the mid-thirties, country blues virtually disappeared, even as Jimmie Rodgers enthusiasts kept its spirit alive and Texas string bands continued to play the black and white blend. The nationalization of country music dealt another blow to country blues, further encouraging the movement toward softer sounds manifest primarily in the country pop fusion. Interest in blues music nationally, however, intensified during the war, bolstered by many of the factors contributing to country music's nationalization (the AFM ban, cultural integration, and so on) as well as the success of blues shouter Louis Jordan. After the war, independent labels gained a stronghold in the new rhythm and blues (R & B) market, with Nathan's King label scoring several of the biggest R & B hits of the late forties. Maintaining a hands-on approach, often to the chagrin of many of his contracted performers, Nathan spurred his country artists to pep up their arrangements and encouraged the cross-fertilization of white country and black blues. In hiring Henry Glover as producer in the late forties, Nathan procured a similarly minded, yet less abrasive A and R man who fleshed out the King country blues fusion with such artists as Moon Mullican and the Delmore Brothers. Mullican and the Delmores, of course, were no strangers to the blues, but in Glover and Nathan they found industry executives seeking to reawaken interest in the passé country subgenre. Largely through its success, King Records became the nucleus of the country blues movement in the late forties and early fifties, eventually eclipsing Capitol as purveyor of the subgenre's biggest hits. [19]

The Delmore Brothers first established a relationship with Syd Nathan in World War II, during their tenure at Cincinnati's WLW. In January 1944, before the duo separated after Rabon accepted a defense job, they recorded their first King sides. Near the end of the war, WLW refused to rehire Rabon, so the Delmores left the city, eventually landing in Memphis, where they began appearing regularly on WMC in 1945. They continued to record for King, developing the country blues approach they established at Decca. One of the principal blues centers of the South, Memphis offered an environment conducive to the maturation of the Delmores' prewar style. While in the area, they met Wayne Raney, a harmonica player from Arkansas whose approach to the instrument reflected his familiarity with and deep appreciation of African American blues styles. Raney immediately clicked with the Delmores and soon became a fixture on their radio shows and records. Recognizing the need to update their sound, the Delmore Brothers embraced amplified accompaniment and the boogie sound that surged in popularity during the war. As skilled guitarists, the two brothers had little difficulty adapting the piano-based sound to their instruments. Applying intricate harmonies, Raney's harmonica, and electric guitar to the up-tempo beat, the Delmore Brothers created some of the liveliest and most modern country music of the postwar period, yet they still proved remarkably capable of playing slow blues as well as folk-based gospel (with the Browns Ferry Four). [20]

In January 1946, the Delmores officially inaugurated their boogie period when they recorded "Hillbilly Boogie," an infectious, lighthearted number with an abundance of guitar bass runs and vocal exclamations. With lyrics that equate the urban honky-tonk with a good time and the presence of Louis Innis's electric guitar, the song represents a conscious effort on the Delmores' part to reach an urban audience. Several other songs from the session, however, point back to their rural, acoustic approach: "She Left Me Standing on the Mountain" and "Midnight Train" indicate that the Delmores were not burning any musical bridges. The brothers continued this mix of rural and urban sounds and lyrical imagery in subsequent sessions, intermingling boogies and country laments. On faster numbers, such as "Boogie Woogie Baby," "Mobile Boogie," and "Stop That Boogie," perfunctory lyrics take a backseat to exciting guitar and harmonica solos, but on slower numbers, the Delmores prove that they never lost their prewar songwriting skills. "Waiting for That Train," "Somebody Else's Darling," and "Home in Dixie" reveal the true extent of their vocal and writing talents, though they continued to score their greatest commercial success with more lively novelty numbers. Raney's harmonica work gives nearly all of their King sides a blues element, lending a Delta feel to a reworking of "Happy on the Mississippi Shore" and adding authenticity to "Rounder's Blues." On the group's biggest hit, "Blues Stay away from Me," the Delmores demonstrate their uncanny ability to marbleize the country and blues traditions. Prompted by Syd Nathan, the two brothers wrote the song and worked out the arrangement with Henry Glover. Haunting harmony, acoustic and electric guitar interplay, and the twin harmonica work of Wayne Raney and Lonnie Glosson all blend together in the creation of a deep, chugging blues with appropriately sullen lyrics. Interestingly, the Delmores moved closer to a mainstream approach after the success of "Blues Stay away from Me" in 1949. A relocation to Texas and personal problems led to a series of difficulties for the Delmores in the early 1950s, and the brothers went their separate ways in 1951. After moving to Detroit, Rabon Delmore embarked on a solo career, which was abruptly halted by a decline in his health. In early 1952, Alton moved north to join Rabon, who soon discovered that he had cancer. On their last recordings before Rabon died later that year, the Delmores reaffirmed their songwriting, singing, and guitar-playing skills with "That Old Train" and "The Trail of Time" ranking among some of their best work. With "I'll Be There," from late 1951, and "I Needed You," from their last session, the Delmores point the way for the soft, country pop harmony popularized by the Everly Brothers in the mid-fifties. To the end, the Delmores maintained the standard of high quality and musical foresight they established in the early thirties. Working with Raney and King executives, they helped rejuvenate the dormant country blues subgenre and reestablished the bond between black and white indigenous southern musical forms at a time when country was moving closer to pop.[21]

As King Records' other primary country blues fusionist, Moon Mullican mixed the barrelhouse piano of the Texas piney woods with southwestern swing and contemporary R & B to forge a style that often trembled more vehemently than early rockabilly. One of country music's most irrepressible performers, Mullican played and sang with a fervor that lent emotional veracity to slower blues pieces and a combustible energy to up-tempo numbers. As a member of Cliff Bruner's Texas Wanderers and Bob Dunn's Vagabonds in the late thirties and early forties, Mullican injected a strong blues element into the Texas swing sound at a time when jazz influence predominated in the idiom. As a solo artist on King Records in the postwar period, he continued to embrace African American blues, incorporating it with country pop, western swing, and Cajun sounds. With his weathered voice and down-home piano playing, Mullican attracted older listeners disenchanted with sophisticated country offerings and a younger crowd that could not relate to honky-tonk's broodishness. Never one to follow in the footsteps of others, Mullican consistently brushed aside country music conventions on the road to developing his own country blues matrix.

Born in 1909, Aubrey "Moon" Mullican grew up on an eighty-acre farm in Polk County, Texas. Within the piney woods of east Texas, a region home to many African Americans working for the lumber companies, a rich blues tradition thrived in the black juke joints and labor camps. Mullican first gained exposure to the blues in his childhood from a black agricultural worker who taught him guitar. When he grew older, the impressionable teenager continued his musical education by stealing away on Saturday nights to hear his neighbors playing. Mullican may have liked the guitar, but he gravitated to the piano at an early age, most probably because of its volume. As a child, he liked to play the family's pump organ at full blast, experimenting with blues chords in defiance of his father's preference for religious music. At age sixteen, Mullican left for Houston, where he began playing cafés and honky-tonks for thirty-five cents a night. When Houston became a hotbed for western swing in the mid-thirties, Mullican joined the Blue Ridge Playboys and later became a member of Cliff Bruner's outfit and Bob Dunn's studio band. Before the war, he made occasional appearances on the records of several notable acts, including the Sunshine Boys, Buddy Jones, and Jimmie Davis. Additionally, Mullican maintained his own band, the Night Riders. Somehow, in late 1941, he ended up in Chicago playing the bars with a member of his group and an otherwise all–African American band. During the war, he toured with Cliff Bruner and campaigned with Jimmie Davis in the Southwest until he settled down momentarily in Port Arthur around 1945. After signing with King Records in 1946, he remained based in Texas, leasing a Beaumont club with Cliff Bruner in 1947 and opening his own nightspot in Hessmer, Louisiana, in 1948. On the strength of several popular singles and with the help of his friend Hank Williams, he began a six-year affiliation with the *Grand Ole Opry* in 1949. In the late fifties, he recorded several interesting rock numbers for the Decca label before returning to his country roots in the early sixties. He remained a dynamic live performer in the last years of his life before suffering a fatal heart attack in 1967.[22]

Moon Mullican's affiliation with the King label proved mutually beneficial. In Mullican, Syd Nathan found an artist capable of playing a variety of eclectic styles, from hard blues to ethnic dance numbers; additionally, Mullican could sing country pop convincingly, making him commercially viable. Nathan never had to worry about Mullican's on-record energy; the pianist was always willing and able to spruce up even sedate numbers with lively rolls and trills. Hence, Mullican's most successful country pop recordings, "Goodnight Irene" and "Mona Lisa," feature sprightly piano work along with his smooth singing. Mullican also made the charts experimenting with Cajun ("New Pretty Blonde") and honky-tonk music ("I'll Sail My Ship Alone"), but blues remained his forte throughout his stay at King. Recording in Texas during the first few years with the label, he dabbled in western swing on numbers "I Left My Heart in Texas" and "What Have I Done That Made You Go Away" and tipped his hat to Jimmie Davis on "Columbus Stockade Blues" and "There's a Chill on the Hill Tonight," but his music remained firmly planted in the blues. "I'm Gonna Move Home Bye and Bye" stands as one of the most striking gospel/blues numbers of the postwar period, and "Wait a Minute" and the relentless "Don't Ever Take My Picture Down" demonstrate Mullican's mastery of urban blues. When Mullican started recording in Cincinnati on a semiregular basis around 1950, he and Henry Glover devised an even more conspicuous R & B sound. Impressed by Mullican's mastery of the boogie-woogie piano technique and his uncanny apprehension of the blues, Glover encouraged him to follow his musical passion. Adding drums and horns and dropping the steel guitar and fiddle all together, Mullican and Glover dismiss the barriers of musical segregation and create straight R & B on several recordings of the period. Syd Nathan sanctioned the musical integration of his King artists' songs, so Mullican covered Tiny Bradshaw's "Well Oh Well" and Roy Brown's "Grandpa Stole My Baby." On the latter number, Mullican steps out of his restrained vocal approach and shouts the blues in deference to its composer's singing style. Other blues highlights include the playful "I Done It" and the stomping "Moonshine Blues." Like Bob Wills and the Delmore Brothers, Moon Mullican proved capable of creating an unadulterated version of African American blues that obfuscated the line between black and white musical forms. [23]

With his incorporation of R & B instrumentation, Moon Mullican more clearly presaged rock and roll than any other contemporary country performer. Two principal factors, however, precluded Mullican's success as a rock performer: his age and his lack of popularity among radio disc jockeys. Mullican and other country blues performers undoubtedly set the stage for rock with their integration of black and white musical forms, but they did not fit the new genre's mold. Performers' success in the rock market depended on three separate but equally important criteria: the musical ability to mix country and urban blues; their appeal to an ever-expanding youth market; and the support of disc jockeys. All of the major country blues performers of the postwar period discussed at length above possessed at least the first of these criteria, but none all three. Mullican and Ford probably had the best chance, but Ford chose pop music and Mullican failed to click with country disc jockeys; additionally, neither connected with teenagers. Ultimately, rock's ascendance was due to the social and business climate in which it matured. Country blues artists of the late forties and early fifties furnished rock with its musical body, but urban teenagers and radio disc jockeys provided the spirit that gave it life.[24]

Prior to the heyday of the radio disc jockey in the late forties and early fifties, live performers and recorded transcriptions provided the bulk of music played on the radio. The history of the disc jockey dates back to early 1932, when Al Jarvis of Los Angeles's KFWB inaugurated a program called the *Make Believe Ballroom*, on which he played records to fill airtime. Within a couple of years, Martin Block in New York developed a similar show. At the time, record companies frowned on the practice, seeing it as encroaching on their sales. Jarvis recalls, "Whenever an announcer would spin a disk, he'd humbly apologize for doing so." In 1940, the disc jockeys received a legal boost from the Supreme Court. The era of the country disc jockey began soon thereafter, with Randy Blake's *Suppertime Frolic* on WJJD in Chicago and Foreman Phillips's *Western Hit Parade* and *Friday Night Merry Go Round* on KRKD, Los Angeles, emerging as important disc spinning shows in the early forties. During the war, disc jockeys gained wider acceptance, most likely because of the lack of available live talent at the time. In the South, Hal Horton's *Hillbilly Hit Parade* on KRLD, Dallas, debuted around 1945 and soon became one of the most popular country disc jockey shows in the region, setting the stage for the postwar surge.[25]

In the decade after World War II, disc jockeys' popularity seemed to grow exponentially with every new year. When the Federal Communications Commission (FCC) granted licenses to hundreds of new independent stations after the war, disc jockeys stepped in to fill airtime in the absence of network programming. Country record spinners usually broadcast in the early morning or noontime hours, but the most popular of all country disc jockeys, Nelson King, broadcast at night. King's *Jamboree* was on the air from 8:00 P.M. to midnight nightly on Cincinnati's WCKY and quickly emerged as the major country record program in the late forties; King was regularly named the "Favorite Folk Disc Jockey" by *Billboard*. Unlike many other popular country disc jockeys who concentrated on humor, such as Tennessee Ernie Ford, King offered listeners information about artists and songs, much as Randy Blake did in Chicago. Consequently, King and Blake attracted listeners who took the music seriously, building up an audience of jukebox operators and record industry executives as well as country music fans. Bob McCluskey, head of RCA-Victor's division of country and western promotion in the late forties and early fifties, comments on the significance of the show: "Nelson's program really controlled that whole section of the country late at night. The people that listened to the station were very, very record conscious at that time because what was played, they bought." Downplaying his influence, King maintained that he based his decision on whether or not to keep playing a record on letters from listeners. Whether they acted as a conduit for audience preferences or actually influenced listeners' tastes, country disc jockeys became the most important promoters of the latest releases, and record companies and artists soon found it to their advantage to curry their favor.[26]

In 1949, *Billboard* approximated there were 450 active country disc jockeys; among the most popular included the aforementioned King and Blake, as well as Johnny Hicks (in Dallas), Don Davis (in Cincinnati), Paul Kallinger (on border station XERF), and Biff Collie (in Houston). Two years later, the trade magazine reported the broadcast of over 1,400 country music disc jockey shows with the accompanying comment: "While the disc jockey is a paramount promotion force in any brand of the music business, nowhere is he more important to the field than in the case of country and western music." The rise of disc jockeys as promoters of personal appearances and recordings signaled the beginning of a new era in country music, one characterized by the importance of hit records as a direct source of income and vehicle for increasing personal appearance revenues. Accompanying this development, the age of live radio soon came to an end. Increasingly, disc jockey shows supplanted live programs; by 1954, stations were devoting over half their airtime to the former and less than 10 percent to the latter. As country music historian Wayne W. Daniel points out, "the role of radio in the dissemination of country music was changing in the early 1950s from that of purveyor of live music to that of promoter of recorded music." Given this development, country music performers could ill afford to ignore the power of the disc jockeys. Many continued to concentrate their efforts on lucrative tours, but the future of the genre was in the hands of the disc jockeys, and those slow to recognize this development soon fell by the wayside.[27]

Through direct contact with listeners, country music disc jockeys both discerned and shaped audience tastes. While major record companies concentrated on marketing product with mass appeal, disc jockeys (like the independent record labels) focused on local and regional preferences. In large, urban areas, an audience of younger listeners began to hold sway, increasingly requesting that disc jockeys play songs applicable to their lives and musical tastes. Television was becoming a home for conservative adult country music, and radio emerged as its more adventurous, youth-oriented counterpart. The barn dances of the postwar decade varied in the types of country music they featured, but as a rule, most remained moderate in musical scope and character. Many popular country music disc jockeys maintained a restrained approach to their work, but a group of more animated radio personalities played the newer styles of music that younger listeners craved. In 1947, Ray Bartlett arrived at KWKH and soon amassed a loyal following with his *Groovie's Boogie* program that featured rhythm and blues records and his own jive talking between discs. In the early fifties, Dewey Phillips spun R & B discs over Memphis's WHBQ nightly, drawing young white listeners in with his charisma and eclectic musical selections. In 1954, Phillips introduced his listeners to Elvis Presley, a country blues performer with a personality and sound that entranced urban teenagers in search of an identifiable symbol for their generation. Together, Phillips and Presley represented the grassroots movement toward the more youth-accommodating music of the mid-fifties known as rockabilly. The popularity of disc jockeys like Phillips and performers like Presley took many by surprise; in retrospect, however, their success appears an inevitability, a product of musical and sociocultural developments of the postwar decade. [28]

In terms of its musical lineage in country, rockabilly can be traced directly from the country blues of the early 1950s back to the honky-tonk of the late 1940s to the Texas swing of the 1930s. The heavy bass sound and electric instrumentation pioneered by western swing bands provided its instrumental makeup, while the percussive guitar effects and thud of honky-tonk furnished its incessant, heavy beat. Presley and the rockabillies took the process one step further, discarding the steel guitar and fiddle in favor of more emphasis on lead guitar work and a thumping rhythm. Several country songs of the 1940s by artists such as Bob Wills, Moon Mullican, the Maddoxes, Hank Williams, and others predate the rockabilly sound, but Presley's recordings possess a novel, almost unidentifiable quality that pushed country music in an entirely new direction. Combining urban attitude with rural earthiness, rockabilly disdains both the sophistication of country pop and the rumination of honky-tonk. As country blues intended for young urbanites, rockabilly disavowed middle-class respectability in favor of primal debauchery. In doing so, it reached a generation of Americans coming of age in the postwar era.

In addition to dramatically altering the lives of America's adult population, World War II had a profound impact on the nation's youths. Just as it opened up employment opportunities for women, so too it brought "youngsters" into the labor force; the number of employed teenagers rose by 2 million during the war. With fathers away and many mothers working, American teens discovered an independence that fostered the development of a rudimentary youth culture. Some young men began wearing zoot suits and hanging around jukeboxes, while many young women termed bobby-soxers read fashion magazines and listened to Frank Sinatra. Gradually, American youths developed their own language, value system, fashion sense, and taste in music. In the mid- to late forties, postwar prosperity and a tenuous atomic peace accelerated the independent youth movement, as did the rise of fragmented families. With less parental supervision and more money, young Americans created their own self-sustaining culture, one that eventually reached full maturity with the help of American business, which supplied the new consumers with the clothing, print material, and music that lent incarnation to the uninhibited youth spirit.[29]

In the postwar decade, youth culture went from an underground fad to a nationwide phenomenon, thanks in large part to the baby boom that occurred during World War II. Between 1941 and 1945, the American population increased by 6.5 million, with 1943 witnessing the highest birthrate in twenty years. These wartime children grew up surrounded by music. During the war, the jukebox craze reawakened adults' interest in records, and postwar affluence led to the number of home record players doubling between 1945 and 1950. The sale of children's records rose steadily during the period, and the success of albums such as Tex Ritter's *Children's Songs and Stories* prompted major labels to release similar selections. By 1948, children's discs accounted for 14 percent of all record sales. With the introduction of the lighter, more durable 45-rpm record in the late forties, "Kidisk" sales figures soared, as did the number of "kiddie players" (an estimated 6 million sold in 1950 alone). A 1949 survey conducted by *American Girl* magazine (published by the Girl Scouts of America) indicated that over two-thirds of junior high school girls had record players, and nearly one-half bought records with their own money. Commenting on the report, *Billboard* astutely asked: "How many [record] dealers are keeping in close touch with this age group as a disk market?" As it turns out, the major record companies that supplied record dealers with musical discs had no trouble in satisfying the tastes of children, but they proved astonishingly nescient in their discernment of what these young listeners wanted to hear once they reached adolescence.[30]

Possessing substantial purchasing power and a keen interest in music as a vehicle for defining themselves, urban teenagers stood on the verge of revolutionizing the American radio and record industries in the late forties and early fifties. As older listeners turned to adult-oriented television, their younger counterparts began to exert more influence on radio programming. Unimpressed with the saccharine offerings of American popular music, they sought out more lively, rhythm-oriented music with honest, straightforward lyrics. Just as many adult Americans found the realism of country music appealing, urban adolescents gravitated toward the emotional wallop of rhythm and blues. With its brashness, danceability, and novelty, R & B offered American youths what they were looking for; additionally, their parents' loathing for the music was a bonus. Although they could not call the music of urban blacks their own, they could at least regard it as their own discovery. In the evening hours, they tuned to R & B radio programs, initially heard exclusively on stations ministering to the tastes of urban African Americans, but eventually broadcast by white disc jockeys as well. The most famous white disc jockey with an R & B show was Alan Freed, who resided in the North. Awakened to white teenagers' interest in rhythm and blues by a Cleveland record storeowner in the early 1950s, Freed contrived a show featuring "rock and roll," originally defined as black music that disc jockeys played for white listeners. In March 1952, he staged the Moon Dog Coronation Ball, an R & B show at Cleveland Arena that drew nearly 25,000 patrons, as many as one-third of them white. A similar non-Freed affair in Knoxville featuring Bull Moose Jackson, a King R & B artist, attracted 700 whites to a segregated event. In tapping into the rhythm and blues fad among young, urban whites, disc jockeys like Freed and Phillips desegregated American radio and exposed underground black music to a white national audience.[31]

Young whites listened to R & B not only on radio and jukeboxes, but on their record players as well. In 1953, sales of rhythm and blues discs reached an all-time high of $15 million; teenagers spearheaded the dramatic increase. In Los Angeles, a record store attributed more than 40 percent of its R & B sales to whites. Latching on to the trend, dealers in predominantly white neighborhoods began stocking the latest releases from Ruth Brown, Big Joe Turner, and Wynonie Harris. Undoubtedly taken aback by the phenomenon and reluctant to cross the racial barrier, the major labels approached the idea of signing rhythm and blues artists tentatively, but they began to flirt with the notion of having white artists cover some of their songs. In the country field, Johnnie and Jack achieved the greatest success with this approach before 1955. In the pop field, an unknown singer named Bill Haley scored major hits with lyrically sanitized, but no less musically invigorating versions of such R & B hits as "Rock the Joint" and "Shake, Rattle, and Roll." Haley was initially lukewarm to the idea of covering R & B material when he recorded Jackie Brenston's "Rocket 88" in early 1951. Encouraged by an independent label owner named Dave Miller and the enthusiastic response he received from audiences, he soon discovered a career in covering material by black songwriters. Haley explains the circumstances that contributed to his success and the musical approach he developed: "Around the early fifties the musical world was starved for something new . . . the days of the solo vocalist and the big bands was gone. . . . I felt that if I could take, say, a Dixieland tune and drop the first and third beats, and accentuate the second and forth, and add a beat the listeners could clap to as well as dance this would be what they were after." Music historian Charlie Gillett terms Haley's saxophone-driven, tightly arranged approach "northern rock and roll," in contrast to its spontaneous, emotionally charged southern counterpart, rockabilly. In 1954 the question remained, however, whether a white southern singer would be as willing to embrace rhythm and blues as Haley did. Not only was there a racial taboo surrounding such a move, but the probabilities of commercial success appeared minimal. Many white southern teenagers knew rhythm and blues, however, and northern adolescents had no patent on alienation and teen culture. Somewhere along the line, a young singer raised in the South was bound to try his hand at creating a southern version of rock and roll, with a record company brave enough to record him. For a variety of reasons, these two elements, distributor and performer, eventually converged in Memphis, Tennessee.[32]

In the early to mid-fifties, Memphis was one of the more likely cities for the country rhythm and blues fusion to take place. Its substantial black population supported R & B radio programming and a burgeoning independent blues label, Sun Records. Additionally, many considered it a "progressive" southern city, one of the few southern urban areas to allow black voting in the era of African American disfranchisement and home to an omnipotent political machine, led by Edward H. "Boss" Crump, that promoted efficiency in government. In the late forties and early fifties, country filled the airwaves on local stations WMPS and WMC, while predominantly black-oriented stations like WDIA broadcast blues music. A list of the most popular radio personalities of Memphis radio during the period includes Eddie Hill, Bob Neal, Dewey Phillips, and B. B. King. Recording in the city dates back to a Ralph Peer field effort in the early 1930s, but by and large, country and blues artists in the forties traveled to other cities to record. When these performers did record in Memphis, they used local radio stations in the absence of formal recording studios within the city. In early 1950, a white man from Florence, Alabama, named Sam Phillips opened the doors to the Memphis Recording Service with the intent of recording artists in the area. Phillips grew up with African American blues and gospel music because he lived in close proximity to blacks on his family's large farm in Alabama; after moving to Memphis in 1945, he became aware of the city's rich blues tradition. In the early 1950s, he recorded several notable R & B artists in the area, including B. B. King, Little Milton, Howlin' Wolf, and Ike Turner. Initially, he leased out his product to independent distributors, but eventually mustered up the confidence to begin his own label in the spring of 1952. Like other independent labels that concentrated on rhythm and blues, such as Modern and Chess, Phillips's Sun Records directed its product at

African Americans who migrated to urban areas during and after World War II. Major labels dominated the national market, releasing over 97 percent of all million-selling records in the first seven years after the war, but the product of the independent labels sold steadily in areas around their home bases. Given a boost by the discovery of magnetic tape, which made recording more economical, another AFM strike in 1948, and the majors' concentration on established artists, the independents reaped a harvest of young talent performing alternative music (bluegrass, jazz, and rhythm and blues). In the country field, King and Imperial were the only independents that steadily produced hit records. Their success was largely due to their signing of artists Moon Mullican, the Delmore Brothers, and Slim Whitman. Phillips occasionally recorded country artists as well; he always had an ear for new talent and a novel sound. The entrepreneur recalls his artistic and business intent: "My main interest even at the outset was in developing something of a combination of black blues and country music. Besides, Nashville was doing a damn good job on country stuff. . . . In the early part of the fifties, I mainly concentrated on the blues, but I always would spend time with a country artist or two if they had any potential." In the recusant Phillips, the first element of the country–rhythm and blues hybrid fell into place, and Sun Records and Memphis, Tennessee, furnished the fertile ground for the music to pullulate.[33]

Sometime in 1953, Phillips met Elvis Presley, a young singer with an appreciation of several types of music and a penchant for flamboyant attire. Born in Mississippi to working-class parents in 1935, Presley moved with his family to Memphis around 1948. As a youngster growing up around Tupelo, Presley acquainted himself with both black and white southern folk music. At age eleven, he acquired his first guitar and received instruction from his uncle and a local pastor. Once in Memphis, the adolescent gained exposure to rhythm and blues, gospel, contemporary country, and pop music via the family radio. When he began singing in public as a teenager, his vocal style reflected the influence of a variety of artists, including Red Foley, Dean Martin, as well as evidencing touches of the Blackwood Brothers (a white gospel quartet) and the Ink Spots (a rhythm and blues group). He enjoyed participating in a gospel-singing program at the city's Ellis Auditorium and spending time at a local record store listening to anything and everything the owner had in stock. As a teenager, he began to set himself apart from his peers through his clothing, hairstyle, and general deportment. He shopped at a black clothing store in the downtown area, and he began to don bold, colorful clothing; the guitar he carried around and the ducktail he wore also caused him to stand out. After graduating from high school, he took a job driving a truck for Crown Electric. Harboring dreams of becoming a singer, he passed by Phillips's studio frequently. One day he worked up the nerve to walk in and introduce himself, and in late 1953 and early 1954, he made several acetates, accompanying his high-register, tentative singing with his own guitar playing. Phillips sensed the talent, but gave no indication of recording the singer until he came up with the idea of teaming him with a country band on his label, the Starlight Wranglers, led by guitarist Scotty Moore.[34]

A native of west Tennessee, Scotty Moore received his first guitar at the age of eight and learned the basics from his father and older brother who played in a country group. Quitting high school, he joined the navy, where he gained considerable exposure to jazz music, and artists Tal Farlow and Barney Kessel peaked his interest. Returning to west Tennessee in 1952, Moore found himself playing country music in the honky-tonks in and around Memphis, patterning his style on Merle Travis and Chet Atkins, two of the genre's more adventurous artists. Moore's Starlight Wranglers, which included bass player Bill Black and singer Doug Poindexter, developed a following, and Moore eventually convinced Sam Phillips to take a chance on recording the group in June 1954. Despite unimpressive sales, Phillips maintained contact with Moore, sensing a synergic capability in the business relationship with the guitarist. Moore explains: "[Sam Phillips] knew there was a crossover coming. He foresaw it. . . . We were all looking for something, we didn't know quite what it was, just some way to get through the door." Remembering Presley, Phillips urged Moore to get together with the young singer to help determine his potential. Showing up at Moore's doorstep in a pink suit and white shoes, Presley caught Moore slightly off guard: "From the beginning, I could see that he had a different outlook on things, just the way he dressed, the way he wore his hair. He was a rebel, really, without making an issue out of it." Overcoming a tawdry first impression, Presley roused enough of the guitarist's interest to earn another audition with Phillips, destined to take place on July 5, 1954.[35]

Country music entered a new era when Elvis Presley, Scotty Moore, and Bill Black gathered at Phillips's Sun studio in the summer of 1954. At that point in time, country music was predominantly conservative, adult-oriented music. Well on their way to taming the honky-tonkers, the Nashville recording industry and the *Grand Ole Opry* were systematically promoting a product that appealed to older, middle-class listeners as well as members of the southern working class. Besieged by television and the retirement of its principal performers, insurgent western swing no longer presented a threat to mainstream country music. Underground movements, such as country blues and postwar traditionalism, continued to thrive in pockets of the Southeast, but country pop and honky-tonk ruled the roost.

The influence of country music's mavericks, located mainly on the West Coast and in Texas, waned as the industry moved to create a homogenized product designed for national consumption. In its push for national acceptance, however, country music overlooked its younger listeners and the quiet revolution taking place in urban areas across the nation. In search of their own distinct identity, many southern youths turned away from the country music their parents listened to and discovered rhythm and blues as an alternative. As Sam Phillips explains, however, they often approached the music with a certain degree of ambivalence: "These records appealed to white youngsters . . . but there was something in many of [them] that resisted buying this music. . . . They liked the music, but they weren't sure whether they ought to like it or not." Phillips realized that by applying R & B's energy and attitude to the country blues matrix established by the West Coast and King artists, he could produce a hybrid that offered younger southerners musical gratification without racial guilt. Presley's age, look, and demeanor all distinguished him from preceding country blues artists. Additionally, his voice knew no constraints; he had no qualms about shouting the blues and absorbing himself completely into the energy of the music. Combining R & B sensuality, gospel emotion, country earthiness, and youthful angst, Elvis Presley offered adolescents the same sense of commonality that prewar listeners found in the schoolhouses and postwar migrants sought in the honky-tonks. Just as members of the nouveau bourgeoisie in the urban South viewed country pop as their music, their sons and daughters looked on rockabilly as the most accurate expression of their worldview.[36]

Understanding the void in country music opened up by the emergence of youth culture helps to explain the circumstances surrounding Elvis Presley's rise, but fails to capture the reasons for his astonishing appeal. It all started with the music. Presley's first recordings with Moore and Black seem innocuous enough; they include a cover of a slow pop song, "Harbor Lights," as well as a rendition of Leon Payne's country classic "I Love You Because." With "That's All Right, Mama," however, the group moves in a completely different direction. Black frenetically slaps the bass, and Moore chimes in with Merle Travis– and Chet Atkins–like licks, while Presley throws himself into an accelerated version of the Arthur Crudup R & B hit. At the center of the group's sound, Presley's acoustic guitar playing gives him the reins with the song's pace, providing him with the freedom to unleash as much energy as he desires. For Scotty Moore, the experience proved liberating as well: "This was the first opportunity, without my really knowing it, that I had to really mix it all up. I mean, it wasn't a planned thing. But I loved blues and I loved country . . . and with the few instruments we had, you just did everything you could to make it sound bigger, you know." For Moore, this meant inserting fingerpicking runs around Presley's vocals and stepping forward with percussive, chord-driven solos. Continually urged by Phillips to keep his jazzy finger rolls to a minimum, Moore increasingly directs his attention to rhythm. On "Good Rockin' Tonight," he sets the standard for all subsequent rockabilly guitarists with a chord progression and walking bass line that defies passive listening. Black contributes to the overall effect of the song with relentless, freewheeling slaps to the upright bass that lend a carefree air to the number. Presley's singing, meanwhile, demonstrates his affinity for blues shouters' and gospel singers' emotional surrender to a song's sentiments. On "Milkcow Blues Boogie," the group completes their musical coup d'état with a complete redefinition of the country blues and boogie idioms. Symbolically, the song starts out slow and bluesy, like earlier western swing versions, before Presley steps back to challenge his band mates (and his listeners) to take an adventurous musical ride. Presley's use of the falsetto, his exclamations during Moore's solo, and his overall enthusiasm push the arrangement to the point of spontaneous combustion, running roughshod over all diffidence and musical orthodoxy. When the group slows things down a bit on "You're a Heartbreaker" and "I'm Left, You're Right, She's Gone," Presley demonstrates just how well he can sing, but Phillips judiciously chose to promote faster numbers, knowing that they would click with younger listeners. [37]

Armed with the initial pressings of "That's All Right, Mama" and "Blue Moon of Kentucky," Sam Phillips began to solicit Presley's recordings to local and regional disc jockeys. As Scotty Moore recalls, Phillips and the group knew they faced a challenge in gaining acceptance for their music: "We thought it was exciting, but what was it? It was just so completely different. But it just really flipped Sam—he felt it really had something. We just sort of shook our heads and said, 'Well, that's fine, but good God, they'll run us out of town.'" When Dewey Phillips played the song on his *Red, Hot, and Blues* radio program, it drew immediate and positive reaction among younger listeners. By the time of its release, Sam Phillips had 5,000 back orders for the single; eventually, in September 1954, it reached the number one position on the Memphis charts. Over the course of the summer, the band played several local appearances, first at honky-tonks but increasingly at places where younger listeners could attend, such as schools and parks. Moore recollects the band began to realize the extent of Presley's popularity among younger listeners when they played at a local shopping center: "This was the first we could see what was happening. 'Cause it was a whole parking lot full of kids, and they just went crazy." While the music certainly helped brew enthusiasm, Presley's stage presence bowled over adolescent listeners more than anything else. The onstage trembles of Hank Williams and Lefty Frizzell furnished Presley with a performance model, but the young man from Tupelo took physical interpretation of the music to a new level, with gyrations that exuded as much sexuality as they did ardent enthusiasm. Presley's mannerisms, hip garb, and unchained passion for the music differentiated him from previous country blues singers and attracted younger audience members, who found in him release from conventional restraints. Many other country music listeners, both young and old, with tastes for established styles failed to see the allure of Presley's music. In hindsight, Presley's cool reception at the *Grand Ole Opry* on October 2, 1954, seems a foregone conclusion; after all, he was moving in a direction diametrically opposed to Nashville's conservative inclinations. The more adventurous *Louisiana Hayride* accepted Presley's individual style and provided the singer with a promotional base until early 1956. Signing Bob Neal as his manager in early 1955, Presley continued a tour of the South begun in the latter part of 1954. Working with Tom Parker, Neal also placed Presley on a package show tour with headliner Hank Snow. Presley's performances garnered ecstatic responses from younger audience members, much to Snow's astonishment: "I was truly amazed at the reaction Elvis received after his first performance on stage. The crowd went wild. For a completely unknown artist to capture an audience in this manner was unbelievable." After signing with RCA-Victor and Parker in late 1955, of course, Presley became a national sensation, turning American culture topsy-turvy. Country music, meanwhile, dealt with the immediate implications of Presley's rise, namely the onset of rockabilly.[38]

In the mid-fifties, Memphis, Tennessee, and Sun Records became the nucleus of the rockabilly movement. According to Scotty Moore, Presley's success vindicated the music that many young country artists were already playing in the honky-tonks: "When Elvis busted through, it enabled all these other groups that had been going along more or less the same avenue—I'm sure there were hundreds of them—to tighten up and focus on what was going to be popular. If they had a steel guitar, they dropped it. The weepers and slow country ballads pretty much went out of their repertoire. And what you had left was country-oriented boogie music." Rockabilly, defined by Carl Perkins as "a country man's song with a black man's rhythm," focuses on emotionally charged singing and lead guitar playing in the absence of familiar country instrumentation. Played primarily by young white southerners, the music stresses spontaneity and rhythmic drive while the lyrics often recall western swing's hedonism. In the hands of pioneers Sidney "Hardrock" Gunter and Carl Perkins, rockabilly offers a vehicle for a variety of alternative musical expressions. Gunter emphasized the music's urban roots in

Alabama boogie and was among the first to record an R & B hit (with a 1951 cover of the Dominos' blockbuster "Sixty Minute Man"). Perkins's music, meanwhile, nearly always bore a folk stamp. Taught guitar by a black sharecropper near his family's home in northwestern Tennessee, Perkins mixed rural African American blues with the country music he heard on the *Grand Ole Opry*. After he formed his own band and began performing in honky-tonks, he learned to add more edge to his playing, but he always managed to keep one foot firmly planted in the music of his youth. On his first recordings from late 1954, he introduces himself in a variety of musical settings, playing a honky-tonk number ("Honky Tonk Girl"), a country waltz ("Turn Around"), and definitive rockabilly ("Gone Gone Gone"). No matter the musical approach, Perkins's singing and songwriting never strayed from country. In addition to attracting Gunter and Perkins, Sun Records also served as Johnny Cash's first record label. Cash grew up on the other side of the Mississippi River, in Arkansas, but eventually moved to Memphis in 1954 after his discharge from the air force. Later that year, he auditioned for Sam Phillips backed by two auto mechanics named Luther Perkins (on guitar) and Marshall Grant (on bass). Cash apologized for his band not sounding professional or country enough, but Phillips liked the stripped down approach and worked out a sound that fit the young singer's style perfectly, more country than rockabilly, but nothing like the product coming out of Nashville. Collectively, Sun's young country artists challenged the complacency of the thriving country music industry at a time when it was moving toward marketing a homogeneous, adult-oriented product suitable for an ever-expanding audience.[39]

In 1954, country music executives could barely hear the rumblings coming from Sun Records. Business was booming: the American public spent $70 million on country entertainment in 1953. With disc sales in excess of $26 million, country music accounted for over 13 percent of the nation's retail record volume. Although personal appearances continued to generate the most money for performers and promoters, all signs pointed toward the importance of radio and records in country music's future. Nationally, total record sales of all types of music would jump from $190 million in 1954 to $325 million in 1956. Recognizing the increasing importance of radio promotion, the country music industry in Nashville moved to create a systematic means of marketing its product. To this end, they focused on the disc jockeys.[40]

In 1952, WSM executives invited country platter spinners from around the country to a convention. Loosely organized and informal, the first gathering of its kind drew only 80 disc jockeys to Nashville. WSM's Second Annual Disc Jockey Festival, however, attracted approximately 500 country disc jockeys to a more structured affair. The convention encouraged dialogue between artists, publishers, writers, radio personalities, and record executives, many of whom already resided in the Nashville area. A resounding success, the event was termed by *Billboard* "one of the greatest public relations coups in the history of radio." Most significant, the convention led to the formation of a formal organization, Country Music Disc Jockeys' Association (CMDJA). Membership increased from 100 to 215 in 1954. Approximately 750 country disc jockeys from across the nation showed up for WSM's third annual event in late 1954. CMDJA members at the meeting went on record stating their primary goal as increased public acceptance of country music and recognition from the nation's music industry of associate status. Governor Clement gave a speech while the state's first lady invited wives of the visiting disc jockeys to tea at the governor's mansion. Two years later, at the 1956 festival, the governor delivered another speech supporting country music, calling it "the heartbeat of America." Additionally, he wholeheartedly endorsed the convention's purpose: "I believe in country music. I want it to be promoted and to prosper." Although many of Nashville's residents failed to see eye to eye with country music's increasing presence, few could ignore it, and some undoubtedly benefited from the income generated by events like the disc jockeys' conventions. Eventually, in 1958, the CMDJA grew into the Country Music Association, an organization dedicated to furthering country music's legitimacy and national acceptance.[41]

When rockabilly struck with full force in 1956, the organizational structure established at the CMDJA conventions provided insulation from the destructive potential of youth-oriented music. Rock and roll rudely awakened everyone to the purchasing power of young, urban Americans and posed a threat to country music's existence. In the mid-fifties, with urban and middle-class listeners purchasing more records, rural southerners no longer comprised the bulk of the country music audience. As records rose in importance, country music artists increasingly directed their product at the share of the market that spent money on discs. This trend began back in the mid- to late forties, when the jukebox industry was thriving and artists targeted patrons of establishments with music machines. After Elvis Presley came on the scene, however, they suddenly realized the importance of attracting younger listeners. Consequently, the mid-fifties witnessed a proliferation of country music songs aimed at a youth market. This represented a complete about-face in the direction of country music lyrics, away from its conservative adult orientation toward a liberal, adolescent focus. Like a fox in a hen house, rockabilly threw country music into a state of chaos. It not only threatened its identity but also upset the fragile peace that existed among country music's subgenres.

After country music's nationalization in World War II, four subgenres emerged directed at certain segments of the country audience. Postwar traditionalists created music for southerners who resided in rural areas and those in cities that preferred older styles. Recognizing that country music needed to evolve, these performers adopted jazz techniques to acoustic instrumentation or applied electric instrumentation to prewar singing and playing styles. Honky-tonk represented the merging of southeast and Texas prewar styles, a mixture of western swing, Jimmie Rodgers blues, and heart-on-sleeve singing all set to lyrics that captured the confusion of neourbanites from southern rural areas. Country pop also embraced western swing instrumentation but interacted more with American popular music in both its lyrical and vocal approach. It offered a product for the South's growing middle class and reached out to a national audience. Country blues, before rockabilly, presented an eclectic mix of western swing instrumentation, nationally popular boogie rhythms, folk blues, and humorous lyrics for Californians and country music listeners across the nation disaffected with honky-tonk's realism and country pop's urbanity. When the centripetal forces of the *Grand Ole Opry* and the Nashville country music industry began pulling in country music's most popular artists, the genre became less heterogeneous, and honky-tonk and country pop artists in particular moved closer to one another in lyrical and musical style. Both country pop and honky-tonk benefited from the new organizational structure that offered effective promotion and a concentrated base of operations. After shedding a great deal of its acrimony, honky-tonk soared in popularity in the early 1950s, eventually climaxing in 1955 with nine of the year's top twelve singles. As it turns out, however, honky-tonk's success was built on sand. With its urban and youth orientation and de-emphasis on fiddles and steel guitars, rockabilly made the western-attired, twangy honky-tonkers look foolish and passé. Most of the country pop singers, on the other hand, wore suits and used steel guitars and fiddles only incidentally. When the rockabilly bomb went off in 1956, the CMDJA offered a safe house for performers who fell in line with their goal of creating a radio-friendly, nationally acceptable product. The CMDJA reconciled country music with the new order by eventually conceding the youth market to the popular music industry and concentrating its efforts on marketing product for urban adults nationwide. In the mid-fifties, several singers emerged that personified the new marketing strategy, eventually known as the Nashville Sound. Some, like Don Gibson, continued in the country pop tradition established by

Red Foley and Eddy Arnold, using a mix of country instrumentation and pop vocal techniques. Others, like Jim Reeves and Ferlin Husky, displayed more willingness to experiment with lush orchestral sounds. Working with the finest singers and musicians in Nashville, producers Chet Atkins and Owen Bradley concentrated their efforts on releasing uptown, professional recordings. In the early sixties, Reeves and Patsy Cline rose above the rest as leading exponents of the Nashville Sound. These mid- to late fifties developments shifted the balance of power on Nashville's Music Row from honky-tonk to country pop. Just as country pop performers adopted elements of honky-tonk in the late forties and early fifties, honky-tonk performers of the late fifties moved closer to country pop as a means to survive. Working without a safety net, western swing and country blues vanished from the country scene, while postwar traditionalists went into hibernation, soon to reemerge in the 1960s with the folk revival. In the short run, rockabilly induced the repudiation of country blues; in the long run, it led to country pop's eclipse of honky-tonk and relegated western swing and postwar traditionalism to permanent underground status.

CONCLUSION

The country music industry had good reason to respond as it did to the rockabilly movement; it had come too far to surrender to the challenge presented by American youths' musical revolt. In the late 1930s, most Americans viewed "hillbilly" music as woefully obsolescent songs listened to by backward rubes. Few recognized the changes taking place within it. When it first appeared on record, country music bore the imprints of its rustic, unsophisticated roots. Male-dominated and rough sounding, it gave little indication that listeners beyond its rural, folk base could ever enjoy it. In the 1930s, however, barn dances domesticated the music, turning it into family entertainment that appealed to listeners across the country reeling in the effects of the Depression. The barn dances and Jimmie Rodgers's success provided a firm foundation, and the progressives of the late thirties began experimenting with different ways to make the music more appealing. On the radio and in the schoolhouses, the progressives accommodated the tastes of their base audience of rural, white, working-class southerners while introducing them to new vocal and musical styles. Overcoming social and economic obstacles, country music burgeoned in the folk culture of the South.

During World War II, country music gained national attention through its transmission across the country via jukeboxes, cultural intermingling, and wartime migration. As a reciprocal process, nationalization not only introduced country music to America but contributed to the dilution of its predominantly rural and regional character as well. In gaining a new audience, country music sacrificed some of its authenticity as a southern folk phenomenon. After nationalization, postwar traditional and honky-tonk music emerged as reaffirmations of country's southern roots, the latter speaking for the South's urban migrants and the former representing those who remained in the southern hinterland. These two subgenres grounded listeners caught up in the swirl of sociocultural changes precipitated by the war in the commonality of shared experience while giving expression to their collective apprehensions.

Many country performers and listeners did not resist the urban impulse; for them, western swing and country pop offered entertainment and escape from the drudgeries of everyday life. Born in Texas, western swing relocated to California in the early forties to become the music of transplanted southerners on the West Coast. Packing dance halls, listeners to western swing enjoyed the heavy beat and big band sound offered by groups led by Bob Wills, Spade Cooley, and Tex Williams. For their own part, western swing musicians reveled in musical experimentation, embracing amplification, drums, and jazz improvisational techniques in the name of musical progress. Their instrumentation, in subdued form, made its way back east, becoming an integral part of both the honky-tonk and country pop sounds. Taking a cue from popular wartime country singers Gene Autry, Tex Ritter, and Al Dexter, country pop vocalists offered a smooth, sophisticated product in tune with the South's ever-increasing middle-class tastes. Refusing to be denied their own music, young southerners sought out the exciting (and forbidden) sounds of rockabilly, wrapping themselves in its rebellious excess.

Behind the scenes, country music producers, promoters, radio announcers, and record company executives sought to sustain the economic advances made by the genre during the war. To this end, they became more involved in the process of country music's dissemination. Increasingly, they supported performers that appealed to a wider array of listeners. They knew not to tamper with country music's southern base, but they continually sought out ways to attract a potential audience of middle-class record buyers, television viewers, and concert audiences. Few country music acts objected to their efforts. They too bore an interest in country music's expansion and national acceptance. Personally and professionally, many objected to the hillbilly epithet, viewing it as an affront not only to their music, but to the people who listened to it as well. Most grew up in the rural South, immersed in its rich culture, and expressed pride in the region's fabric of folk tradition and communal ethos.

Country music in the 1940s and early 1950s reflected the struggle of its performers and listeners trying to come to terms with the modernizing forces pushing and pulling them away from their folk roots. While some embraced the opportunities presented by nationalization and modernization, others mourned the disappearance of country music's prewar identity. In its flexibility and dynamism, the genre continued to accurately depict the lives of its listeners even as they scattered in different directions. When Elvis Presley burst on the scene in 1954, country music stood at a crossroads, forced to choose between accommodating a new audience (and renouncing its adult orientation) or following through on its commitment to moving closer to the American mainstream (thereby risking the loss of its folk individuality). Country music took steps toward the former but ultimately chose the latter course of action. Between 1939 and 1954 it built upon the folk tradition in the process of forging the genre's modern form. After 1954, the subgenres established during the period of modernization became traditions themselves, the musical pillars of all country music that followed.

Ever evolving and adapting to the needs of each generation of listeners, country music continued to manifest the worldview of its ever-changing audience. In the late 1940s and early 1950s, it communicated the thoughts and emotions of white southerners coping with the realities of modern life. In the process of doing so, it captured the interest and respect of many listeners previously indifferent to or in some cases hostile toward the music. Demonstrating extraordinary elasticity, country music, in all its various forms, maintained its core audience of white, working-class southerners while attracting urban and middle-class listeners throughout the nation. From an economic and cultural standpoint, country music in the forties and early fifties succeeded in its pursuit of profitability and respectability. More important, however, it achieved this goal while remaining steadfast to the principals of lyrical unpretentiousness and musical simplicity that initially gave it life in the rural South. Striking a delicate balance between folk art form and commercial product, country music proved itself a source of communal ethos, an exponent of southern culture, and a musical genre perfectly suited to encapsulating the universality of the human condition.

APPENDIX

Table 1

Predominant Country Music Performers, by Subgenre, 1939–1954

Progressive	*Western Swing*
Roy Acuff	Bill Boyd
Blue Sky Boys	Cliff Bruner
Callahan Brothers	Spade Cooley
Carlisle Brothers	Tommy Duncan
Jimmie Davis	Bob Dunn's Vagabonds
Delmore Brothers	Leon McAuliffe
Mainer's Mountaineers	Hank Penny
Bill Monroe	Hank Thompson
Morris Brothers	Tex Williams
Shelton Brothers	Bob Wills

Postwar Traditional	*Honky-tonk*
Bailes Brothers	Lefty Frizzell
Flatt and Scruggs	Hank Locklin
Jim and Jesse	Webb Pierce
Johnnie and Jack	Ray Price
Grandpa Jones	Carl Smith
Louvin Brothers	Floyd Tillman
Bill Monroe	Ernest Tubb
Molly O'Day	Kitty Wells
Reno and Smiley	Hank Williams
Stanley Brothers	Faron Young

Country Pop	*Country Blues*
Eddy Arnold	Delmore Brothers
Red Foley	Tennessee Ernie Ford
Pee Wee King	Maddox Brothers and Rose
George Morgan	Moon Mullican
Hank Snow	Elvis Presley
Jimmy Wakely	Merle Travis

Table 2
Chart Points of Country Music Subgenres, 1939–1954

Year	Progressive	Western Swing	Honky-tonk	Postwar Traditional	Country Pop	Country Blues
1939	119	41	0	0	50	0
1940	111	32	18	0	49	0
1941	72	52	35	0	51	0
1942–43	66	16	44	0	84	0
1944	3	32	41	0	135	0
1945	8	70	19	0	116	0
1946	0	46	12	0	119	37
1947	6	37	21	0	105	41
1948	0	24	6	0	168	13
1949	0	0	47	0	145	18
1950	0	0	65	0	136	24
1951	0	0	96	5	95	14
1952	0	24	120	0	69	0
1953	0	8	118	5	82	14
1954	0	3	126	1	99	0

Source: Table generated from information in Charles Faber, *The Country Music Almanac: 1922–1943,* vol. 1 (Lexington: Charles F. Faber, 1978), 59–60; Joel Whitburn, *The Billboard Book of Top Forty Country Hits* (New York: Billboard Books, 1996); "Best Selling Country and Western Records—1946–1953," *Billboard* 66, no. 21 (22 May 1954): 19; "1954's Top Country and Western Records . . . According to Retail Sales," *Billboard* 66, no. 52 (25 December 1954): 17.

Table 3

Percentage of Country Songs Appearing on Charts, by Lyrical Category, 1939–1954

Year	Love Songs	Love Lost	Breakup without Regret	Self-pity	Individualism	Nostalgic	Novelty	Topical	Religious	Instrumental
1939	8	0	0	0	21	17	25	13	8	8
1940	3	12.5	12.5	6.5	12.5	9.25	9.25	9.25	9.25	16
1941	9	33	7	9	15	9	9	3	3	3
1942–43	16	36	4	4	8	8	8	8	8	0
1944	6	34	18	3	0	9	12	15	3	0
1945	8	22	30	2	2	2	10	22	0	2
1946	9	16	15	3	4	4	34	9	0	6
1947	15	13	11	0	4	4	49	2	0	2
1948	11	26	4	5	3	4	32	6	5	4
1949	15	28	11	6	2	7	26	2	1	2
1950	18.5	13.5	10	4	5	6	36	2	4	1
1951	17	22	11.5	1.5	3	9	29	3	4	0
1952	27	22	14	3	0	2	29	3	0	0
1953	14	13	13	8	4	1	39	4	4	0
1954	25	15.5	18	8	0	4	28.5	1	0	0

Source: Table generated from information in Charles Faber, *The Country Music Almanac: 1922–1943*, vol. 1 (Lexington: Charles F. Faber, 1978), 59–60; Joel Whitburn, *The Billboard Book of Top Forty Hits* (New York: Billboard Books, 1996).

Table 4

Population Distribution of White Southerners, by Percentage, 1940

State	Large Cities (50,000+)	Urban	Rural
Alabama	13.6	29.2	70.8
Arkansas	4.5	22.3	77.7
Florida	27.5	54.9	45.1
Georgia	17.5	34.0	66.0
Kentucky	12.6	27.8	72.2
Louisiana	27.0	44.0	56.0
Mississippi	3.4	23.0	77.0
North Carolina	9.0	26.3	73.7
Oklahoma	14.8	37.6	62.4
South Carolina	7.3	27.3	72.7
Tennessee	19.9	31.0	69.0
Texas	24.0	45.4	54.6
Virginia	16.0	34.9	65.1
West Virginia	11.0	28.0	72.0
Total	*16.0*	*34.5*	*65.5*

Source: Bureau of the Census, *Sixteenth Census of the United States. 1940. Population. Characteristics of the Population. United States Summary* (Washington, D.C.: United States Printing Office, 1943), tables 50 and 52.

Table 5

Population Distribution of White Southerners, by Percentage, 1950

State	Large Cities (50,000+)	Urban	Rural
Alabama	19	43	57
Arkansas	5	33	67
Florida	26	65	35
Georgia	17.5	45	55
Kentucky	15	35	65
Louisiana	31	57	43
Mississippi	5	31	69
North Carolina	11	34	66
Oklahoma	19	51	49
South Carolina	10.5	42	58
Tennessee	20	40	60
Texas	38	63	37
Virginia	11	34	66
West Virginia	19	47	53
Total	*21*	*46.9*	*53.1*

Source: Bureau of the Census, *A Report of the Seventeenth Decennial Census of the United States. Census of the Population: 1950. Characteristics of the Population* (Washington, D.C.: United States Printing Office, 1952), tables 15 and 33.

NOTES

Introduction

1. Hank Thompson quoted in Rich Kienzle, *Hank Thompson and His Brazos Valley Boys, 1946–1964* (Hambergen: Bear Family Records, 1996), 6.

2. Ronnie F. Pugh, *Ernest Tubb: The Texas Troubadour* (Durham: Duke University Press, 1996), 105; Charles Faber, *The Country Music Almanac: 1922–1943*, vol. 1 (Lexington: Charles F. Faber, 1978), 59–60, and Joel Whitburn, *The Billboard Book of Top Forty Country Hits* (New York: Billboard Books, 1996); "Best Selling Country and Western Records—1946–1953," *Billboard* 66, no. 21 (22 May 1954): 19, and "1954's Top Country and Western Records . . . according to Retail Sales," *Billboard* 66, no. 52 (25 December 1954): 17.

3. Art Satherley, interview by Douglas B. Green, Hollywood, 27 June 1974, Country Music Foundation Oral History Collection (hereafter CMFOHC), Nashville.

4. Ray Price quoted in Alton Brooks, "Golf, Horses, and Country Music," *WENO Country* (November 1967), Ray Price vertical file, Country Music Foundation, Nashville; Roy Acuff with William Neely, *Roy Acuff's Nashville: The Life and Good Times of Country Music* (New York: Putnam, 1983), 10; Johnny Cash, liner notes, *Unchained,* American Recordings CD CT 69404, 1996; Maybelle Carter, introduction to *Fifty Years at the Grand Ole Opry,* by Myron Tassin and Jerry Henderson (Gretna: Pelican, 1975), 11.

5. Richard Peterson and Melton McLaurin, introduction to *You Wrote My Life: Lyrical Themes in Country Music,* ed. Melton McLaurin and Richard Peterson (Philadelphia: Gordon and Breach, 1992), 6–7; Merle Travis, interview by Douglas B. Green, n.p., 17 October 1975, CMFOHC.

6. Statistics generated from information in Whitburn, *The Billboard Book of Top Forty Country Hits* and Barry McCloud, et al., *Definitive Country: The Ultimate Encyclopedia of Country Music and Its Performers* (New York: Perigee, 1995).

7. Wilbur Zelinsky, "Where the South Begins: The Northern Limit of the CIS-Appalachian South in Terms of Settlement Landscape," *Social Forces* 30, no. 2 (December 1951): 172; W. J. Cash, *The Mind of the South* (1941; reprint, New York: Vintage Books, 1991), vii; George Tindall, *Ethnic Southerners* (Baton Rouge: Louisiana State University Press, 1976), 86; Charles Pierce Roland, *The Improbable Era: The South since World War II* (Lexington: University Press of Kentucky, 1975), 2–9; John Shelton Reed, *One South: An Ethnic Approach to Regional Culture* (Baton Rouge: Louisiana State University Press, 1982), 17–171; John Shelton Reed and Benjamin K. Hunnicutt, "Leisure," *Encyclopedia of Southern Culture,* ed. Charles Reagan Wilson and William Ferris (Chapel Hill: University of North Carolina Press, 1989), 1208–09.

8. David M. Potter, "The Enigma of the South," *Yale Review* 51, no. 1 (1961): 150; Edward B. Reuter, *Handbook of Sociology* (New York: Dryden Press, 1941), 118.

9. Bureau of the Census, *Sixteenth Census of the United States: 1940. Housing—General Characteristics* (Washington, D.C.: United States Printing Office, 1943), tables 6, 8, and 10.

10. Howard W. Odum, *The Way of the South toward the Regional Balance of America* (New York: Macmillan, 1947), 61; Fred W. Voget, "The Folk Society: An Anthropological Application," *Social Forces* 31, no. 2 (December 1954): 107; Reed, *One South,* 43, 170–71; C. Vann Woodward, *The Burden of Southern History* (New York: Vintage Books, 1960), 19.

11. Lawrence W. Levine, *Black Culture and Black Consciousness: Afro-American Folk Thought From Slavery to Freedom* (New York: Oxford University Press, 1978), 5; Odum, *The Way of the South,* 70; Clifford Geertz quoted in Charles Reagan Wilson, introduction to *Encyclopedia of Southern Culture,* xvi.

12. Minnie Pearl quoted in Les Pouliot, *John Thayer and Don Bruce Together Present the History of Country Music; A Thirty-six-Hour Radio Documentary* (Memphis: J. Thayer and D. Bruce Together, 1970), 154.

13. Robert Cantwell, *Bluegrass Breakdown: The Making of the Old Southern Sound* (Urbana: University of Illinois Press, 1984), 74.

14. Richard A. Peterson, *Creating Country Music: Fabricating Authenticity* (Chicago: University of Chicago Press, 1997), 220.

15. Roy Acuff quoted in Russell B. Nye, *The Unembarrassed Muse: The Popular Arts in America* (New York: Dial Press, 1970), 342; Hank Williams quoted in Rufus Jarman, "Country Music Goes to Town," *Nation's Business* 41, no. 2 (February 1953); Bill C. Malone, "Growing Up with Texas Country Music," *What's Going On? (In Texas Folklore),* ed. Francis Edward Abernathy (Austin: Encino Press, 1976), 245.

16. Bureau of the Census, *Sixteenth Census of the United States: 1940. Population. Characteristics of the Population. United States Summary* (Washington, D.C.: United States Printing Office, 1943), tables 50 and 52; Bureau of the Census, *A Report of the Seventeenth Decennial Census of the United States. Census of the Population: 1950. Characteristics of the Population* (Washington, D.C.: United States Printing Office, 1952), tables 15 and 33; Bill C. Malone, *Southern Music, American Music* (Lexington: University Press of Kentucky, 1979), 64.

1. Radio Barn Dances, Schoolhouse Shows, and "Hillbilly" Domestication

1. David R. Goldfield, *Promised Land: The South since 1945* (Arlington Heights: H. Davidson, 1987), 1.

2. Merle Travis quoted in Rich Kienzle, *Merle Travis: Guitar Rags and a Too Fast Past* (Hambergen: Bear Family Records, 1994), 4; Charles K. Wolfe, *Louvin Brothers: In Close Harmony* (Vollsode: Bear Family Records, 1992), 2; Charles K. Wolfe, introduction to *Truth Is Stranger Than Publicity,* by Alton Delmore (Nashville: Country Music Federation Press, 1995), ix; Johnny Cash, liner notes, *Unchained,* American Recordings CD CT 69404,

1996; Jack Temple Kirby, *Rural Worlds Lost: The American South, 1920–1960* (Baton Rouge: Louisiana State University Press, 1987), 208–9; Ivan M. Tribe, liner notes, *Molly O'Day and the Cumberland Mountain Folks,* Bear Family CD BCD 15565, 1992.

3. Kirby, *Rural Worlds Lost,* 181; Suzy Lowry Geno, "Charlie and Ira—The Louvin Brothers," *Bluegrass Unlimited* 17, no. 9 (March 1983): 12; Robert Cantwell, *Bluegrass Breakdown: The Making of the Old Southern Sound* (Urbana: University of Illinois Press, 1984), 74; Michael Streissguth, *Eddy Arnold, Pioneer of the Nashville Sound* (New York: Schirmer Books, 1997), 11–13; Bill C. Malone, "Country Music," *Encyclopedia of Southern Culture,* ed. Charles Reagan Wilson and William Ferris (Chapel Hill: University of North Carolina Press, 1989), 1003; Roy Acuff with William Neely, *Roy Acuff's Nashville: The Life and Good Times of Country Music* (New York: Putnam, 1983), 12.

4. Johnnie Wright quoted in Walt Trott, "The Johnnie and Jack Story," *Johnnie and Jack and the Tennessee Mountain Boys,* by Eddie Stubbs and Walt Trott (Vollersode: Bear Family Records, 1992), 3; Wayne Erbsen, "Wiley and Zeke: The Morris Brothers," *Bluegrass Unlimited* 15, no. 2 (August 1980): 40.

5. Bill C. Malone, *Country Music, U.S.A.,* 2d ed. (Austin: University of Texas Press, 1985), 1; William J. Ivey, foreword to *Country Gentleman,* by Chet Atkins with Bill Neely (Chicago: Henry Regnery, 1974), viii; D. K. Wilgus, "Country-Western Music and the Urban Hillbilly," *The Urban Experience and Folk Tradition,* ed. Americo Paredes and Ellen J. Stekert (Austin: University of Texas Press, 1971), 138; Malone, "Music," *Encyclopedia of Southern Culture,* 985.

6. Wilgus, "Country-Western Music and the Urban Hillbilly," 139; Norm Cohen, "America's Music: Written and Recorded," *John Edwards Memorial Foundation Quarterly* 16, no. 59 (fall 1980): 124.

7. Cohen, "America's Music," 124–25; Charles K. Wolfe, *Tennessee Strings: The Story of Country Music in Tennessee* (Knoxville: University of Tennessee Press, 1977), 8; Bill C. Malone, *Singing Cowboys and Musical Mountaineers: Southern Culture and the Roots of Country Music* (Athens: University of Georgia Press, 1993), 50–53, 57; Malone, *Country Music, U.S.A.,* 6; Acuff, *Roy Acuff's Nashville,* 35; Wilgus, "Country-Western Music and the Urban Hillbilly," 140; Malone, *Country Music, U.S.A.,* 16.

8. Malone, *Singing Cowboys and Musical Mountaineers,* 38; Malone, *Country Music, U.S.A.,* 25–27.

9. Malone, *Singing Cowboys and Musical Mountaineers,* 73–74; Malone, "Music," 988.

10. Bill C. Malone, *The Smithsonian Collection of Classic Country Music* (Washington, D.C.: Smithsonian Institution, 1981), 1; Malone, *Country Music, U.S.A.,* 35–36; Jacquelyn Dowd Hall, et al., *Like a Family: The Making of a Southern Cotton Mill World* (Chapel Hill: University of North Carolina Press, 1987), 259; Malone, *Country Music, U.S.A.,* 37–38.

11. Malone, *Country Music, U.S.A.,* 27; Norm Cohen, liner notes, *Minstrels and Tunesmiths: The Commercial Roots of Early Country Music,* John Edwards Memorial Foundation LP 109, 1981; Wilgus, "Country-Western Music and the Urban Hillbilly," 142; Richard

A. Peterson, *Creating Country Music: Fabricating Authenticity* (Chicago: University of Chicago Press, 1997), 194–95; Archie Green, "Hillbilly Music: Source and Symbol," *Journal of American Folklore* 78, no. 309 (July–September 1965): 213, 221.

12. Richard Spottswood, "Country Music and the Phonograph," *Bluegrass Unlimited* 21, no. 8 (February 1987): 18; Wolfe, *Tennessee Strings*, vii; Malone, *Country Music, U.S.A.*, 81; Ralph Peer, "Rodgers' Heritage: Influence Inspires Industry of Today," *Billboard* 66, no. 21 (21 May 1954): 17; Mark Humphrey, "Interview: Merle Travis," *Old Time Music* 36 (summer 1981): 8; Ronnie F. Pugh, *Ernest Tubb: The Texas Troubadour* (Durham: Duke University Press, 1996), 54–55; Atkins with Neely, *Country Gentleman,* 56.

13. Ralph Peer, "Discovery of the First Hillbilly Great," *Billboard* 65, no. 20 (16 May 1953): 35; Nolan Porterfield, *Jimmie Rodgers: The Life and Times of America's Blue Yodeler* (Urbana: University of Illinois Press, 1979), 107, 249–50, 313–14; Hank Snow and Ernest Tubb, "Rodgers's Influence on Country Music," *Billboard* 65, no. 20 (16 May 1953): 20–35.

14. Malone, "Country Music," 1003; Robert Coltman, "Across the Chasm: How the Depression Changed Country Music," *Old Time Music* 23 (winter 1976–77): 6, 7, 11.

15. Ivey, foreword, xi.

16. Timothy A. Patterson, "Hillbilly Music among the Flatlanders: Early Midwestern Radio Barn Dances," *Journal of Country Music* 6, no. 1 (spring 1975): 12; Wayne W. Daniel, *Pickin' on Peachtree: A History of Country Music in Atlanta, Georgia* (Urbana: University of Illinois Press, 1990), 173; Atkins, *Country Gentleman,* 74; Rich Kienzle, *Hank Thompson and His Brazox Valley Boys, 1946–1964* (Hambergen: Bear Family Records, 1996), 12.

17. Bill C. Malone, *Southern Music, American Music* (Lexington: University Press of Kentucky, 1979), 58; John Lomax III, *Nashville: Music City USA* (New York: Abrams, 1985), 83; Alan Havig, "Radio and American Life," *Reviews in American History* 8, no. 3 (September 1980): 404; Green, "Hillbilly Music: Source and Symbol," 209, 219; Bureau of the Census, *Sixteenth Census of the United States: 1940. Housing—General Characteristics* (Washington, D.C.: United States Printing Office, 1943), table 10; Malone, *Country Music, U.S.A.,* 33; "WLS National Barn Dance Thirtieth Anniversary on Twenty-fourth," *Billboard* 66, no. 15 (10 April 1954): 5.

18. George Biggar, "The WLS National Barn Dance Story: The Early Years," *John Edwards Memorial Foundation Quarterly* 7, no. 23 (autumn 1971): 106; Wayne W. Daniel, "WLS National Barn Dance: Uptown Downhome Music in the Old Hayloft," *Old Time Country* 8, no. 1 (spring 1992): 14–16; Loyal Jones, "Who is Bradley Kincaid?" *John Edwards Memorial Foundation Quarterly* 12, no. 43 (autumn 1976): 122, 126–27; D. K. Wilgus, "Current Hillbilly Recordings: A Review Article," *Journal of American Folklore* 78, no. 309 (July–September 1965): 274; WLS vertical file, Country Music Foundation, Nashville; George Biggar quoted in Renfro Cole Norris, "The Ballad on the Air" (master's thesis, University of Texas, Austin, 1951), 110; Patterson, "Hillbilly Music among the Flatlanders," 14–16.

19. Charles K. Wolfe, *Kentucky Country: Folk and Country Music of Kentucky* (Lexington: University Press of Kentucky, 1982), 46; Charles K. Wolfe, "The Triumph of the Hills: Country Radio, 1920–1950," *Country: The Music and the Musicians,* ed. Paul Kingbury and Alan Axelrod (New York: Abbeville Press, 1988), 70–77; Ivan M. Tribe, *Mountaineer Jamboree: Country Music in West Virginia* (Lexington: University Press of Kentucky, 1984), 43, 53; Barbara Kempf, "Meet Doc Williams: Country Music Star, Country Music Legend," *John Edwards Memorial Foundation Quarterly* 10, no. 33 (spring 1974): 2, 6; Charles K. Wolfe, *Carl Smith: Satisfaction Guaranteed* (Hambergen: Bear Family Records, 1996), 4; "American Folk Tunes," *Billboard* 59, no. 32 (9 August 1947): 116; Bill C. Malone, "Country Music in the Depression Southwest," *The Depression in the Southwest,* ed. Donald W. Whisenhunt (Port Washington: Kennikat Press, 1989), 61; George Carney, "Country Music and the Radio: A Historical Geographic Assessment," *Rocky Mountain Social Science Journal* 11, no. 2 (April 1974): 18, 28; Acuff, *Roy Acuff's Nashville,* 43.

20. Malone, *Country Music, U.S.A.,* 70–71; Wolfe, *Tennessee Strings,* 54–58; Richard A. Peterson and Paul DiMaggio, "The Early Opry: Its Hillbilly Image in Fact and Fancy," *Journal of Country Music* 4, no. 2 (summer 1973): 40; Robert K. Oermann, "The Grand Ole Opry," *Frets Magazine* 4, no. 12 (December 1982): 22–25; Jack Harris, "The True Story of the Famous WSM Grand Ole Opry," *Rural Radio* 1, no. 10 (November 1938), 5.

21. Charles K. Wolfe, *The Grand Ole Opry: The Early Years, 1925–35* (London: Old Time Music, 1975), 17–18; Peterson and DiMaggio, "Early Opry," 43; David Cobb, interview by John W. Rumble, Nashville, 18 August 1983, Country Music Foundation Oral History Collection (hereafter CMFOHC), Nashville; Bradley Kincaid quoted in Jones, "Who is Bradley Kincaid?" 131; Grandpa Jones, *Everybody's Grandpa: Fifty Years behind the Mike* (Knoxville: University of Tennessee Press, 1984), 105.

22. Sam McGee quoted in Dob Krueger, "Sam McGee, He Was a Country Guitar Legend," *Guitar Player* 10, no. 6 (June 1976), 38; Wolfe, *Tennessee Strings,* 64, 66; Wolfe, *The Grand Ole Opry,* 117; Harris, "The True Story of the Famous WSM Grand Ole Opry," 5; Mel Foree, "Down the Smoky Mountain Trail," *Mountain Broadcast and Prairie Recorder* 1, no. 3 (November 1939): 4; Myron Tassin and Jerry Henderson, *Fifty Years at the Grand Ole Opry* (Gretna: Pelican, 1975), 75.

23. Wolfe, *Kentucky Country,* 52, 76; Wayne W. Daniel, "Renfro Valley, Kentucky: The Valley Where Time Stands Still," *Bluegrass Unlimited* 22, no. 7 (January 1988): 56; Malone, *Country Music, U.S.A.,* 184; "A Hillbilly Colony Built Up around One Thousand-Seat Barn Run by John Lair," *Billboard* 142, no. 12 (28 May 1941): 31; Nat Green, "Fantastic Grosses with Folkshows," *The Billboard 1944 Music Year Book* (New York: Billboard, 1944), 344–45; Henry "Homer" Haynes and Kenneth "Jethro" Burns, "From Moonshine to Martinis, Part Two," *Journal of Country Music* 16, no. 1 (1994): 4; Old Joe Clark, interview by John W. Rumble, Berea, 3 December 1985, CMFOHC.

24. Robert K. Oermann, "Honky-tonk Angels: Kitty Wells to Patsy Cline," *Country: The Music and the Musicians,* 320; Robert Coltman, " 'Sweethearts of the Hills': Women in

Early Country Music," *John Edwards Memorial Foundation Quarterly* 14, no. 52 (winter 1978): 162; Malone, *Country Music, U.S.A.,* 22; Norm and Anne Cohen, "Folk and Hillbilly Music: Further Thoughts on Their Relation," *John Edwards Memorial Foundation Quarterly* 13, no. 46 (summer 1977): 50–57; Mary A. Bufwack, *Finding Her Voice: The Saga of Women in Country Music* (New York: Crown Publishers, 1993), 102–4.

25. Malone, *Country Music, U.S.A.,* 22; Coltman, " 'Sweethearts of the Hills,' " 161–62; Oermann, "Honky-tonk Angels," 321; Robert K. Oermann, "Mother, Sister, Sweetheart, Pal: Women in Old-Time Country Music," *Southern Quarterly* 22, no. 3 (spring 1984): 125.

26. Ruth A. Banes, "Dixie's Daughters: The Country Music Female," *You Wrote My Life: Lyrical Themes in Country Music,* ed. Melton A. McLaurin and Richard A. Peterson (Philadelphia: Gordon and Breach, 1992), 90–91; Malone, *Country Music, U.S.A.,* 65–67; Coltman, " 'Sweethearts of the Hills,' " 164–65.

27. Banes, "Dixie's Daughters," 90–91; Bufwack, *Finding Her Voice,* 96–98, 100; Malone, *The Smithsonian Collection of Classic Country Music,* 29; Malone, *Country Music, U.S.A.,* 118–19; Coltman, " 'Sweethearts of the Hills,' " 169.

28. Bufwack, *Finding Her Voice,* 100–102.

29. Coltman, " 'Sweethearts of the Hills,' " 175; Bufwack, *Finding Her Voice,* 102–5.

30. Wolfe, "The Triumph of the Hills," 83; Charlie Louvin quoted in Ed Bumgarduer, "Remaining Half of the Louvin Brothers Preserves the Legacy," *Winston-Salem Journal,* 12 July 1987; Merle Travis quoted in Mark Humphrey, "Interview: Merle Travis, Part 2," *Old Time Music* 37 (autumn 1981): 22.

31. Atkins, *Country Gentleman,* 74; Ruth Sheldon Knowles, *Bob Wills: Hubbin' It* (1938; reprint, Nashville: Country Music Foundation Press, 1995), 79; Malone, *Country Music, U.S.A.,* 95; Eddy Arnold quoted in Les Pouliot, *John Thayer and Don Bruce Together Present the History of Country Music; A Thirty-six-Hour Radio Documentary* (Memphis: J. Thayer and D. Bruce Together, 1970), 223.

32. Neil V. Rosenberg, *Bluegrass: A History* (Urbana: University of Illinois Press, 1985), 18–19; Malone, *Country Music, U.S.A.,* 28–29; Tom Yarbro, letter, *Mountain Broadcast and Prairie Recorder* 2, no. 3 (February 1941): 5; Geno, "Charlie and Ira," 13; Trott, "The Johnnie and Jack Story," 4; Marty Licklider, letter, *Mountain Broadcast and Prairie Recorder* 2, no. 4 (April 1941): 7; Karl Davis, interview by Douglas B. Green, n.p., 8 June 1974, CMFOHC; Edwin J. Malechek, letter, *Mountain Broadcast and Prairie Recorder* 2, no. 6 (September 1941): 9.

33. Bumgarduer, "Remaining Half of the Louvin Brothers Preserves the Legacy"; Russell and Pat Jackson, interview by the author, Franklin, 21 October 1998.

34. Bill Bolick, "I Always Liked the Type of Music That I Play: An Autobiography of the Blue Sky Boys," John Edwards Memorial Foundation LP 104, 1977; Steve Sholes, interview by Tandy Rice, Nashville, 8 February 1968, CMFOHC; Malone, *Country Music, U.S.A.,* 95; Charles K. Wolfe, "Cliff Carlisle," *Bluegrass Unlimited* 19, no. 6 (December 1984): 59; Russell and Pat Jackson, interview.

35. Wolfe, "Cliff Carlisle," 59; Hank Snow, *The Hank Snow Story* (Urbana: University of Illinois Press, 1994), 154; Merle Travis, interview by Douglas B. Green, n.p., 17 October 1975, CMFOHC; Rosenberg, *Bluegrass,* 23–24; Peterson, *Creating Country Music,* 190; Jones, *Everybody's Grandpa,* 77.

36. Dale Vinnicur, *Jim and Jesse: Bluegrass and More* (Vollersode: Bear Family Records, 1993), 3; Acuff, *Roy Acuff's Nashville,* 57–58; Erbsen, "Wiley and Zeke," 45; Russell and Pat Jackson, interview; Bolick, "I Always Liked the Type of Music That I Play"; Atkins, *Country Gentleman,* 95.

37. Russell and Pat Jackson, interview; Grandpa Jones quoted in Robert K. Oermann, "Grandpa Jones Cherishes Country Traditions with His Own Old-Time Manner," *Tennessean* 5 December 1990; David Cobb, interview.

38. Erbsen, "Wiley and Zeke," 45; Snow, *Hank Snow Story,* 127; Atkins, *Country Gentleman,* 95; Nelson Sears, *Jim and Jesse: Appalachia to the Grand Ole Opry* (Lancaster: Nelson Sears, 1976), 19.

39. Malone, *Country Music, U.S.A.,* 14–16; Dorothy Horstman, *Sing Your Heart Out, Country Boy,* 3d ed. (Nashville: Country Music Foundation Press, 1996), 97; Art Satherley quoted in Maurice Zolotow, "Hillbilly Boom: Uncle Art Satherley Seeks Out Country Music in the Bayous, Canebrakes, and Hills," *Saturday Evening Post* 216, no. 33 (12 February 1944): 38.

40. Alton Delmore, *Truth Is Stranger Than Publicity* (Nashville: Country Music Federation Press, 1995), 2.

41. Colin Escott, *Hank Williams: The Biography* (Boston: Little, Brown, 1994), 19; Roy Acuff quoted in William Price Fox, "Grand Ole Opry," *Alabama Heritage* 30, no. 2 (February/March 1979): 96; Acuff, *Roy Acuff's Nashville,* 63–64; Cantwell, *Bluegrass Breakdown,* 79.

42. Wolfe, *Tennessee Strings,* 41; Norm Cohen, "The Skillet Lickers: A Study of a Hillbilly String Band and Its Repertoire," *Journal of American Folklore* 78, no. 309 (July–September 1965): 238–39; Rich Kienzle, "Country Music Instruments and Players," *The Country Music Book,* ed. Michael Mason (New York: Scribner's Sons, 1985), 139, 177; Malone, *Country Music, U.S.A.,* 125; Fred Hoeptner and Bob Pinson, "Clayton McMichen Talking, II," *Old Time Music* 2 (summer 1971): 14; Wilgus, "Country-Western Music and the Urban Hillbilly," 147.

43. Malone, *Country Music, U.S.A.,* 50, 54; Hazel Meyer, *The Gold in Tin Pan Alley* (Philadelphia: Lippincott, 1958), 74; Vito Pellettieri quoted in Elizabeth Schlappi, *Roy Acuff, the Smoky Mountain Boy* (Gretna: Pelican, 1978), 34–35; John W. Rumble, liner notes, *Roy Acuff: Columbia Historic Edition,* Columbia CD 39998, 1985; Schlappi, *Roy Acuff,* 39; Rufus Jarman, "Country Music Goes to Town," *Nation's Business* 41, no. 2 (February 1953): 48.

44. Colin Escott, liner notes, *The Essential Roy Acuff,* Columbia CD CK 48956, 1992; Schlappi, *Roy Acuff,* 8–9, 17–18, 23, 26–27, 30–32; Acuff, *Roy Acuff's Nashville,* 18–35; Willie J. Smyth, "Early Knoxville Radio (1921–1941): WNOX and 'Midday Merry

Go-Round,' " *John Edwards Memorial Foundation Quarterly* 18, nos. 67–68 (fall–winter 1982): 111; some biographical information for Roy Acuff compiled from Roy Acuff vertical file, Country Music Foundation, Nashville; Malone, *Country Music, U.S.A.,* 190; Pouliot, *History of Country Music,* 112; Roy Acuff quoted in Jack Hurst, "Phenom of the Opry: Roy Acuff Celebrates Fifty Years on Center Stage," *Chicago Tribune* 14 February 1988; David P. Stone, interview by John W. Rumble, Nashville, 24 May 1983, CMFOHC; Rumble, liner notes, *Roy Acuff: Columbia Historic Edition.*

45. Roy Acuff quoted in Alana Nash, "Home Is Where the Gig Is: Life on and off the Road," *Country: The Music and the Musicians,* 258; Roy Acuff quoted in Hurst, "Phenom of the Opry"; Nat S. Green, "King Korn Klondike: Hillbilly Troupes Roll Up Dizzy Box Office Scores in One-Day and Repeat Stands," *Billboard* 55, no. 10 (6 March 1943): 7; Malone, *Country Music, U.S.A.,* 193; Hank Williams quoted in Colin Escott, *Hank Williams: The Biography* (Boston: Little, Brown, 1994), 19; Merle Travis, "Recollections of Merle Travis, 1944–1955," *John Edwards Memorial Foundation Quarterly* 15, no. 54 (summer 1979): 109.

46. Kienzle, "Country Music Instruments and Players," 163–64; Malone, *Country Music, U.S.A.,* 191; John W. Rumble, *Roy Acuff* (Alexandria: Time-Life Records, 1983), 11; Bev King, "Bashful Brother Oswald: Dobro Pioneer," *Sing Out* 33, no. 1 (fall 1987): 2–3.

47. Beecher "Pete" Kirby, interview by Douglas B. Green, Nashville, 28 February 1975, CMFOHC; Old Joe Clark, interview by John W. Rumble, Berea, 5 December 1987, CMFOHC; Minnie Pearl quoted in Pouliot, *History of Country Music,* 166; Rumble, *Roy Acuff,* 14; Schlappi, *Roy Acuff,* 109.

48. John W. Morris, liner notes, *Sacred Songs of Mother and Home: A Tribute to Wade Mainer,* Old Homestead LP 90001, 1971; E. N. Tarantino, "Wade Mainer: Portrait of a Country Gentleman," *Bluegrass Unlimited* 18, no. 5 (November 1983): 26; Malone, *Country Music, U.S.A.,* 122–23; Wade Mainer, interview by Doug Smith, n.p., n.d., CMFOHC; Brad McCuen, "Mainer's Discography," *Country Directory* 4 (1962): 17–24.

49. Constance Keith, "Gulf Coast Gossip," *Mountain Broadcast and Prairie Recorder* 2, no. 4 (April 1941): 4; Morris, liner notes, *Sacred Songs of Mother and Home;* Tarantino, "Wade Mainer," 26, 28; Robert Shelton, *The Country Music Story: A Picture History of Country and Western Music* (Indianapolis: Bobbs-Merrill, 1966), 143; Malone, *Country Music, U.S.A.,* 123.

50. Mark A. Humphrey, liner notes, *Cliff Carlisle: Blues Yodeler and Steel Guitar Wizard,* Arhoolie CD 7039, 1996; Wolfe, "Cliff Carlisle," 57–58; Wayne W. Daniel, "The Traditional Roots of Jumpin' Bill Carlisle, Veteran Singer of Novelty Songs," *Bluegrass Unlimited* 26, no. 12 (June 1992): 41–42; Malone, *Smithsonian Collection of Classic Country Music,* 27; Tony Russell, *Blacks, Whites and Blues* (New York: Stein and Day, 1970), 95–96.

51. Cary Ginell, *The Decca Hillbilly Discography, 1927–1945* (New York: Greenwood Press, 1989), 151–52; Wolfe, *Kentucky Country,* 65; Daniel, "Traditional Roots of Jumpin' Bill Carlisle," 42–43.

52. Ivan M. Tribe, liner notes, *Roy Hall and His Blue Ridge Entertainers,* County LP CO-406, 1979; Kip Lornell, liner notes, *Virginia Traditions: Early Roanoke Country Radio,* Blue Ridge Institute Records LP 010, 1988; Rosenberg, *Bluegrass,* 49; Kip Lornell, "Roanoke Country Radio from 1929–1954," *Old Time Herald* 1, no. 4 (May–July 1988): 25–26.

53. Rodney McElrea and August J. Vrchota, "The Hall Brothers and Roy Hall and His Blue Ridge Entertainers," *Country News and Views* 3, no. 4 (January 1964): 23–26; Lornell, liner notes, *Virginia Traditions: Early Roanoke Country Radio.*

54. Hank Penny quoted in Ken Griffis, "Hank Penny: The Original 'Outlaw'?" *John Edwards Memorial Foundation Quarterly* 18, nos. 65–66 (spring–summer 1982): 5.

55. Norm Cohen, "Clayton McMichen: His Life and Music," *John Edwards Memorial Foundation Quarterly* 11, no. 39 (autumn 1975): 121–22; Cohen, "The Skillet Lickers," 240.

56. Wilgus, "Country-Western Music and the Urban Hillbilly," 148; Rich Kienzle, "Steel," *Country Music* 4, no. 4 (January 1976): 37–38.

57. Grady McWhiney and Gary B. Mills, "Jimmie Davis and His Music," *Journal of American Culture* 6, no. 2 (summer 1983): 54–55; Jason Berry, "The Sunshine Man: A Tale of Stardom, Political Heart, and Legendary Music," *Reckon* 1, no. 3 (fall 1995): 50–51; Stephen R. Tucker, " 'Louisiana Saturday Night': A History of Louisiana Country Music" (Ph.D. diss., Tulane University, 1995; Ann Arbor, Mich.: UMI, 1996), 136, 155–58; Jimmie Davis, interview by Douglas B. Green, Nashville, 8 July 1976, CMFOHC; Ronnie F. Pugh, liner notes, *Jimmie Davis,* MCA CD MCAD-10087, 1991; Malone, *Country Music, U.S.A.,* 107; Ginell, *Decca Hillbilly Discography,* 167–70.

58. Ivan M. Tribe, liner notes, *The Shelton Brothers: Bob and Joe,* Old Homestead LP OHS-201, 1993; Malone, *Country Music, U.S.A.,* 169–70; Tucker, " 'Louisiana Saturday Night,' " 77–78, 104.

59. Ginell, *Decca Hillbilly Discography,* 254–56.

60. Zeke Morris quoted in Erbsen, "Wiley and Zeke," 46; Charles K. Wolfe, "The White Man's Blues, 1922–1940," *Journal of Country Music* 15, no. 3 (1993): 38–43.

61. Malone, *Country Music, U.S.A.,* 87.

62. Ibid., 110; Ivan M. Tribe, "Bill and Joe Callahan: A Great Brother Duet," *Old Time Music* 16 (September 1975): 16.

63. Bob Pinson, "The Callahan Brothers," *Country Directory* 2 (April 1961): 5–6; Tribe, "Bill and Joe Callahan," 15–18; Malone, *Country Music, U.S.A.,* 110–12; Daniel C. Cooper, *Lefty Frizzell: The Honky-tonk Life of Country Music's Greatest Singer* (Boston: Little, Brown, 1995), 93–94.

64. Bob Artis, *Bluegrass: From the Lonesome Wail of a Mountain Love Song to the Hammering Drive of the Scuggs-Style Banjo, the Story of an American Musical Tradition* (New York: Hawthorn Books, 1975), 14.

65. Delmore, *Truth Is Stranger Than Publicity,* 1–19, 61, 89; Malone, *Singing Cowboys and Musical Mountaineers,* 28–30; Malone, *Country Music, U.S.A.,* 21–22; Charles K. Wolfe, "The Delmore Brothers on the Opry," *Bluegrass Unlimited* 24, no. 4 (October

1989): 16, 17; John Lilly, "The Delmore Brothers," *Old Time Herald* 3, no. 5 (fall 1992): 9, 10; Lynn Pruett, "The Delmore Brothers," *Alabama Heritage* 5 (summer 1987): 25–26.

66. Wolfe, *The Grand Ole Opry*, 124; Delmore, *Truth Is Stranger Than Publicity*, 215.

67. William A. Bolick, "Bill Bolick's Own Story of the Blue Sky Boys," *Sing Out* 17, no. 2 (April–May 1967): 19.

68. Bolick, "I Always Liked the Type of Music That I Play"; Daniel, *Pickin' on Peachtree*, 155; Bill Bolick quoted in Wayne W. Daniel, "Bill and Earl Bolick Remember the Blue Sky Boys," *Bluegrass Unlimited* 16, no. 3 (September 1981): 18.

69. Daniel, "Bill and Earl Bolick Remember the Blue Sky Boys," 18.

70. Constance Keith, "Gulf Coast Gossip," *Mountain Broadcast and Prairie Recorder* 2, no. 6 (September 1941): 5; Bolick, "I Always Liked the Type of Music That I Play"; William A. Bolick, liner notes, *The Blue Sky Boys on Radio, Volume One*, Copper Creed CD CCCD-0120, 1993; Douglas B. Green, liner notes, *The Blue Sky Boys*, Bluebird LP AXM2–5525, 1976.

71. Malone, *Country Music, U.S.A.*, 113; Wolfe, *Kentucky Country*, 53–55; Karl Davis, interview.

72. Rodney McElrea, "The Morris Brothers," *Country News and Views* 3, no. 4 (April 1965): 6–8; Erbsen, "Wiley and Zeke," 40–50.

73. McElrea, "The Morris Brothers," 9–10.

74. Erbsen, "Wiley and Zeke," 42; Mark Humphrey, *The Essential Bill Monroe and His Blue Grass Boys: 1945–1949* (New York: Sony Music Entertainment, 1992), 11–12; Kienzle, "Country Music Instruments and Players," 220–22.

75. Rosenberg, *Bluegrass*, 28–32; Bill Monroe quoted in Charles K. Wolfe, "Bluegrass Touches: An Interview with Bill Monroe," *Old Time Music* 16 (September 1975): 6; Malone, *Country Music, U.S.A.*, 324–25; Wolfe, *Kentucky Country*, 98–100.

76. Malone, *Country Music, U.S.A.*, 115–16; Rosenberg, *Bluegrass*, 34–35, 42; Karl Davis, interview; Edward Morris, liner notes, *The Essential Bill Monroe and the Monroe Brothers*, RCA CD RCA07863-67450-2, 1997; Bill Monroe quoted in Wolfe, "Bluegrass Touches," 11; Neil V. Rosenberg, "Blue Moon of Kentucky: Bill Monroe, Flatt and Scruggs, and the Birth of Bluegrass," *Country: The Music and the Musicians*, 191.

77. Morris, liner notes, *The Essential Bill Monroe and the Monroe Brothers*.

78. Rosenberg, *Bluegrass*, 52, 62.

79. Ibid., 41, 48; Patrick Carr, "Will the Circle Be Unbroken: The Changing Image of Country Music," *Country: The Music and the Musicians*, 486.

80. Joe Talbot, interview by Douglas B. Green, Hendersonville, 3 May 1974, CMFOHC; Harris, "True Story of the Famous WSM Grand Ole Opry," 30; Wolfe, *Tennessee Strings*, 61; "WSM, Nashville Host to N.Y. Admen," *Variety* 139, no. 4 (3 July 1940): 24; Minnie Pearl, *Minnie Pearl: An Autobiography* (New York: Simon and Schuster, 1980), 142; Zolotow, "Hillbilly Boom," 38.

81. Kirby, *Rural Worlds Lost*, 324; Tribe, *Mountaineer Jamboree*, 109; Roy Acuff quoted in Rumble, *Roy Acuff*, 21; Delmore, *Truth Is Stranger Than Publicity*, 87.

82. Bolick, "I Always Liked the Type of Music That I Play"; Tommy Gentry, letter, *Mountain Broadcast and Prairie Recorder* 1, no. 5 (March 1940): 5–6; Cliff Carlisle, letter, *Mountain Broadcast and Prairie Recorder* 1, no. 5 (March 1940): 5.

83. Clayton McMichen quoted in Fred Hoeptner and Bob Pinson, "Clayton McMichen Talking, IV," *Old Time Music* 5 (spring 1972): 20, 30; Ernest Tubb quoted in John Etheredge, "Ernest Tubb: The Legend," *Country Music* 8, no. 8 (May 1980): 31; Acuff, *Roy Acuff's Nashville*, 115.

84. Malone, *Country Music, U.S.A.*, 42; H. L. Mencken quoted in James C. Cobb, "Country Music and the 'Southernization' of America," *All That Glitters: Country Music in America*, ed. George H. Lewis (Bowling Green: Bowling Green University Popular Press, 1993), 76; unidentified *Variety* writer quoted in Carr, "Will the Circle Be Unbroken," 486; James C. Cobb, "Does *Mind* No Longer Matter? The South, the Nation, and *The Mind of the South*, 1941–1991," *Journal of Southern History* 57, no. 4 (November 1991): 685; Bufwack, *Finding Her Voice*, 99.

85. Bill C. Malone, "Will Hays," *Encyclopedia of Southern Culture*, 1061–62; Malone, *Singing Cowboys and Musical Mountaineers*, 74; Wolfe, *Tennessee Strings*, 56; Malone, *Country Music, U.S.A.*, 42–43, 56, 128–29; Jones, "Who Is Bradley Kincaid?" 126–27; Neil V. Rosenberg, introduction to *Transforming Tradition: Folk Music Revivals Examined*, ed. Neil V. Rosenberg (Urbana: University of Illinois Press, 1993), 8; David E. Whisnant, *All That Is Native and Fine: The Politics of Culture in an American Region* (Chapel Hill: University of North Carolina Press, 1983), 184; Delmore, *Truth Is Stranger Than Publicity*, 87.

86. Robert Shelton, *The Country Music Story: A Picture History of Country and Western Music* (Indianapolis: Bobbs-Merrill, 1966), 53; Steve Sholes, interview by Tandy Rice, Nashville, 8 February 1968, CMFOHC.

2. *The Great Breakthrough*

1. George B. Tindall, *The Emergence of the New South, 1913–1945* (Baton Rouge: Louisiana State University Press, 1967), 703; Pete Daniel, "Going among Strangers: Southern Reactions to World War II," *Journal of American History* 77, no. 3 (December 1990): 886, 898; David R. Goldfield, *Promised Land: The South since 1945* (Arlington Heights: H. Davidson, 1987), 5–8; C. Vann Woodward, *The Burden of Southern History* (Baton Rouge: Louisiana State University Press, 1960), 4–6; Jack Temple Kirby, *Rural Worlds Lost: The American South, 1920–1960* (Baton Rouge: Louisiana State University Press, 1987), 304–5; Francis Edward Abernathy, "Texas Folk and Modern Country Music," *Texas Country: The Changing Rural Scene*, ed. Glen E. Lich and Dona B. Reeves-Marquardt (College Station: Texas A & M University Press, 1986), 165.

2. Daniel, "Going among Strangers," 886, 899–905; Agnes Meyer of the *Washington Post* and John Dos Passos quoted in Carl Abbott, *The New Urban America: Growth and Politics in Sunbelt Cities* (Chapel Hill: University of North Carolina Press, 1981), 110.

3. Robert G. Spinney, "World War II and Nashville, Tennessee, 1938–1951: Social Changes and Public Sector Expansion" (Ph.D. diss., Vanderbilt University, 1995), 39; Daniel, "Going among Strangers," 898; Kirby, *Rural Worlds Lost,* 317; Bill C. Malone, *Country Music, U.S.A.,* 2d ed. (Austin: University of Texas Press, 1985), 182; "Hillbillies Rolling in Coin and What They Want Most Are More Pumping Pianos," *Variety* 150, no. 11 (10 March 1943): 1; "Band Buyers Eye Territory Faves: Folk Artists Big," *Billboard* 55, no. 1 (2 January 1943): 27; "Hillbilly Tunes Are Tops in Baltimore War Plant Section," *Billboard* 55, no. 23 (5 June 1943): 62; "Hillbilly Disks Hit New Mid-West High." *Billboard* 55, no. 31 (31 July 1943): 16.

4. Malone, *Country Music, U.S.A.,* 186; Nat Green, "Fantastic Grosses with Folkshows," *The Billboard 1944 Music Year Book* (New York: Billboard, 1944), 345; "American Folk Tunes," *Billboard* 55, no. 42 (16 October 1943): 65; James B. Hamilton, "West of the Mississippi," *Mountain Broadcast and Prairie Recorder,* n.s., 1 (September 1944): 19; Stephen R. Tucker, " 'Louisiana Saturday Night': A History of Louisiana Country Music" (Ph.D. diss., Tulane University, 1995; Ann Arbor, Mich.: UMI, 1996), 395; Nat S. Green, "King Korn Klondike," *Billboard* 55, no. 10 (6 March 1943): 7; "American Folk Records," *Billboard* 55, no. 8 (20 February 1943): 65; Ronnie F. Pugh, *Ernest Tubb: The Texas Troubadour* (Durham: Duke University Press, 1996), 78–79; Bill C. Malone, "Country Music in the Depression Southwest," *The Depression in the Southwest,* ed. Donald W. Whisenhunt (Port Washington: Kennikat Press, 1989), 62; Roy Acuff and William Neely, *Roy Acuff's Nashville: The Life and Good Times of Country Music* (New York: Putnam, 1983), 120–21.

5. Floy Case, "Down Blue Bonnet Way," *Mountain Broadcast and Prairie Recorder* 3, no. 4 (March 1943): 1; "American Folk Tunes and Tunesters," *Billboard* 55, no. 39 (25 September 1943): 68; Otto Kitsinger, *Pee Wee King and His Golden West Cowboys* (Hambergen: Bear Family Records, 1994), 12.

6. Green, "King Korn Klondike," 8–9; "American Folk Tunes," *Billboard* 56, no. 27 (1 July 1944): 66; Bill McCluskey quoted in Green, "King Korn Klondike," 9; Neil V. Rosenberg, *Bluegrass: A History* (Urbana: University of Illinois Press, 1985), 50.

7. Bill and Cliff Carlisle, interview by Bill Williams, Nashville, 18 September 1968, Country Music Foundation Oral History Collection (hereafter CMFOHC), Nashville; Alton Delmore, *Truth Is Stranger Than Publicity* (Nashville: Country Music Federation Press, 1995), 269; Bill Callahan, interview by Ronnie Pugh and David Hayes, Dallas, 4 January 1979, CMFOHC; Roland Gelatt, *The Fabulous Phonograph,* 2d rev. ed. (New York: J. B. Lippincott, 1955), 276–77; Russell Sanjek, *Pennies from Heaven: The American Popular Music Business in the Twentieth Century* (New York: Da Capo Press, 1996), 216; Kevin Coffey, *Cliff Bruner and His Texas Wanderers* (Hambergen: Bear Family Records, 1997), 31; Art Satherley, interview by Douglas B. Green, Hollywood, 27 June 1974, CMFOHC; Harold Humphrey, "Talent and Tunes on Music Machines," *Billboard* 53, no. 14 (5 April 1941): 72; "More Shellac for Records," *Billboard* 56, no. 3 (15 January 1944): 63; "Folk Music Here to Stay in Jukes," *Billboard* 57, no. 9 (3 March 1945): 92–93.

8. "65 Years of Juke Box Growth," *Billboard* 65, no. 21 (23 May 1953): 53; John Morthland, "Jukebox Fever," *Country Music* 6, no. 8 (May 1978): 35; Richard Spottswood, "Country Music and the Phonograph," *Bluegrass Unlimited* 21, no. 8 (February 1987): 20; Pugh, *Ernest Tubb*, 55; "Open Alabama Taverns to Jukes: Lift Five-Year Ban on Music," *Billboard* 59, no. 48 (29 November 1947): 156; Wanda Marvin, "Hillbillies Win in New York," *Billboard* 56, no. 30 (22 July 1944): 11, 16, 64–65; "Folk Music Takes Hold in the Jukes," *The Billboard 1944 Music Year Book*, 343; Joli Jensen, *The Nashville Sound: Authenticity, Commercialization, and Country Music* (Nashville: Vanderbilt University Press, 1998), 42.

9. Jensen, *Nashville Sound*, 43–44; Charlie Gillett, *The Sound of the City: The Rise of Rock and Roll* (New York: Dell, 1970), 10; "What Is ASCAP," *Variety* 138, no. 4 (3 April 1940): 26; "What is BMI," *Variety* 138, no. 4 (3 April 1940): 27; Llewellyn White, *The American Radio: A Report on the Broadcasting Industry in the United States* (New York: Arno Press, 1971), 51; Hazel Meyer, *The Gold in Tin Pan Alley* (Philadelphia: Lippincott, 1958), 89–96.

10. Floyd Tillman, interview by John W. Rumble, Nashville, 13 October 1986, CMFOHC; Art Satherley, interview by Douglas B. Green, Nashville, 17 October 1974, CMFOHC; Malone, *Country Music, U.S.A.*, 178–80.

11. White, *The American Radio*, 51; Gelatt, *The Fabulous Phonograph*, 278–80, 326; Louis R. Cook quoted in Renfro Cole Norris, "The Ballad on the Air" (master's thesis, University of Texas, Austin, 1951), 27.

12. Gillett, *The Sound of the City*, 11–12; Martin W. Laforse and James A. Drake, *Popular Culture and American Life: Selected Topics in the Study of American Popular Culture* (Chicago: Nelson-Hall, 1981), 54; Sanjek, *Pennies from Heaven*, 251–52.

13. Douglas B. Green, "Gene Autry," *Stars of Country Music: Uncle Dave Macon to Johnny Rodriguez*, ed. Bill C. Malone (Urbana: University of Illinois Press, 1975), 152–54.

14. Green, "Gene Autry," 146; Jonathan Guyot Smith, "The Brilliant Artistry of Gene Autry," *Movie Collector's World* 438 (14 January 1994): 67; Larry Willoughby, *Texas Rhythm, Texas Rhyme: A Pictorial History of Texas Music* (Austin: Texas Monthly Press, 1984), 28.

15. Douglas B. Green, "The Sons of the Pioneers," *Southern Quarterly* 22, no. 3 (spring 1984): 53; Thomas F. Johnson, "That Ain't Country: The Distinctiveness of Commercial Western Music," *John Edwards Memorial Foundation Quarterly* 17, no. 62 (summer 1981): 75, 78; Abernathy, "Texas Folk and Modern Country Music," 145.

16. Willoughby, *Texas Rhythm, Texas Rhyme*, 29–30; Malone, *Country Music, U.S.A.*, 151; Johnny Bond, *The Tex Ritter Story* (New York: Chappell Music, 1976), 20–49; Tex Ritter, spoken introduction to "Rye Whiskey," *Tex Ritter: An American Legend*, Capitol LP SKC-11241, 1973; Douglas B. Green, "The Singing Cowboy: An American Dream," *Journal of Country Music* 7, no. 2 (May 1978): 27.

17. Al Dexter quoted in John W. Moody, "Wine, Women and Song," *Denton-Record Chronicle*, 27 June 1980; Bill C. Malone, *The Smithsonian Collection of Classic Country*

Music (Washington, D.C: Smithsonian Institution, 1981), 36; Nick Tosches, "Al Dexter," *Old Time Music* 22 (autumn 1976): 4.

18. Art Satherley, interview by Douglas B. Green, Hollywood, 27 June 1974, CMFOHC; " 'Pistol Packin' Mama,' Hillbilly Tune, Likewise Clicks in Class Cafes," *Variety* 151, no. 11 (25 August 1943): 1; " 'Pistol' in Black Market Demand," *Variety* 152, no. 1 (13 September 1943): 45; " 'Pistol Packin' Mama,' " *Billboard* 15, no. 11 (11 October 1943): 43; Dexter's chart success was calculated using information in Joel Whitburn, *The Billboard Book of Top Forty Country Hits* (New York: Billboard Books, 1996).

19. Rich Kienzle, liner notes, *Bob Wills and His Texas Playboys Anthology, 1935–1973*, Rhino CD R2 70744, 1991; "Inside Stuff—Music," *Variety* 150, no. 17 (28 April 1943): 48; M. H. Orodenker, "On the Records," *Billboard* 53, no. 34 (21 August 1941): 13; M. H. Orodenker, "On the Records," *Billboard* 54, no. 29 (18 July 1942): 22; "Hillbilly Record Reviews," *Billboard* 55, no. 32 (7 August 1942): 66; Rosenberg, *Bluegrass*, 61.

20. "Gold in Them Thar Hillbillies," *Billboard* 55, no. 34 (21 August 1943): 12; Ian Whitcomb, *After the Ball: Pop Music from Rag to Rock* (London: Penguin Press, 1974), 198; Ted Daffan, interview by Garna Christian, Houston, 24 October 1977, CMFOHC.

21. Janet Schaefer and Marjorie Allen, "Class and Regional Selection in Fatal Casualties of the First 18–24 Months of World War II," *Social Forces* 23, no. 2 (December 1944): 167–69; Stephen R. Tucker, "The Western Image in Country Music" (master's thesis, Southern Methodist University, 1976), 78–80; "American Folk Records," *Billboard* 54, no. 40 (3 October 1942): 70; Tindall, *Emergence of the New South*, 688; Jennie A. Chinn, " 'There's a Star-Spangled Banner Waving Somewhere': Country-Western Songs of World War II," *John Edwards Memorial Foundation Quarterly* 16, no. 58 (summer 1980): 80.

22. Gene Fowler and Bill Crawford, *Border Radio* (Austin: Texas Monthly Press, 1987), 115–42; "Hillbilly Music Is Step to Political Success in Texas," *Billboard* 53, no. 38 (20 September 1941): 66; "Another Senator-to-Be Uses Hillbilly Troupe to Campaign," *Billboard* 56, no. 28 (8 July 1944): 6; Nat Green, "American Folk Tunes," *Billboard* 56, no. 45 (4 November 1944): 66.

23. Malone, *Country Music, U.S.A.*, 18; Charles K. Wolfe, *Tennessee Strings: The Story of Country Music in Tennessee* (Knoxville: University of Tennessee Press, 1977), 22; "Hillbilly Song in Louisiana Free-For-All Governor Race," *Billboard* 55, no. 40 (2 October 1943): 1; Jimmie Davis, interview by Ronnie F. Pugh, Nashville, 10 October 1983, CMFOHC; Johnny Gimble, interview by Rick Balsom, n.p., c. 1975, CMFOHC; Ronnie F. Pugh, liner notes, Jimmie Davis, MCA CD MCAD-10087, 1991; Gus Weill, *You Are My Sunshine: The Jimmie Davis Story* (Gretna: Pelican, 1987), 77–84; Tucker, " 'Louisiana Saturday Night,' " 144, 166, 173–80.

24. Elizabeth Schlappi, *Roy Acuff, the Smoky Mountain Boy* (Gretna: Pelican, 1978), 184–96; "Acuff Quits Guv Race, Tension Off," *Variety* 153, no. 10 (16 February 1943): 3; "Hamblen Runs Hot and Dry," *Billboard* 63, no. 47 (24 November 1951): 1; Irwin Stambler and Grelun Landon, *The Encyclopedia of Folk, Country and Western Music*, 2d ed. (New York: St. Martin's Press, 1984), 170–71.

25. Steve Sholes, interview by Tandy Rice, Nashville, 8 February 1968, CMFOHC; Mina Kerstein Curtiss, *Letters Home* (Boston: Little, Brown, 1944), 205; Malone, *Country Music, U.S.A.,* 182–83; Steven D. Price, *Take Me Home: The Rise of Country and Western Music* (New York: Praeger Publishers, 1974), 130; Jack Stapp quoted in Paul Hemphill, *The Nashville Sound: Bright Lights and Country Music* (New York: Simon and Schuster, 1970), 151; Nelson Sears, *Jim and Jesse: Appalachia to the Grand Ole Opry* (Lancaster: Nelson Sears, 1976), 22; D. K. Wilgus, "Country-Western Music and the Urban Hillbilly," *The Urban Experience and Folk Tradition,* ed. Americo Paredes and Ellen J. Stekert (Austin: University of Texas Press, 1971), 149; Betty Casey, *Dance across Texas* (Austin: University of Texas Press, 1985), 44; "G.I.s Tab Their Favorites," *Billboard* 56, no. 38 (16 September 1944): 12; "American Folk Songs," *Billboard* 56, no. 2 (8 January 1944): 64; Jack Penkola quoted in "American Folk Tunes and Tunesters," *Billboard* 55, no. 40 (2 October 1943): 65.

26. Johnny Gimble, interview; Nick Tosches, "The Hank Thompson Saga: Reflections of the King of Swing," *Country Music* 3, no. 10 (July 1975): 32; Leon McAuliffe, interview by Cecil H. Whaley, Nashville, 19 August 1969, CMFOHC; Ferlin Husky quoted in Whitcomb, *After the Ball,* 199; "American Folk Tunes and Tunesters," *Billboard* 55, no. 39 (25 September 1943): 68; Bob and Maggie Atcher, interview by John W. Rumble, Nashville, 1 May 1987, CMFOHC; Rich Kienzle, "Joe Maphis," *Country Musicians: From the Editors of Guitar Player, Keyboard, and Frets Magazines,* ed. Judie Eremo (Cupertino: Grove Press, 1987), 68; Grandpa Jones, *Everybody's Grandpa: Fifty Years behind the Mike* (Knoxville: University of Tennessee Press, 1984), 90–91.

27. Hugh Cherry, "Country DJs Carry Music to the People," *Music City News* 18, no. 4 (October 1980): 18; Lou Frankel, "Army Broadcasting Selling the World as It Entertains G.I.s on All Six Continents," *Billboard* 56, no. 6 (5 February 1944): 3; D. K. Wilgus, "Current Hillbilly Recordings: A Review Article," *Journal of American Folklore* 78, no. 309 (July–September 1965): 276; William M. Freeman, "Ol' Mountain Music Drowns Oh-h Frankie," Roy Acuff scrapbook, Country Music Foundation, Nashville; Schlappi, *Roy Acuff,* 108; Wolfe, *Tennessee Strings,* 75; I. W. Peters to Roy Acuff, 12 April 1944, Roy Acuff scrapbook, Country Music Foundation, Nashville.

28. Colin Escott, *Hank Williams, the Biography* (Boston: Little, Brown, 1994), 105; John W. Rumble, *Roy Acuff* (Alexandria: Time-Life Records, 1983), 11; Pugh, *Ernest Tubb,* 85; David P. Stone, interview by John W. Rumble, Nashville, 24 May 1983, CMFOHC.

29. Pugh, *Ernest Tubb,* 83; Bill C. Malone, *Singing Cowboys and Musical Mountaineers: Southern Culture and the Roots of Country Music* (Athens: University of Georgia Press, 1993), 76–77; Patrick Carr, "Will the Circle Be Unbroken: The Changing Image of Country Music," *Country: The Music and the Musicians,* ed. Paul Kingbury and Alan Axelrod (New York: Abbeville Press, 1988), 488.

30. Dorothy Horstman, *Sing Your Heart Out, Country Boy,* 3d ed. (Nashville: Country Music Foundation Press, 1996), 321; Buck Rainey, "The 'Reel' Cowboy: Myth Versus Realism," *Red River Valley Historical Review* 2, no. 1 (spring 1975): 25; Holly George-Warren,

"Cowboy Cool and Kitsch: The Western Motif in America," *Songs of the West* (Los Angeles: Rhino Records, 1993), 29; Charlie Seemann, "Cowboy Music: A Historical Perspective," *Songs of the West,* 11; Malone, *Country Music, U.S.A.,* 89–90, 122; Willoughby, *Texas Rhythm, Texas Rhyme,* 26; Green, "The Singing Cowboy," 5; Wilgus, "Country-Western Music and the Urban Hillbilly," 146.

31. Green, "Gene Autry," 154; Malone, *Country Music, U.S.A.,* 148; Richard A. Peterson and Marcus V. Gowan, "What's in a Country Music Band Name?" *Journal of Country Music* 2, no. 4 (winter 1971): 4–5; Ronnie F. Pugh, "The Texas Troubadour: Selected Aspects of the Career of Ernest Tubb" (master's thesis, Stephen F. Austin State University, 1978,) 73; Wade Austin, "Hollywood Barn Dance: A Brief History of Country Music in Films," *Southern Quarterly* 22, no. 3 (spring 1984): 114; Green, "Singing Cowboy," 40–41, 54–59; Roy Acuff quoted in unidentified clipping, Roy Acuff scrapbook, Country Music Foundation, Nashville; Roy Acuff quoted in Schlappi, *Roy Acuff,* 200; Daniel C. Cooper, *Lefty Frizzell: The Honky-tonk Life of Country Music's Greatest Singer* (Boston: Little, Brown, 1995), 155–56; Pugh, *Ernest Tubb,* 94.

32. Pugh, *Ernest Tubb,* 65–67, 84, 94, 113, 363–65; Ernest Tubb quoted in John Etheredge, "Ernest Tubb: The Legend," *Country Music* 8, no. 8 (May 1980): 32; Floy Case, "Grand Ole Opry Time," *Mountain Broadcast and Prairie Recorder,* n.s., 5 (September 1945): 12.

33. Ted Daffan, interview by Dorothy Gable, Nashville, 31 January 1968, CMFOHC; Nich Tosches, "Ted Daffan," *Old Time Music* 30 (autumn 1978): 6; Ted Daffan, interview by Garna Christian, Houston, 24 October 1977, CMFOHC; Bob Healy, "The Ted Daffan Story," *Country Directory* 4 (1962): 27; Tom Dunbar, *From Bob Wills to Ray Benson: A History of Western Swing Music* (Austin: Term Publications, 1988), 54–55.

34. John W. Rumble, liner notes, Floyd Tillman, MCA Records CD MCAD-10189, 1991; Malone, *Country Music, U.S.A.,* 166; Floyd Tillman quoted in Bob Claypool, "Floyd Tillman—Original Cosmic Cowboy," *Houston Post,* 21 July 1979; Adam Komorowski, "Floyd Tillman," *Hillbilly Researcher,* 15 (1992): 14, 18–19; Ed Ward, " 'Retired' Floyd Tillman's Still Making Music," *Austin American Statesman,* 30 January 1981; Floyd Tillman, interview by John W. Rumble, Nashville, 13 October 1986, CMFOHC.

3. The Southwestern Component

1. Bob Pinson, liner notes, *Bill Boyd's Cowboy Ramblers,* Bluebird LP AXM2-5503, 1975; "Music Grapevine," *Billboard* 56, no. 43 (21 October 1944): 19; Bob Wills quoted in Charles R. Townsend, *San Antonio Rose: The Life and Music of Bob Wills* (Urbana: University of Illinois Press, 1976), 38; Hank Thompson quoted in Rich Kienzle, *Hank Thompson and His Brazos Valley Boys, 1946–1964* (Hambergen: Bear Family Records, 1996), 6; Al Cunniff, liner notes, *Western Swing, Volume One,* Franklin Mint Record Society LP FMRS-CW-075/076, 1984; Tony Russell, *Blacks, Whites, and Blues* (New York: Stein and Day, 1970), 88; Garna L. Christian, "It Beats Picking Cotton: The Origins of

Houston Country Music," *Red River Valley Historical Review* 7, no. 3 (summer 1982): 39–40; Robert Coltman, "Across the Chasm: How the Depression Changed Country Music," *Old Time Music* 23 (winter 1976–77): 11; D. K. Wilgus, "Current Hillbilly Recordings: A Review Article," *Journal of American Folklore* 78, no. 309 (July–September 1965): 278.

2. "Country Instruments and Players," *The Country Music Book,* ed. Michael Mason (New York: Scribner's Sons, 1985), 175–76, 185; Bill C. Malone, *Singing Cowboys and Musical Mountaineers: Southern Culture and the Roots of Country Music* (Athens: University of Georgia Press, 1993), 33, 36–38, 175–76; George Carney, "Music and Dance," *This Remarkable Continent: An Atlas of United States and Canadian Society and Culture,* ed. John F. Rooney Jr. et al. (College Station: Texas A & M University Press, 1982), 234; Bill C. Malone, *Country Music, U.S.A.,* 2d ed. (Austin: University of Texas Press, 1985), 16, 23–24; Charles R. Townsend, "A Brief History of Western Swing," *Southern Quarterly* 22, no. 3 (spring 1984): 31; Charles Seemann, liner notes, *Bob Wills: Fiddle,* Country Music Foundation Records LP CMF-010-L, 1987.

3. Carney, "Music and Dance," 239; Francis Edward Abernathy, "Texas Folk and Modern Country Music," *Texas Country: The Changing Rural Scene,* ed. Glen E. Lich and Dona B. Reeves-Marquardt (College Station: Texas A & M University Press, 1986), 152; Patrick Carr, "Country Music: The Rich Texas Connection and Its Evolution," *Houston Chronicle,* 30 September 1979; Lawrence W. Levine, *Black Culture and Black Consciousness: Afro-American Folk Thought from Slavery to Freedom* (New York: Oxford University Press, 1978), 294; Malone, *Country Music, U.S.A.,* 152; "Texas Hoofing Can't Make Up Its Mind—Hillbilly or Waltzes," *Variety* 138, no. 4 (3 January 1940): 217.

4. Christian, "It Beats Picking Cotton," 38; Cary Ginell, *Milton Brown and the Founding of Western Swing* (Urbana: University of Illinois Press, 1994), xvii–xxxi, 16–112; Larry Willoughby, *Texas Rhythm, Texas Rhyme: A Pictorial History of Texas Music* (Austin: Texas Monthly Press, 1984), 11.

5. Townsend, *San Antonio Rose,* 1–90; Ruth Sheldon Knowles, *Bob Wills: Hubbin' It* (1938; Nashville: Country Music Foundation Press, 1995), 84; William J. Ivey, liner notes, *The Bob Wills Anthology,* Columbia LP KG 32416, 1973.

6. Townsend, *San Antonio Rose,* 98, 151–52; Leon McAuliffe, interview by Cecil H. Whaley, Nashville, 19 August 1969, Country Music Foundation Oral History Collection (hereafter CMFOHC), Nashville; Bob Pinson, liner notes, *Leon McAuliffe and His Western Swing Band,* Columbia LP FCT 38908, 1984; Rich Kienzle, "Country Music Instruments and Players," *The Country Music Book,* ed. Michael Mason (New York: Scribner's Sons, 1985), 170; Rich Kienzle, *Bob Wills* (Alexandria: Time-Life, 1982), 14; Mark Humphrey, "Playboy Days, Part I: Eldon Shamblin Talking to Mark Humphrey," *Old Time Music* 23 (winter 1976–77): 15, 20.

7. Knowles, *Hubbin' It,* 84, 89–90; Malone, *Country Music, U.S.A.,* 172; Eldon Shamblin quoted in Humphrey, "Playboy Days, Part I," 20; Al Stricklin and Jon McConal, *My Years with Bob Wills* (San Antonio: Naylor, 1976), 14; Townsend, *San Antonio Rose,* 134, 150–52, 201; Robert Shelton, *The Country Music Story: A Picture History of Country*

and Western Music (Indianapolis: Bobbs-Merrill, 1966), 173; Art Satherley, interview by Douglas B. Green, Hollywood, 30 June 1974, CMFOHC; Bob Wills quoted in Townsend, *San Antonio Rose*, 152.

8. Stricklin and McConal, *My Years with Bob Wills*, 32–33; Eldon Shamblin quoted in Humphrey, "Playboy Days, Part I," 20.

9. Stephen R. Tucker, "'Louisiana Saturday Night': A History of Louisiana Country Music" (Ph.D. diss., Tulane University, 1995; Ann Arbor, Mich.: UMI, 1996), 120; Townsend, *San Antonio Rose*, 201–9; Art Satherley, interview by Douglas B. Green, Nashville, 15 October 1974, CMFOHC; Smokey Dacus quoted in Townsend, *San Antonio Rose*, 105; Humphrey, "Playboy Days, Part I," 19, 21; Bob Wills quoted in "Strictly by Ear," *Time* Vol. 47, No. 6 (11 Februrary 1946): 50.

10. Pinson, liner notes, *Bill Boyd's Cowboy Ramblers;* Tom Dunbar, *From Bob Wills to Ray Benson: A History of Western Swing Music* (Austin: Term Publications, 1988), 15–17.

11. Pinson, liner notes, *Bill Boyd's Cowboy Ramblers;* Brad McCuen, "Bill Boyd and His Cowboy Ramblers," *Disc Collector 3* (c. 1961): 15–20.

12. "Second Bill Boyd Bond Tour of West Coast," *Bill Boyd's Ranch House News* 1, no. 3 (August–September 1943): 1; "Bill Boyd and His Cowboy Ramblers on Navy Appearances," *Bill Boyd's Ranch House News* 3, no. 1 (1946): 2; "Bill Boyd," *Bill Boyd's Ranch House News* 4, no. 6 (June 1947): 1; "Bill Boyd a Hit in Pictures," *Mountain Broadcast and Prairie Recorder* 18 (January 1944): 7.

13. Pinson, liner notes, *Bill Boyd's Cowboy Ramblers.*

14. Daniel C. Cooper, *Lefty Frizzell: The Honky-tonk Life of Country Music's Greatest Singer* (Boston: Little, Brown, 1995), 101; Stephen Tucker, "The Western Image in Country Music" (master's thesis, Southern Methodist University, 1976), 76–77; Martin V. Melosi, "Dallas–Fort Worth, Marketing the Metroplex," *Sunbelt Cities: Politics and Growth since World War II,* ed. Richard M. Bernard and Bradley R. Rice (Austin: University of Texas Press, 1983), 163–64; Pete Daniel, "Going among Strangers: Southern Reactions to World War II," *Journal of American History* 77, no. 3 (December 1990): 901; Willoughby, *Texas Rhythm, Texas Rhyme,* 15.

15. Malone, *Country Music, U.S.A.,* 168; Tony Russell, liner notes, *South Texas Swing,* Arhoolie CD-7029, 1994.

16. Jerry Irby, interview by Garna Christian, n.p., 20 November 1977, CMFOHC; Leon Selph, interview by Garna Christian, n.p., 28 September 1977, CMFOHC; Hank Thompson quoted in Kienzle, *Hank Thompson and His Brazos Valley Boys,* 23.

17. Malone, *Country Music, U.S.A.,* 158; Mark Humphrey, "Playboy Days, Part II: Eldon Shamblin Talking to Mark Humphrey," *Old Time Music* 24 (spring 1977): 17.

18. Kevin Coffey, "Bob Dunn: Steel Colossus," *Journal of Country Music* 17, no. 2 (1995): 47–51; Rich Kienzle, "Steel," *Country Music* 4, no. 4 (January 1976): 38; Rich Kienzle, "The Electric Guitar in Country Music: Its Evolution and Development," *Guitar Player* 13, no. 11 (November 1979): 30; Kevin Coffey, "The Bob Dunn Story," *Western*

Swing Society Music News 12, no. 4 (April 1997): 7; Kevin Coffey, *Cliff Bruner and His Texas Wanderers* (Hambergen: Bear Family Records, 1997), 19–20.

19. Coffey, "Bob Dunn: Steel Colossus," 53–55.

20. Leon Selph, interview.

21. Floyd Tillman, interview by John W. Rumble, Nashville, 13 October 1986, CMFOHC; Russell Sanjek, *Pennies from Heaven: The American Popular Music Business in the Twentieth Century* (New York: Da Capo Press, 1996), 137; "Jack Kapp Teases Boys on Melody," *Variety* 148, no. 5 (7 October 1942): 68.

22. Coffey, *Cliff Bruner and His Texas Wanderers*, 1–10; Cliff Bruner quoted in Coffey, *Cliff Bruner and His Texas Wanderers*, 3; Leo Raley quoted in Coffey, *Cliff Bruner and His Texas Wanderers*, 7.

23. Coffey, *Cliff Bruner and His Texas Wanderers*, 52–58.

24. Ibid., 8–9; Nick Tosches, "The Grand Tour," *Journal of Country Music* 16, no. 3 (1994): 24.

25. Carl Abbott, *The New Urban America: Growth and Politics in Sunbelt Cities* (Chapel Hill: University of North Carolina Press, 1981), 103; Mary A. Bufwack, *Finding Her Voice: The Saga of Women in Country Music* (New York: Crown Publishers, 1993), 129; "Hillbilly Disks Pull Most Nickels, Calif. Juke Ops Say," *Billboard* 56, no. 36 (2 September 1944): 62; Dick Schofield quoted in Richard P. Stockdell, "The Evolution of the Country Radio Format," *Journal of Popular Culture* 16, no. 4 (spring 1983): 147.

26. Nat Green, "Fantastic Grosses with Folkshows," *The Billboard 1944 Music Year Book* (New York: Billboard Publishing, 1944), 344–45; "American Folk Tunes," *Billboard* 56, no. 34 (9 August 1944): 67; "American Folk Tunes and Tunesters," *Billboard* 55, no. 42 (16 October 1943): 65; Billie Green, "Foreman Phillips," *Bill Boyd Ranch House News* 5, no. 3 (March 1947): 15; Cliffie Stone, "Western Dances Still Drawing Especially in Southern California," *Capitol News* 4, no. 10 (October 1946): 14; Merle Travis, interview by Douglas B. Green, n.p., 17 October 1975, CMFOHC; Gerald F. Vaughn, "Foreman Phillips: Western Swing's Kingmaker," *John Edwards Memorial Foundation Quarterly* 15, no. 53 (spring 1979): 28.

27. Leon McAuliffe quoted in Townsend, *San Antonio Rose*, 63; Douglas B. Green, "Tumbling Tumbleweeds: Gene Autry, Bob Wills, and the Dream of the West," *Country: The Music and the Musicians*, ed. Paul Kingbury and Alan Axelrod (New York: Abbeville Press, 1988), 109–14.

28. Ginell, *Milton Brown*, xxix–xxx.

29. Al Quaglieri, liner notes, *Spadella: The Essential Spade Cooley*, Columbia CD CK 57392, 1994; Rich Kienzle, "When a Country Star Turns Murderer: The Strange, Tragic Case of Spade Cooley," *Country Music* 5, no. 10 (July 1977): 34–38; Dunbar, *From Bob Wills to Ray Benson*, 67–68; Jimmy Wakely, liner notes, *Spade Cooley*, Columbia LP FC 37467, 1982; "Profiling the Folk Artists," *The Billboard 1944 Music Year Book*, 364; Malone, *Country Music, U.S.A.*, 201; success of "Shame on You" determined from information

in Joel Whitburn, *The Billboard Book of Top Forty Country Hits* (New York: Billboard Books, 1996); "Spade Cooley: Cherokee to His Western Swing," *Billboard* 58, no. 9 (2 March 1946): 18; "Cooley Exits Rancho for Palisades; Spot Seven-Night Op in June," *Billboard* 58, no. 13 (30 March 1946): 39.

30. "Record Reviews," *Billboard* 59, no. 45 (8 November 1947): 31; Rich Kienzle, *Merle Travis: Guitar Rags and a Too Fast Past* (Hambergen: Bear Family Records, 1994), 32; Dunbar, *From Bob Wills to Ray Benson,* 68; C. Phil Henderson, "Spade Cooley Defies Western Music Standards with Sensational Band," *Top Hand* 1, no. 4 (July 1946): 1; *Billboard* 62, no. 21 (27 May 1950): cover; "Cooley Joins H.B. Pop Parade," *Billboard,* 61, no. 19 (7 May 1949): 18.

31. "Spade Cops TV Laurels in L.A.," *Billboard* 63, no. 33 (18 August 1951): 3; "Folk Talent and Tunes," *Billboard* 63, no. 39 (29 September 1951): 98; "Cooley Grosses 220G in 1953," *Billboard* 66, no. 5 (30 January 1954): 26.

32. "Cooley Exits RCA, Switches to Decca Wax," *Billboard* 63, no. 10 (10 March 1951): 33; Quaglier, liner notes, *Spadella,* 8; Kienzle, "When a Country Star Turns Murderer," 34–38.

33. Billie Green, "Tex Williams," *Bill Boyd Ranch House News* 4, no. 8 (August 1947): 9; Ken Griffis, "The Tex Williams Story," *John Edwards Memorial Foundation Quarterly* 15, no. 53 (spring 1979): 5–7.

34. Griffis, "Tex Williams Story," 5–7; C. Phil Henderson, "Tex Williams Fronts New Co-op Band of Ex Spade Cooley Men," *Top Hand* 1, no. 4 (July 1946): 1; "American Folk Tunes," *Billboard* 58, no. 42 (19 October 1946): 100; Tex Williams quoted in "American Folk Tunes," *Billboard* 58, no. 47 (23 November 1946): 106.

35. Griffis, "Tex Williams Story," 9.

36. Rich Kienzle, "Hank Penny," *Old Time Music* 28 (spring 1978): 5–6; Cary Ginell, liner notes, *Tobacco State Swing,* Rambler LP 103, 1980; Hank Penny quoted in Wayne W. Daniel, *Pickin' on Peachree: A History of Country Music in Atlanta, Georgia* (Urbana: University of Illinois Press, 1990), 189–90.

37. Kienzle, "Hank Penny," 7–10; Kienzle, *Merle Travis,* 22; Johnny Sippel, "Folk Talent and Tunes," *Billboard* 62, no. 26 (1 July 1950): 98.

38. Hank Penny quoted in Ken Griffis, "Hank Penny: The Original 'Outlaw'?" *John Edwards Memorial Foundation Quarterly* 18, nos. 65–66 (spring–summer 1982): 6; Rich Kienzle, "Steel Guitar: The Western Swing Era," *Guitar Player* 13, no. 12 (December 1979): 50–53.

39. Kienzle, *Merle Travis,* 22.

40. Rich Kienzle, "Hank Penny Discography," *Old Time Music* 28 (spring 1978): 11–15; Alan Fischler, "Western Caravan," *Billboard* 61, no. 13 (26 March 1949): 17.

41. "Nut Cuts Number of Newies: Costly Sidemen, Arrangers, Up Infant Ork Investments," *Billboard* 56, no. 30 (22 July 1944): 15; Townsend, *San Antonio Rose,* 229; Townsend, "A Brief History of Western Swing," 41; Richard R. Peterson, *Creating*

Country Music: Fabricating Authenticity (Chicago: University of Chicago Press, 1997), 190.

42. Townsend, "A Brief History of Western Swing," 43; Eldon Shamblin quoted in Mark Humphrey, "Playboy Days, Part III: Eldon Shamblin Talking to Mark Humphrey," *Old Time Music* 25 (summer 1977): 25; Sanjek, *Pennies from Heaven,* 312; "Tele Audience Now 325,000: Viewer Total Goes up 600 percent in Two Years," *Billboard* 59, no. 27 (5 July 1947): 1, 19; "Three out of Ten Now Watch TV: Figures Show Two-Year Growth as Fantastic," *Billboard* 60, no. 45 (6 November 1948): 1, 14; Merle Travis, "Recollections of Merle Travis, 1944–1955, Part 2," *John Edwards Memorial Foundation Quarterly* 15, no. 55 (fall 1979): 140; Johnny Bond, *Reflections: The Autobiography of Johnny Bond* (Los Angeles: John Edwards Memorial Foundation, 1976).

43. "If You Own a TV Set in the Los Angeles Area You Go to Movies 25 percent Less Often, Survey Determines," *Billboard* 61, no. 9 (26 February 1949): 1; Lucky Moeller, interview by Douglas B. Green, Nashville, 20 November 1974, CMFOHC.

44. Townsend, *San Antonio Rose,* 225, 228–29, 236; "Hillbilly Band Tops Swing Kings on Coast," *Variety* 153, no. 7 (26 January 1944): 45; Nat Green, "American Folk Tunes," *Billboard* 56, no. 40 (30 September 1944): 66; "On the Stand: Bob Wills and His Texas Playboys," *Billboard* 56, no. 30 (22 July 1944): 26.

45. Bob Pinson, "Bob Wills Discography" in Townsend, *San Antonio Rose,* 339–59.

46. Joe Holley, liner notes, *The Tiffany Transciptions,* vol. 5, Edsel CD 325, 1986; Kienzle, *Bob Wills,* 15.

47. Kienzle, *Bob Wills,* 15; Townsend, *San Antonio Rose,* 253; Johnny Sippel, "Folk Talent and Tunes," *Billboard* 60, no. 34 (21 August 1948): 31.

48. Rich Kienzle, *Papa's Jumpin': The MGM Years of Bob Wills* (Bremen: Bear Family Records, 1985), 6–8, 11–13; Greg Drust, liner notes, *Tommy Duncan: For the Last Time,* Longhorn LP LH 1237; Townsend, *San Antonio Rose,* 254–65; Joe Carr and Alan Munde, *Prairie Night to Neon Lights: The Story of Country Music in West Texas* (Lubbock: Texas Tech University Press, 1995), 62–63.

49. Rich Kienzle, liner notes, *Texas Moon,* Bear Family CD BCD 15907, 1996.

50. Leon McAuliffe, interview; Kienzle, "Steel Guitar: The Western Swing Era," 48–52; Bob Pinson, liner notes, *Leon McAuliffe and His Western Swing Band;* Sonya Colberg, " 'Mr. Steel Guitar' Leon McAuliffe Dies at Age Seventy-one after Long Illness," *Tulsa World,* 21 August 1988; Stricklin and McConal, *My Years with Bob Wills,* 100–101; John W. Rumble, *Roy Acuff* (Alexandria: Time-Life Records, 1983), 19.

51. Leon McAuliffe, interview; biographical information for Leon McAuliffe compiled from Leon McAuliffe vertical file, Country Music Foundation, Nashville; Pinson, liner notes, *Leon McAuliffe and His Western Swing Band;* Humphrey, "Playboy Days, Part I," 15.

52. Leon McAuliffe, interview; Johnny Sippel, "Folk Talent and Tunes," *Billboard* 61, no. 6 (5 February 1949): 30; Johnny Sippel, "Folk Talent and Tunes," *Billboard* 60, no. 36 (4 September 1948): 31; Townsend, "A Brief History of Western Swing," 44.

53. Carr and Munde, *Prairie Nights to Neon Lights,* 65–66.

54. Kienzle, *Hank Thompson and His Brazos Valley Boys,* 3–15; Nick Tosches, "The Hank Thompson Saga: Reflections of the King of Western Swing," *Country Music* 3, no. 10 (July 1975): 32–34.

55. Hank Thompson quoted in Kienzle, *Hank Thompson and His Brazos Valley Boys,* 16; Tosches, "The Hank Thompson Saga," 32–34; Malone, *Country Music, U.S.A.,* 227.

56. Kienzle, *Hank Thompson and His Brazos Valley Boys,* 16, 22, 28; Kienzle, *Merle Travis,* 59.

57. Carr and Munde, *Prairie Nights to Neon Lights,* 62; Les Pouliot, *John Thayer and Don Bruce Together Present the History of Country Music; A Thirty-six-Hour Radio Documentary* (Memphis: J. Thayer and D. Bruce Together, 1970), 137; Ronnie F. Pugh, *Ernest Tubb: The Texas Troubadour* (Durham: Duke University Press, 1996), 151–52; Hank Thompson quoted in Pugh, *Ernest Tubb,* 152; Kienzle, *Hank Thompson and His Brazos Valley Boys,* 31.

4. Alternative String Bands and Old-time Revivalists

1. Neil V. Rosenberg, "Bluegrass, Rock and Roll, and 'Blue Moon of Kentucky,'" *Southern Quarterly* 22, no. 3 (spring 1984): 67.

2. L. Mayne Smith, "An Introduction to Bluegrass," *Journal of American Folklore* 78, no. 309 (July–September 1965): 245–50; Robert Cantwell, *Bluegrass Breakdown: The Making of the Old Southern Sound* (Urbana: University of Illinois Press, 1984), 68–76; Neil V. Rosenberg, "Bluegrass," *Encyclopedia of Southern Culture,* ed. Charles Reagan Wilson and William Ferris (Chapel Hill: University of North Carolina Press, 1989), 993–94; Charles K. Wolfe, *Kentucky Country: Folk and Country Music of Kentucky* (Lexington: University Press of Kentucky, 1982), 96–97; Robert Cantwell, "Mimesis in Bill Monroe's Bluegrass Music," *All That Glitters: Country Music in America,* ed. George H. Lewis (Bowling Green: Bowling Green University Popular Press, 1993), 9; Alan Lomax, "Bluegrass Background: Folk Music with Overdrive," *Esquire* 52, no. 4 (October 1959): 108.

3. Bill Monroe quoted in Charles K. Wolfe, "Bluegrass Touches: An Interview with Bill Monroe," *Old Time Music* 16 (September 1975): 7; Bill Monroe quoted in Les Pouliot, *John Thayer and Don Bruce Together Present the History of Country Music; A Thirty-six-Hour Radio Documentary* (Memphis: J. Thayer and D. Bruce Together, 1970), 140–41; Rosenberg, "Bluegrass, Rock and Roll, and 'Blue Moon of Kentucky,'" 190; Clyde Moody, interview by Douglas B. Green, Nashville, 2 April 1974, Country Music Foundation Oral History Collection (hereafter CMFOHC), Nashville; Cantwell, *Bluegrass Breakdown,* 73; Neil V. Rosenberg, *Bluegrass: A History* (Urbana: University of Illinois Press, 1985), 68–71.

4. Neil V. Rosenberg, *Flatt and Scruggs* (Alexandria: Time-Life Records, 1982), 4–7; Rosenberg, *Bluegrass,* 69.

5. Bill Monroe quoted in Wolfe, "Bluegrass Touches," 11; Earl Scruggs, interview by Douglas B. Green, Madison, 21 June 1974, CMFOHC; Earl Scruggs quoted in Pouliot, *History of Country Music,* 693; Rosenberg, *Bluegrass,* 69–71.

6. Rosenberg, *Bluegrass,* 71–74; Rosenberg, *Flatt and Scruggs,* 7–10; Charles K. Wolfe, *Tennessee Strings: The Story of Country Music in Tennessee* (Knoxville: University of Tennessee Press, 1977), 84; Chubby Wise quoted in Wayne W. Daniel, "Chubby Wise: Dean of the Bluegrass Fiddlers," *Bluegrass Unlimited* 21, no. 10 (April 1987): 33.

7. Mark Humphrey, *The Essential Bill Monroe and His Blue Grass Boys: 1945–1949* (New York: Sony Music Entertainment, 1992), 23.

8. Johnny Sippel, "Folk Talent and Tunes," *Billboard* 61, no. 46 (12 November 1949): 35; Humphrey, *The Essential Bill Monroe and His Blue Grass Boys,* 31; Rosenberg, "Bluegrass: 1950–1958," *Bill Monroe: Bluegrass, 1950–1958* (Vollersode: Bear Family Records, 1989), 57–62.

9. Neil V. Rosenberg, liner notes, *Flatt and Scruggs: The Golden Era,* Rounder CD SS 05/SMSP A 22614, 1992; Rosenberg, *Flatt and Scruggs,* 11–12; Neil V. Rosenberg, *Flatt and Scruggs, 1948–1959* (Vollersode: Bear Family Records, 1991), 1–3.

10. Ibid.

11. Smith, "An Introduction to Bluegrass," 252–53; Linda Stanley, "Don Reno: A Bluegrass Family Tradition," *Bluegrass Unlimited* 15, no. 2 (August 1980): 18–21; Rosenberg, *Bluegrass,* 105; Bob Artis, *Bluegrass: From the Lonesome Wail of a Mountain Love Song to the Hammering Drive of the Scruggs-Style Banjo, the Story of an American Musical Tradition* (New York: Norton Publications, 1975), 61–62.

12. Artis, *Bluegrass,* 62–63; Don Reno quoted in Rhonda Strickland, "Don Reno, Reflections," *Bluegrass Unlimited* 19, no. 6 (December 1984): 10; Bill Vernon and Gary B. Reid, *Don Reno and Red Smiley and the Tennessee Cut-Ups, 1951–1959* (Dearborn: Highland Music, 1993), 2–13; Stanley, "Don Reno," 22; Bill C. Malone, *Country Music, U.S.A.,* 2d ed. (Austin: University of Texas Press, 1985), 336.

13. Jack Temple Kirby, *Rural Worlds Lost: The American South, 1920–1960* (Baton Rouge: Louisiana State University Press, 1987), 80; Harry K. Schwarzweller, *Mountain Families in Transition: A Case Study of Appalachian Migration* (University Park: Pennsylvania State University Press, 1971), 6–9, 58–75.

14. Kirby, *Rural Worlds Lost,* 85–93; Ralph Stanley quoted in Ken Ringle, "The Natural King of Bluegrass: Virginia's Ralph Stanley, the Old-Timey Singer Whose Time Has Come," *Washington Post,* 20 March 1993; Anthony Dellaflora, "True Colors: Bluegrass Legend Ralph Stanley Holds onto Musical Roots," *Rio-Albuquerque Journal,* 14 April 1994; Charles K. Wolfe, liner notes, *The Complete Columbia Stanley Brothers,* Columbia CD CK 53798, 1996; Ralph Stanley, interview by Thomas D. Warren, Nashville, 19 October 1968, CMFOHC; Jack Tottle, "The Stanley Brothers: For Most of Their Brilliant First Decade, Bristol Was Home," *Bluegrass Unlimited* 22, no. 4 (October 1987): 27; Rich Kienzle, "The Stanley Brothers," *CMSA Newsletter* (July–August 1989): 36D–36E; Ralph

Stanley quoted in Ringle, "The Natural King of Bluegrass"; Malone, *Country Music, U.S.A.,* 341.

15. Ralph Stanley quoted in Ringle, "The Natural King of Bluegrass."

16. Artis, *Bluegrass,* 31–33; Rosenberg, "Bluegrass, Rock and Roll, and 'Blue Moon of Kentucky,'" 196; Tottle, "The Stanley Brothers," 27–29; Ralph Stanley quoted in Dellaflora, "True Colors."

17. Rosenberg, *Bluegrass,* 100; Malone, *Country Music, U.S.A.,* 343–44; Artis, *Bluegrass,* 34.

18. Malone, *Country Music, U.S.A.,* 337–38; Rosenberg, *Bluegrass,* 117; Artis, *Bluegrass,* 71.

19. Tottle, "The Stanley Brothers," 29; Rosenberg, *Bluegrass,* 81–82; Richard Spottswood, "Country Music and the Phonograph," *Bluegrass Unlimited* 21, no. 8 (February 1987): 22; Kip Lornell, liner notes, *Virginia Traditions: Early Roanoke Country Radio,* Blue Ridge Institute LP 010, 1988.

20. Malone, *Country Music, U.S.A.,* 223; Robert Cogswell, "'We Made Our Name in the Days of Radio': A Look at the Career of Wilma Lee and Stoney Cooper," *John Edwards Memorial Foundation Quarterly* 11, no. 38 (summer 1975): 67–73; Wayne W. Daniel, "Wilma Lee Cooper: America's Most Authentic Mountain Singer," *Bluegrass Unlimited* 16, no. 8 (February 1982): 15; Wilma Lee Cooper quoted in Daniel, "Wilma Lee Cooper," 14.

21. Ivan M. Tribe and John W. Morris, "Molly O'Day and Lynn Davis," *Bluegrass Unlimited* 9, no. 3 (September 1974): 10–14; Ivan M. Tribe, liner notes, *Molly O'Day and the Cumberland Mountain Folks,* Bear Family CD BCD 15565, 1992; Malone, *Country Music, U.S.A.,* 219.

22. Ivan Tribe and Richard Weize, "Molly O'Day and the Cumberland Mountain Folks," in Tribe, liner notes, *Molly O'Day and the Cumberland Mountain Folks.*

23. Grandpa Jones, *Everybody's Grandpa: Fifty Years behind the Mike* (Knoxville: University of Tennessee Press, 1984), 44–101; Charles K. Wolfe, "The Music of Grandpa Jones," *Journal of Country Music* 8, no. 3 (1981): 47–48, 65–66, 70–72; Malone, *Country Music, U.S.A.,* 217.

24. Malone, *Country Music, U.S.A.,* 126; Rich Kienzle, "Country Music Instruments and Players," *The Country Music Book,* ed. Michael Mason (New York: Scribner's Sons, 1985), 144–48.

25. Charles K. Wolfe, "Grandpa Jones Discography," *Everybody's Grandpa,* 237–45; Jones, *Everybody's Grandpa,* 110–12.

26. Wolfe, "Grandpa Jones Discography," 245–48; Jones, *Everybody's Grandpa,* 127–28.

27. Ivan M. Tribe and John W. Morris, "The South's Favorite Trio: The Story of the Anglin Brothers," *Bluegrass Unlimited* 13, no. 5 (November 1978): 30–32; Walt Trott, "The Johnnie and Jack Story," *Johnnie and Jack and the Tennessee Mountain Boys* (Vollersode: Bear Family Records, 1992), 2–9; Eddie Stubbs, "Johnnie and Jack: The Recordings,"

Johnnie and Jack and the Tennessee Mountain Boys, 10; Douglas B. Green, "Kitty Wells: The Queen Still Reigns," *Country Music* 8, no. 9 (June 1980): 41–42.

28. Johnnie Wright quoted in A. C. Dunkleberger, *Queen of Country Music: The Life Story of Kitty Wells* (Nashville: Ambrose Publishing, 1977), 42; Stubbs, "Johnnie and Jack: The Recordings," 10–18.

29. Stubbs, "Johnnie and Jack: The Recordings," 19–29.

30. Nelson Sears, *Jim and Jesse: Appalachia to the Grand Ole Opry* (Lancaster: Nelson Sears, 1976), 13–66; Joy McReynolds, letter to Bill Ivey, 27 January 1997, Jim and Jesse vertical file, Country Music Foundation, Nashville; Jim McReynolds quoted in Dixie Deen, "'Diesel on My Tail': Jim and Jesse," *Music City News* 4, no. 11 (May 1967): 6; Jim McReynolds quoted in Robert K. Oermann, "Music Is Our Life: Bluegrass Brothers Jim and Jesse Celebrate Fifty Years of Making Music," *Tennessean,* 29 March 1997; Jim McReynolds quoted in Linda Jean Morris, "Bluegrass Music and Good Times," *Yorka Record,* 27 October 1989; Artis, *Bluegrass,* 77–78; Dale Vinicur, liner notes, *Jim and Jesse, 1952–1955,* Bear Family CD BCD 15635, 1992; Dale Vinicur, *Jim and Jesse: Bluegrass and More* (Vollersode: Bear Family Records, 1993), 2–8.

31. Malone, *Country Music, U.S.A.,* 345; Artis, *Bluegrass,* 79.

32. Vinicur, *Jim and Jesse: Bluegrass and More,* 9.

33. Charles K. Wolfe, *The Louvin Brothers: In Close Harmony* (Vollersode: Bear Family Records, 1992), 2–9; Charlie Louvin quoted in Ed Bumgardner, "Remaining Half of the Louvin Brothers Preserves the Legacy," *Winston-Salem Journal,* 12 July 1987.

34. Wolfe, *The Louvin Brothers,* 4, 10–13; Eddie Stubbs, Richard Weize, and Charles Wolfe, "The Louvin Brothers," *The Louvin Brothers,* 42–43; Charlie Louvin, interview by Douglas B. Green, Nashville, 30 November 1977, CMFOHC; Malone, *Country Music, U.S.A.,* 214–15; James C. Cobb, "From Rocky Top to New York City: Country Music and the Economic Transformation of the South," *You Wrote My Life: Lyrical Themes in Country Music,* ed. Melton A. McLaurin and Richard A. Peterson (Philadelphia: Gordon and Breach, 1992), 70–71; Bumgardner, "Remaining Half of the Louvin Brothers Preserves the Legacy"; Charlie Louvin quoted in Suzy Lowry Geno, "Charlie and Ira—The Louvin Brothers," *Bluegrass Unlimited* 17, no. 9 (March 1983): 16; Joel Whitburn, *The Billboard Book of Top Forty Country Hits* (New York: Billboard Books, 1996), 190.

35. Malone, *Country Music, U.S.A.,* 10–13; W. J. Cash, *The Mind of the South* (1941; reprint, Vintage Books, 1991), 58; George Lipsitz, *Rainbow at Midnight: Labor and Culture in the 1940s* (Urbana: University of Illinois Press, 1994), 261; William Gerald McLoughlin Jr., *Modern Revivalism: Charles Grandison Finney to Billy Graham* (New York: Ronald Press, 1959), 472–81; Asa A. Allen quoted in David E. Harrell, *All Things Are Possible: The Healing and Charismatic Revivals in Modern America* (Bloomington: Indiana University Press, 1975), 97; Merle Curti, *The Growth of American Thought* (New York: Harper and Row, 1964), 771; Roy L. Moore, *Mass Communication Law and Ethics* (Hillsdale: Erlbaum, 1994), 372; "Strong Faith with Fans, Sacred Music Is Just That," *Billboard* 67, no. 23 (21 May 1955): 22.

36. Johnny Cash, liner notes, *Unchained,* American Recordings CD CT 69404, 1996; for a discussion of country music's takes on postwar sociopolitical developments and the advent of the atomic age see Jens Lund, "Socio-Political Aspects of Right Wing County Music" (master's thesis, Bowling Green State University, 1975), and Charles K. Wolfe, "Nuclear Country: The Atomic Bomb in Country Music," *Journal of Country Music* 7, no. 1 (January 1978): 4–21.

37. Bailes Brothers, interview by Ronnie F. Pugh, Nashville, 9 June 1983, CMFOHC; Ivan M. Tribe, "The Bailes Brothers," *Bluegrass Unlimited* 9, no. 8 (February 1975): 8–12; Ivan M. Tribe, *Mountaineer Jamboree: Country Music in West Virginia* (Lexington: University Press of Kentucky, 1984), 110–12; Stephen R. Tucker, " 'Louisiana Saturday Night': A History of Louisiana Country Music" (Ph.D. diss., Tulane University, 1995; Ann Arbor, Mich.: UMI, 1996), 404–5, 411–12; "American Folk Tunes," *Billboard* 58, no. 11 (16 March 1946): 112; "Folk Talent and Tunes," *Billboard* 60, no. 26 (26 June 1948): 110; Malone, *Country Music, U.S.A.,* 214.

38. Bill C. Malone, *The Smithsonian Collection of Classic Country Music* (Washington, D.C.: Smithsonian Institution, 1981), 36; Bailes Brothers, interview; "Record Reviews," *Billboard* 58, no. 47 (23 November 1946): 30.

39. C. Vann Woodward, *The Burden of Southern History* (New York: Vintage Books, 1960), 10; Kirby, *Rural Worlds Lost,* 328–33; Lawrence W. Levine, *Black Culture and Black Consciousness: Afro-American Folk Thought from Slavery to Freedom* (New York: Oxford University Press, 1978), 297.

40. Tribe, *Mountaineer Jamboree,* 153.

41. "Folk Parks to Take Foothold in Ohio, South This Summer," *Billboard* 60, no. 23 (5 June 1948): 38; Ford Rush, "Acuff's Dunbar Cave Rich in Lore, Visitors," *Billboard* 65, no. 49 (5 December 1953): 54.

5. Country Music at the Dawn of the Sunbelt Era

1. Steven Mintz and Susan Kellogg, *Domestic Revolutions: A Social History of American Family Life* (New York: Free Press, 1988), 155; David R. Goldfield, *Promised Land: The South since 1945* (Arlington Heights: H. Davidson, 1987), 6–10; Jack Temple Kirby, *Rural Worlds Lost: The American South, 1920–1960* (Baton Rouge: Louisiana State University Press, 1987), 326–28; Lewis M. Killian, "The Adjustment of Southern White Migrants to Northern Urban Norms," *Social Forces* 32, no. 1 (October 1953): 66.

2. Goldfield, *Promised Land,* 8–10; Pete Daniel, "Going among Strangers: Southern Reactions to World War II," *Journal of American History* 77, no. 3 (December 1990): 898; H. Clarence Nixon, "The South after the War," *Virginia Quarterly Review* 20, no. 3 (summer 1944): 321.

3. Goldfield, *Promised Land,* 28; James C. Cobb, *Industrialization and Southern Society, 1877–1984* (Chicago: Dorsey Press, 1984), 42–52; Kirby, *Rural Worlds Lost,* xiv;

Carl Abbott, *The New Urban America: Growth and Politics in Sunbelt Cities* (Chapel Hill: University of North Carolina Press, 1981), 101.

4. Ronnie F. Pugh, *Ernest Tubb: The Texas Troubadour* (Durham: Duke University Press, 1996), 322; Bill C. Malone, *Honky-tonkin'* (Alexandria: Time-Life Records, 1983), 5; Joli Jensen, *The Nashville Sound: Authenticity, Commercialization, and Country Music* (Nashville: Vanderbilt University Press, 1998), 27–29.

5. Rich Kienzle, "Country Music Instruments and Players," *The Country Music Book,* ed. Michael Mason (New York: Scribner's Sons, 1985), 184; Joe Carr, *Prairie Nights to Neon Nights: The Story of Country Music in West Texas* (Lubbock: Texas Tech University Press, 1995), 62; Bill C. Malone, "Honky Tonk: The Music of the Southern Working Class," *Folk Music and Modern Sound*, eds. William R. Ferris and Mary L. Hart (Jackson: University Press of Mississippi, 1982), 123.

6. Bill Porterfield, *The Greatest Honky-tonks in Texas* (Dallas: Taylor, 1983), 16; Killian, "The Adjustment of Southern White Migrants to Northern Urban Norms," 66–67; John Morthland, "Honky Tonk Music: The Raw Sound of Hard Country," *Country Music* 5, no. 10 (July 1977): 42; Bill C. Malone, *Country Music, U.S.A.*, 2d ed. (Austin: University of Texas Press, 1985), 154–55; Malone, *Honky-tonkin'*, 5–6; Colin Escott, *Hank Williams, the Biography* (Boston: Little, Brown, 1994), 125; Russell Sanjek, *Pennies from Heaven: The American Popular Music Business in the Twentieth Century* (New York: Da Capo Press, 1996), 305; Steve Schickel, "Acceptance of C & W. Jukes in Big Role for Passing Word," *Billboard* 66, no. 21 (22 May 1954): 28.

7. Huey Meaux quoted in Nick Tosches, "The Grand Tour," *Journal of Country Music* 16, no. 3 (1994): 22; "Texas Bill Defines 'Honky Tonks' for Officers' Guidance," *Billboard* 55, no. 27 (3 July 1943): 62.

8. Carl Perkins quoted in Patrick B. Mullen, "Hillbilly Hipsters of the 1950s: The Romance of Rockabilly," *Southern Quarterly* 22, no. 3 (spring 1984): 86; Bob Claypool, "Floyd Tillman—Original Cosmic Cowboy," *Houston Post*, 21 July 1979; Floyd Tillman quoted in Claypool, "Floyd Tillman—Original Cosmic Cowboy."

9. Donna Fielder, "Honky-tonk Melody Brought Dexter Fame," *Denton Record-Chronicle*, 27 June 1980; Al Dexter vertical file, Country Music Foundation Oral History Collection (hereafter CMFOHC), Nashville; Adam Komorowski, "Floyd Tillman," *Hillbilly Researcher* 15 (1992): 18–22.

10. Komorowski, "Floyd Tillman," 14–15; Claypool, "Floyd Tillman—Original Cosmic Cowboy"; "Five Years Ago This Week," *Billboard* 65, no. 11 (14 March 1953): 44.

11. Ernest Tubb quoted in Ronnie Pugh, "The Texas Troubadour: Selected Aspects of the Career of Ernest Tubb" (master's thesis, Stephen F. Austin State University, 1978), 58; Porterfield, *The Greatest Honky-tonks in Texas*, 24; Pugh, *Ernest Tubb*, 113–14, 318–19.

12. Pugh, *Ernest Tubb*, 10–54, 64–68, 93–94, 100–103; Malone, *Country Music, U.S.A.*, 155–56.

13. Pugh, *Ernest Tubb*, 365–73.

14. George Lipsitz, *Rainbow at Midnight: Labor and Culture in the 1940s* (Urbana: University of Illinois Press, 1994), 45–47; Pugh, *Ernest Tubb,* 111.

15. Pugh, *Ernest Tubb,* 373–87.

16. Roger M. Williams, *Hank Williams* (Alexandria: Time-Life Records, 1981), 6–8; Escott, *Hank Williams, the Biography,* 12–37, 51–98, 251; Colin Escott, *Hank Williams: The Original Singles Collection . . . Plus* (New York: Polygram Records, 1990), 2–14; Bob Pinson, liner notes, *Hank Williams, the First Recordings,* Country Music Foundation LP CMF-007, 1986; Joel Whitburn, *The Billboard Book of Top Forty Country Hits* (New York: Billboard Books, 1996), 358; "Opry Bounces Hank Williams," *Billboard* 64, no. 34 (23 August 1952): 21.

17. Williams, *Hank Williams,* 22; Escott, *Hank Williams, the Biography,* 52–54; Mark Humphrey, "Interview: Merle Travis, Part I," *Old Time Music* 36 (summer 1981): 8; Chet Atkins with Bill Neely, *Country Gentleman* (Chicago: Henry Regnery, 1974), 175.

18. Escott, *Hank Williams, the Biography,* 61–63.

19. Ibid., 118.

20. Hank Williams quoted in Williams, *Hank Williams,* 4; Ray Price, interview by Hugh Cherry, California, 10 March 1967, CMFOHC.

21. Nev Gehman, "Fans Clamour for Disks of Late Singer," *Billboard* 65, no. 3 (17 January 1953): 1, 25; "In-Pouring of Tributes to Williams Continues," *Billboard* 65, no. 5 (31 January 1953): 15; Williams, *Hank Williams,* 20; Malone, *Country Music, U.S.A.,* 243; Bailes Brothers, interview by Ronnie F. Pugh, Nashville, 9 June 1983, CMFOHC; "Hank Williams Day," *Billboard* 66, no. 40 (2 October 1954): 41–42.

22. Lawrence W. Levine, *Black Culture and Black Consciousness: Afro-American Folk Thought from Slavery to Freedom* (New York: Oxford University Press, 1978), 234–35; Steve Goodson, "Hillbilly Humanist: Hank Williams and the Southern Working Class," *Alabama Review* 46, no. 2 (April 1993): 109–14.

23. Rich Kienzle, *Ray Price and the Cherokee Cowboys: The Honky Tonk Years, 1950–1966* (Hambergen: Bear Family Records, 1995), 4, 8; Ray Price, interview; Mike Elswick, "Country Star Ray Price Travels World, but Likes East Texas Best," *Longview News,* 12 June 1985; David Mankelow, "Ray Price," *Hillbilly Researcher* 12: 13–14; Daniel Cooper, "Being Ray Price Means Never Having to Say You're Sorry," *Journal of Country Music* 14, no. 3 (1992): 24–26.

24. Kienzle, *Ray Price and the Cherokee Cowboys,* 6–21; Tommy Hill quoted in Kienzle, *Ray Price and the Cherokee Cowboys,* 15; Cooper, "Being Ray Price Means Never Having to Say You're Sorry," 26; Richard Weize and Rich Kienzle, "Ray Price: The Bullet and Columbia Discography, 1950–1966," in Kienzle, *Ray Price and the Cherokee Cowboys,* 64.

25. Mintz and Kellogg, *Domestic Revolutions,* 152–54, 161; Mary A. Bufwack, *Finding Her Voice: The Saga of Women in Country Music* (New York: Crown Publishers, 1993), 142; Lipsitz, *Rainbow at Midnight,* 49–52, 268.

26. Mark Humphrey, *The Essential Bill Monroe and His Blue Grass Boys: 1945–1949*

(New York: Sony Music Entertainment, 1992), 25; Bufwack, *Finding Her Voice,* 164; Mintz and Kellogg, *Domestic Revolutions,* 170–72.

27. Bufwack, *Finding Her Voice,* 166–67.

28. A. C. Dunkleburger, *Queen of Country Music: The Life Story of Kitty Wells* (Nashville: Ambrose Publishing, 1977), 12; Charles K. Wolfe, *Kitty Wells: The Queen of Country Music* (Hambergen: Bear Family Records, 1993), 2–4; Bufwack, *Finding Her Voice,* 177–78; Johnnie Wright quoted in Walt Trott, "The Johnnie and Jack Story," *Johnnie and Jack and the Tennessee Mountain Boys* (Vollersode: Bear Family Records, 1992), 8.

29. Chet Atkins quoted in Wolfe, *Kitty Wells,* 4; Johnnie Wright quoted in Trott, "The Johnnie and Jack Story," 9.

30. Wolfe, *Kitty Wells,* 4–5; Kitty Wells quoted in Dunkleburger, *Queen of Country Music,* 14; Bob Pinson, "Discography: 1949–1958," in Wolfe, *Kitty Wells,* 24–25; Whitburn, *The Billboard Book of Top Forty Country Hits,* 328; Robert K. Oermann, "Honky-tonk Angels: Kitty Wells to Patsy Cline," *Country: The Music and the Musicians,* ed. Paul Kingbury and Alan Axelrod (New York: Abbeville Press, 1988), 328; Mary A. Bufwack, "The Feminist Sensibility in Postwar Country Music," *Southern Quarterly* 22, no. 3 (spring 1984): 138.

31. "Gals from the Hills: Kitty and Goldie Start Country-Girl Search," *Billboard* 65, no. 25 (20 June 1953): 1, 23.

32. Bufwack, *Finding Her Voice,* 169–74, 185–86; Bob Allen, liner notes, *Welcome to the Club: Charline Arthur,* Bear Family LP BFX 15234, 1986; Mintz and Kellogg, *Domestic Revolutions,* 201.

33. Kevin Coffey, *Hank Locklin: Send Me the Pillow You Dream On* (Hambergen: Bear Family Records, 1996), 7; Charles K. Wolfe, *Lefty Frizzell: Life's like Poetry* (Hambergen: Bear Family Records, 1992), 15–17; Daniel C. Cooper, *Lefty Frizzell: The Honky-tonk Life of Country Music's Greatest Singer* (Boston: Little, Brown, 1995), 73; "Satherley Quits Columbia Job," *Billboard* 64, no. 23 (7 June 1952): 17; Charles K. Wolfe, *Carl Smith: Satisfaction Guaranteed* (Hambergen: Bear Family Records, 1996), 8.

34. Merle Haggard quoted in Robert Hilburn, "Hail to the Real King," *Los Angeles Times,* 9 May 1993.

35. Wolfe, *Lefty Frizzell,* 4–92; Cooper, *Lefty Frizzell,* 18–129; Lefty Frizzell quoted in Wolfe, *Lefty Frizzell,* 5; Malone, *Country Music, U.S.A.,* 231–32; Whitburn, *The Billboard Book of Top Forty Country Hits,* 151–52.

36. Coffey, *Hank Locklin,* 2–25.

37. Ibid., 24–25; Kevin Coffey et al., "Hank Locklin: Gold Star, Royalty, Four-Star, and Decca Discography," in Coffey, *Hank Locklin,* 28–31; Malone, *Country Music, U.S.A.,* 235.

38. Ronnie F. Pugh, liner notes, *Webb Pierce: King of the Honky-tonk from the Original Decca Masters, 1952–1959,* Country Music Foundation CD CMF-019D/MSD-35500, 1994; Stephen R. Tucker, " 'Louisiana Saturday Night': A History of Louisiana Country Music" (Ph.D. diss., Tulane University, 1995; Ann Arbor, Mich.: UMI, 1996), 447–50; Nat Green,

"American Folk Tunes," *Billboard* 57, no. 34 (25 August 1945): 75; "1954's Top Country and Western Records . . . according to Retail Sales," *Billboard* 66, no. 52 (25 December 1954): 1; Whitburn, *The Billboard Book of Top Forty Country Hits,* 244–45; Otto Kitsinger, *Webb Pierce: The Wandering Boy, 1951–1958* (Vollersode: Bear Family Records, 1990), 2–8.

39. Whitburn, *The Billboard Book of Top Forty Country Hits,* 244–45; Rich Kienzle, "Steel," *Country Music* 4, no. 4 (January 1976): 61; John Haggard, "Bud Isaacs," *Guitar Player* 10, no. 11 (November 1976): 31.

40. Webb Pierce quoted in Mindy Tate, "Hall of Fame Award Is Ultimate to Pierce," *Brentwood Journal,* 19 September 1990; Webb Pierce quoted in Kitsinger, *Webb Pierce,* 19; Malone, *Country Music, U.S.A.,* 232–33; Webb Pierce quoted in Les Pouliot, *John Thayer and Don Bruce Together Present the History of Country Music; A Thirty-six-Hour Radio Documentary* (Memphis: J. Thayer and D. Bruce Together, 1970), 419.

41. Lefty Frizzell quoted in Geoff Lane, "The Last of Lefty Frizzell," *Country Music* 4, no. 2 (November 1975): 42; Kitsinger, *Webb Pierce,* 19; Nick Tosches, " 'Honky Tonkin': Ernest Tubb, Hank Williams, and the Bartender's Muse," *Country: The Music and the Musicians,* 244; Ernest Tubb quoted in Hank Snow, *The Hank Snow Story* (Urbana: University of Illinois Press, 1994), 351–52; Nolan Porterfield, *Jimmie Rodgers: The Life and Times of America's Blue Yodeler* (Urbana: University of Illinois Press, 1979), 361–62.

42. Snow, *The Hank Snow Story,* 352–57; "Jimmie Rodgers: Hillbilly World to Honor His Memory," *Billboard* 65, no. 20 (16 May 1953): 1, 16; Bert Braun, "Jimmie Rodgers Day: Folk Artists and Execs Stage Great Tribute," *Billboard* 65, no. 23 (6 June 1953): 1, 17, 44.

43. Ted Daffan, interview by Garna Christian, Houston, 24 October 1977, CMFOHC; Floyd Tillman paraphrased in Marty Racine, "Tillman Takes His Talent on Stage," *Houston Chronicle,* 18 October 1984; Escott, *Hank Williams, the Biography,* 46; Ernest Tubb quoted in Pugh, *Ernest Tubb,* 132; Fred Rose quoted in "American Folk Tunes," *Billboard* 58, no. 31 (3 August 1946): 123; Ernest Tubb quoted in Marshall Fallwell, "E.T. Remembers: On His Last Night at the Rhyman, Ernest Tubb Talks about the Old Days," *Country Music* 2, no. 8 (April 1974): 77; Pugh, *Ernest Tubb,* 133; Whitburn, *The Billboard Book of Top Forty Country Hits,* 8.

44. Pugh, *Ernest Tubb,* 48–50, 135; "Hillbilly Bash in Carnegie Perks Stem Interest," *Billboard* 59, no. 38 (27 September 1947): 1, 21; "Hillbilly Nitery Makes Bow in Chicago July 1," *Billboard* 64, no. 17 (26 April 1952): 17; Lee Zhito, "Merchandising Pays Off: Stone Does Well by Folk, Both on Disks and in Store," *Billboard* 61, no. 48 (26 November 1949): 17; Bill Simon, "Merchandising Pays Off: Hillbilly Center (54th Street, New York) Not in Hills, but All Is Rosie," *Billboard* 61, no. 53 (31 December 1949): 14.

45. "Hillbillies May Get Their Day," *Billboard* 65, no. 8 (21 February 1953): 1, 29; "Congress to Go Hillbilly? Invite House Members to Meridian Festival," *Billboard* 66,

no. 21 (22 May 1954): 41; Joe Martin, "Politicians Descend on Meridian Fete," *Billboard* 66, no. 23 (5 June 1954): 14, 26; "Hillbilly Week: Hoppers Bill in Congress for National Fete," *Billboard* 66, no. 20 (15 May 1954): 16.

46. Joe Martin, "Country Music Field Full of Green Stuff—Folding Kind, That Is," *Billboard* 66, no. 21 (22 May 1954): 1, 30; Paul Ackerman, "Country and Western Fans Like Their Talent Alive: Personal Appearances in the Field Nudge $50,000,000 per Year," *Billboard* 67, no. 23 (21 May 1955): 1, 15, 48; Neil V. Rosenberg, *Bluegrass: A History* (Urbana: University of Illinois Press, 1985), 95–96; Johnny Sippel, "New Horizons for Country Western Platter Spinners," *Billboard* 65, no. 9 (28 February 1953): 58; Johnny Sippel, "Dixie Successes Spur Rustic Headlines to Seek More Dates," *Billboard* 63, no. 51 (22 December 1951): 44–45; "RCA 'Country Caravan': Artist Tour to Hit Ten Big Cities in Fifteen Days," *Billboard* 66, no. 3 (16 January 1954): 1; Escott, *Hank Williams, the Biography,* 100–101; "Personal Appearances Boom along the Suburban Trails: Rural Stars Thrive as City Acts Strive," *Billboard* 65, no. 38 (19 September 1953): 1, 15.

47. Bill Bolick, "I Always Liked the Type of Music That I Play: An Autobiography of the Blue Sky Boys," *Presenting the Blue Sky Boys,* John Edwards Memorial Foundation Quarterly LP 104, 1977; Old Joe Clark, interview by John W. Rumble, Berea, 5 December 1985, CMFOHC; Escott, *Hank Williams, the Biography,* 47; Bob and Maggie Atcher, interview by John W. Rumble, Nashville, 2 May 1987, CMFOHC; George Biggar, "The WLS National Barn Dance Story: The Early Years," *John Edwards Memorial Foundation Quarterly* 7, no. 23 (autumn 1971): 111; Jonny Whiteside, *Ramblin' Rose: The Life and Career of Rose Maddox* (Nashville: Country Music Foundation Press, 1997), 138; "Barn Dance Back on Net, Hypes WLS," *Billboard* 61, no. 6 (5 February 1949): 6.

48. Bureau of the Census, *Sixteenth Census of the United States: 1940. Housing— General Characteristics* (Washington, D.C.: United States Printing Office, 1943), table 10; Bureau of the Census, *A Report of the Seventeenth Decennial Census of the United States: 1950. Housing—General Characteristics* (Washington, D.C.: United States Printing Office, 1952), table 20; "Facts on Country and Western Radio Jamborees," *Billboard* 65, no. 49 (5 December 1953): 88–89; Paul Lazarsfield and Harry Field, *The People Look at Radio* (Chapel Hill: University of North Carolina Press, 1946), 101; Wayne W. Daniel, *Pickin' on Peachtree: A History of Country Music in Atlanta, Georgia* (Urbana: University of Illinois Press, 1990), 173; Edward Morris, "New, Improved, Homogenized: Country Radio since 1950," *Country: The Music and the Musicians,* 89, 96–97; Ronnie F. Pugh, "Country across the Country," *Country: The Music and the Musicians,* 171.

49. Stephen R. Tucker, "Louisiana Folk and Regional Popular Music Traditions on Records and the Radio: An Historical Overview with Suggestions for Further Research," *Louisiana Folklife: A Guide to the State,* ed. Nicholas R. Spitzer (Baton Rouge: Louisiana Folklife Program, 1985), 224; Tucker, " 'Louisiana Saturday Night,' " 402–15, 439; Kyle Bailes, interview by Ronnie F. Pugh, Nashville, 19 July 1980, CMFOHC; Malone, *Country Music, U.S.A.,* 207.

50. "American Folk Tunes," *Billboard* 59, no. 31 (2 August 1947): 114; Escott, *Hank Williams, the Biography,* 105; David Cobb, interview by John W. Rumble, Nashville, 18 August 1983, CMFOHC; Elizabeth Schlappi, *Roy Acuff, the Smoky Mountain Boy* (Gretna: Pelican, 1978), 53; Jimmy Wakely, interview by Douglas B. Green, Burbank, 25 June 1974, CMFOHC.

51. Malone, *Country Music, U.S.A.,* 205; Escott, *Hank Williams, the Biography,* 77.

52. Tucker, " 'Louisiana Saturday Night,' " 422–23; Joe Martin, "Country Music Field Full of Green Stuff—Folding Kind, That Is," 30; Escott, *Hank Williams, the Biography,* 110; Sippel, "Dixie Successes Spur Rustic Headlines to Seek More Dates," 44; WSM Artists' Service Bureau, advertisement, *Billboard* 65, no. 15 (11 April 1953): 91; Charlie Louvin, interview by Douglas B. Green, Nashville, 30 November 1977, CMFOHC; Ernest Tubb quoted in Fallwell, "E.T. Remembers: On His Last Night at the Rhyman, Ernest Tubb Talks about the Old Days," 72.

53. Pouliot, *History of Country Music,* 368–69; Wolfe, *Carl Smith,* 2–12; Ronnie F. Pugh, *Carl Smith,* Columbia LP FC 38906, 1984.

54. Otto Kitsinger and Richard Weize, "Carl Smith: The Columbia Discography, 1950–1959," in Wolfe, *Carl Smith,* 30–34; Wolfe, *Carl Smith,* 16, 28; Carl Smith quoted in Rich Kienzle, "Carl Smith: You Can't Roll Back Time," *Country Music* 113 (May–June 1985): 38; Malone, *Country Music, U.S.A.,* 228.

55. Tucker, " 'Louisiana Saturday Night,' " 452–54; Faron Young quoted in Pouliot, *History of Country Music,* 400; Daniel Cooper, liner notes, *Faron Young: Live Fast, Love Hard, Original Capitol Recordings, 1952–1962,* Country Music Foundation CD CMF-020D/S21-18678, 1995; Colin Escott, *Faron Young: The Classic Years, 1952–1962* (Vollersode: Bear Family Records, 1992), 2–38; Whitburn, *The Billboard Book of Top Forty Country Hits,* 372–74.

56. Otto Kitsinger, Don Roy, and Richard Weize, "The Capitol Discography," in Escott, *Faron Young,* 40.

57. Richard A. Peterson, *Creating Country Music: Fabricating Authenticity* (Chicago: University of Chicago Press, 1997), 187–89; Levine, *Black Culture and Black Consciousness,* 273; Ted Daffan, interview.

58. Williams, *Hank Williams,* 27; Escott, *Hank Williams: The Original Singles Collection . . . Plus,* 11; "Golden Oatunes: Hank Williams Clefs Twenty-two Hillbilly Toppers," *Billboard* 63, no. 43 (27 October 1951): 15; "Bouncin' the Pop Bayou: 'Jambalaya' Man Makes It Again on Big-Time Charts," *Billboard* 64, no. 35 (30 August 1952): 20; Sanjek, *Pennies from Heaven,* 240; John W. Rumble, "Fred Rose and the Development of the Nashville Music Industry, 1942–1954" (Ph.D. diss., Vanderbilt University, 1980; Ann Arbor, Mich.: UMI, 1983), 298.

59. Floyd Tillman, interview by John W. Rumble, Nashville, 13 October 1986, CMFOHC; Bruce Feiler, "Has Country Music Become a Soundtrack for White Flight?" *New York Times,* 20 October 1996; Kirby, *Rural Worlds Lost,* 305.

6. The Sophistication of Country Music

1. Bureau of the Census, *Sixteenth Census of the United States: 1940. Housing—General Characteristics* (Washington, D.C.: United States Printing Office, 1943), table 6; Bureau of the Census, *A Report of the Seventeenth Decennial Census: 1950. Housing—General Characteristics* (Washington, D.C.: United States Printing Office, 1952), table 7; Rupert B. Vance, "The Urban Breakthrough in the South," *Regionalism and the South: Selected Papers of Rupert Vance,* ed. John Shelton Reed and Daniel J. Singal (Chapel Hill: University of North Carolina Press, 1982), 177–82; Carl Abbott, *The New Urban America: Growth and Politics in Sunbelt Cities,* rev. ed. (Chapel Hill: University of North Carolina Press, 1987), 16; David R. Goldfield, *Promised Land: The South since 1945* (Arlington Heights: H. Davidson, 1987), 7; Robert G. Spinney, "World War II and Nashville, Tennessee, 1938–1951: Social Change and Public Sector Expansion" (Ph.D. diss., Vanderbilt University, 1995), 84; Charles P. Roland, *The Improbable Era: The South since World War II* (Lexington: University Press of Kentucky, 1975): 183.

2. Old Joe Clark, interview by John W. Rumble, Berea, 3 December 1985, Country Music Foundation Oral History Collection (hereafter CMFOHC), Nashville; David Cobb, interview by John W. Rumble, Nashville, 18 August 1983, CMFOHC; "Roy Acuff: Getting away from the Mike," *Billboard* 58, no. 17 (27 April 1946): cover; "Foley Takes over Reynold's Ole Opry as Acuff Travels," *Billboard* 58, no. 14 (6 April 1946): 5; John W. Rumble, liner notes, *Red Foley,* MCA CD MCAD-10084, 1991; "American Folk Tunes," *Billboard* 59, no. 31 (2 August 1947): 114; John W. Rumble, "Fred Rose and the Development of the Nashville Music Industry, 1942–1954" (Ph.D. diss., Vanderbilt University, 1980; Ann Arbor, Mich.: UMI, 1983), 293–95.

3. Hazel Meyer, *The Gold in Tin Pan Alley* (Philadelphia: Lippincott, 1958), 129; Frank Sinatra quoted in Ian Whitcomb, *After the Ball* (London: Allen Lane Penguin Press, 1972), 203; Bill C. Malone, "Honky Tonk: The Music of the Southern Working Class," *Folk Music and Modern Sound,* ed. William R. Ferris and Mary L. Hart (Jackson: University Press of Mississippi, 1982), 122; Johnny Sippel, "Rustic Rhythm Reaps $$ Reward," *Billboard* 61, no. 43 (22 October 1949): 97; Roland, *The Improbable Era,* 166; John W. Rumble, *Roy Acuff* (Alexandria: Time-Life Records, 1983), 23; Bill C. Malone, *Country Music, U.S.A.,* 2d ed. (Austin: University of Texas Press, 1985), 211.

4. Nolan Porterfield, *Jimmie Rodgers: The Life and Times of America's Blue Yodeler* (Urbana: University of Illinois Press, 1979), 209; Malone, *Country Music, U.S.A.,* 60–61.

5. Pee Wee King, "A Little Bit about Myself," rec. 1952, *Pee Wee King and His Golden West Cowboys,* Bear Family CD 15727, 1994; Pee Wee King quoted in Alana Nash, "Pee Wee King: He Changed the Course of Country Music," *Country Music* 3, no. 11 (August 1975): 55; Pee Wee King quoted in Otto Kitsinger, *Pee Wee King and His Golden West Cowboys* (Hambergen: Bear Family Records, 1994), 2; Kitsinger, *Pee Wee King and His Golden West Cowboys,* 2–7.

6. Charles K. Wolfe, *Kentucky Country: Folk and Country Music of Kentucky* (Lexington: University Press of Kentucky, 1982), 92–95; Pee Wee King quoted in Kitsinger, *Pee Wee King and His Golden West Cowboys,* 9; Kitsinger, *Pee Wee King and His Golden West Cowboys,* 7–19; "American Folk Tunes," *Billboard* 60, no. 12 (20 March 1948): 106; "Pee Wee King: The Golden West Cowboy," *Old Time Country* 7, no. 3 (summer 1981): 10–12; Joel Whitburn, *The Billboard Book of Top Forty Country Hits* (New York: Billboard Books, 1996), 176.

7. Otto Kitsinger and Richard Weize, "Pee Wee King and His Golden West Cowboys: The 1946–1958 Discography," in Kitsinger, *Pee Wee King and His Golden West Cowboys,* 56–63; Wesley Rose quoted in Les Pouliot, *John Thayer and Don Bruce Together Present the History of Country Music; A Thirty-six-Hour Radio Documentary* (Memphis: J. Thayer and D. Bruce Together, 1970), 328–29.

8. Kitsinger and Weize, "Pee Wee King and His Golden West Cowboys: The 1946–1958 Discography," 57–58.

9. "1952's Top Popular Records, According to Retail Sales," *Billboard* 64, no. 52 (27 December 1952): 19; "Pee Wee King's Flying W Ranch (TV)," *Billboard* 66, no. 44 (30 October 1954): 13.

10. Michael Streissguth, *Eddy Arnold, Pioneer of the Nashville Sound* (New York: Schirmer Books, 1997), 7–60; Michael Streissguth, *Eddy Arnold: The Tennessee Plowboy and His Guitar* (Hambergen: Bear Family Records, 1998), 2–15.

11. "Folk Record Reviews," *Billboard* 57, no. 4 (27 January 1945): 64; Richard Weize, "Eddy Arnold: The Discography, 1944–1950," in Streissguth, *Eddy Arnold: The Tennessee Plowboy and His Guitar,* 32, 35; Streissguth, *Eddy Arnold, Pioneer of the Nashville Sound,* 95; "Best Selling Country and Western Records—1946–1953," *Billboard* 66, no. 21 (22 May 1954): 19; Whitburn, *The Billboard Book of Top Forty Country Hits,* 27–28.

12. Richard Weize, "Eddy Arnold: The Discography, 1944–1950," 35; Streissguth, *Eddy Arnold: The Tennessee Plowboy and His Guitar,* 2; Ronnie F. Pugh, *Ernest Tubb: The Texas Troubadour* (Durham: Duke University Press, 1996), 137; "American Folk Tunes," *Billboard* 59, no. 50 (13 December 1947): 102; Streissguth, *Eddy Arnold, Pioneer of the Nashville Sound,* 100, 121, 130; "Arnold and RCA Ink Seven-Year Pact," *Billboard* 60, no. 51 (18 December 1948): 41; Charles K. Wolfe, *Tennessee Strings: The Story of Country Music in Tennessee* (Knoxville: University of Tennessee Press, 1977), 80; *Billboard* 62, no. 34 (26 August 1950): cover; Frank M. Folsom, "Thirty Million Records Ago It Was Tough Plowing for Eddy," *Billboard* 67, no. 3 (15 January 1955): 18; Eddy Arnold quoted in Streissguth, *Eddy Arnold, Pioneer of the Nashville Sound,* 121; Eddy Arnold quoted in Pouliot, *History of Country Music,* 504; Whitburn, *The Billboard Book of Top Forty Country Hits,* 27–28.

13. Streissguth, *Eddy Arnold, Pioneer of the Nashville Sound,* 134–47, 226–32.

14. George Morgan, interview by Douglas B. Green, Nashville, 13 May 1975, CMFOHC; Colin Escott, *George Morgan: Candy Kisses* (Hambergen: Bear Family Records, 1996), 2–

14, 20; George Morgan quoted in Pouliot, *History of Country Music*, 268; Johnny Sippel, "Folk Talent and Tunes," *Billboard* 63, no. 27 (7 July 1951): 26.

15. Otto Kitsinger, Richard Weize, and Larry Zwisohn, "George Morgan: The Columbia Discography," in Escott, *George Morgan*, 40; Whitburn, *The Billboard Book of Top Forty Country Hits*, 216.

16. Immanuel Wallerstein, "What Can One Mean by Southern Culture?" *The Evolution of Southern Culture*, ed. Numan V. Bartley (Athens: University of Georgia Press, 1988), 11–12; Kurt Blaser, " 'Pictures from Life's Other Side': Hank Williams, Country Music, and Popular Culture in America," *South Atlantic Quarterly* 84, no. 1 (winter 1985): 14; "New Trends Evolve in Hillbilly Field," *Billboard* 67, no. 7 (14 February 1953): 16, 44.

17. Porterfield, *Jimmie Rodgers*, 159; Ronnie F. Pugh, "Country across the Country," *Country: The Music and the Musicians*, ed. Paul Kingbury and Alan Axelrod (New York: Abbeville Press, 1988), 153–61; Rumble, "Fred Rose and the Development of the Nashville Music Industry," 193–95; John W. Rumble, "The Emergence of Nashville as a Recording Center: Logbooks from the Castle Studio, 1952–1953," *Journal of Country Music* 7, no. 3 (December 1978): 24, 28; Eddie Stubbs, "Johnnie and Jack, the Recordings," *Johnnie and Jack and the Tennessee Mountain Boys* (Vollersode: Bear Family Records, 1992); Charles K. Wolfe, *Kitty Wells: The Queen of Country Music* (Hambergen: Bear Family Records, 1993), 7; "Tin Pan Valley," *Time* 58, no. 7 (13 August 1951): 61–62; John W. Rumble, "Grand Ole Opry," *Encyclopedia of Southern Culture*, ed. Charles Reagan Wilson and William Ferris (Chapel Hill: University of North Carolina Press, 1989), 1059–60.

18. Paul Fryer, "Local Styles and Country Music: An Introductory Essay," *All That Glitters: Country Music in America*, ed. George H. Lewis (Bowling Green: Bowling Green University Popular Press, 1993), 72; "Questions and Answers Reveal Approach, Policies of A & R Men," *Billboard* 65, no. 49 (5 December 1953): 54.

19. Hank Snow, *The Hank Snow Story* (Urbana: University of Illinois Press, 1994), 27–28, 83, 116–30, 190–240, 281–96, 323–24; Charles K. Wolfe, *Hank Snow, the Singing Ranger: 1949–1953* (Vollersode: Bear Family Records, 1988), 1–4; Charles K. Wolfe, *Hank Snow: The Yodeling Ranger: The Canadian Years, 1936–1947* (Hambergen: Bear Family Records, 1993), 2; Peter Guralnick, "Hank Snow, the Singing Ranger: Still Movin' On," *Country Music* 7, no. 2 (November–December 1978): 28–30; Marshall Fallwell, "Hank Snow Moves on in the Old Tradition," *Country Music* 2, no. 3 (November 1973): 69–70; Ruth Lee Miller, "Hank the Singing Ranger," *Mountain Broadcast and Prairie Recorder*, n.s., 4 (June 1945): 17; "Best Selling Country and Western Records—1946–1953," 19; Whitburn, *The Billboard Book of Top Forty Country Hits*, 299–300.

20. Joe Talbot, interview by Douglas B. Green, Hendersonville, 3 May 1974, CMFOHC; Wolfe, *Hank Snow, the Singing Ranger*, 3–5.

21. Joe Talbot, interview; Richard Weize, "The Recording Information," in Wolfe, *Hank Snow, the Singing Ranger*, 5–7; Hank Snow quoted in Dennis Henslcy, "Hank Snow," *Country Musicians: From the Editors of Guitar Player, Keyboard, and Frets Magazines*, ed. Judie Eremo (Cupertino: Grove Press, 1987), 120.

22. "Red Foley: Exclusive Decca Recording Artist," unidentified clipping, Red Foley vertical file, Country Music Foundation, Nashville; Pouliot, *History of Country Music,* 292; Reta Spears-Stewart, "The Ozark Jubilee Saga—Red Foley," Red Foley vertical file, Country Music Foundation, Nashville; Rumble, liner notes, *Red Foley;* Jinnie Rodgers, "Corn Belt Comments," *Mountain Broadcast and Prairie Recorder* 2, no. 1 (September 1940): 7; George A. Barker, "A Traveling Man's Gotta Zigzag," *Tennessean,* 2 February 1964; Ronnie F. Pugh, liner notes, *Vintage Country,* Franklin Mint Record Society LP FMRS CW 021—FMRS CW 022, 1982; Rich Kienzle, "Red Foley," unidentified clipping, Red Foley vertical file, Country Music Foundation, Nashville; Wolfe, *Kentucky Country,* 134; "American Folk Tunes," *Billboard* 56, no. 32 (5 August 1944): 64; "Profiles of Folk Artists: Ramblin' Red Foley," *The Billboard 1944 Music Year Book* (New York: Billboard Publishing, 1944), 364; Red Foley, advertisement, *Billboard* 57, no. 7 (17 February 1945): 16; "American Folk Tunes," *Billboard* 57, no. 27 (7 July 1945): 75.

23. Red Foley quoted in Barker, "A Traveling Man's Gotta Zigzag"; Whitburn, *The Billboard Book of Top Forty Country Hits,* 111–13; Wolfe, *Kentucky Country,* 135–36; Allen Churchill, "Tin-Pan Alley's Git-tar Blues," *New York Times Magazine,* 15 July 1951; *Billboard* 62, no. 8 (25 February 1950): cover; "Foley Grosses 31G on Coast," *Billboard* 65, no. 23 (6 June 1953): 44; "Coast One-Nighters for Opry Folk," *Billboard* 65, no. 14 (4 April 1953): 17; "Red Foley Quits as 'Opry' Star after Seven Years," *Billboard* 65, no. 18 (2 May 1953): 3; "Foley Signs with RadiOzark, TT for Personal Appearances," *Billboard* 66, no. 16 (17 April 1954): 16; "Foley to Air from Ozarks," *Billboard* 66, no. 32 (7 August 1954): 1; "Radio Ozark-ABC, Set C & W Video Series," *Billboard* 67, no. 1 (1 January 1955): 2; George Carney, "Country Music and the Radio: A Historical Geographic Assessment," *Rocky Mountain Social Science Journal* 11, no. 2 (April 1974): 25; Howard Turtle, "Ozark Folk Tunes and Comedy Make Springfield a TV Center," *Kansas City Star,* 29 January 1956; Clarence B. Newman, "Homespun Harmony: Hillbilly Music Sells Rural Customers, Keeps Record Counters Busy," *Wall Street Journal,* 3 May 1957; Rumble, liner notes, *Red Foley.*

24. Colin Escott, *Hank Williams, the Biography* (Boston: Little, Brown, 1994), 61, 89; Johnny Sippel, "Folk Talent and Tunes," *Billboard* 60, no. 46 (13 November 1948): 38; Roger M. Williams, *Hank Williams* (Alexandria: Time-Life Records, 1981), 24; Pugh, liner notes, *Vintage Country,* 3; Rich Kienzle, "Hank Garland," *Country Musicians: From the Editors of Guitar Player, Keyboard, and Frets Magazines,* 45–46; "Recent Foley Diskings Sell Half a Million Copies," *Billboard* 64, no. 46 (15 November 1952): 20.

25. Rich Kienzle, liner notes, *Jimmy Wakely: Vintage Collections,* Capitol CD 7243–8-36591–2-8, 1996; Jimmy Wakely, interview by Douglas B. Green, Burbank, 25 June 1974, CMFOHC; Douglas B. Green, "The Singing Cowboy: An American Dream," *Journal of Country Music* 7, no. 2 (May 1978): 48; Malone, *Country Music, U.S.A.,* 234; Gerald F. Vaughn, "Foreman Phillips: Western Swing's Kingmaker," *John Edwards Memorial Foundation Quarterly* 15, no. 53 (spring 1979): 27; "Jimmy Wakely," *Billboard* 60, no. 17 (24 April 1948): 42; "Capitol Records Biography: Jimmy Wakely," Jimmy Wakely vertical

file, Country Music Foundation, Nashville; "Jimmy Wakely," *Billboard* 64, no. 31 (2 August 1952): 74; "Top Male Singers on Juke Boxes—1949," *Billboard* 62, no. 9 (4 March 1950): 76; Bep Roberts, "Hank Thompson Survives Plane Crash," *Capitol News* 8, no. 12 (December 1950): 10; Bep Roberts, "Eddie Dean, Seventh Son of Seventh Son, Etches New Discs for Western Fans This Month," *Capitol News* 9, no. 2 (February 1951): 11; "Folk Talent and Tunes," *Billboard* 62, no. 42 (21 October 1950): 35; "Folk Talent and Tunes," *Billboard* 62, no. 2 (14 January 1950): 95; Johnny Sippel, "Folk Talent and Tunes," *Billboard* 61, no. 7 (13 February 1949): 30.

26. Jimmy Wakely, interview; "NBC and CBS Ban 'One Has My Name,' " *Billboard* 61, no. 9 (26 February 1949): 20; "Music—As Written," *Billboard* 61, no. 47 (19 November 1949): 40; *Billboard* 61, no. 41 (8 October 1949): cover; "Folk Talent and Tunes," *Billboard* 63, no. 37 (15 September 1951): 149; "Margaret Whiting," *Billboard* 64, no. 31 (2 August 1952): 74.

7. Across the Great Divide

1. Joe Bleeden, "Hollywood Now Hillbilly H.Q.," *Billboard* 63, no. 47 (24 November 1951): 1, 18.

2. Bleeden, "Hollywood Now Hillbilly H.Q."; Norman Nelson, "Spotlight on Southern California: The Hard to Believe Market," *Billboard* 65, no. 17 (25 April 1953): 36, 38; Cliffie Stone, "Western Dances Still Drawing Especially in Southern California," *Capitol News* 4, no. 10 (October 1946): 14.

3. Johnny Sippel, "Country and Western," *Billboard* 64, no. 11 (15 March 1952): 82; June Bundy, "Names Make Rapid Strides of TV Webs; Corral Not Full Yet," *Billboard* 67, no. 23 (21 May 1955): 15; Daniel C. Cooper, *Lefty Frizzell: The Honky-tonk Life of Country Music's Greatest Singer* (Boston: Little, Brown, 1995), 156–57; Cliffie Stone, interview by John W. Rumble, Nashville, 27 March 1992, Country Music Foundation Oral History Collection (hereafter CMFOHC), Nashville; Rich Kienzle, *Tennessee Ernie Ford, Masters* (Nashville: Liberty Records, 1994), 7–9; "Cliffie Stone's Hometown Jamboree," *Billboard* 61, no. 51 (17 December 1949): 10; *Billboard* 62, no. 17 (29 April 1950): cover.

4. Bill C. Malone, *Country Music, U.S.A.,* 2d ed. (Austin: University of Texas Press, 1985), 202; Johnny Bond, *The Tex Ritter Story* (New York: Chappell Music, 1976): 152–54; Rich Kienzle, *Merle Travis: Guitar Rags and a Too Fast Past* (Hambergen: Bear Family Records, 1994), 48; Cliffie Stone, interview; Edward Morris, "New, Improved, Homogenized: Country Radio since 1950," *Country: The Music and the Musicians,* ed. Paul Kingbury and Alan Axelrod (New York: Abbeville Press, 1988), 97; "Midwestern Hayride," *Billboard* 64, no. 21 (24 May 1952): 9; Colin Escott, *Hank Williams, the Biography* (Boston: Little, Brown, 1994), 199; Ronnie F. Pugh, *Ernest Tubb: The Texas Troubadour* (Durham: Duke University Press, 1996), 198; Bundy, "Names Make Rapid Strides of TV Webs," 15; Gene Plotnik, "Big Push Due on 'Opry' TV," *Billboard* 66, no. 46 (13 November 1954): 1, 100.

5. Russell Sanjek, *Pennies from Heaven: The American Popular Music Business in the Twentieth Century* (New York: Da Capo Press, 1996), 217; "A Decade of Growth and Success," *Billboard* 64, no. 31 (2 August 1952): 51; "Capitol Drive in Folk Field," *Billboard* 62, no. 35 (2 September 1950): 12; "Capitol Folk Chief Goes Nashville," *Billboard* 62, no. 30 (29 July 1950): 12; "Cliffie Stone Heads Capitol Westerns," *Capitol News* 4, no. 4 (April 1946): 12; Ken Nelson, interview by Douglas B. Green, Ventura, 2 April 1975, CMFOHC.

6. Steve Sholes, "Developing Country Scene: Styles Change and Quality Improves: Artists, Firms, Increase in Ten Years," *Billboard* 66, no. 21 (22 May 1954): 18.

7. Charles K. Wolfe, *Kentucky Country: Folk and Country Music of Kentucky* (Lexington: University Press of Kentucky, 1982), 110; Rich Kienzle, "The Evolution of Country Fingerpicking: From Sylvester Weaver to Chet Atkins and Beyond," *Guitar Player* 18, no. 5 (May 1984): 38–39; Mark Humphrey, "Merle Travis," *Country Musicians: From the Editors of Guitar Player, Keyboard, and Frets Magazines,* ed. Judie Eremo (Cupertino: Grove Press, 1987), 124–25; Merle Travis, interview by Douglas B. Green, n.p., 17 October 1975, CMFOHC; Rich Kienzle, liner notes, *The Best of Merle Travis*, Rhino CD R2 70993, 1990; Bob Baxter, "Merle Travis: The Man, the Music," *Guitar Player* 10, no. 9 (September 1976): 28; Merle Travis quoted in Les Pouliot, *John Thayer and Don Bruce Together Present the History of Country Music; A Thirty-six-Hour Radio Documentary* (Memphis: J. Thayer and D. Bruce Together, 1970), 215.

8. Rich Kienzle, *Merle Travis*, 6, 10, 22, 39; Mark Humphrey, "Interview: Merle Travis," *Old Time Music* 36 (summer 1981): 10; Chet Atkins with Bill Neely, *Country Gentleman* (Chicago: Henry Regnery, 1974), 56; Merle Travis quoted in Dorothy Horstman, "Merle Travis: Memories of a Country Guitar Genius," *Country Music* 4, no. 1 (October 1975): 32; "Boone County Jamboree," *Billboard* 55, no. 12 (20 March 1943): 8; Merle Travis, "Recollections of Merle Travis, 1944–1955, Part 2" *John Edwards Memorial Foundation Quarterly* 15, no. 55 (fall 1979): 137–39; Mark Humphrey, "Interview: Merle Travis, Part 4," *Old Time Music* 39 (winter 1982–spring 1983): 24–25.

9. Kienzle, *Merle Travis,* 22; Merle Travis quoted in Mark Humphrey, "Interview: Merle Travis, Part 3," *Old Time Music* 38 (summer–autumn 1982): 15; Lee Gillette, "Cliffie Stone Hops from Control Booth to 'Mike' with New Capitol Contract," *Capitol News* 5, no. 1 (January 1947): 14; Joel Whitburn, *The Billboard Book of Top Forty Country Hits* (New York: Billboard Books, 1996), 325–26.

10. Kienzle, *Merle Travis,* 2, 27.

11. Tennessee Ernie Ford, *This Is My Story, This Is My Song* (Englewood Cliffs: Prentice-Hall, 1963), 75; Jan Hampton, "Tennessee Ernie Ford: Talking with the Pea Picker," Tennessee Ernie Ford vertical file, Country Music Foundation, Nashville; Kienzle, liner notes, *The Ultimate Tennessee Ernie Ford Collection,* Razor and Tie CD RE 2134-2, 1997; Kienzle, *Tennessee Ernie Ford, Masters,* 4–14; Tennessee Ernie Ford, interview by Hugh Cherry, San Francisco, c. 1968, CMFOHC; "Cliffie Stone's Hometown Jamboree," *Billboard* 61, no. 51 (17 December 1950): 10.

12. Tennessee Ernie Ford, advertisement, *Billboard* 61, no. 14 (2 April 1949): 43; Rich Kienzle, "The Electric Guitar in Country Music: Its Evolution and Development," *Guitar Player* 13, no. 11 (November 1979): 31, 33; Rich Kienzle, "Steel," *Country Music* 4, no. 4 (January 1976): 61; Rich Kienzle, "Country Music Instruments and Players," *The Country Music Book,* ed. Michael Mason (New York: Scribner's Sons, 1985), 246; Kienzle, *Tennessee Ernie Ford, Masters,* 10, 29–37; Whitburn, *The Billboard Book of Top Forty Country Hits,* 114.

13. "Kay Starr," *Billboard* 64, no. 31 (2 August 1952): 74; Leigh Vance, "Night Club— Vaude Reviews," *Billboard* 65, no. 16 (18 April 1953): 13, 50.

14. Mary A. Bufwack, *Finding Her Voice: The Saga of Women in Country Music* (New York: Crown Publishers, 1993), 156–63; Robert K. Oermann and Mary A. Bufwack, "Rockabilly Women," *Journal of Country Music* 8, no. 1 (May 1979): 65, 88; Hazel Meyer, *The Gold in Tin Pan Alley* (Philadelphia: Lippincott, 1958), 112–13; Jonny Whiteside, *Ramblin' Rose: The Life and Career of Rose Maddox* (Nashville: Country Music Foundation Press, 1997), 97.

15. Bill C. Malone, *Honky-tonkin'* (Alexandria: Time-Life Records, 1983), 3; Whiteside, *Ramblin' Rose,* 4–158; Rose Maddox quoted in Bufwack, *Finding Her Voice,* 128; Fred Maddox quoted in Whiteside, *Ramblin' Rose,* 58–59; Stephen R. Tucker, " 'Louisiana Saturday Night': A History of Louisiana Country Music" (Ph.D. diss., Tulane University, 1995; Ann Arbor, Mich.: UMI, 1996), 480–81; Bufwack, *Finding Her Voice,* 124–29; Johnny Sippel, "Folk Talent and Tunes," *Billboard* 61, no. 8 (19 February 1949): 35; Daniel C. Cooper, "The Maddox Brothers," *The All Music Guide to Country,* ed. Michael Erlewine et al. (San Francisco: Miller Freeman Books, 1997), 287–88; Keith Oleson, liner notes, *The Maddox Brothers and Rose,* vol. 1, *America's Most Colorful Hillbilly Band,* Arhoolie CD-391, 1993.

16. Fred Maddox quoted in Whiteside, *Ramblin' Rose,* 130.

17. Fred Maddox quoted in Whiteside, *Ramblin' Rose,* 136.

18. Richard L. Gordon, "The Man Who Is King," *Saga* 1951. Reprinted in *John Edward Memorial Foundation Quarterly* 4, no. 10 (June 1968): 63–64; Ian Whitcomb, *After the Ball* (London: Allen Lane Penguin Press, 1972), 213; Malone, *Country Music, U.S.A.,* 208–9.

19. John W. Rumble, "Roots of Rock and Roll: Henry Glover at King Records," *Journal of Country Music* 14, no. 2 (1992): 33–36.

20. Charles K. Wolfe, "Editor's Postscript," *Truth Is Stranger Than Publicity,* by Alton Delmore (Nashville: Country Music Foundation Press, 1995), 286–88; Ian Whitcomb, *After the Ball,* 145; Cooper, *Lefty Frizzell,* 149; Kienzle, "Country Music Instruments and Players," 215.

21. Charles K. Wolfe, "The Delmore Brothers Discography," *Truth Is Stranger Than Publicity,* 306–18; Wolfe, "Editor's Postscript," 287–90, 292–95; Johnny Sippel, "Folk Talent and Tunes," *Billboard* 65, no. 1 (3 January 1953): 28; Whitburn, *The Billboard Book of Top Forty Country Hits,* 93.

22. Gordon Baxter, "Pop Never Wanted Me to Be a Musician," *Music City News* 4, no. 8 (February 1967): 27; Rich Kienzle, liner notes, *Seven Nights to Rock,* Western LP 2001, 1982; Rich Kienzle, liner notes, *Moon's Rock,* Bear Family CD BCD 15607, 1992; Phillip J. Tricker, liner notes, *Moonshine Jamboree,* Ace/King CD CDCHD 458, 1993; Johnny Sippel, "Folk Talent and Tunes," *Billboard* 60, no. 34 (21 August 1948): 31.

23. Rumble, "Roots of Rock and Roll," 30–38.

24. "Favorite Country and Western Artists," *Billboard* 63, no. 37 (15 September 1951): 62; "Favorite Country and Western Artists," *Billboard* 65, no. 9 (28 February 1953): 60.

25. Al Jarvis, "Spotlight on Turntables: The Disc Jockey," *Billboard* 65, no. 17 (25 April 1953): 39; Peter Fornatle and Joshua E. Mills, *The Radio in the Television Age* (Woodstock: Overlook Press, 1980), 12–13; Martin Block, "Disc Jockey in Key Music Biz Spot," *Variety* 157, no. 4 (3 January 1945): 135, 155; Hugh Cherry, "Country DJs Carry Music to the People," *Music City News* 18, no. 4 (October 1980): 18; Foreman Phillips, letter, *Mountain Broadcast and Prairie Recorder* 3, no. 1 (March 1942): 13–14; Gerald F. Vaughn, "Foreman Phillips: Western Swing's Kingmaker," *John Edwards Memorial Foundation Quarterly* 15, no. 53 (spring 1979): 27–28; *Hillbilly Hit Parade,* advertisement, *Billboard* 57, no. 26 (30 June 1945): 19; Tucker, " 'Louisiana Saturday Night,' " 400.

26. Cherry, "Country DJs Carry Music to the People," 18–19; "Special Disc Jockey Supplement," *Billboard* 60, no. 40 (2 October 1948): 74–76; Colin Escott, *Hank Williams, the Biography* (Boston: Little, Brown, 1994), 87; Bob McCluskey quoted in Michael Streissguth, *Eddy Arnold, Pioneer of the Nashville Sound* (New York: Schirmer Books, 1997), 118; "Favorite Folk Disc Jockeys," *Billboard* 61, no. 43 (22 October 1949): 101; "Favorite Folk Disc Jockeys," *Billboard* 62, no. 40 (7 October 1950): 31; "Nelson King Repeats Past Wins as Jockey's Favorite Spinner," *Billboard* 65, no. 9 (28 February 1953): 62; "C and W Disk Jockeys . . . Favorites," *Billboard* 66, no. 46 (13 November 1954): 78; Nelson King, "Billboard Charts: A Prime Source for Programming," *Billboard* 65, n. 9 (28 February 1953): 44; Russell Sanjek, *Pennies from Heaven: The American Popular Music Business in the Twentieth Century,* (New York: Da Capo Press, 1996), 217–18.

27. Johnny Sippel, "Rustic Rhythms Reaps $$ Reward," *Billboard* 61, no. 43 (22 October 1949): 97; Gene Fowler and Bill Crawford, *Border Radio* (Austin: Texas Monthly Press, 1987), 171; Johnny Sippel, "The Hillbilly Deejay, Prime Asset to Country and Western Music," *Billboard* 63, no. 37 (15 September 1951): 61; "Airtime," *Billboard* 66, no. 46 (13 November 1954): 34; Wayne W. Daniel, *Pickin' on Peachtree: A History of Country Music in Atlanta, Georgia* (Urbana: University of Illinois Press, 1990), 206.

28. Neil V. Rosenberg, *Bluegrass: A History* (Urbana: University of Illinois Press, 1985), 96–97; Hazel Meyer, *The Gold in Tin Pan Alley* (Philadelphia: Lippincott, 1958), 130–34; Whitcomb, *After the Ball,* 217; Tucker, " 'Louisiana Saturday Night,' " 428; Peter Guralnick, *Last Train to Memphis: The Rise of Elvis Presley* (London: Abacus, 1994), 4, 38, 96–97.

29. Steven Mintz and Susan Kellogg, *Domestic Revolutions: A Social History of American Family Life* (New York: Free Press, 1988), 166–75, 199–200; H. F. Mooney, "Popular

Music since the 1920s: The Significance of Changing Taste," *American Quarterly* 20, no. 1 (spring 1968): 75.

30. Mintz and Kellogg, *Domestic Revolutions*, 154; Sanjek, *Pennies from Heaven*, 246, 318; "No Junking of Jukes," *Billboard* 55, no. 39 (25 September 1943): 166; "American Folk Tunes," *Billboard* 58, no. 30 (27 July 1946): 128; "Development of Kidisk Market," *Billboard* 63, no. 28 (14 July 1951): 79; Tony Wilson and Jerry Wexler, "Specialized Disk Sales Advance," *Billboard* 60, no. 25 (19 June 1948): 20; "Dealer Doings," *Billboard* 62, no. 2 (14 January 1950): 30.

31. Fornatale and Mills, *Radio in the Television Age*, 15, 37-38; "Lowdown on Bands: Teen-Agers Give out Frank Opinions," *Billboard* 63, no. 16 (21 April 1951): 24; Charlie Gillett, *The Sound of the City: The Rise of Rock and Roll* (New York: Dell Publishing, 1970), 15-19, 32; George Lipsitz, *Rainbow at Midnight: Labor and Culture in the 1940s* (Urbana: University of Illinois Press, 1994), 319-20; Bob Rolontz and Joel Friedman, "Teen-Agers Demand Music with a Beat, Spur Rhythm-Blues," *Billboard* 66, no. 17 (24 April 1954): 1, 18, 24.

32. Rolontz and Friedman, "Teen-Agers Demand Music with a Beat, Spur Rhythm-Blues," 1, 18; Lipsitz, *Rainbow at Midnight*, 319; Malone, *Country Music, U.S.A.*, 246-47; Steve Schnickel, "R & B Music Invades Pop Market: Jukes, Disk Stores Feeling Trend," *Billboard* 66, no. 33 (14 August 1954): 13; Chris Gardner, liner notes, *Rockin' Rollin' Bill Haley*, Bear Family LP BFX 15068, 1981; Bill Haley quoted in Gillett, *The Sound of the City*, 34; Gillett, *The Sound of the City*, 41.

33. Roger Biles, "Memphis," *Encyclopedia of Southern Culture*, ed. Charles Reagan Wilson and William Ferris (Chapel Hill: University of North Carolina Press, 1989), 1460; Colin Escott, *The Sun Country Years: Country Music in Memphis, 1950-1959* (Bremen: Bear Family Records, 1986), 10-13, 21-27; Colin Escott, *B. B. King: King of the Blues* (Universal City: MCA Records, 1992), 7-10; James Austin, liner notes, *The Sun Story*, Rhino LP 71103, 1986; Robert Palmer, "Get Rhythm: Elvis Presley, Johnny Cash, and the Rockabillies," *Country: The Music and the Musicians*, 287-94; Guralnick, *Last Train to Memphis*, 328-31; Martin Hawkins, "Bullet Records: A Shot in the Dark," *Journal of Country Music* 8, no. 3 (1981): 34; Richard Spottswood, "Country Music and the Phonograph," *Bluegrass Unlimited* 21, no. 8 (February 1987): 20-21; Cooper, *Lefty Frizzell*, 50; Fornatale and Mills, *Radio in the Television Age*, 40; Sam Phillips quoted in Escott, *The Sun Country Years*, 18-19; "Indies Move up in C & W Field," *Billboard* 66, no. 8 (20 February 1954): 17; Joe Martin, "Status Quo in R & B: Years Been Good to Talent, Indies, Some Majors Subside," *Billboard* 66, no. 17 (24 April 1954): 13.

34. Guralnick, *Last Train to Memphis*, 6-91.

35. Peter Guralnick, *Lost Highway: Journeys and Arrivals of American Musicians* (Boston: D. R. Godine, 1979), 96-100; Scotty Moore quoted in Guralnick, *Lost Highway*, 99, 101.

36. Sam Phillips quoted in Guralnick, *Last Train to Memphis*, 96; James C. Cobb, *The Most Southern Place on Earth: The Mississippi Delta and the Roots of Regional Identity*

(New York: Oxford Press, 1992), 303; Patrick Mullen, "Hillbilly Hipsters of the 1950s: The Romance of Rockabilly," *Southern Quarterly* 22, no. 3 (spring 1984): 79.

37. Scotty Moore quoted in Dan Forte, "Roots of Rockabilly," *Country Musicians: From the Editors of Guitar Player, Keyboard, and Frets Magazines,* ed. Judie Eremo (Cupertino: Grove Press, 1987), 100; Guralnick, *Last Train to Memphis,* 92–104; Palmer, "Get Rhythm," 302–8.

38. Scotty Moore quoted in Peter Guralnick, *Elvis, the King of Rock 'n' Roll: The Complete Fifties Masters* (New York: BMG Music, 1992), n.p.; "C and W Territorial Best Sellers—Memphis," *Billboard* 66, no. 37 (11 September 1954): 54; Scotty Moore quoted in Guralnick, *Last Train to Memphis,* 124; Guralnick, *Last Train to Memphis,* 97–184; Guralnick, *Lost Highway,* 102, 127–28; Bill C. Malone, "Elvis, Country Music, and the South," *All That Glitters: Country Music in America,* ed. George H. Lewis (Bowling Green: Bowling Green University Popular Press, 1993), 55; Robert Hilburn, "Hail to the Real King," *Los Angeles Times,* 9 May 1993; Bill C. Malone, "Growing Up with Texas Country Music," *What's Going On? (In Texas Folklore),* ed. Francis Edward Abernathy (Austin: Encino Press, 1976), 252; Tucker, " 'Louisiana Saturday Night,' " 482–91; Hank Snow, *The Hank Snow Story* (Urbana: University of Illinois Press, 1994), 384.

39. Scotty Moore quoted in Guralnick, *Lost Highway,* 104; Carl Perkins quoted in Colin Escott, *The Classic Carl Perkins* (Vollersode: Bear Family Records, 1990), 4; Nick Tosches, "Hardrock Gunter, the Mysterious Pig-Iron Man," *Journal of Country Music* 10, no. 1 (1985): 36–39; Escott, *The Classic Carl Perkins,* 3–5; Colin Escott, *Johnny Cash, the Sun Years* (London: Charly Records, 1984), 2, 7–8.

40. Joe Martin, "Country Music Field Full of Green Stuff—Folding Kind That Is," *Billboard* 66, no. 21 (22 May 1954): 1; Clarence B. Newman, "Homespun Harmony: Hillbilly Music Sells Rural Customers, Keeps Record Counters Busy," *Wall Street Journal,* 3 May 1957.

41. "WSM Invites 900 DJs to 'Opry' Anniversary," *Billboard* 65, no. 46 (14 November 1953): 17; Paul Ackerman, "Public Relations Coup: WSM DJ Festival Packs Real Wallop," *Billboard* 65, no. 48 (28 November 1953): 1, 42; "Country Music Jocks Build for the Future," *Billboard* 66, no. 48 (27 November 1954): 11; Bill Sachs and Paul Ackerman, "WSM Country Fest Pulls Record Crowd," *Billboard* 66, no. 48 (27 November 1954): 11; Sanjek, *Pennies from Heaven,* 247; "Over One Thousand to Fete WSM's Twenty-ninth Year," *Billboard* 66, no. 47 (20 November 1954): 13; Frank Clement, "A Free People's Music: A Talk by Frank G. Clement," National Disc Jockey Festival, Nashville, 9 November 1956; Rosenberg, *Bluegrass,* 132.

INDEX

Rodgers, Jimmie, 24–26, 41; influence of, on other performers, 24–25, 46, 50, 52, 53, 54, 119, 133, 166, 171, 180, 181, 182, 184–85, 204, 211, 213; "Jimmie Rodgers Day," 185, 186

Rose, Fred, 152, 169, 195

Satherley, Art, 76, 95–96, 139, 179

schoolhouse shoes ("kerosene circuit"), 37–38, 65

Scruggs, Earl, 132, 133

Seckler, Curly, 134

Selph, Jimmie, 143

Selph, Leon, 99, 100, 102, 103

Shamblin, Eldon, 94, 96, 118, 121

Shepard, Jean, 177, 178

Sherrill, Homer, 55, 58

Sholes, Steve, 80

Shuffler, George, 140

Sibert, Johnny, 193

Sims, Benny, 134

Smith, Arthur, 40

Smith, Carl, 191–93

Smith, Ralph, 164

Snow, Hank, 185, 211–14

Snydor, Glenn, 27

Sons of the Pioneers, 106

southern culture: folk qualities of, 8, 10–11, 19–20; as reflected in country music, 12–13, 39–40

southerners, in northern cities, 71, 162

southwestern migrants, in California, 106, 221

southwestern vocalists, in honky tonk, 178, 191. *See also* Frizzell, William Orville "Lefty"; Locklin, Hank; Pierce, Webb

square dance phenomenon (circa 1950), 110

Stanley Brothers, 133, 137–40

Stanton, Jim, 141, 179

Stapp, Jack, 82, 192

Stewart, Redd, 203

Stockard, Ocie, 92, 120

Stone, Cliffie, 111, 222, 223, 229, 236

Stone, David, 82, 200, 202

Stone, Harry, 30, 70, 82, 190, 200, 202, 205

Stricklin, Al, 94

string-band tradition: reconfiguration of, 45–51 passim; repudiation of, 40–43, 55, 57

Sunbrock, Larry, 69

Sun Records, 251

sustaining programs, 36–37

Suttee, Madge, 180

Talbot, Joe, 44, 213

Taylor, Harty, 35, 57

teenagers, 242–44

television: country music programs on, 221–23; impact of, on country music, 114–16

Texas Ruby (Ruby Agnes Owens), 177

Texas triumvirate (Gene Autry, Tex Ritter, Al Dexter), 73–77

Thompson, Hank, 81, 122–24

Tillman, Floyd, 81, 86–87, 101, 102, 164–65, 195

Town Hall Party, 180, 222

Travis, Merle, 112, 114, 124, 144, 145, 225–27, 229

Tubb, Ernest, 69, 85–86, 123, 165–68, 185, 192, 212; influence of, on other performers, 191

Turner, Zeb, 216

Turner, Zeke, 216

Upson, Dean, 189

urbanization: the rural-urban transition, 199–200; of the South, 8, 14–15, 67–68, 156–57, 159, 199–200; of the Southwest, 49

Vaden, Tommy, 213
Vandevender, Clifton Howard (Van Howard), 173
Venice Ballroom, 106–7, 109
vocalists, southwestern, 178, 191. *See also* Frizzell, William Orville "Lefty"; Locklin, Hank; Pierce, Webb

Wagnon, William, 222
Wakely, Jimmy, 109, 218–20
Warren, Paul, 148, 176, 177
Weis, Johnny, 112
Wells, Kitty (Muriel Deason), 175–77
Wesbrooks, Willie Egbert ("Cousin Wilbur"), 59
West, Wesley W. "Speedy," 114
western swing (country music subgenre), 2, 86–90; California, 105–6; demise of, 114–16; lyrical orientation of, 107, 108, 123; roots of, 90–91
western swing dances, 94–95, 116
Whitewing, Wayma K. "Pee Wee," 124
Whiting, Margaret, 219
Whitley, Ray, 107
Whitman, Slim, 209, 246
Wiggins, Little Roy, 205, 206, 207, 212
Williams, Hank, 168–72, 195; influence of, on other performers, 173, 193, 194

Williams, Tex, 109, 110, 111–12, 114
Williamson, LaVerne (Molly O'Day), 142–43
Wills, Bob, 92–96, 106, 107, 116–19; influence of, on other performers, 113, 123
Winkle, Jimmy, 232
Winterhalter, Hugo, 207
Wise, Chubby, 60, 132, 133
Wiseman, Mac, 140
WLS Artists' Bureau, 70
WLS Barn Dance, 27, 28, 33, 188
women in country music, 13–14, 141, 175–78, 219, 230–31; career opportunities for, in radio, 32–34, 141; as comediennes, 33. *See also individual female performers*
World War II: appeal of country music during, 78; country music tours during, 68–70, 97; interregional cultural exchange during, 80–81; migration during, 67–68, 99; women in, 174–75
Wright, Johnnie, 175
WSM, disc jockey festivals of, 251–52
WSM Artists' Service Bureau, 30, 82, 188, 190
Wyble, Jimmy, 110, 117, 120

Young, Faron, 193–94